SILENT KNIGHTS

SILENT KNIGHTS

Blowing the Whistle on Military Accidents and Their Cover-Ups

Alan E. Diehl, Ph.D.

Foreword by
Lt. Col. John J. Nance, USAFR

BRISTOL PARK BOOKS / NEW YORK

First Bristol Park Books edition published in 2007.

Published by Bristol Park Books
252 W. 38th Street
NYC, NY 10018

Bristol Park Books is a registered trademark of
Bristol Park Books, Inc.

Published by arrangement with Potomac Books, Inc.

Library of Congress Catalog Number: 2001052726

ISBN 10: 0-88486-406-5
ISBN 13: 978-0-88486-406-6

Printed in the United States of America

Dedication

To the half-million American troops who died from preventable illnesses and accidents. Whether you perished from frostbite at Valley Forge or friendly fire in the Gulf War, your passing was painful. May an aroused nation finally acknowledge your sacrifice and redeem itself by reforming the system that claimed your lives.

Contents

Foreword

The United States of America exists and endures because of the individual courage of the men and women who have gone before us. We know this—it's the basic stuff of American history. Washington, Jefferson, Madison, Lincoln, and a seemingly endless line of those in and out of uniform spoke their minds at critical times for the good of their nation, unfettered by the very real concerns of personal consequence from institutions and individuals to whom the status quo had become a deity. We are a people who exist because of the courage to stand up, speak up, and exercise our Constitutional rights to free speech when things are wrong and we know it. That is where the story of the author of this work begins.

These concepts should be anchored in your understanding, because selfless courage was required of Dr. Alan Diehl in the face of overwhelming pressure not to write this book. That lonely, personal determination not to remain silent is squarely within the mainstream of the traditions that have made us not only the most powerful nation on earth, but the most relevant and enduring of the last century. Whether we continue to merit that distinction as a nation will be determined by the way we deal with and accept the type of constructive criticism inherent in this work.

I have been an Air Force pilot since 1968, both active and reserve, and I revere our great defense establishment, which daily must deal with a mind-numbing array of challenges. I have also been a journalist, writer, and newsman for most of my life, and that's how I got to know Alan Diehl. I helped connect him with the Air Force in 1987 by encouraging Al to come help my service understand the challenges of human performance shortcomings when he was entertaining a job offer from the Air Force Inspection and Safety Center. And while I'm proud to have been a part of that professional marriage, I am anything but proud of the way the Air Force responded to him over the years.

When Dr. Alan Diehl filed a whistle-blowing complaint with the Department of Defense and Congress in 1994, he was the top safety expert and the only Ph.D. within the Air Force Safety Center. His act was one of ultimate desperation: No one had listened. He had no choice in such a circumstance, because there were specific, monumental problems with military safety attitudes and procedures, and no one was heeding the warnings.

The shock waves of that whistle-blowing filing reverberated throughout America's military establishment, specifically because Dr. Diehl had exposed one of our nation's best-kept dirty secrets: More troops are killed by the Pentagon's seriously flawed approach to safety and health matters than die in combat, and many—if not most—of those deaths are easily preventable. Moreover, he had exposed a staggering inability of not only the Air Force, but of all Department of Defense (DoD) arms to investigate themselves honestly when accidents occur, so as to extract the lessons and make the corrections that would prevent repetitions of the same accident. By his act of courageous desperation, Dr. Diehl had single-handedly faced the most powerful organization on the planet and challenged it to admit its mistakes openly and to reform what is a fundamentally dysfunctional safety system.

This book has been long in coming, primarily because the author, during his long battle to change a badly flawed system, retained hope that the needed corrections could be made internally. That hope, however, has proven stillborn.

These pages reveal how the U.S. military's clandestine safety procedures evolved and how staggeringly high the costs and consequences are of maintaining such a pat-the-public-on-the-head-and-assure-them-we've-got-it-under-control methodology of denying the utter failures of the present safety structure while doing little, if anything, to correct it. Make no mistake about it, this is an exposé made necessary by the grossly misguided stonewalling of the established structure. This book documents the waste of countless billions of dollars and the excruciating pain inflicted on individual victims of military accidents—victims that include wives and husbands and children and parents. How a debacle of this scope could take root within one of the republic's most trusted and vital institutions is yet another repeat of the classical admonition of history that absolute power corrupts absolutely. It is also a deadly serious lesson and warning that allowing American institutions to escape the "sunshine" of public scrutiny to the extent afforded the DoD on safety matters inevitably leads to self-serving institutional decisions which metastasize over time into dishonesty, cover-up, denial, and, finally, wholesale, mindless attacks on anyone who would attempt to surgically remove or irradiate that very real organizational cancer.

Equally important for this work is Diehl's explanation of how "military reform," a buzzword of the 2000 political campaign, should now be translated into an action plan by the new presidential administration and Congress. Both branches of government must exert their full power and determination to overhaul this cancerous system of secrecy and denial in safety matters, not only to protect American GIs, but also to vastly improve the ability of the system to learn rapidly and effectively from its past safety mistakes.

Even in the tumultuous free-market jungle of the deregulated commercial airlines, we've learned these lessons through the husbandry of a professional investigative agency known as the National Transportation Safety Board. The NTSB uses world-class scientists and experienced professionals, mostly uninfluenced by industry or governmental pressures, in its constant rendering of safety recommendations made for the sake of safety. Sadly, we have no such capability within the Department of Defense, and as Diehl argues, that must change immediately.

Diehl's crusade did not begin with his 1994 complaint. It had its roots in his earlier work, much of which was seminal for aviation safety. A decade earlier, while doing basic research for what became my own much-heralded work on aviation safety, *Blind Trust* (William Morrow, 1986), I began haunting the National Transportation Safety Board offices in Washington, trying to soak up decades of knowledge in preparation for writing about the aviation human-factors revolution, then in its Bastille days. Three investigators in a row suggested I interview one of their former colleagues, a man who had led a successful campaign to reinvent the NTSB's approach to accident investigation by inclusion of full human-factors issues. I chased down the progenitor, Dr. Diehl, who by then was working as a senior scientist for the FAA. I found him in the midst of an energetic campaign to get the regulation-oriented FAA to embrace human factors in commercial aviation by establishing a heretofore unheard of "invention of necessity" at United Airlines that eventually became the planet-wide, culture-changing course called Crew Resource Management (CRM). It took some arm-twisting and credential-presenting on my part to get him to discuss in detail his work with the NTSB, but in the end he agreed to help my project. His contributions became very pivotal in the critical success and usefulness of the book that resulted, which, in some ways, was the first work to popularly introduce into mainstream America this innovative, human-based approach to system safety.

The NTSB's evolution was fascinating and instructive. Previously, the NTSB had considered itself incapable of dealing with a human-caused accident other than to label it "pilot error" and walk away. There was no better or more sophisticated an accident investigatory agency on the planet at discovering the causes of mechanically based mishaps, but until the early 1980s, the prevailing response at NTSB when a pilot caused an accident was, "We can't get in a pilot's head." Thus, scores of terribly important accident investigations ended with stillborn conclusions that failed to address the true human causative factors as well as potential remedies such as reformed cockpit culture and communication. Diehl had been one of the key innovators on the NTSB's staff, arguing tirelessly that "pilot error" was, in the vernacular, an investigative cop-out. *Human* error, Diehl insisted, is quite different from pilot error. Pilot error involves discretion, such as a pilot who crashes because he or she purposefully, knowingly violates rules or procedures. A *human* error, on the other hand, involves mistakes resulting directly from human imperfection, such as perceiving something incorrectly and acting on that misperception (such as a pilot landing with the gear retracted). Human error, insofar as it results from *being* human (a state we can't change), is thus impervious to 1) disciplinary responses (fire the offending pilot to send a message to all the others never to make that human mistake again, as if the mistake had been voluntary), and to 2) glib investigatory conclusions that fail to probe the underlying causes of human failure ("the crash occurred because the pilot took off with the flaps in the wrong position," versus analyzing *why* the crew mistakenly left the flaps up). Diehl's persistence and personal expertise were critical at NTSB in ultimately changing staff attitudes by one hundred and eighty degrees and thus changing the course of their human-factors procedures and investigations.

By 1987, I had come to know and respect Al Diehl, and in urging him to accept the Air Force job offer, I hoped he could lend his considerable expertise to Air Force safety programs. I urged him to do so on the erroneous and ultimately naïve supposition that his superior credentials and contributions would be appreciated, not considered a threat at what was, after all, called the safety center.

I was wrong.

Throughout my career I had watched in frustration as fellow blue suiters had perished in unnecessary crashes, including the pivotal 1975 loss of a C-141 from my own McChord AFB wing in the Cascade Mountains of Washington State, an accident caused by command arrogance and massive human-factors problems induced by gross misunderstanding of human-performance issues. I had learned personally at that point that candor and professionalism in Air Force accident investigations were often thwarted, if not destroyed, by parochial interests, and that the system had become amateurish and dishonest. Furthermore, when commanders interfered with accident investigations, it seemed to me as a lawyer that the system bordered on being criminally negligent. Certainly I knew what all Air Force officers knew: that we demonstrated on a monthly basis why we could not be trusted to investigate ourselves, both because we did not possess the expertise of an NTSB to conduct such investigations and because the results were constantly tainted or dishonestly altered through the unfettered operation of self-interest. I had hoped that a world-class expert like Dr. Diehl could help guide my service out of that quagmire, but I should have suspected that his honesty and integrity would irritate, challenge, alarm, and ultimately invite the retaliation of those who, with grossly misguided loyalty and a shocking lack of integrity, sought to preserve the status quo of self-investigation at all costs.

The first few years, however, gave me reason to hope that Dr. Diehl's presence was ultimately making a large difference. I was amazed and pleased to see him win over reform-minded admirals and generals in all the services, many of whom began implementing his recommendations on various topics such as CRM training. My personal role in bringing Dr. Diehl's work—and the need for CRM—to the attention of the leader of my command, CINCMAC Gen. Duane Cassidy, led directly to the adoption of the first CRM program for the Military Airlift Command and put us in a leadership position within the Air Force. But there were storm clouds on the horizon of Dr. Diehl's advocacy whenever he pushed beyond CRM into investigatory reform, and it became obvious by 1993 that this gifted scientist was essentially tap-dancing through a mine field and one day would step in the wrong place.

The sentinel event that became that "trigger" occurred in the skies over Iraq in April 1994. Two Air Force F-15s accidentally shot down two U.S. Army Black Hawk helicopters, killing twenty-six soldiers and civilians. Coordination had broken down between elements such as AWACS (radar plane) and the fighters and the helicopter crews in a deadly environment—a classic example of the type of accident thoroughly preventable through the implementation of the CRM principles, which Diehl had been instrumental in developing. The DoD leaders had already ignored too many of these lessons, but they were about to make another significant mistake. First they formally assigned Dr. Diehl to the accident investigation to probe the human-factors aspects of the shoot-down, then they removed him from the investigation and ignored his findings when they failed to toe the official line.

President Clinton and Defense Secretary Perry injected themselves into the fray by promising a thorough and open investigation, a promise that froze the blood of those generals in the Air Force who wanted anything but an open probe. In fact, with the deafening sound of wagons being circled within the DoD in the background, it became very apparent that there was no way the military would allow senior officers who had pointedly ignored the urgent CRM recommendations of the only Ph.D.-level member of the Air Force safety function to be held accountable for their decisions—decisions that had essentially perpetuated the atmosphere of poor coordination and communication of which this tragic shoot-down was a product. Dr. Diehl realized the consequences of objecting to their purposely incomplete investigation, but he stood up and objected anyway, and for the Air Force, that was the final straw: The uncontainable scientist had to be silenced.

Dr. Diehl's safety job was quickly abolished. While at least a dozen additional Ph.D.-level scientists were, in fact, desperately needed in such positions, his job was specifically declared unnecessary by a threatened colonel and a threatened brigadier general. Diehl fought back with a whistle-blowing complaint carefully crafted to comply with all laws and security requirements, one which he mistakenly thought would reach the ears and the hearts of men and women of integrity at the top of the military and civilian food chain.

This time, *he* was wrong.

Instead, the entire defense establishment fell into an active and collective state of denial, and hundreds more victims would die in the intervening years, arguably as a result of the DoD's refusing—not failing—to learn and incorporate the necessary lessons. Chief among those lessons is the reality that neither the DoD nor any individual service has the expertise or the ultimate integrity to investigate its own accidents and incidents and report honestly and fully thereon.

Dr. Diehl did not decide to write this book on his own. I have urged him to do so; the media has urged him to do so; outraged and grief-stricken families of military personnel unnecessarily killed in the line of duty by preventable accidents have urged him to do so. The result is a very important work for America, because Diehl's experiences and his insights into the problems of dealing with human error and insulating systems against its effects are those of a pioneer in a new and important field. The troops, in Diehl's words, have become "silent knights" on the flawed theory that whatever their sacrifice, it serves the interests of America's defense—when, in actuality, unnecessary accidents imperil everything from the support of the American people (the ultimate authority) to the viability of the DoD's budget. We can't afford to waste lives or money, and we're wasting scandalous amounts of both.

This is the clarion call of a patriot. We all have a serious duty to listen, heed, and implement. The founders of this nation would say nothing less.

Lt. Col. John J. Nance, USAFR

Acknowledgments

This book would not have happened without the moral support, tutelage, and information provided by many people. I am particularly grateful for the assistance of several groups.

I am thankful for the many teachers and professors who stressed the need for scholarship and perseverance in the quest for wisdom. I remember one history professor, Major Philip Flammer, who emphasized the high price of misplaced loyalty in military affairs. Their influences cannot be overestimated, but some of the most important lessons are learned outside of school, such as those that came from my parents, Technical Sergeant Aloysius Diehl and Edna Diehl, who always stressed the values of courage and candor.

Others who influenced me include our neighbors. These hardworking GIs and their families loved this country and made great sacrifices to serve it. They personified what Tom Brokaw described in his book *The Greatest Generation*. But I have since concluded that such people have always been there when we needed them, and they still stoically stand their watches today.

Then there were many progressive-thinking senior military officers and officials whose actions convinced me that maybe, just maybe, the system could be changed. One of the most important was Eric Thorson, who served as an assistant secretary of the Air Force and continued to fight for safety reform long after he left office.

Another group of individuals, who have been lavish in their private praise and of necessity otherwise quiet, are my fellow investigators from the three military safety centers. As with most of the senior officials, their names cannot be mentioned for fear of retaliation. Interestingly, most of these individuals have confided their concurrence with my message, although some have questioned my use of the media.

That is certainly understandable, for professional investigators generally avoid all contact with the media. This is because these hardworking investigators fear that things they say might be misunderstood or, worst yet, intentionally sensationalized. In fact, for many years while working as an investigator, I followed that path—until I met Mr. John Nance.

Nance was writing a book about civil aviation and had a great reputation for accuracy and integrity. It helped that he was a professional pilot, as well as a lawyer. By the time he finished his classic tome, *Blind Trust*, I was convinced that members of the fourth estate were neither dangerous nor disruptive to the investigative process.

Over the years, I learned a great deal from him about how the media works. His many suggestions were invaluable in reassuring this nervous scientist that most people in the industry were dedicated, not just to getting the story, but also to getting it right. Moreover, because military safety endeavors were always highly secretive, I felt a special obligation to get involved and thereby insure the accuracy of their work.

I soon concluded that the vast majority of reporters were trying to get at the truth, just as I was. This was reinforced when I spoke with people like Mark Thompson from *Time*, Bob Davis from *USA Today*, Matt Brelis from the *Boston Globe*, and many others who labored over their keyboards.

Then there were the networks with their producers and on-the-air talent. This was another group that John Nance, who by now was the ABC national aviation consultant, helped me understand. It was a pleasure working with the likes of ABC's Diane Sawyer, CBS's Morley Safer, CNN's Lou Waters, Fox's Laurie Dhue, and NBC's Brian Williams. I certainly appreciated their patience in listening to this reluctant whistle-blower.

We are all products of our times, and no one can truly know the impact that the visionaries have had on our society. People like Ralph Nader have always inspired me. Another group of individuals whom I was proud to emulate were the whistle-blowers. They were people of conviction and courage who were not afraid to endure risks to protect society. While most did not have to pay the ultimate price that Karen Silkwood did, all suffered for righteous causes.

Such people include Chuck Miller of the National Transportation Safety Board. He steadfastly resisted White House pressures while exposing problems with FAA's aircraft certification process. His courage helped Congress create an independent NTSB—and cost him his health. Pentagon management analyst Ernest Fitzgerald exposed massive cost overruns and was summarily fired. His family endured economic hardship for years. It was a privilege to follow in such footsteps.

Another group I must acknowledge are those who helped bring this story out. My agent, Francis Kuffel of the Jean V. Naggar Literary Agency, suggested contracting with Brassey's, Inc. because of their reputation in producing the highest-quality books on military, aviation, and technical history topics. I found their publisher, Don McKeon, most gracious in dealing with a naïve first-time author. I want to thank him and my editors, Don Jacobs and Paul Merzlak, who labored to turn a rough manuscript into this polished product.

I also want to acknowledge my long-suffering wife, Marlyn, for ably catching my many errors while tracking down countless references. Her knowledge and insight made this a much less arduous undertaking. Her beauty, grace, and humor helped get this writer through this often depressing exercise. She also heard the often not-so-veiled threats I received, and she urged me to stay on course and deliver the message.

But perhaps those who contributed the most to this crusade were the victims and their loved ones. The families of the victims had already lost their most precious possessions and could expect nothing but grief in hearing the story of their loved ones' suffering again. But they did not demur as they provided me with the intimate details needed to properly convey what happened in these accidents. Their sacrifices drove me forward in trying to help right these unspeakable wrongs. There were literally dozens of people who asked me to tell the story of a child, spouse, or relative.

These families and victims (in alphabetical order) include: Connie and Cleon Bass, parents of Cornelius (Anthony) Bass; Joe Bowers, father of Paul Bowers; Darrell Darling, father of Adam Darling; Shirley Dostal and Gertrude Sandor, mother and godmother of Mark Dostal; Kathy Kubicina, sister of Clayton Hartwig; William Leland Jr., father of William

Leland III; Cathy, Joyce, and Myrna Levens, wife, mother, and aunt of Kenneth Levens; Norman Levine, uncle of Alan Levine; Anne McHugh, mother of Robert Weinman; Heidi and Peter Mueller, parents of Thomas Mueller; Joan and Danny Piper, parents of Laura Piper; Candida, Cathy, and Allen Rogers, wife and parents of Robert Rogers; Neta and Stan Sharp, parents of Mark Sharp; Debra Shelton-Harris, mother of Lance Fielder; Sally Spears, mother of Kara Hultgreen; Sharon and James Svoboda, parents of Amy Svoboda; and Hank Weber, father of Pace Weber.

While nothing can truly ease their suffering, perhaps this exposé can prevent others from having to undergo such torture in the future.

Introduction

As a kid growing up on military bases named for dead heroes, I developed a profound respect for those who served. Each evening, when taps rang out, everybody stood at attention to honor fallen comrades. I soon discovered that many had died in preventable accidents, rather than in combat. Somehow, that seemed wrong.

I joined up and quickly learned why this was such a dangerous profession. Safety was rarely a top priority for military leaders, partly because of time, resource, and expertise limitations. Years later, after becoming a military safety professional myself, I knew that somehow I had to change this sad reality. This book describes what happened, why I failed, and what needs to happen now.

This manuscript explains the profound problems facing military personnel and describes the highly dysfunctional system used to investigate mishaps—one that often leads to bungled investigations and cover-ups. The book documents both historic and contemporary events, as well as the cumulative costs of ignoring such problems.

This book is a factual description of what happened, my observations of why such tragedies occurred, and how they could have been avoided. My scientific judgment has been shaped by years of investigating accidents and by graduate study in the safety and health fields, buttressed by intimate familiarity with military equipment.

I wanted to capture the enormity of this tragedy—the deaths of over one-half million American troops from accidents and illnesses—but not to lose sight of their individual sacrifices. Doing this would prove to be a challenge.

Using "psychological autopsy" techniques, I've tried to take readers into the minds of these victims. This process is based on the physical evidence and on statements of people closely associated with each particular mishap, along with my interviews of others who survived similar accidents.

Perhaps the most difficult part of writing this book involved dealing with the victims' families, who struggled to understand why our government would not tell them the truth. I had no answer for their questions, nor could I explain why such a system has been allowed to exist unchallenged for so many years.

These chivalrous troops and their families have suffered in silence far too long. It is now time to tell their story, and hope that as America launches into this difficult war on international terrorism, it won't repeat past mistakes that have claimed so many of our troops.

Disclaimer: The views expressed herein are those of the author and do not necessarily reflect the official positions of the Department of Defense or any other agency of the United States government.

PART

I

Betrayal of Trust

1

Nexus of the Nightmare

First Lieutenant Laura Piper watches the rugged Iraqi terrain glide by a hundred feet below as the wind whips through her chopper's crowded passenger compartment. She glances at another U.S. Army UH-60 Black Hawk[1] while shadows of both craft dance across the valley floor.

It's April 14, 1994. This twenty-three-year-old Air Force intelligence analyst knows she is a long way from her home in San Antonio, Texas. But seeing the oversized red-white-and-blue flag emblazoned on the side of the nearby chopper reminds her why she volunteered for this mission.[2]

The United States has promised to use its vast aerial armada to protect the Kurds from Saddam Hussein. Piper wants to be part of this important show-the-flag operation. But America's high-tech arsenal is a two-edged sword, and today, its massive firepower is about to explode in the lieutenant's face.

For her helicopter is being unknowingly stalked by two sleek fighters. These U.S. Air Force F-15 Eagles[3] bristle with deadly missiles as they patrol the so-called no-fly zone. Unfortunately, headquarters has failed to tell the F-15 pilots that friendly Black Hawks are *also* operating in this area today.

In the fighter cockpits, Captain Eric Wickson and Lieutenant Colonel Randy May stare at their radarscopes. At 10:22 A.M., they pick up the two unidentified blips forty miles away.[4] Wickson pushes a button on his throttles that sends a signal to electronically interrogate the targets. Black boxes aboard the helicopters fail to respond with the proper code identifying them as "friendlies." Seeing no response on his radar, the captain pushes the throttles forward, lighting his afterburners.

The two jets quickly intercept the "bogies" from behind. Captain Wickson, in the lead jet, closes to within one thousand feet. Staring through his canopy, he mistakenly identifies the two helicopters as Soviet-made Mi-24 Hinds.[5] He knows the Iraqis often use such choppers to strafe civilians—and those clowns are not going to get away with that on his watch.

As an Air Force Academy cadet, his nickname was "Blinky"—because of an eye-twitch[6]—and the stress of this situation is not helping him see any better. He asks Colonel May, flying a mile behind him, to verify this identification. Wickson mistakenly believes that May's terse reply is confirmation that these are indeed enemy craft. The two pilots eagerly maneuver into firing position behind the unsuspecting choppers.

More than a hundred miles away, other eyes are watching. Captain Jim Wang is the senior weapons director aboard an Air Force E-3, Airborne Warning and Control System (AWACS).[7] Seated deep in the belly of this flying radar station, he peers at the confusing and ever-changing picture on his scope. Wang was born in Taiwan, and, like Wickson and Piper, he is a graduate of the United States Air Force Academy. But such a classic military education is not adequate preparation for decision making on the frontiers of the new world order.

Captain Wang has been recently upgraded to senior director because the Air Force decided to retire many of its veteran AWACS controllers early. This post–Cold War economy measure is about to become very costly, as this inexperienced young officer will soon be overwhelmed by the myriad challenges facing him today.

First, he and his crew of junior radar observers, two lieutenants, arrived "in theater" only yesterday. They have not had time to master its arcane rules of engagement. He is also struggling with the ergonomically deficient AWACS radar control panel. The letters on his keyboard are arranged alphabetically, rather than in the familiar personal computer format.[8] The alphabetical arrangement forces this computer geek to constantly guard against typos rather than concentrating on the radar picture.

His crew was tracking the Black Hawks earlier, but the icons dropped off their scopes several minutes ago. The steep mountains in the area often conceal low-flying helicopters from the AWACS' prying radar. Now the fighter pilots are saying they are going to attack two enemy Hind helicopters that they have visually identified.

In the Air Force pecking order, fighter jocks are at the top of the food chain. Wang's previous experience has taught him not to question such customs. Furthermore, his lieutenants, staring at their radarscopes, are reluctant to even bring up the possibility that the fighters might be about to engage the friendly Black Hawks.

Four years earlier, I had recommended the Air Force adopt an innovative type of training designed to facilitate interpersonal communication in just such situations. This training is called Crew Resource Management (CRM). It teaches team members how to coordinate their efforts and avoid distractions. This optimizes judgment in stressful, time-critical conditions. Subordinates are also encouraged to speak up if they ever suspect leaders do not understand critical information.

But a few senior officers thought CRM might undermine military discipline. Because the brass dragged its feet, Wang and his fellow airmen have *not* received this vital training. Along with the other safety glitches, this folly has set the stage for disaster.

Captain Wickson and Colonel May aggressively maneuver their craft into firing position. At 10:30 A.M. Wickson has dropped to five miles behind the trailing chopper. He quickly selects his most sophisticated weapon, the radar-guided AMRAAM missile.[9] When he presses the firing button on his control stick, this rocket instantly drops from beneath his jet. Its high-tech guidance system has already locked on to the quarry.

Laura Piper and the others in her chopper drone on, oblivious to the lethal threat streaking toward their hindquarters at supersonic speeds. Seconds later, the powerful missile explodes beside its target—like a sledgehammer hitting a Swiss watch. Blam!

The lead helicopter immediately dives for cover, hoping that clutter from the hills below will shield it from radar. But May has already launched a heat-seeking Sidewinder missile.[10] It relentlessly closes in on the second Black Hawk and explodes. Blam!

Laura Piper cries only for a moment, and then the helicopter's tumbling fuselage flails her unconscious body around like a pit bull shaking a rag doll.[11] Villagers look up in horror, but the roar of the nearby F-15s drowns out her voice. This knight without armor is forever silenced when her Black Hawk shatters itself across the valley floor.

Flames immediately erupt from ruptured fuel tanks on both helicopters. Smutty black smoke billows from the twisted wreckage of the twin funeral pyres. Overhead, the two jets pilots circle victoriously as they stare down through their canopies.

With fighter pilots, the two most dangerous substances are adrenaline and testosterone. Oblivious to the nationality of their victims, they resort to humor—to protect their psyches from the carnage of the scene below. Like two chefs at a family barbecue, they use some culinary clichés. May quips to Wickson, "Stick a fork in him," and adds, "Yeah, he's done."[12] Standard fare for fighter jocks who must be prepared to dish out death without remorse.

Lieutenant Piper's body will burn for hours. Her twenty-five companions in death include soldiers from the U.S. Army, Britain, France, and Turkey, as well as American and Kurdish civilians. The military's worst nightmare has come true—friendly-fire deaths. Furthermore, video cameras have caught this fratricidal debacle on tape. Soon, my job will require me to take a front-row seat.

The wreckage is still smoldering when I arrive at the headquarters of Air Education and Training Command. This impressive brick facade is located at Randolph Air Force Base (AFB) in San Antonio, Texas. As I open the massive wooden door, an ashen-faced captain says, "Dr. Diehl, hurry up, *it's* on TV."

We scurry down the hall to his office. There we watch in disbelief as Secretary of Defense Perry and President Clinton appear on CNN. The accident has occurred in broad daylight, but the president and his defense secretary are both totally in the dark about what has happened.

Prodded by handlers and Pentagon spin-meisters, they apologize to the victims' families and promise a full and complete investigation. They also pledge to make all this information public and to hold those responsible accountable.

"If that happens, it will be a first," I exclaim to the young captain, and excuse myself. I hastily depart this officer's cramped office, for I need to brief a general in a nearby building in a few minutes.

Ambling down the stately headquarters corridors, I am reminded of the countless military crashes I have studied. But unlike this latest debacle, such mishaps usually go almost unnoticed by the press, public, and politicians.

Typically, there is just a brief blurb on page seven of the local newspaper. "Military officials announced this morning that a jet crashed last night forty miles east of Heartland Air Force Base. It was on a routine training mission. The pilot, whose name was not released, died of injuries. A team of military officers is investigating the mishap."

Several weeks later, an even shorter follow-up piece will appear on page eight: "The Public Affairs Office at Heartland Air Force Base announced today the completion of their investigation into last month's crash. The inquiry has concluded the mishap was caused by pilot error." Period, end of story.

The stealthy meat grinder whirls on, unabated. Our finest young people quietly join the ranks of its victims. Their families will never be given the real reasons for their deaths. Furthermore, the nation is kept in the dark about the cumulative cost of such tragedies. The biggest secret is that unnecessary accidents and illnesses actually kill more troops than do enemy action. These thoughts haunt me as I step outside.

I walk across the headquarters parking lot, passing a row of Air Force staff cars. But not all of the staff vehicles are here right now. One is parked on the other side of San Antonio. It is in front of Lieutenant Laura Piper's home.

The casualty notification team has just arrived to tell her family she was aboard one of the helicopters shot down over Iraq. They explain there are no survivors, and the Air Force will try to return her body in several days. They then offer their deepest condolences and depart for the base.

Meanwhile, I walk into the office of Brigadier General Marcie Harris, Director of Technical Training. This woman, a former maintenance officer, has previously developed innovative training programs for other commands. Today, this no-nonsense lady says she wants to see the statistical evidence on the effectiveness of Crew Resource Management training. I quickly load my slides into the projector and turn down the lights.

This slide show soon answers her questions. My research has revealed that CRM can reduce military flying accidents by up to 81 percent and maintenance errors by up to 64 percent.[13] She is convinced but asks why CRM did not help the crew members in the today's friendly-fire incident.

Pausing for a second, I explain that they had *not* received CRM training, because some commanders do not recognize its value. I suggest the tragedy will certainly accelerate the pace of CRM training in the United States Air Force. But I am sadly mistaken, as I learn a few days later.

On April 17, I am eating lunch at my desk in the Air Force Safety Agency at Kirtland Air Force Base in Albuquerque, New Mexico. Our secretary appears at my door. She tells me a colonel from Ramstein Air Base in Germany has phoned earlier and will be calling me again in a few minutes.

I know the call is probably related to the friendly-fire accident because Ramstein is the location of the headquarters of the United States Air Forces Europe (USAFE). That command was in charge of air operations over northern Iraq. Under the service's procedures, when a command has an accident, it gets to investigate itself. As I scarf down my sandwich, I remember just how this dysfunctional safety system operates.

The command that had the accident appoints members to its so-called Safety Investigation Board (SIB). Commanders never like surprises, so they always ensure that the "voting members" of the inquiry are people they know and trust. These subordinates are line officers such as pilots, who have little training, not to mention experience, in the complex protocols employed by professional accident investigators. They work for this commander and will try to keep him happy above all else.

The command then calls consultants like myself. We are asked to provide expert opinions and technical reports in a variety of specialized areas such as psychology, meteorology, and metallurgy. But the Safety Investigation Board is free to ignore this data should it conflict with what they want to report back to their commanding general.

These SIB reports are supposed to be kept privileged and *never* released outside the Department of Defense (DoD). The official purpose of the SIB report is to establish *why* the mishap occurred so that steps can be taken to prevent a future reoccurrence.

But this fundamentally flawed system is often abused to protect commanders from embarrassment and accountability. The obvious problems with such an incestuous and clandestine system have not gone unnoticed by critics.

To get around such criticism, the services have commanders conduct another, separate, investigation. This second type of inquiry is called an Accident Investigation Board (AIB). Its ostensive purpose is to establish *legal* responsibility, but its real objective is public relations. The military has learned the value of keeping two sets of books on each mishap.

These Accident Investigation Boards suffer many of the same problems as the SIBs, namely, handpicked subordinates who are amateur investigators. But AIBs have additional limitations. Unlike the SIBs, witnesses who are interviewed by the AIBs do not have immunity. Thus, they understandably will not reveal information that could later be used to prosecute them. Furthermore, these *accident* reports, unlike the *safety* reports, *will* be released to the public, including the victim's families, Congress, and the press. Thus, investigators preparing such reports are usually *very* careful about their contents.

Consequently, these accident reports are less informative than the safety reports.[14] At best they simply describe what may have happened and whom the investigators think should be punished. Not surprisingly, such reports are even less likely than the safety reports to find fault with the commander, who, after all, convened the whole process. Nor do such reports usually blame other senior officers in their command or even such individuals in other commands—professional courtesy, no doubt, for next time they could be investigating your actions.

There is another pandemic problem with military investigations. The part-time investigators all have important "real" jobs. So, while these officers are off pretending to be accident investigators, the paperwork is piling up on their desks back home. Their critical "officer performance ratings" are based on how well they do their day jobs. Thus, they are very eager to come up with quick, simplistic, answers so they can go back to their own units.

Obviously, the key to preventing future accidents is an independent and thorough investigation. Watching the military's self-serving and highly dysfunctional system clunk along for years was particularly disturbing to me because I know how the process *should* work—from previous experience. Before taking my military position, I served as an investigator for the National Transportation Safety Board (NTSB).

The NTSB is the federal agency charged with investigating civilian airline and other transportation crashes. This elite group of about four hundred dedicated experts is arguably the most effective accident investigation organization on the planet.

In 1974, Congress made the Board independent of the giant Department of Transportation because of the obvious difficulties of allowing *any* organization to investigate itself.[15] In 1994, Congress also closed a loophole that allowed most government departments to investigate their own crashes. Unfortunately, the DoD was excluded from this law.[16]

In the seven years since taking the senior civilian job with the Air Force Safety Agency, I have watched unnecessary accidents cost the Pentagon billions of dollars and kill hundreds of troops. But explaining the drawbacks of the current system to the brass was so much mental masturbation. A former secretary of the Air Force has privately asked me, "You don't think the generals and admirals will ever *willingly* give up the current system, do you?"

The ringing phone brings me back to reality. I pick up and immediately recognize a familiar voice. Colonel Jimmy Hollerin[17] is a senior official in USAFE headquarters. This colleague is very familiar with my many years of conducting civil and military investigations as well as my safety research. He explains that I am being asked to become a consultant to this important investigation.

He nervously says they are being directed *not to* perform a safety investigation. Instead, USAFE will just do an accident investigation. I ask him who made that decision, but he ignores the question. The colonel then explains that many of the Air Force's best lawyers have been assigned to this inquiry. Changing the subject, he tells me that I need to travel to Incirlik Air Base in Turkey, which is where the board is meeting.

He then asks me what issues I would expect to investigate. I tell him, things like 1) the confusing rules of engagement, 2) the poorly designed equipment, and 3) the visual illusions involved in the misidentification of the helicopters. He quickly agrees these are all important issues.

I then tell the colonel how the lack of CRM training also appears to be a factor in this accident. I note how USAFE and other major commands

(MAJCOMs) have so far failed to implement such training. He then asks me if I am *sure* of these facts. I explain that I was in the room when the responsible safety official blew off this training as unnecessary.

Colonel Hollerin has heard my briefings before and knows my well-documented data on CRM effectiveness. He agrees such training deficiencies *are* significant and asks me to fax copies of my studies and briefings directly to the accident board in Turkey. He concludes the conversation by saying the board's flight surgeon will call me in the next several hours.

At 2 A.M., my bedroom phone rings. Half awake, I flip the lights on and soon realize it is the doctor calling from the accident board in Turkey. Major Chris Lasanti states that he has received my fax. He has read the materials and wants to know how fast I can join the board. I reply that I should be able to leave tomorrow, as soon as they cut my travel orders.

The major and I start poring over the details of the accident. I pick up a cold cup of coffee as I shuffle toward my cluttered desk. From years of doing this drill, I know these are never quick calls.

An hour later the major concludes by lamenting that the process of accident investigation is so confusing. He remarks that he has done only a couple of previous investigations. I remind him that's probably two more than most officers who are assigned to Air Force accident boards, and then I hang up.

Shortly after arriving at work the next morning, I hear from a senior lawyer at Kirtland Air Force Base. It seems that his counterparts assigned to the investigation have contacted him. They apparently have strong reservations about some of the areas that I have proposed investigating. He reminds me of the high level of interest in this investigation. Moreover, this is a very unusual situation in that all information uncovered will supposedly become public domain—because this is an *accident* rather than a *safety* investigation.

He remarks that twelve of the victims were not members of the U.S. Armed Services. Quick translation: Our GIs[18] and their families cannot sue in wrongful death situations, but it is theoretically possible for the other families to file embarrassing lawsuits. It sounds like an all too familiar situation—a cover-up is already under way!

The suspected conspiracy is confirmed a few hours later when Colonel Hollerin calls me from Ramstein. An unusual tremor distorts his voice. He clears his throat and says there is *a problem:* "Al, they don't want *your* kind of investigation." I know immediately what he means. Before I can say anything, he apologetically adds, "They only want the *whats,* not the *whys.*" I instinctively ask, "Who is the *they?*" The colonel reluctantly replies that the order came from headquarters. The die is cast.

Over the next several days the twenty-six victims are laid to rest. Nine weeks later, Secretary of the Air Force Sheila Widnall quietly signs a regulation requiring CRM training for all air crew members.[19] Twelve weeks later, Secretary of Defense William Perry presents a two-thousand-plus-page document to the television cameras.[20]

In this Pentagon press briefing, he claims the tome is a "full and complete" documentation of the incident. This accident report does not mention the CRM training deficiencies or the many other problems that contributed to the disaster. Secretary Perry adds—in what has to be the understatement of the age—"It is a tragedy that never should have happened."[21]

This catastrophe should have been a wake-up call for the entire Defense Department to mend its ways and stop ignoring widespread safety problems. Instead, Secretary Perry and the Pentagon sycophants will slip into a collective state of denial, suggesting this friendly-fire incident was a freak accident rather than a symptom of a dysfunctional system. These problems will soon claim more victims, including two of Perry's personal associates.

In the months that follow, the press and Congress will begin asking embarrassing questions as the families of victims cry out in vain for justice. Laura Piper's mother, Joan, will soon discover that the organization to which she entrusted her daughter's life lacks accountability. She will eventually capture her frustrations in a compelling book, *Chain of Events.*[22] This same military establishment has already begun a hunt for low-ranking scapegoats to deflect criticism from senior officials. Meanwhile the real culprit, the "safety process," will continue unchanged. This situation soon would convince me that I *had* to file a whistle-blowing complaint to bring about needed reforms.

The American people would shortly begin hearing about another tragedy, one involving thousands of Gulf War veterans who are suffering from mysterious illnesses. In their standard modus operandi, the Pentagon officials will insist, first, that there is no "real" problem, and secondly, that they alone must be allowed to investigate all matters pertaining to the safety and health of *their* troops. But this "just trust us" refrain is wearing a little thin, as the evidence of a massive cover-up emerges regarding the exposure of *our* GIs to deadly chemicals.

Some of the Black Hawk shoot-down victims are buried in Arlington National Cemetery. The serenity of this place is interrupted only by the periodic passage of airliners en route to nearby National Airport. These fallen warriors are some of this country's most chivalrous people. Like so many of their comrades, they have paid the ultimate price for a flawed system. They are truly "silent knights" who would be turning over in their graves at the specter of shameful events occurring behind a nearby façade.

This most sacred piece of American real estate overlooks both the Pentagon and a historical U.S. Army post—Fort Myer. Such juxtaposition represents at once both a colossal contradiction and a supreme irony, because the Pentagon is normally where self-righteous statements originate—demands that *other* nations provide *all* information concerning U.S. military personnel who are "killed in action." This same building houses those who insist the families, not to mention the American people, have *no* right to know what happened to our troops killed in accidents. Furthermore, it was on the parade grounds of Fort Myer, literally a stone's throw from this cemetery, that a military plane crash three quarters of a century ago changed the world forever.

2

First Blood

In early September 1908, hundreds of people gathered at Fort Myer, Virginia, just across the river from Washington, D.C. The crowd included members of Congress, senior military officers, government officials, as well as many of the capital's common citizens. Three unnoticed army lieutenants huddled together at the edge of the parade ground. Two would go on to long, distinguished careers as generals in the future Air Service; the other would be dead within a fortnight.

Reporters and photographers were also in evidence. Their stories had set the entire city abuzz with talk about how the Army was *actually* testing its first "flying machine." These crowds reflected the growing public fascination with what was happening in this open field adjacent to Arlington Cemetery.

Many spectators had come to see if men could *really* fly. Most people remembered how the government had sponsored another aeronautical experiment five years earlier. The director of the Smithsonian Institution, the renowned scientist Dr. Samuel Langley, had designed a prototype aircraft. On its maiden flight attempt, the flimsy craft crashed into the Potomac several miles south of the city.[1] While the pilot escaped unscathed, the government's interest in things aeronautical definitely took a plunge. After this spectacular failure, the pundits of the day concluded that human flight was *impossible*. These same experts dismissed claims that two brothers named Wright, who were mere bicycle mechanics, had successfully flown an aircraft just weeks before at some remote beach called Kitty Hawk.

The Wright brothers had offered to build an aircraft for the Army in 1905, but they were soundly rebuffed. After all, the government was still smarting from the 1903 Langley fiasco. By 1907, President Teddy Roosevelt had heard stories about the successes of the publicity-shy Wrights.

This president was fascinated by technical innovation and was aware that fledgling aviators were beginning to attract the attention of certain European governments. He suggested that his secretary of war, one William Howard Taft, look into the matter. The upwardly mobile bureaucrat knew how to take a hint.

On December 23, 1907, the Army Signal Corps released Specification Number 486.[2] It called for bids on an airplane that could fly forty miles per hour, carry a passenger in addition to the pilot, and stay aloft for one hour. On February 10, 1908, the Army signed a contract with the Wrights for its first airplane. This $25,000 contract, however, had a stiff penalty clause for speeds less than forty miles per hour. The Army identified Fort Myer as the location for test flying the aircraft.

The Army soon selected the Wrights' basic design. The two-place craft was designated the Model A. It was a scaled-up version of their Flyer, which first soared over the dunes of Kitty Hawk in 1903.

The new biplane had a wingspan of just over thirty-six feet. It had a small upholstered bench-style seat for the pilot and passenger located on the leading edge of the lower wing. The craft had two wing-like horizontal elevators mounted on a truss structure that projected several feet in front of the crew seat. Dual landing skids ran aft under the lower wing and connected to the twin vertical rudders. Criss-crossed steel wires provided the necessary rigidity to the craft's wooden structure.

This box-kite-like craft weighed 1,360 pounds fully loaded. A catapult mechanism helped launch it along a sixty-foot wooden rail lying on the ground. A twenty-five horsepower, four-cylinder motor was located just left of the passenger seat. It drove the two propellers mounted behind the wings via a bicycle chain-and-sprocket mechanism. This type of transmission must have seemed natural to these bicycle mechanics.

Orville Wright arrived at Fort Myer on August 23, 1908, with the newly manufactured biplane. He and his two mechanics assembled the fragile craft over the next two weeks. They fine-tuned the engine in preparation for the first shakedown flight. But some things bothered Orville, who had always been safety conscious.

He knew that several of the pioneering balloonists had died in accidents. Furthermore, both he and his brother had been involved in minor crack-ups, though neither was seriously hurt. A colleague of theirs, Dr. Otto Lilienthal, however, had died a decade earlier in a glider crash.

Lilienthal's death was partially blamed on the fact that he had removed a safety bar from the front of his glider. That was one reason why the Wrights had located the horizontal tail structure in front of the occupants on their craft. But Orville also knew that to date, *nobody* had ever perished in an airplane accident.

Orville had other safety concerns, not the least of which was the environment that the Army had selected for these tests. He noted the small size of the ersatz flying field. The parade ground was only one thousand feet long, about the size of a modern aircraft carrier flight deck. Because of the possibility of having to make a forced landing, he wanted to keep the flight path close to this field.

This would require him to make sharp turns and fly tight racetrack patterns around the field because most of the surrounding terrain was unsuitable. A series of barracks, artillery sheds, and stables were directly to the west. He planned to take off to the south, and, after traveling over the parade grounds, he would turn left over a small tree-filled gully. He would then cross the Arlington Cemetery wall to the east. After flying back to the north over the cemetery, he planned to make another left turn and fly over the take-off point on the field. Flying this tight oval pattern would require lots of skill, with little margin for error.

By September 3, everything was ready. Six hundred excited spectators had gathered to watch the event, which must have compared with the moon rocket launches of later decades, because in 1908, this vehicle represented an *astounding* piece of technology.

In the crowd were several people who were aviation pioneers in their own right and others who would soon become so. Dr. Alexander Graham Bell, the inventor of the telephone, had also helped to develop a series of flying machines with the assistance of the first aviation organization that he founded, the Aerial Experiment Association. Glen Curtis, who was already famous as a racecar builder and driver, would in future years develop the world's first successful seaplane.

Also present at Fort Myer were the three U.S. Army lieutenants who would soon be riding as passengers. These young officers were not just guinea pigs. They were assigned major responsibilities for testing of the Wright machine. But today Orville would be flying solo.

For the first demonstration, Orville flew for only one minute and eleven seconds, gracefully flying in a single oval circuit around the field—but that was enough. It convinced the elated spectators that man could *really* fly. The morning papers broadcast the news. Reporters had once asked in print of the Brothers Wright, "Are they fliers or liars?" Now they were eating crow and printing praiseful retractions.

Over the next two weeks Orville would "expand the envelope." He was flying longer, faster, and higher in seemingly endless oval circuits around the field. He even added innovations, such as performing spectacular figure-eight patterns and flying directly over the crowd at times. Orville was soon carrying a passenger aboard and was practically setting new world's records on almost a daily basis.

This series of convincing demonstrations had resulted in mob scenes as more and more spectators surrounded the parade grounds, mesmerized by the seemingly effortless accomplishments of this marvelous machine. There was a growing sense of euphoria as officials and the press began issuing statements about the potential of the new invention. But the modest pilot said little, knowing that the formal Army test protocols still lay ahead.

The ever-cautious Orville was also beginning to worry over a few noisome problems. One of the skids had been fractured during a hard landing on the parade ground's uneven terrain. Much more troubling, the wood near the tip of one of the craft's propeller blades had developed a split. Orville knew that all aircraft fly safely *only* when various forces are in proper balance.

A split in a propeller could propagate and eventually cause the rapidly spinning blade to break apart. If this happened, the blade fragment could fly off and cut a rudder control wire or even break one of several guide wires, which held the tail surfaces in place. Being "wired" was even more critical in those days, and these vital steel lines ran perilously close to the whirling blades.

Moreover, a failure in one of the two propellers would kill the thrust on that side, thus upsetting the delicate balance of forces holding the craft in the air. The airplane would then want to turn violently. The pilot would have to react instantly by doing one of two things—either cut the power and glide, or try to resist the asymmetric forces with control surface inputs. The latter maneuver is especially tricky at the low speeds, because the air passing over the control surfaces might not have enough force to resist the high asymmetric engine thrust. Orville, like every aviator who would follow in his footsteps, knew the danger implicit in this situation.

At Orville's direction, his mechanics repaired this potentially dangerous split in the propeller tip with nails and glue. The test flights continued, but Orville kept a watchful eye on the situation. He was also concerned because the craft was not quite performing up to the forty-miles-per-hour speed requirement set by the Army. This was particularly troubling because Orville had not flown with the heaviest of the three lieutenants, the robust Thomas Selfridge. Carrying Selfridge, who was almost six feet tall and weighed over 175 pounds, would be the most demanding test for the craft.

So after a dozen days of successful flying, Orville decided to replace the original propellers with a new set of oversized blades. The original props were eight and one-half feet in diameter, while the new ones were nine feet. These new props were expected to increase the craft's performance by taking a bigger bite of air and hopefully producing the needed increase in speed. But they would also place the propeller tips only a few inches from the critical guide wires on the tail.

Orville somewhat reluctantly agreed to fly with Selfridge on the first test flight with the bigger props, but his reluctance involved more than this lieutenant's large stature. Selfridge earlier had been assigned to work with Dr. Bell's Aerial Experiment Association, and, in 1907, the lieutenant had written the Wrights asking about details of their airplane's design. The Wrights freely revealed their hard-earned secrets—for scientific purposes only. When similar features appeared on aircraft being built for sale by other members of the association, the Wrights complained that their ideas were being stolen. Orville had personally blamed Selfridge for disclosing the information to potential competitors, but Selfridge knew that he was only trying to spread the word on what worked.

The stoic officer exuded integrity. His relatives had had distinguished naval careers, but Tom Selfridge ended up attending West Point. This highly sensitive young man idolized the Wrights for what they had accomplished but was still embarrassed by Orville's angst. Orville, for his part, knew this was neither the time nor place to open old wounds. Selfridge, after all, represented the customer, the United States Army.

Thomas Selfridge certainly understood the depth of the Wrights' accomplishments, for he had studied aeronautical science for many years. He had, in fact, designed the Aerial Experiment Association's first aircraft. It flew, but because it lacked the Wright-invented features, it was difficult to control. He had also personally piloted the association's second aircraft, but it too was crude compared to the Wright craft.

For the last two weeks, he had reverently watched the tour-de-force provided by Orville's impressive flying demonstrations. Now he was going to get a chance to ride with this master aircraft designer. By the late afternoon of September 17, all was in readiness. The shadows of the tombstones in nearby Arlington Cemetery had begun their daily march eastward. An even noisier than usual crowd of two thousand people pressed close to the aircraft. Meanwhile, the early twentieth-century paparazzi had positioned their tripod-mounted cameras in front of the crowd. They were no doubt hoping to get a photo prior to a subsequent disaster. Lieutenant Selfridge in his uniform sat ramrod straight on the passenger seat. He watched Orville in his business suit carefully performing the preflight inspection. The catapult weight was hoisted to the top of a twenty-five-foot tower.

At 5:14, Orville climbs over the wooden structure, slipping through the series of brace wires that cross directly in front of the men's faces. Orville, sitting to the left of Selfridge, places his hands on the controls. The crowd grows quiet with anticipation. Orville gives the command as two mechanics grab the new propellers and simultaneously pull downward. The engine roars to life.

Orville carefully listens to the sounds of the engine. Satisfied that all is well, he reaches over and pulls the wire, releasing the catapult weight. The craft is hurled down the rail. Orville pulls the elevator control stick, causing the craft to leap into the air.

As they climb to 150 feet, the aviators can hear the cheers of the crowd over the roar of the engine. In the distance they can see the city of Washington. After completing four flawless circuits around the parade grounds, Orville begins a left turn toward Arlington Cemetery. Then both aviators hear an ominous tapping sound. Orville decides to turn the craft rapidly left, toward the safety of the parade grounds. He wants to make an immediate landing.

Seconds later, they hear loud cracking sounds coming from behind them. Terrified, both men glance back to see a vertical rudder flip over into a horizontal position. Orville kills the engine immediately as the craft begins to buck and wobble. Now the plane suddenly lurches to the right. Orville jerks the control stick to force the errant craft to turn back toward the parade grounds. The craft then rolls violently leftward, and its nose pitches almost straight down. Both men know they are in a dangerous predicament. The stoic lieutenant looks into Orville's eyes and utters "Oh! Oh!"[3] in an almost inaudible voice as the craft plunges toward the terrain.

Orville frantically manipulates the controls, managing to partially right the craft at fifty feet above the ground. The lowered left wing has almost come back to the horizontal. But the craft is still tilted forty-five degrees nose down when its front structure, with the landing skids and wing-like elevators, digs into the dirt.

The wooden struts snap like matchsticks. The structure's progressive destruction absorbs much of the impact force—just as it was designed to do. But the men, unrestrained by seat belts or shoulder harnesses, are thrown forward into the wires, splintering struts, and sod. A large cloud of dust surrounds the wreckage as a chorus of screams arises from the incredulous crowd.

Dozens of would-be rescuers reach the victims in a matter of seconds. Willing hands lift the wreckage from the fallen airmen. They find the badly dazed Orville with his right arm outstretched in a vain effort to shield his passenger. Orville, who appears to be less badly hurt, is extricated first.

Selfridge lies unconscious, pinned under the craft's engine. Blood is gushing from a deep wound to the lieutenant's forehead over his right eye. Stretcher-bearers remove his battered body and momentarily place it on the ground as physicians examine his injuries.

These doctors, recognizing the seriousness of Selfridge's injuries, immediately order him taken to the post hospital. There, surgeons quickly realize he has a badly fractured skull. At 8:10 P.M. this gallant young officer dies without ever regaining consciousness.

Orville, who had three fractures of his hip and four broken ribs, spent the next six weeks in the hospital. When he was told of Selfridge's death, he became remorseful, perhaps because of the harsh way he had treated this young man for releasing the Wright trade secrets.

That evening, in downtown Washington, Alexander Graham Bell's wife, Mabel, was preparing dinner to celebrate the lieutenant's flight with Orville. When told of Tom Selfridge's death, she became distraught. This elderly woman had virtually adopted him as a surrogate son while he worked with her husband on aerial experiments. He had always shown chivalry to her and everyone else with whom he came in contact. She wrote to her husband three days later, referring to Lieutenant Selfridge as that "knightly boy."[4]

This "knightly boy" was buried in Arlington Cemetery one week after his accident. He was literally the first person in the world, military or civilian, to die in an airplane accident. This tragedy was a harbinger of things to come, for countless thousands of military personnel would perish in unnecessary accidents over the next decades.

The Army had experienced its first accident even before it owned an airplane. It quickly convened a board of inquiry. Orville Wright was only slightly injured, there were literally hundreds of eyewitnesses, and the wreckage was totally recovered. It did not take long to establish what happened.

Interestingly, this board was not an all-Army affair—that is, an organization investigating itself. It actually consisted of officers from all of the services and civilians, a concept that the military would later fervently denounce. The board also appears to have conducted a thorough, objective, open, and unrushed investigation. It then publicly released *all* information related to their inquiry—again, concepts that would later be opposed for future military mishap investigations. Nor did the board attempt to blame the pilot, as would become the standard practice in future mishaps.

On February 19, 1909, the board issued its findings. It concluded that the mishap " . . . was due to the accidental breaking of a propeller blade and a consequent loss of control which resulted in the machine falling to the ground. . . . "[5] The board recovered a two-and-one-half-foot piece of the right propeller.[6] This fragment had been seen flying off the craft shortly before it went out of control. It appeared to have struck the upper right-hand guide wire running to the rear rudder. The ensuing vibrations caused the rudder to come out of its socket and fall over, resulting in the loss of control.

In June 1909, a recovered Orville Wright returned to Fort Myer with an aircraft almost identical to the ill-fated craft that had killed Selfridge. It quickly exceeded the Army's speed requirement of forty miles per hour. Orville set several new world records in the process of the tests. The U.S. Army purchased the craft, becoming the first military organization in the world to have an airplane.

A decade later, Selfridge's successors would be called "Knights of the Air" as they achieved glory in the skies over France. Little more than three decades would pass before their sons would man America's vast air armadas that would swarm over far-flung battlefields around the globe. Five decades and a day after Lieutenant Selfridge's mishap, on September 18, 1947, the United States Air Force would be established as an independent service.

Orville lived to see aviation accomplishments beyond his wildest dreams, but he could never forget that fateful day when Tom Selfridge died. Shortly before his own death on January 30, 1948, the publicity-shy Orville Wright would grant what turned out to be his last interview. With a tremor in his voice he said, "You know, my hip still bothers me. It's God's way, I believe, of never letting me forget the Fort Myer incident."[7]

The government eventually named the sprawling base near Mount Clemens, Michigan, in honor of First Lieutenant Thomas Selfridge. In 1952, a technical sergeant drove to his new assignment at this base. His wife, Edna, sat beside him, while his two young sons bounced on the backseat of their maroon 1949 Ford sedan. The sergeant looked weary, for he was still recovering from illness contracted during the Korean conflict.

As he drove through the main gate, he explained to his family that Selfridge Air Force Base was named after the first person who died in an airplane crash. The younger boy looked enviously at the pilots scrambling to board their jets on the flight line. This youngster would one day become a crack fighter pilot himself. Two decades later, he would blast a MiG out of the sky over Vietnam, and four decades later, he would lead the first formation of strike fighters over Baghdad. The older boy simply asked his dad why Lieutenant Selfridge died. To which the sergeant replied: "I don't know son—why don't you try to find out someday?" That simple question would launch my lifelong quest to enhance aviation safety.

3

Deadly Debacles

Serving in the military has always been a dangerous endeavor, because you can die from one of three causes: enemy action, disease, or accidents. The latter two non-battle causes are often lumped together as *other* (see Table 1).[1]

This table does not convey the total picture, because many "battle deaths" result from accidents occurring in a war zone. One famous example was the crew of the *Lady Be Good*, a World War II B-24 that got lost at night over the Mediterranean. Their deaths were counted as "battle deaths" because their aircraft and bodies were not found until many years after the war—in the middle of the Sahara desert.

In addition to these *unintentional* distortions, sometimes embarrassing battlefield mishaps were *deliberately* recorded as combat losses.[2] Furthermore, only a small fraction of all troops were actually in the front lines. The majority served in rear areas and stateside where accidents were the real threat. As one newspaper reported, "In fact, a recent Army analysis found that more of its soldiers had been killed from non-combat causes during World War II, Korean, Vietnam and Persian Gulf Wars than died in battle."[3]

Thus, enemy action has historically *not* been the biggest killer of our troops. Prior to the twentieth century, illness, disease, and poor medical

TABLE 1. CASUALTIES IN AMERICA'S WARS

	Battle Deaths	Other Deaths
Revolutionary War	4,435	Unknown
War of 1812	2,260	Unknown
Mexican War	1,733	11,550
Civil War		
(Union)	140,414	224,097
(Confederate)	74,524	124,000[4]
Spanish-American War	385	2,061
World War I	53,402	63,114
World War II	291,557	113,842
Korean War	33,651	3,262[5]
Vietnam War	47,378	10,799
Persian Gulf War[6]	148	145

treatment were usually the greatest threats to military personnel. Accidents, in contrast, have grown increasingly more numerous in the past one hundred years.

In fact, during America's last three major military campaigns in the Persian Gulf, Kosovo, and Afghanistan, the first casualties were all GIs killed in accidents. Such was also the case in this nation's bloodiest conflict, the Civil War.

The war began when the South decided to capture a Union fort located on an island in the harbor at Charleston, South Carolina. At first, both sides hoped this gentleman's conflict would not lead to full-scale hostilities. During this siege of Fort Sumter, the combatants fired thousands of rounds at each other's fortified positions without inflicting a single casualty. After weeks of artillery duels, the Confederates offered to end this so-far bloodless bombardment. They would permit the Union forces to evacuate the fort by sea, under a flag of truce.

This would accomplish the Confederates' objective of ejecting the Yankees from Southern territory. Moreover, this could be accomplished without imposing the indignity of a formal surrender on their former West Point comrade who commanded the Union garrison.

This officer, Major Robert Anderson, realizing the hopelessness of his situation, quickly accepted the generous Confederate terms—but only if he was allowed to perform an important piece of protocol, one dictated by the code of chivalry. Major Anderson wanted to fire a one-hundred-gun salute to commemorate the evacuation of the fort.

On April 14, 1861, Private Daniel Hough was standing beside the twenty-seventh cannon when it exploded. Shrapnel from this blast tore off the arm of this young Irish immigrant, who died shortly thereafter.[7] Of course, Private Hough would certainly not be the last accident victim in this bloody conflict.

A little more than a fortnight after the Confederate surrender at Appomattox, the steamboat *Sultana* was churning her way up the Mississippi River. Her decks were packed with newly released Union prisoners. These men, most of them desperately ill from their prolonged incarceration, were eager to get home.

But just north of Memphis, on April 26, 1865, the steamboat's overworked boiler exploded without warning. The horrific blast hurled her battered human cargo into the muddy waters. Thus, the final event of this most tragic war killed seventeen hundred soldiers.[8]

Not all of this war's casualties would be obscure characters, relegated to the footnotes of history. Perhaps the best-known Civil War accident involved General Thomas "Stonewall" Jackson. This dashing Confederate officer was famous for his tactical skills and gallantry, so much so that the Confederate commanding general, Robert E. Lee, called Stonewall his "right arm."

In the evening hours of May 2, 1863, General Jackson was returning from personally reconnoitering Union forces near Chancellorsville, Virginia. He had intended to launch a daring night attack. Riding toward Confederate lines in the dark, he was mistaken for an enemy cavalry patrol and cut down by a volley of rifle shots from his own troops.

Confederate surgeons would amputate his left arm in a vain attempt to save his life. Robert E. Lee said, "Jackson has lost his left arm, but I have lost my right arm."[9] Lee felt the Confederacy never recovered from this friendly-fire incident. Stonewall Jackson was arguably the most brilliant tactical commander that the nation produced during the nineteenth century.

Eight decades later, the most brilliant tactical commander of the twentieth century would die in another freak accident. This gallant tank general had recently led the charge to sweep the Nazi legions from two continents. But on December 9, 1945, General George Patton was taking a peaceful ride in his staff car through a small burg near Mannheim, Germany.[10] His vehicle rammed head-on into a U.S. Army truck that had suddenly veered into its lane. Patton was being chauffeured and did not have a seat belt. He was thrown against the front seat by this violent impact. A military ambulance rushed the semiconscious general to a nearby hospital where it was soon realized that his neck was broken.

Lying there, Patton may have remembered his earlier motor-vehicle accident.[11] Five years before, he had watched from the grandstands as his tanks demonstrated their power to a large crowd at Fort Benning, Georgia. His tankers had been crushing small trees with ease, but the impulsive general decided that a more spectacular show was in order.

Patton seized the microphone and promised to show the audience what these new tanks could *really do*. Directing their attention to an abandoned farmhouse in the distance, he announced he would personally knock it down. He then jumped into the driver's seat of a nearby tank over the protest of his sergeant.

Patton crashed his tank into the side of the dilapidated wooden structure, only to disappear. Unbeknownst to the general, the farmhouse had a basement. His celebrated luck held that day, as he emerged uninjured from the debris. But five years and one bloody war later, the general would not be so fortunate.

General Patton died several days after his automobile accident—still complaining about the supreme irony of America's greatest combat leader dying in a car crash. "Old Blood and Guts," as he was frequently called, who'd never been injured in combat, would perish in a manner similar to that of British Princess Diana five decades later. The general would also be in good company, because motor-vehicle accidents would someday become the second most common cause of military deaths—after air crashes.[12]

Another famous Army officer was more fortunate than General Patton. On the eve of World War II, a lieutenant colonel assigned to General Douglas MacArthur's staff decided to take flying lessons. Aviation was becoming critical to military operations, and this officer wanted to experience and understand it firsthand.

One day he was preparing his training plane for flight by placing a sandbag into the rear cockpit. This was where his flight instructor normally sat, but today the colonel would be flying solo. This extra weight was needed to keep the light plane in balance. He hurriedly secured this ballast with the seat's lap belt. He understood that any loose object in an unoccupied rear compartment could be dangerous if it impinged on the aircraft controls.

Everything was fine until he began to land. He felt his control stick suddenly push forward. The nose of his craft dove toward the ground. The neophyte aviator knew immediately what had occurred. Somehow the sandbag had come loose and fallen forward onto the rear cockpit controls. He also knew he had no chance of reaching back to dislodge this bag or of bailing out. Realizing he had scant seconds to react, he adroitly maneuvered the craft using all his strength. He felt the sandbag miraculously shift off the control stick as the craft recovered.[13]

This U.S. Army officer learned a valuable lesson about the innate hazards of aviation. His superiors heard about his harrowing experience, as well as his initiative of learning to fly in his spare time. His familiarity with aviation and his reputation for coolness in critical situations helped him quickly move up through the ranks of the rapidly expanding wartime Army.

A few years later, he would have reason to call upon the aviation insight he gained as a lieutenant colonel, for this erstwhile infantry officer was selected as the Supreme Commander of all Allied Forces in Europe. General Dwight Eisenhower soon learned that airpower was the key to victory against the German war machine. But he also discovered that its employment could be a two-edged sword when he directed his strategic bombers to be used for close support of his embattled infantry units.

During the Normandy invasion, as Allied units tried to push inland from the beaches, waves of bombers attacked German positions near St. Lo. Unfortunately, during these desperate days, some bombs missed their intended targets and fell on American troops. Over one hundred GIs died on July 25, 1944, alone. Among the victims was Lieutenant General Lesley McNair, the highest-ranking U.S. casualty of World War II.[14]

This same knowledge would later be invaluable when General Eisenhower became the president of the United States. "Ike" used airpower as the cornerstone of *Pax Americana*. And it all began with a young lieutenant who took an airplane ride at Fort Myer, fell to earth, and ended up in Arlington Cemetery.

When Tom Selfridge was interred in 1908, he certainly was not the only accident victim in the cemetery. In 1898, dozens of other young American servicemen had been killed in their sleep. These were sailors who died in their bunks when the battleship *Maine* exploded in Havana Harbor the night of February 15, 1898. This famous disaster changed the course of history.[15]

On January 25, 1898, the USS *Maine* entered Havana Harbor. The battleship's mission was a "friendly visit" to show the flag. America wanted to convince the Spanish government that we were growing increasingly displeased with its treatment of the Cuban people. America was not so subtly asserting the Monroe Doctrine by suggesting that this nation would not countenance European colonial powers abusing the people of the Western Hemisphere.

For three weeks, the powerful warship, pride of the United States Navy, sat at anchor in the shallow harbor. As warm tropical breezes blew across her decks, the relations between the two countries grew ever cooler. America's jingoistic press was stirring up sentiment for a war.

At sundown on the evening of February 15, 1898, the bugler played taps as the crew turned in for the evening. At 9:40 P.M. on this quiet, overcast, Caribbean night, a blast ripped the stately ship. As the ship's ammunition magazines exploded, its bow rose from the water, bending its keel.

Within thirty minutes the once proud vessel settled on the muddy bottom, its superstructure still protruding above the water's surface. Of the 350 men in the ship's company, only 84 would survive.[16]

Nobody knew what caused the explosion, but the ship's master, Captain Charles Sigsbee, sent a cryptic message to Washington. It stated he suspected that an underwater mine had caused the blast. The supposedly secret communiqué was quickly leaked to the press. A Navy board of inquiry was soon dispatched to Havana. This panel began its investigation on February 25, 1898, and quickly concluded that the explosion was most likely due to a mine.[17]

The panel had little physical evidence to support this very self-serving finding. Furthermore, their conclusions conveniently exonerated the Navy as well as its associates, the *Maine*'s officers. This finding of sabotage, by implication, suggested the hated Spanish government must have somehow been responsible. The report was quickly leaked to the press.

The Spanish also conducted an investigation that noted there was no evidence of mine fragments or components. It also noted none of the eyewitnesses saw a blast or a water gusher outside the hull—the telltale signature of a marine mine explosion. This latter investigation was soon dismissed as Spanish propaganda.

On April 25, 1898, America declared war on Spain. "Remember the *Maine*" became the rallying cry. This "splendid little war" lasted just three months and resulted in a decisive defeat for the Spanish forces. When the smoke cleared, the United States had suffered 385 battle deaths—not counting the *Maine*'s victims. But 2,061 other servicemen perished, mainly from disease.[18]

Ten years later, the remains of sixty-seven sailors were still entombed inside the rusting hull of the *Maine*. In 1908, America decided to raise the ship and recover these bodies. Many people were uncomfortable with the Navy's original inquiry, so the Navy agreed to another inquiry. Although their second investigation was not as rushed, it again could find no definitive evidence of a mine—only a couple of bent hull plates. Nonetheless, this second board of inquiry concluded that the mine theory of the first investigation was correct.

Because of doubts about the two original investigations, a third inquiry was launched in 1974. Rear Admiral Hyman Rickover, the father of the nuclear submarine and a man known for his intellect and candor, headed this one. Rickover and his team examined all the evidence from the two earlier Navy investigations as well as data from other battleship explosions. They published their findings in a book titled *How the Battleship Maine Was Destroyed*.[19]

This third inquiry would come to some *very* different conclusions. The explosion came from *inside* the ship's hull; thus a Spanish mine could not have destroyed the vessel. The most probable explanation was spontaneous combustion in the ship's coal bunker.

This compartment was located adjacent to an ammunition bunker. This was an unfortunate juxtaposition that allowed a relatively minor combustion of coal dust to precipitate the catastrophic explosion of the ship's ammunition supply. This third investigation finally uncovered the *true* cause of the explosion by identifying this highly critical design flaw.

Rickover's no-holds-barred investigation also noted the *Maine*'s commanding officer, as well as the members of the earlier accident boards, knew of the very real dangers posed by coal dust. These dangers were exacerbated by poor housekeeping practices. Moreover, ships that were under this particular captain's command had failed earlier inspections for just such problems. But both previous accident boards, staffed by the officer's contemporaries, had conveniently overlooked this factor.

Self-serving or poor quality military mishap investigations often lead to additional problems, but rarely have they had such profound consequences. Here, a preventable accident sank a battleship, killing hundreds of servicemen. Then a bungled investigation—or worse, an intentional cover-up—actually led to a bloody war, costing thousands of lives.

Perhaps the only man to benefit from this battleship's demise was a little-known assistant secretary of the Navy by the name of Theodore Roosevelt. He would resign his Navy post, join an Army cavalry unit called the "Rough Riders," lead a charge up a hill at San Juan, and become a national hero. Years later, while he was vice president, an assassin's bullet would propel him into the White House.

Roosevelts, it seems, are lucky when it comes to battleships. Forty-five years later, Teddy's cousin Franklin Delano Roosevelt was aboard another battleship. This ship, the USS *Iowa*, was among the most powerful and stately warships ever to sail.[20] She had just completed her maiden voyage, and this second sailing would be an important mission. She was to transport FDR and all the service chiefs across the sub-infested waters of the North Atlantic. The top brass was en route to the 1943 Tehran Conference. There the president and America's military brain trust would meet with their counterparts from the other allied countries. Collectively, they would map out a global war-fighting strategy.

The chief of naval operations (CNO), Admiral Ernest J. King, had personally selected this super dreadnought partly because of the security it afforded. But he also knew the massive battleship would help insure the frail president's comfort during this wintertime passage across the choppy North Atlantic. Although a much younger FDR had been an assistant secretary of the Navy, this paraplegic commander in chief no longer had his sea legs.

The *Iowa* and her three escorting destroyers made twenty-five knots[21] as they departed the Virginia coast on November 12, 1943. In war, it is often said that "speed is life," but twenty-five knots was well beyond the normal sustained cruising speed for the three diminutive escorts in heavy seas. Moreover, because of wartime secrecy, the destroyers' crews were not told who was aboard the *Iowa*. At this point in the conflict, ultimate victory was still uncertain, and nobody would quibble with this need for speed. Besides, sailors were expected simply to cope with such hardships.

Two days later, on the clear Sunday afternoon, it was decided that a firepower demonstration might entertain these august guests. With the presidential party watching, an anti-aircraft gunnery demonstration began with the release of balloons. The battlewagon's gunners quickly sighted in on and dispatched these makeshift targets.

But unbeknownst to those aboard the *Iowa*, someone else had the battleship's silhouette in *their* sights. Without warning, the ship lurched as she suddenly changed course. Alarms sounded as the public address system screamed, "Torpedo defense! This is *not* a drill!"[22] Seconds later an explosion erupted off the ship's stern that shook the massive vessel.

The chief of naval operations raced across the bridge to find out what the hell was going on. The *Iowa*'s red-faced captain explained that one of the escorting destroyers, the USS *William D. Porter*, had accidentally launched a torpedo. It seems the destroyer had been using the battleship as a target for torpedo aiming practice, and someone had forgotten to remove the firing primer from a torpedo tube.

Fortunately, the *Iowa*'s crew was warned in time by a radio message from the embarrassed *Porter*'s bridge. The torpedo's warhead had exploded harmlessly when it hit the Iowa's propeller wash. But in terms of its potential consequences, this was arguably the most embarrassing friendly-fire incident in the history of the republic.

Perhaps the second most interesting aspect of this incident was FDR's reaction when the CNO explained that he was recommending a court-martial for the destroyer's captain. The president quickly vetoed that idea because he apparently did not want to risk the adverse publicity.[23]

The *most* interesting thing about the situation was revealed in the recent biography of General Hap Arnold by historian Major General John Huston.[24] Arnold was aboard the *Iowa* as the chief of the Army Air Forces. His diary entries describe the explosion but do not mention that he was ever told what caused the blast.[25] It is fascinating to consider that the Navy brass may have kept this embarrassing information from the other members of the joint chiefs of staff, who were almost victims themselves.

While FDR never even got wet during the *Iowa* incident, sometimes an accident can help sink an entire administration. When President Jimmy Carter took office, he allowed America's military readiness to dangerously deteriorate. This was the era of the so-called hollow force.

Carter then decided to dance with the devil, the Ayatollah Khomeini. When this Islamic cleric came to power in Iran, our highly religious president thought that he could deal with this other holy man. Carter's reward was the seizure of the American embassy in Tehran, when its entire staff was taken hostage in late 1979.

After several months of unsuccessful diplomatic maneuvers, the president chose a bold plan of military action. The four services would cooperate to rescue the hostages with a commando-style raid.

Senior generals and admirals rarely say "no" when their commander in chief has decided he wants something. This "can do" attitude sometimes leads to a disaster—which low-ranking personnel, the "grunts," pay for with their lives.

This extremely complex operation has come to be called "Desert One,"[26] after the name of a landing site in Iran. It involved flying four Air Force C-130 "Hercules" transports loaded with Army Green Berets. They would fly from an island off the coast of Oman to this remote landing site in the Iranian desert 265 miles from Tehran. These aircraft would then rendezvous with eight Navy RH-53 "Sea Stallion" helicopters launched from the carrier *Nimitz* steaming in the Gulf of Oman six hundred miles away. The C-130s were then to refuel the RH-53s at this remote landing site at night.

The next step of the plan called for the helicopters to transfer the assault force to a mountain hideaway located sixty-five miles from Tehran. These rescuers were then to be secreted into the capital by local trucks under the cover of darkness. They would subsequently storm the embassy, free the hostages, and escort them to a pre-determined spot where the helicopters would land for the pickup and escape.

The plan required that at least six of the eight helicopters be fully operational to haul all the hostages and commandos. The "Washington warriors" who did the planning decided against using Air Force MH-53s, which were designed for just such operations. Their logic for rejecting this particular aircraft apparently was that the Air Force choppers lacked folding rotors at that time. These were needed for below-deck storage aboard the carrier. Theoretically, the Soviets might spot this strange collection of specialized helicopters and notify the Iranians.

These Pentagon planners decided that Marine CH-53 crews would fly Navy RH-53 helicopters, which have a slightly larger payload. But when these officials requested to "borrow" eight of these choppers from a Navy unit in Norfolk, Virginia, they did not mention that the craft were going to be used for a mission of paramount national importance.

Consequently, this Navy unit sent them eight of their "hangar queens," aircraft that had a history of maintenance problems.[27] Years of budget cuts had degraded the reliability of such equipment, and complex helicopters like the RH-53 are especially vulnerable to such neglect.

When President Carter ordered the attack to proceed on April 24, things went wrong almost from the get-go. Two of the eight RH-53s soon had to abort en route. A third chopper developed a hydraulic leak in its control system at the refueling site. Amazingly, this leak was due to a single cracked nut.[28] When it was determined the craft could not be repaired, Washington was notified. Knowing that six choppers were required, the president's people reluctantly decided to cancel the operation.

To make matters worse, a sand storm had unexpectedly blown up, drastically restricting visibility. The five remaining helicopters and four transports kept their engines running, which churned up more dust as they maneuvered on this noisy, dark, confined airstrip. In the confusion, one helicopter collided with a transport, causing both craft to explode instantly.

Eight would-be rescuers died in the ensuing fire, and three others were severely burned. The disoriented survivors then hastily abandoned the remaining helicopters—along with much secret equipment and documents—and fled this fiery cauldron in the remaining C-130s.[29]

The Iranians soon discovered the crash location and brought the media to the site of this catastrophe. This Islamic government next discovered a new way of embarrassing the "great Satan." Videos of Iranian officials glibly handling the charred remains of our accident victims were flashed around the globe. The American government had these images indelibly burned into its collective psyche.

Moreover, this debacle destroyed public confidence in the Carter Administration and contributed to its defeat in the next election. In geopolitics, the enemy of my enemy is my friend. This credo helped persuade the victorious Reagan Administration to provide Iraqi dictator Saddam Hussein with extensive military and intelligence materials, for he was soon at war with Iran.

This in turn led Hussein to a misguided conclusion that his *ally*, America, would not interfere when he decided to invade Kuwait several years later. So this first debacle, in the Iranian desert, helped sow the seeds for a far greater tragedy in another nearby desert. In that sense, "Desert One" was well named.

Furthermore, America's arms merchants were encouraged to sell the Iraqis the materials that could be used to manufacture things like poison gas. Saddam Hussein would soon turn these weapons against not only the Iranians, but also the Kurds living in his own country. Within a decade, our own troops would be faced with these same deadly weapons. Perhaps most disturbing is the fact that as many as 100,000 Americans may suffer grievous illnesses as a consequence of this nation's willingness to assist Saddam Hussein, a move made largely to avenge the taking of our embassy and the humiliation of the Desert One accident.

4

Safety Last

The cartoon character Pogo once remarked: "We have met the enemy and he is us." Our traditional military mind-set is that *mission* comes first, and anything else, such as safety, is secondary. This "mission myopia" has proven to be a costly problem for those who serve under arms. Because military operations *are* so innately dangerous, one would expect safety to also be a paramount concern.

But this was not the case, as I learned from many years of close observation. The biggest problems were those leaders who undervalued the importance of safety. This was not something that the generals or admirals liked to discuss. Too many senior officials were intent on protecting their unsafe peers from public accountability at all costs.

But this was not always the case. A number of future military leaders were present when Tom Selfridge shed his blood on the soil of Fort Myer. They, along with others, joined together to try to improve safety—at least for embryonic military aviation. Two individuals would stand out as pillars of integrity across the sands of time.

One officer in the forefront of this effort was Lieutenant Henry "Hap" Arnold, who eventually became chief of the Army Air Force. He began his military flying career in 1911 after taking lessons from the Wright brothers. In those early years, things were very dangerous, with the life expectancy of army aviators literally measured in hours. In that year, 1911, there was a fatal accident for every 65 hours flown. By 1914, this figure had improved to one fatal accident for every 125 hours flown.

Arnold received pilot license number twenty-nine. Of his twenty-eight civilian and military pilot predecessors, ten would die in crashes, fourteen would quit flying, and only four would live long enough to die of natural causes.[1] Hap Arnold, a workaholic, would live until 1950, when he would succumb to a heart attack, but not before changing the world and saving countless other flyers with his staunch advocacy for improving aviation safety.

Hap Arnold had a healthy respect for the hazards of flying and avoided taking unnecessary risks. After nearly crashing in 1912, he asked to be grounded. "I cannot even look at a machine in the air without feeling that some accident is going to happen to it,"[2] he said.

Arnold was reassigned to a desk job in Washington, D.C. This move was fortuitous for a couple of reasons. First, it just may have saved his life given the high fatality rates in these early years. Second, Arnold got to know the other pillar of aviation safety, Billy Mitchell. Captain Mitchell was his boss in those days, and he learned much from this brilliant but very outspoken officer.

Four years later, Arnold would return to the sky as an ever-vigilant airman. Perhaps he remembered Wilbur Wright's saying, "Carelessness and overconfidence are more dangerous than deliberately accepted risks."[3]

During World War I, the usually tactful Arnold would quickly rise to the rank of colonel and fight the thankless bureaucratic battles on the home front. Meanwhile, Mitchell became a brigadier general and commander of the Air Service in combat. Mitchell was highly decorated for his war work, but his strident advocacy for airpower angered many of his superiors.

After the war, the "peace dividend" cut the Air Service, along with the rest of the military, to dangerous levels. Without wartime funding, training and maintenance suffered, eventually causing safety problems, which bothered both officers.

Mitchell soon decided to show Congress and the public that the bomber could do a better job of defending America's shores than the battleship. In tests, beginning in 1921, Mitchell's aircraft sank a series of warships. This was much to the chagrin of the Navy as well as to the traditionalists in the Army. Billy Mitchell had become the darling of the press with his outspoken pleas for more and better aircraft.

These were times of austerity. The senior military and naval officials resented Mitchell's public statements that the Air Service should get a bigger part of the shrinking budgetary pie. The proactive general's exploits soon got him ostracized.

In 1925, several of Mitchell's close friends died in military crashes, one of whom was the captain of the Navy's ill-fated dirigible *Shenandoah*. Billy Mitchell lashed out against the system that had contributed to these accidents. He *alleged* that senior leaders should be held accountable for " . . . incompetency, criminal negligence and almost treasonable administration of the national defense by the War and Navy Departments."[4] This, not surprisingly, led to a swift court-martial for conduct prejudicial to military discipline.

Hap Arnold would help lead the vain effort to defend Mitchell by testifying at his court-martial. Arnold knew how to lead and was willing to put his career on the line whenever safety was involved. But Mitchell was convicted and resigned from the Army. General Mitchell died in 1938—many think from a broken heart because senior officers would not listen to his pleas.

That was not the last time Arnold would find himself embroiled in a safety controversy. In 1934, the Roosevelt administration decided to kick the commercial airlines out of the postal contract business and require the Army to haul the mail. Many of the same gutless military leaders who ruined Mitchell's career did not speak up in protest although they knew their obsolete equipment and limited training were not up to airline standards.

With the traditional military *can do* spirit, they launched this ill-advised air-mail effort using aircraft that lacked the instruments needed to safely fly in adverse weather and at night. The results were all too predictable. The fiasco lasted three months and ended only after sixty-six crashes, which claimed eleven lives. World War I flying ace Captain Eddie Rickenbacker called this experiment "legalized murder."[5]

Hap Arnold was assigned to manage the western routes. His crews were forced to handle the worst terrain in the nation, including the Rocky

Mountains, and they had the least developed ground-support structure. But because of his leadership and emphasis on safety, his division suffered the fewest casualties.

However, Arnold's greatest accomplishment as a safety advocate would come later, when he commanded the Army Air Forces in World War II. In 1943, there were 5,024 U.S. Army aircraft destroyed in stateside accidents compared with 3,847 destroyed in actual combat.[6] General Arnold, after receiving this information, directed a major expansion of the Army Air Forces accident-prevention efforts.

But even these numbers do not convey the tremendous suffering involved for the victims and their loved ones. Russia's World War II leader, Joseph Stalin, once remarked, "A single death is a tragedy. A million deaths is a statistic."[7]

As a school kid I became familiar with one such tragic death when I was required to memorize the world's best-known aviation poem, "High Flight." It was written by a young American who joined the Royal Canadian Air Force before the United States entered World War II. He was posted to a besieged Britain, where he would pen these immortal words:

Oh, I have slipped the surly bonds of earth
And danced the skies on laughter-silvered wings
Sunward I've climbed, and joined the tumbling mirth
Of sun-spit clouds – and done a hundred things
You have not dreamed of – wheeled and soared and swung
High in the sunlit silence. Hovering there,
I've chased the shouting wind along, and flung
My eager craft through footless hall of air.
Up, up the long, delirious burning blue
I've topped the windswept height with easy grace
Where never lark, or even eagle flew.
And, while with silent, lifting mind I've trod
The high untrespassed sanctity of space,
Put out my hand and touched the face of God.[8]

(John Gillespie Magee Jr., "High Flight")

On December 11, 1941, this brave nineteen-year-old Spitfire pilot slipped the surly bonds of earth one last time, but he did not die at the hands of the enemy. Like so many other casualties of that conflict, John Gillespie Magee Jr. would perish in a tragic accident. He had a midair collision with another British aircraft.

Growing up on Selfridge Air Force Base in the 1950s, I soon learned that even dedicated efforts by General Arnold could not overcome the fundamental problems with the military's approach to safety. I would discover this by visiting the base salvage yard and viewing the ever-changing collection of wrecked aircraft.

Many of these crashes were not discussed in the newspapers, so I would ask around until I found someone who would explain why a particular crash occurred. I was constantly amazed at how most of these accidents were preventable. This early fascination with aviation safety would later help me understand important details on confusing investigations.

In 1963, I received an appointment to the U.S. Air Force Academy. I could not wait to report, because it would allow me to continue my studies of aviation and safety. After becoming part of the system, I soon realized another problem was the macho culture that encourages unnecessary risk taking.

As a cadet, I remember standing in formation and watching a visiting Royal Air Force plane make a high-speed pass just a few hundred feet overhead. This "Britannia" transport was loaded with British Air Force Academy cadets. Its four turbo-prop engines made an impressive roar at that distance. The low-flying craft quickly disappeared behind a hill, only to reappear a short time later with one of its engines shut down. As it flew over the American cadets again and disappeared, you could hear puzzled whispers coming from our ranks.

The gleaming craft returned again, this time with *two* engines out. The Yanks were duly impressed as its giant shadow raced across our formation and disappeared. The Britannia soon returned on a fourth pass. This time they passed with only a *single* engine running. Military protocol broke down as we rubbernecked, astonished at this dangerous air show designed just to impress the cadets of a rival institution.

I would not see another Britannia for years—until I examined the twisted wreckage of one lying in the woods near Boston.[9] I was an NTSB investigator assigned to find out why this former Royal Air Force transport crew had attempted to take off with ice on its wings—an often fatal mistake. Hours later I went into the morgue to assist with the autopsies of the crew. I noted the Royal Air Force insignias on their jackets and remembered that other Britannia crew's stunt years before.

After earning a Ph.D. in human factors and systems safety, I joined the staff of the U.S. Navy training command as an aviation psychologist. My first assignment was to examine the requirements for the next generation of training aircraft. This involved flying with instructors in the current TA-4 Skyhawk jets. I remember talking with an older instructor pilot after landing one day.

He was complaining that he did not like the Skyhawks because they were "too easy to fly." He explained why he preferred the early generation training jets, the TF-9 Cougars. Even though the Cougars had suffered lots of accidents, they "weeded out the weaklings." Better they should die in obsolete training jets before they got to the fleet and wasted brand-new F-14 Tomcats. Such Darwinian views were not all that uncommon in the Navy.

Flyers don't have a monopoly on macho. Attending U.S. Army Parachute School was interesting, partly because of the swagger of drill sergeants. These instructors loved to taunt neophytes with questions like "You don't want to live forever, do you?" This was sometimes asked as you "stood in the door" and momentarily glanced at the windy abyss.

Such attitudes that devalue safety do not originate with sergeants or flight instructors. It comes from their leaders—and therein lies the problem. Perhaps this is best illustrated by a statement from the officer who was then in charge of safety for the Air Force. Brigadier General Orin Godsey was being interviewed by the *Washington Post* after the crash of a CT-43 transport in 1996. This was the infamous accident that killed thirty-five people, including Commerce Secretary Ronald Brown.

The CT-43 was a military version of the Boeing 737 airliner, but it lacked many safety devices required by the FAA for its civilian counterpart. Chief of Safety Godsey said the Air Force had decided not to install such devices because " . . . we wouldn't have enough money for anything else."[10] Such attitudes lie at the heart of many of the military's profound safety problems.

Unfortunately, many of these officers have no training or experience in safety before they're asked to assume critical but temporary assignments. The Air Force actually abolished safety as a career field for officers in the early 1970s. The service was thereby sending a strong message: Safety was *not* an important endeavor—ergo *only* enlisted personnel or civil servants should spend much time on this subject. In the military's hierarchy, the latter people have little influence.

Air Force officers have a saying about this activity: "Don't get that safety *stink* on you." Translation: If you have to take a job in this field, okay, but don't stay too long. Thus, those who need to know the most about safety, the senior leaders, never become experts on this topic.

The other services have similar problems, although the Army does allow *warrant* officers to become safety professionals. Such specialist officers, like the civil servants and enlisted personnel, are very talented and dedicated, but they too are not permitted to hold critical leadership positions. In recent years, it seems that senior people in the Pentagon do not want to be reminded about their many institutional safety problems. I became painfully aware of this fact years ago.

In 1986 I got a phone call from one of the Air Force's top safety experts, Dr. David Porterfield. He was a brilliant military physician who had done post-graduate work in safety and human factors.

He was looking for an eminent scientist to serve as the senior civilian at the Air Force Inspection and Safety Center.[11] Finding none who would work under the military's demanding conditions, he called me. He knew I was already fully engaged in a similar position with the FAA. The colonel kept playing on my sympathy for the many victims of unnecessary military crashes.

He reminded me that this USAF technical advisor's responsibilities would include developing a comprehensive computerized data system, which was aptly called the Aircraft Mishap Prevention system. The software-intense system would allow the commanders and their subordinates to better understand where safety problems were occurring throughout the Air Force. Armed with such vital information, they then could implement appropriate countermeasures to prevent similar accidents from occurring. At least that was the theory.

I accepted this Air Force safety position in June of 1987. Dr. Porterfield soon introduced me to another lieutenant colonel, Jim Miholick, who was in charge of reviewing all Air Force safety data. Miholick was another of the center's best and brightest. Furthermore, he had been stationed there for more than a decade. This type of tenure was extremely rare for officers. Since he was the Air Force's top data expert, I would need to work closely with him to develop the new computer system.

Colonel Miholick had graduated from the Air Force Academy and was a highly decorated combat fighter pilot. Because of his intellect and experience, he had been assigned to many important studies, including those with the Army and Navy safety centers. He had also served as a consultant on a presidential commission into crew workload. I liked working with this dedicated safety expert who enjoyed a reputation for integrity and candor. I would soon learn, however, that this stoic officer had a dark secret—one that he was about to share with me.

Much of the safety data he had worked with was simply *fraudulent.* Many individual accident reports, as well as the statistical data that he reviewed and sent on to the Pentagon and Congress, contained *false* information. Miholick had tried to correct these records whenever possible, but the powers-that-be usually thwarted his efforts. Moreover, the top Air Force generals had to know that this was going on. Meanwhile, the other services had similar problems. Other officers confirmed such problems were widespread.

This fakery took on many guises. These will be discussed in detail in later chapters, but typical forms included:

- Unreported Accidents: Sometimes units or major commands (MAJ-COMs) simply did not report embarrassing accidents.
- Misclassified Accidents: The MAJCOMs or the safety center would intentionally "dump" accidents into a lower category by using false accounting data, such as saying that engines were going to be repaired when they had actually had been scrapped.
- Secretly Repairing Wrecks: This was often done by surreptitiously removing parts from other aircraft or warehouses.
- Hiding Real Causes: This trick was sometimes used to protect high-ranking officers who failed to institute safety or training measures.
- Oversimplified Investigations: Investigators failed to examine critical issues, such as cockpit design deficiencies, that the board members could not understand.

- Assigning Wrong Causes: This ruse typically involved saying a crash was due to something, such as suicide or a bird strike, when investigators had no concrete evidence of such causes.
- Lost Evidence: Sometimes boards would inadvertently misplace a critical component and did not want to admit it.
- Hasty Investigations: Boards failed to examine complex issues such as visual illusions because they can be complicated, contentious, or time consuming.
- Ignoring Key Witnesses: Boards have been known *not* to interview critical witnesses for a variety of inappropriate reasons, such as to avoid ruining the witnesses' careers.
- Ignoring Unpopular Recommendations: When MAJCOM commanders said they did not want to hear anything more about certain problems, such as installing a particular safety device, boards would dutifully comply.
- Scapegoating: Boards sometimes blamed the wrong person, usually a convenient low-ranking individual, in order to protect higher-ups.

These problems were improper, if not outright unlawful. However, in addition to the illegal practices, the Pentagon had a whole series of ways to *legally* keep from reporting the truth. Remember, they made up their own rules. Several of the schemes included:

- Deflated Labor Repair Costs: The services reported hourly repair costs at only $16 per hour when they usually paid several times that rate.
- Deflated Personnel Replacement Costs: Dead pilots were written off at $1.1 million each, though the service typically had invested more than $5 million in their training alone.
- Non-Flight Mishap Loopholes: Aircraft destroyed while taxiing to or from runways were not counted as major flight accidents, the basic barometer of aviation safety.
- Special Category Loopholes: In-flight engine explosions, for instance, often result in multimillion dollar losses but were not counted as major flight accidents, further obscuring actual numbers of in-flight accidents.

- Combat Crash Loopholes: Some very embarrassing crashes occurring in a war zone were not counted as accidents—even if no enemy action was involved.

In addition to systematically understating the various direct costs, the military's bogus cost-accounting system totally ignored the indirect cost of inadequate safety—such as conducting mishap investigations, undertaking search and rescue efforts, and purchasing extra "attrition" aircraft. My master's thesis dealt with cost-benefit analyses of aviation safety devices.[12] I'm sure my graduate advisor would have instantly flunked me had I tried to float the kinds of absurd assumptions invented by Pentagon safety gurus.

In Pentagon-speak, attrition seemed like a euphemism for "aircraft destroyed in accidents." So, in 1989, I decided to examine what proportion of USAF aircraft were being lost to accidents. I knew from my work with the NTSB that about 1 or 2 percent of jetliners are destroyed over the course of their operational lifetimes in the United States. I looked at the USAF statistics of aircraft types that were nearing the end of their operational flying lives and was shocked to find how high the attrition rates were.[13]

- Fighters (e.g., F-4, F-111)   20 percent destroyed
- Trainers (e.g., T-37, T-38)   20 percent destroyed
- Helicopters (e.g., H-3)   20 percent destroyed
- Bombers (e.g., B-52)   10 percent destroyed
- Transports (e.g., C-130 A/B/E)   5 percent destroyed

Obviously George Orwell would have been proud of the Pentagon spin-meisters who coined the term *attrition*.

The Pentagon contends it annually loses approximately *$3 billion* in all types of accidents, with about half this figure being aircraft crashes. But nobody has ever publicly stated what the true financial burden is. It is a safe bet that the real figure is many times the advertised amount.

In my several years at this military safety agency, I watched these sloppy and/or fraudulent practices contribute to many additional accidents. The taxpayers were picking up the tab while the grunts paid with their blood. But nobody got very excited about this situation.

Moreover, it seemed impossible to break the cycle. I would, of course, try to bring such information to the attention of senior leaders, but I was often told by my superiors at the safety center that I was "upsetting the generals." This was often followed by not-so-veiled threats of retaliation.

But I was not the only one at the center worried about what was happening. The new director, Brigadier General Joel Hall, had arrived with the usual minimal background in safety. He, however, listened well, learned quickly, and was not afraid to ask the tough questions. Moreover, he seemed to be genuinely disturbed by the things he was seeing.

On March 26, 1991, he wrote an extremely candid and forceful letter to the top officer, Chief of Staff of the Air Force, General Merrill McPeak. In it, Hall, who was getting ready to retire, emphasized the gravity of a number of the problems noted above. The seven-page letter[14] began: "I am deeply concerned with the continued effectiveness and legitimacy of the Air Force safety program . . . I sincerely believe that as events and decisions are now occurring we are *headed for a disaster."*

The letter continued: " . . . I have witnessed command manipulation of mishap cost/classification to improve the command statistics/image, shallow and incomplete investigations into mishap causes, interference by MAJCOM staffs with the investigative board process, and punishment of board members for unpopular findings. . . . Even more troubling is the acceptance by senior leaders of a mishap investigation process which frequently obscures supervisory culpability . . . [The] investigative process has been politicized to the point of dysfunction."

Later on, the one-star general courageously asks his four-star boss for more independence and resources. As will be illustrated in later chapters, General McPeak's actions suggest he had little interest in or understanding of safety issues.

On April 1, General Hall got a terse letter[15] telling him to enjoy his retirement. Insiders referred to General McPeak's response as the "April Fool's reply" because he was obviously going to ignore Hall's plea.

But events, some of which McPeak set in motion, would eventually come back to haunt him and his new chief of safety. Within three years of Hall's departure, the reported rate for major USAF aircraft accidents would increase by more than 25 percent at a time when the other services were improving their safety records.

By 1994, things were spinning out of control, so I began looking at the costs of all the DoD's tragic accidents over the past two decades (1975 to 1994). I quickly reviewed these losses, which included:

- Over $50 billion in *reported* economic losses. Who knows what the real number is?
- More than two thousand military aircraft destroyed compared with fewer than one hundred airliners.
- More than fifteen thousand military deaths in all on-duty and off-duty accidents compared with fewer than six hundred from hostile action.

After reviewing these unacceptable losses, it was apparent to me that the Pentagon simply undervalues safety. But what was also obvious was that these losses were caused by deep-seated institutional problems that somehow had to be exposed.

5

Institutionalized Abuses

Sometimes institutional problems start at the top. Robert McNamara served as the defense secretary for Presidents Kennedy and Johnson. As such, he was the architect of America's war in Vietnam. Although he was arguably the most intelligent person to hold that job, McNamara had a character flaw, which was revealed in his book, *In Retrospect*.[1]

Secretary McNamara admitted that, after watching the war in Vietnam go downhill for years, he knew the conflict was not winnable. But, at the time, he could not bear to tell this critical fact to the president, Congress, or the American people. By valuing loyalty over truth, he ignored his Constitutional responsibilities.

He apparently did not want to embarrass himself, the administration, or the military establishment. So he continued to argue that America should fight on. Mr. McNamara had to know this was a death sentence for thousands. But this cabinet officer felt compelled to do this to protect the "system."

Another recent book, *Dereliction of Duty: Lyndon Johnson, Robert McNamara, the Joint Chiefs of Staff, and the Lies That Led to Vietnam*, suggests that these problems were not limited to the secretary of defense.[2] Interestingly, the author, H.R. McMaster, is a U.S. Army lieutenant colonel and an academically trained historian. This officer's penetrating analysis reveals some long-whispered secrets about other people who helped lead this nation down that disastrous path decades ago.

McMaster did a detailed examination of the government's decision making during a critical phase of our history, 1964 to 1965—the period when America decided to expand its involvement in this war. He brilliantly explains how many top civilian and military officials engaged in a "conspiracy of deception" during this critical two-year phase of the conflict.

I discovered similar problems in the safety arena. But in the safety arena the pathology was not limited to a brief period during a confusing war. Unfortunately, this epidemic has lingered for decades, infecting too many who serve in the upper echelons of the Defense Department.

Over the years, I worked with dozens of generals and admirals, as well as their top civilian counterparts. While doing so, I met lots of brilliant and well-meaning people, some of whom failed to demonstrate integrity when dealing with safety issues. They were exhibiting a protracted form of "McNamara's Syndrome."

But these individuals were in the minority. More disturbing was the unwillingness of the majority of their contemporaries to confront such wrongdoers. Most officials simply would not challenge the system and thereby risk ruining their own or their colleagues' careers.

This corrupt system operates with impunity because of several factors. Moreover, it has operated like this for decades—unchallenged. As such, it has become the perfect manifestation of how absolute power corrupts absolutely. It simply has no effective checks and balances. Leaders are not above the law—they *are* the law. Furthermore, they like it that way.

They are simply not held accountable for their safety decisions. A senior Pentagon official once told me, "We don't need independent investigations because we own the equipment and the people." I respectfully disagreed by reminding him that the equipment belonged to the taxpayers and that the American people had entrusted us to safeguard their loved ones. I also noted that our troops have no union to protect them, only *our* sense of integrity.

This official then noted the two bedrock requirements for all military organizations. First was the "chain of command"—that is, orders from superiors are not optional. The second was the concept that the "mission comes first," especially in war. He asked me if independent safety investigations would interfere with these two military necessities.

I replied that independent safety investigations would not hinder either, but commanders would have to learn how to manage safety issues, just as they adroitly balance all other requirements today. I then noted that in the past, our officers were not really held accountable for sexual harassment or environmental pollution as they are today.

So maybe there is hope for overhauling military safety in this uphill battle against organizational inertia. Later chapters will describe what needs to happen to bring these reforms about. But it is important to understand how the military safety system currently differs from its civilian counterpart.

The civilian world has a legally mandated system of checks and balances, which involves well-established "fire walls" between different, critical domains. In U.S. aviation, for instance, the operators (commercial airlines), the investigators (National Transportation Safety Board), and the regulators (Federal Aviation Administration) are separate and totally independent from one another, as depicted in Figure 1 below.

But in the military, these functions are merged into one all-powerful organization. The operators (major commands), the investigators (safety centers), and the regulators (Defense Department), are all a part of the same monolithic organization. Moreover, an impenetrable wall of secrecy surrounds this cluster of functions, as depicted in Figure 2.

Perhaps the biggest problem in making meaningful reforms is the sheer size of the military establishment. The critical role that the defense establishment has played to protect the republic's vital interests is actually part of the problem. Most of our institutions—including Congress,

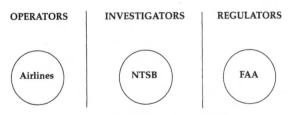

Figure 1. Civil Aviation Safety

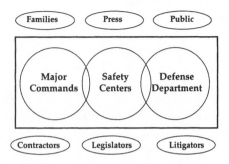

Figure 2. Military Aviation Safety

presidential administrations, and the courts—seem very comfortable with the *status quo,* or they are at least reluctant to confront this behemoth. Critics of the military are frequently viewed as being unpatriotic.

A further long-standing institutional problem lies in the government's position that it cannot be held financially liable for the deaths or injuries of service personnel. This sovereign immunity concept is called the Feres Doctrine after the 1950 Supreme Court decision named for a soldier, Rudolph Feres, who was killed in a barracks fire.[3]

This ruling put an end to the rash of lawsuits against the military, which followed a 1946 act passed by Congress. This act had allowed citizens to sue the government under the Federal Torts Claims Act. It understandably barred claims arising out of combatant activities. But, as noted earlier, accidents are a far greater threat to our troops.

Basically, what this legal exemption means is that the services cannot be held accountable for the safety of their personnel. It also allows contractors to get away with poor design practices when building products for the military—so long as they follow the provisions of the government contract. For instance, if a manufacturer's negligence causes the death of a serviceman traveling home on leave in a commercial airliner crash, his survivors can sue that firm for damages. But they cannot sue if he is killed flying on the same type of aircraft used by the military services.

Privilege, as discussed earlier, represents another barrier to improving safety. This concept permits the military to conduct two separate investigations. The first, called the safety investigation, is designed to establish why the accident occurred and to hopefully prevent future reoccurrences. This is an "internal use only" document. The second, the accident investigation, is a legalistic exercise designed only to establish who is to be blamed for the crash. The latter report is, of course, public domain and is intended to placate criticism.

The military contends the concept of executive privilege permits results of its safety inquiries to be kept "secret." Of course, because the information usually has nothing to do with national security, they have to do some very creative thinking to justify *not* releasing the contents of such investigations. Their specious logic contends they have a "covenant" with their employees not to reveal the most important information contained in the safety report.

This bogus argument holds that Congress, who authorized the funding for the service, has no right to know why the accident occurred. Likewise, the taxpayers who paid for the equipment, personnel, and operations have no right to know why the accident occurred. Most ludicrous, this logic must hold that the next of kin also should be denied the right to know why their loved one died.

None of this makes much sense, so the military adds another argument. The military claims it must promise witnesses that their testimony will be protected by "privilege" so that these people will agree to tell the truth. This is another self-serving ploy, because the service could just grant them testimonial immunity, which would prevent prosecutors or commanders from later using information from a witness's statements against that witness.

Another specious idea often cited by the military is that witnesses would not testify if they thought the information would become public. This is also nonsense, because these people know that safety reports will be briefed to their comrades throughout the service.

The military even contends that it is a criminal offense for any service member or civilian employee to reveal certain kinds of information contained in safety reports. The proscribed privileged information includes witness testimony and the deliberations, findings, causes, and recommendations of the safety investigation board.

If one discusses information from any privileged "safety" report with outsiders, military regulations prohibit releasing detailed data that might identify the particular accident. Thus, specific information such as the date and place of the mishap or the aircraft's serial number cannot be given.

This is why such details are missing from many of the cases described in this text. In places where I've used the names of people involved or other details that would identify a particular incident, this information came from "accident" reports or other public domain sources.

I remember one glaring example of the abuse of "privilege." In 1993 I was attending a military lawyers meeting when they discussed how to mislead federal judges by invoking "privilege." Sitting in that room in the bowels of the Air Force Safety Agency listening to such conspiracies made me nauseous. These guys were very self-assured because the law was on their side.

One smug Pentagon lawyer even bragged how he had used this ploy to avoid having to admit the government's liability in a domestic water-heater explosion. The accident had seriously burned a soldier and his family at an Army post. This military officer of the court pointed out how naïve judges were about buying the "national security argument." He quipped, "After all, we weren't talking about the design of the Army's Abrams tank."[4] This abuse of privilege thus shields the Pentagon and those commanders who routinely ignore safety issues from some much-needed accountability.

After one recent accident, an interesting article appeared in the *Wall Street Journal*.[5] It described how the increased information being released " . . . has raised some hopes that the military, steeped for decades in a culture of concealment, will stop covering up deadly mishaps as if they were defense secrets." Unfortunately, the article was referring to the Russian military and the loss of their submarine *Kursk*. This culture of concealment is still alive and well in the American military and continues to put our GIs in jeopardy.

Air Force Lieutenant Tony Armstrong[6] was one such victim. This young man was on his first flight after being checked out in fighters when his flight commander decided to attempt an unauthorized maneuver. None of the experienced aviators in the formation spoke up.

At the time, fighter pilots in this command did not receive CRM training, which encourages subordinates to tactfully challenge a leader's questionable decisions. This rookie subsequently became disorientated and had to hastily eject from his jet at a very low altitude.

A rescue helicopter soon picked up this confused but very lucky aviator and brought him back to base where a flight surgeon,[7] Tim Goldman,[8] was standing by. This highly motivated captain had been in the service for only a short time, but he knew what needed to be done.

The flight doc approached the chopper and quickly transferred his patient, who was complaining of neck pain, to the waiting ambulance. Neck injuries are common after ejection, and because of the omnipresent danger of spinal injuries causing permanent paralysis, the good doctor began to fit his patient with a neck brace.

But before he can install this collar-like device, a staff car screeches to a halt in front of the parked ambulance. A colonel strides up to the ambulance and announces he is the interim safety board president and demands to see the pilot.

Captain Goldman replies, "This is Lieutenant Armstrong. He seems to be okay except for some potential neck injuries and—"

"I need to interview this pilot," the colonel says.

Dr. Goldman, knowing the potential dangers posed by such injuries, says, "Yes sir, but we need to fit him with this neck brace first and get him X-rayed right away. I should also draw some blood and get a urine sample. We'll have him ready for you in about one hour, sir."

If the colonel's facial expressions don't communicate his pique at this answer, his words do as he shouts, "Captain, I'm giving you a *direct* order. Get out of this vehicle, *now!*" Dr. Goldman knows the Hawkeye Pierce routines only work on the *M.A.S.H.* television episodes. He steps down from the ambulance holding the trauma collar.

Concerned about his patient, the doc stands outside where he overhears what is happening in the ambulance. The colonel starts in on the lieutenant by demanding that he tell him everything. A few minutes into the interview, the pilot states, "Okay, sir, I'm fully responsible for the accident. Now can I have my neck brace?" The colonel replies, "No, not until you answer some more of my questions." The young physician is furious by the time the interrogation ends nearly fifteen minutes later. The colonel steps out of the ambulance and glibly says, "He's all yours, Doc."

Goldman quickly fits the lieutenant with the brace and rushes him to the base hospital. Within the hour, the flight surgeon sees the X-rays, which reveal that the pilot has only a badly sprained neck.

When I arrive at the base a few days later, Goldman is still mad about this incident and wants to talk with me. He asks me how we could prevent such incidents. I offer to report the abuse when I get back to the center, but I note that senior leaders rarely show an interest in such matters.

I then remark that it's too bad the lieutenant was not an Iraqi prisoner of war. When the doc looks puzzled, I add that the Geneva Accords protect such people. They specifically forbid withholding medical treatment to obtain information. Our troops who are involved in accidents, it seems, don't have such protections from overzealous investigators. We both nod in sad agreement.

PART
II

Flying Fiascoes

6

Beneath Human Error

"Pilot error" is often singled out as *the* cause of aviation disasters. In fact, most statistical studies conclude that crew or operator error is the most common cause of accidents. Typically, between 60 and 90 percent of all accidents are blamed on human error, but safety experts have long noted such conclusions are often the by-product of superficial investigations.

These shallow explanations usually illustrate the investigator's own naïveté about the mechanisms that precipitate different types of human errors. Sophisticated investigators, by contrast, know that most mishaps do not occur because of a single failure, be it human or material. Rather, there is a deadly "chain of events," usually a series of seemingly minor problems or deficiencies that cascade in a particular situation to precipitate the accident.

This phenomenon is called the "chain" because if any one of the links is removed, the chain is broken—and the accident does not occur. Typically, the operator is merely the last link in a long sequence of events. Thus, he or she usually just represents the final chance of disrupting the accident chain. The operator's chronological proximity to the accident event often leads to the de facto assignment of blame.

Many underlying factors obviously contribute to crashes, but military safety investigations are particularly fond of citing "pilot error" as

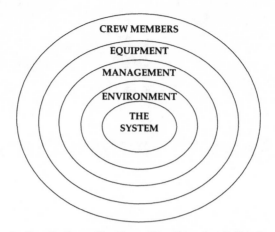

In-Depth Investigation: "Peeling the Onion"

the cause of mishaps, especially when the pilot is dead. This practice institutionalizes the egregious process by literally adding insult to injury.

But on rare occasions, the truth will out. This happens only when members of the investigation have the insight, patience, and courage to expose *all* the factors that contributed to the accident. By doing so, they are refusing to stop at merely identifying *what* has happened and are endeavoring to explain *why* the crash occurred.

Such investigators are willing to uncover the truth no matter where it lies. They simply keep digging until they have uncovered the underlying causes. They often find that, besides the crew performance, several other problems—such as the machine's design, management decisions, and environmental conditions—also played a role in the accident chain.

But more often than not, when one gets to the core of the matter, "the system" is the underlying culprit. The investigative process is not unlike peeling back the layers of an onion. By digging deeper and deeper, one gets at the truth, which is illustrated by the figure above. Often, the deeper one digs, the uglier the truth, and most military investigators simply cannot handle the truth.

Such a comprehensive approach to investigating human error was not always the case, even in civil investigations, as aviation expert and best-selling author John Nance notes in his classic book, *Blind Trust.*[1] But in the late 1970s, with some internal prodding from myself, the NTSB changed the way it investigated human factors issues.

The same cannot be said for the vast majority of today's military inquiries. However, occasionally they at least try to come close. One example of this occurred after an F-117 Stealth fighter crashed in 1995.

The F-117's official name is the Nighthawk. This superlative weapon system illustrates America's approach to warfare in the waning decades of the twentieth century. Visionary leaders such as Hap Arnold had long ago recognized the need to employ innovative technologies to defeat potential adversaries. By the end of World War II, radar had proved critical to military aviation. Therefore, anything that could negate an enemy's radar would provide an invaluable advantage.

The Stealth fighter sprang from the genius of two of America's most fertile minds. One was Lockheed Aircraft Corporation's premier designer, Mr. Kelly Johnson, whose previous successes included the high-flying U-2 and the world's fastest aircraft, the tri-sonic SR-71. These spy planes were but two products of his celebrated design facility, which was called the Skunk Works.

The other man was a brilliant but little-known Stanford University professor who had been a Department of Defense technocrat. He would soon be called "the father of stealth." Circumstances would later thrust this introverted scientist, one Dr. William Perry, into the Pentagon's top job.

The Pentagon would eventually place an order for fifty-nine of the black jets even though the craft had several latent deficiencies. These problems, in combination with its hazardous operational environment and a series of management blunders, would cost the lives of unsuspecting pilots. Apparently, neither man fully understood the dangers posed by the military's casual approach to safety. To paraphrase a 1992 political slogan, "It's the *system*, stupid!"

Part of the problem was that these Stealth jets were developed and tested in a highly classified environment. Having worked on other super-secret programs, I was well aware of the compromises often associated with these environments.

One of the dangers is that the programs are highly compartmentalized. This means, for security purposes, that people working on one component cannot always talk with others working on related components. Thus, if they fail to use good ergonomic design conventions, such equipment may be incompatible. For example, one engineer may arbitrarily decide to use triangles as icons to symbolize *enemy* aircraft on one cockpit display, while the individual designing a different cockpit instrument uses similar triangles to symbolize *friendly* aircraft.

Thus, a pilot may become confused when these two instruments are juxtaposed in the operational cockpit. Such features eventually lead to errors. Aviation psychologists call this phenomenon "design induced error." As part of my master's thesis, I spent many hours in graduate school studying how these problems occur.

Furthermore, the test pilots often overlook such problems. These highly experienced and very skillful individuals have years to become intimately familiar with all the nuances of the particular design. These aviators can cope with such idiosyncrasies during test flights. The same isn't always true for the line pilots who first encounter design features while they are being checked out in the operational craft.

Because of my experience with other classified programs, I was not surprised when I was informed of a series of dangerous incidents involving the F-117. For years, I tried unsuccessfully to persuade senior officers at the Air Force Safety Agency to investigate such deficiencies *before* an accident occurred. Unfortunately, such proactive concepts were foreign to that place.

Thus, in October 1994, I included my concerns about the F-117's problems as part of my whistle-blowing complaint. Ironically, my letter was addressed to Dr. William Perry, who by then was not just "the father of stealth," but also the Secretary of Defense. For the sake of brevity, my letter did not document all the deficiencies of these jets. But Dr. Perry surely must have known, at least after the fact, that his invention had more than a few warts.

One such problem involves the F-117's highly angular lines, which disrupt the smooth flow of air across the aircraft's surface. It also has a stubby arrowhead-shaped planform. Both features are designed to insure that radar signals are reflected away from enemy receivers. However, the net result is a machine that lacks innate stability—so much so that the aircraft requires a computer to electronically augment its performance. Hence, the craft has earned its unofficial moniker, the "wobbly goblin."

The craft's instability also requires the use of a sophisticated automatic pilot. Another reason for such equipment is that the goblin's pilot flies and fights alone. There is no copilot, navigator, or bombardier to assist this very busy solo act. High workloads increase the potential for errors.

The autopilot's functions range from simply keeping the aircraft upright (in straight-and-level flight) to following a complex course on an extended cross-country sortie. The human pilot can "type" (program) various altitudes and airspeeds as well as way points into the device. It will then dutifully follow these commands, allowing the pilot time to think about other things, such as potential enemy actions, changing weather conditions, or fuel management calculations (as the one thing that is certain in military aviation is uncertainty).

But like any piece of equipment, these computerized devices sometimes fail at inopportune times, so the human pilot always has the option of quickly shutting off the autopilot and "hand flying" the aircraft. Turning off the device usually can be done by either throwing a switch or just by pulling on the stick with sufficient force.

One critical function in designing any cockpit is providing clear indications to tell the pilot *when* the autopilot is turned off or has failed. Accident annals describe many mishaps where confused pilots thought a disengaged autopilot was still flying the craft. Perhaps the best-known example was the 1972 Eastern Airlines crash into the Florida Everglades.[2] This Lockheed 1011 jumbo jet's autopilot did not have adequate cues to alert crew members when it was disconnected, and neither did early production F-117s.

After a fatal 1987 crash, the Air Force decided to modify all its F-117s by installing a newer model autopilot, one that *clearly* announces when it has been disconnected. But by May 1995, the Air Force had not yet installed these updated autopilot-warning systems on all F-117s. What was worse, it had not told its pilots which individual jets were still unmodified.

All designs are compromises, and sometimes these compromises are deadly. The F-117's lack of aerodynamic features limit it to subsonic speeds. Thus it can be flown only at night in combat, for in daylight, it could be spotted visually and shot down by faster fighters. Night operations, however, are intrinsically risky for a variety of reasons, and they are several times more dangerous (per hour) when compared with day-only flying.

While flying in the dark, pilots have always been much more dependent on their instrumentation. This means cockpit designers have to be especially careful of ergonomic issues. The most important of these instruments is the so-called artificial horizon. As the name implies, this device looks like a miniature horizon. The real horizon, of course, is invisible in the dark. This vital instrument allows a pilot to quickly understand his aircraft's "attitude."

Thus, pilots can visualize their pitch angle (nose up, down, or level) and roll angle (wings banking left, right, or level). In recent years the name of this vital instrument has changed to the Attitude Director Indicator (ADI).

Because knowing one's attitude is so critical, this instrument is usually located directly in front of the pilot's eyes, near the top of the instrument panel. That location insures the ADI is always highly visible. Unfortunately, the designers of the F-117 eventually placed this vital instrument on the lower left-hand side of the instrument panel.

This is a particularly bad location, because they positioned the F-117's Data Entry Panel (DEP) directly in front of the pilot, near the top of the panel (where the ADI should be). DEP is a keyboard-like device that the pilot uses to type in a vast amount of data, such as altitudes and navigational way points. Unfortunately, fighter control sticks have several control buttons designed only to fit the pilot's right hand.

The problem arises because the pilot has to use his left hand to make inputs into the DEP. During this time, his arm literally blocks his view of the vital ADI. This is particularly dangerous when the pilot is maneuvering his craft at night. In a matter of seconds, a pilot can become disoriented.

Without knowing his aircraft's attitude, he literally cannot tell which way is up. A series of vestibular illusions often follows, because the pilot's sense of balance is playing tricks on his mind. When this happens, the aircraft's nose drops as the machine enters into a turn. The confused pilot then allows the craft's bank angle to progressively steepen while its nose plunges farther earthward. This often-fatal phenomenon is appropriately called the "graveyard spiral."

After two earlier F-117 crashes involving so-called spatial disorientation, the service should have redesigned the cockpit. Unnecessary design deficiencies force the pilot to compensate for the machine's inadequacies. These shortcomings invariably add to the pilot's already high workload, increasing the probability of error with potentially fatal results.

Such aircraft design deficiencies—compounded by difficulties posed by the operational environment and management problems—often cascade with tragic results. This is precisely what happened in the night skies over western New Mexico on May 10, 1995.

While officially the mishap was caused by "pilot error," the report did an unusually thorough job of explaining how this particular aviator died. The Accident Investigation Board documented the factors *underlying* his mistakes.[3]

It was almost dusk as Captain Kenneth Levens donned his flight suit in his bedroom. The loose-fitting greenish-gray outfit concealed the thirty-five-year-old's athletic build. This handsome young man grew up in rural Texas and gave up a potential spot on the Olympic judo team to fly for the Air Force.

He is a former F-16 pilot who has recently completed his initial checkout in the F-117. He has just been assigned to the Ninth Fighter Squadron, the so-called Flying Knights. At 5:00 P.M., he passionately kisses his pretty wife, Cathy, and their one-year-old daughter, Jacie, good-bye, and then he drives to nearby Holloman Air Force Base. This sprawling complex in southern New Mexico is the operational home to the Stealth fighters.

The whole Levens family is just recovering from a week-long bout with head colds, but Ken knows he cannot afford to stay away from work much longer. Cathy, who is a nurse, has some exciting news. A few days earlier, she has told her husband their second child is on the way. He reminds Cathy to take care of herself. The captain is delighted with the news, but he has other things on his mind recently.

For the last several days, Captain Levens has been anxiously planning an "open house" that will involve hosting a group of local dignitaries invited to tour the base. This thankless job was added on top of his other time-consuming duties as the squadron scheduling officer.

The scheduler job is always one of the most demanding positions in any military flying unit. It involves constantly juggling and updating "the board" due to the ever-changing availability of equipment, crews, facilities, weather, and missions. Normally, such duties are assigned only to people after they are highly experienced with the squadron's equipment. Captain Levens was a highly experienced F-16 pilot but is still only a neophyte in the F-117.

Military personnel have always been expected to perform such non-job-related tasks, but in the downsized Air Force, these so-called collateral duties have reached oppressive levels. Yet officers, who want to be promoted and stay in the service, dare not complain about such onerous practices.

Ken Levens wants to make a career of the Air Force, and he knows his commanders expect this open house to come off without a hitch. This will require him to juggle his other full-time duties as squadron scheduler. Thus, flying the jet this week has become a tertiary function for this overworked airman.

His concerns about these non-flying duties have even caused him to uncharacteristically break down and complain to Cathy. But he quickly regained his composure, not wanting to worry her. For Captain Levens also knows that he is still struggling to master the vagaries of the complex F-117, and the next few days would be very demanding.

Tonight Captain Levens *must* put all such distractions out of his mind and concentrate on being an aviator. Pilots are usually good at leaving such problems behind when they get to the flight line. They call this process "compartmentalization,"[4] meaning they have different mental compartments for family, officer duties, flying, and the like. When this aviator arrives at the squadron, he will have to be totally immersed in the extremely complex process of mission planning for tonight's sortie.

The mass briefing promptly begins at 6:45 P.M. Tonight's mission is a routine round-robin surface-attack sortie. The flight plan calls for Levens to depart in trail of two other Nighthawks. He and another neophyte Nighthawk pilot will follow an experienced flight leader. They will rendezvous with a tanker to refuel and then fly a complex course across the breadth of the state of New Mexico. During this mission, each craft will conduct several simulated bombing runs. The three jets will then return to Holloman for debriefing, all before the sun rises. At least that's the plan.

Captain Levens wants to study the "mission package" to carefully review the complex course, timing, and target depictions. But he soon learns he must go to the scheduling shop to handle his other duties not related to tonight's mission. He then rushes to the flight line but arrives five minutes late because he has had to retrieve a vital piece of equipment that he almost forgot.

As his mechanic helps Captain Levens strap himself into the cockpit, he tells the pilot the jet is "good to go." Neither man is aware that this jet is one of six F-117s in the squadron that has not had the updated autopilot installed.

Before this three-ship formation can depart, the plan begins to unravel. The lead jets aborts for mechanical reasons, so the two neophytes depart shortly after 9:15 P.M. while their leader tries to find a flyable jet. Captain Levens's call sign is Spear 26. He will be following behind the other rookie by about three minutes, but for all practical purposes, these are separate missions—everyone is on his own.

In the stratosphere over eastern New Mexico, Spear 26 rendezvouses with a giant KC-10 tanker to practice refueling. Captain Levens then asks the air traffic controllers for permission to descend to sixteen thousand feet to avoid reported weather at higher altitudes, a scattered-to-broken layer of clouds. At the lower level, the jet will burn more fuel, but the F-117 infrared viewing systems do not work in clouds. He subsequently turns westward to begin his "bombing runs."

Since his jet shares the airspace with airlines, Levens must maintain radio contact with the appropriate FAA air traffic control center. Albuquerque Center will be his eyes for weather and traffic as he proceeds along his route. Stealth jets are not equipped with a radar transmitter for such functions because such signals would give away their location in combat. These controllers will watch their scopes for Spear 26's transponder signals to identify the otherwise invisible craft.

Off his right wing tip, Captain Levens can see the bright lights of Albuquerque disappear in the distance. About seventy-five miles west of the city, the overhead clouds vanish. Now the stars and the widely scattered ground lights form a continuum, a thousand points of light with no visible horizon. The various windows of his diamond-shaped canopy catch and reflect these lights, as well as the glowing lights from his cockpit instruments.

Time wise, he knows he is now about halfway through tonight's mission as he approaches checkpoint eighteen, the Zuni Indian Pueblo.

Below lies the vast rolling chaparral where proud Native Americans once rode mustangs. Tonight, the descendants of these ancient warriors are shepherds, watching over their grazing flocks.

Ironically, their ancestors once worshipped bird figures, carved from black rocks, which bore an uncanny resemblance to modern stealth fighters. Before this night has passed, their quiet homeland will become a tragic scene of death, for a modern warrior will fall from the sky on his arrowhead-shaped steed.

Captain Levens has planned to let his autopilot do most of the flying tonight so he can mentally focus on the procedures needed for the upcoming bomb runs. These are the critical items that he did not have time to review during the preflight briefing. As he passes over the Zuni Pueblo, Levens expects this friendly robot to change course, turn the aircraft to the left, and head for its next stored checkpoint. This autopilot procedure is called auto-sequencing, but failures are very common.

When such a failure happens, five miles after the plane passes its last known checkpoint, the autopilot is programmed to direct a gradual, fifty-degree, banked turn. This maneuver is designed to bring the jet back toward the last programmed checkpoint. This same problem actually befell the F-117 flying in front of Levens this evening. However, that pilot noticed the problem and stopped the errant maneuver.

As Captain Levens passes over the Zuni Pueblo checkpoint, he also decides it is time to get up to his planned altitude. Shortly after 10:24 P.M. he requests permission to climb to twenty-two thousand feet. About this time, he probably reaches across his instrument panel to begin typing this altitude into his data entry panel in front of his face. But the controller denies this request and instead approves a twenty-one-thousand-foot level. Captain Levens acknowledges this clearance while his fingers quickly try to enter the new numbers on this panel.

In his haste, the captain may have inadvertently dropped a digit, entering twenty-one *hundred* feet instead of twenty-one *thousand* feet into the data entry panel. This is not an uncommon error. The dumb and dutiful computer will then gently lower the jet's nose and dive toward this accidentally selected altitude. These altitude figures are given in feet above sea level. Unfortunately, Levens's jet cannot descend to twenty-one hundred feet because the terrain under his jet is more than six thousand feet above sea level.

During this critical period, the jet's autopilot somehow becomes disengaged. It is no longer electronically keeping this naturally unstable jet upright. What is worse, unlike the newer versions of this device, it does not provide a clear warning when this has occurred. Moreover, the collage of reflections off his canopy windows helps to conceal the fact that the stars and scattered ground lights have begun to swap places as the jet steadily rolls over.

Unfortunately, when this is happening, Captain Levens's left arm is blocking his view of the Attitude Director Indicator. This is the one instrument that can quickly provide the vital information needed to recover from spatial disorientation. Without such cues, Levens does not realize his jet has inverted and entered a near vertical dive.

In just twenty seconds, Captain Kenneth Levens and his high-tech mount are doomed as they plummet to earth like an invisible meteorite. A few seconds past 10:25 P.M., they hit the ground at more than six hundred miles per hour. The craft is in a 70-plus degree dive, upside down, with 120 degrees of right bank. The jet blasts a crater thirty feet deep, hurling dirt, parts, fuel, and human fragments hundreds of feet across the terrain. Seconds later a crackling fireball rises over this grisly scene.

No humans witness Levens's demise, only the panicked sheep grazing the nearby range and an orbiting U.S. Air Force satellite, which detects the flash from space. Zuni tribal police and fire department members soon observe the fireball rising into the dark sky and head toward the scene.

Minutes after the jet disappears, the airways are alive with radio calls asking in vain for Spear 26 to acknowledge his position. Shortly after midnight, an H-60 Black Hawk helicopter is dispatched to the scene from Kirtland AFB in Albuquerque. Its crew finds the gaping crater, surrounded by smoldering aircraft fragments.

Back at the Levens's house, the family dogs begin to bark, awakening Cathy shortly after midnight. Looking out the window, she sees Ken's commander and the chaplain walking toward the front door. She knows instinctively what has happened. It's every military spouse's worst nightmare—but she knows she is not sleeping.

Before the commander can speak, Mrs. Levens says, "Don't tell me anything bad, because we're about to have another baby." In a monotone, the commander says he's sorry, but Ken's jet has crashed, and they don't know his fate yet. Her heart stops as Cathy grabs her stomach. She knows that Ken won't be coming home. An eternity of minutes ticks by before the phone rings at 7:00 A.M. with the dreaded confirmation.

From watching other widows, Mrs. Levens also knows that the *real* agony is about to begin. Within days, Cathy will have to lay Ken's remains to rest and then deal with the Safety Investigation Board. She is well aware that they will undoubtedly ask a lot of prying and very personal questions. They will then go away and likely conclude that the crash was all Ken's fault. Next, they will add insult to injury by informing her that she is not entitled to see this "privileged" report.

Mrs. Levens will subsequently be faced with a second inquiry, the accident investigation board. Its job is not to find out why, but merely to establish what happened and who should be blamed. Although this second investigation seems to be looking at many things, she also is aware that neither type of investigation tends to hold commanders or other officials responsible for crashes. Cathy is told she will get a copy of this report in several weeks, once the 12th Air Force commanding general approves it.

But when this general very abruptly leaves this command, his replacement will not view the report as a priority. Weeks become months, until finally the document is released to the family. Cathy is not surprised at its "pilot error" conclusion.

But Ken's parents are crushed by this stigma. His despondent dad will die two years later with a broken heart, for the elder Levens had encouraged his boy's decision to give up his chance for an Olympic gold medal for wings of silver.

Cathy sometimes wonders what is in the "privileged" safety report, which the Air Force will not let her see. She remembers how one widow did get to see her husband's safety report. A family friend serving on the inquiry illegally gave Janet Harduvel a copy of her husband's fatal F-16 investigation. This 1982 report claimed her husband died after becoming spatially disoriented and flying his jet into the ground using full afterburner.

Mrs. Harduvel was so angered by what she read that she conducted her own investigation, exposing many of the deficiencies in the Air Force's safety investigation. She also independently discovered that these jets had a history of electrical problems caused by bad wiring. In fact, she sued the manufacturer (because it had not followed "government specifications") and convinced a jury of these facts. She later testified before a Congressional committee, and for a time, got the television networks interested in her plight. HBO was so impressed that they even did a docu-drama about her efforts titled *Afterburn*.

The whole Harduvel saga was unfolding shortly after I arrived at the Air Force Inspection and Safety Center in 1987. Having just come from the relatively open civilian accident-investigation world, it was strange to watch the military leaders' angst over this situation. The brass were beside themselves trying to figure out just who the hell had given this privileged report to the widow.

In the civilian world, the next of kin are handled with respect because they are also considered to be victims. But here, you would think Mrs. Harduvel had just sold our national secrets to the Russians. I remember one general saying that somebody's head was going to roll over the unauthorized release of this report. Furthermore, if the *60 Minutes* crew showed up outside the building, somebody other than he was going to do the interview.

Cathy Levens realizes Janet Harduvel's experience was very unique. She knows most widows never learn what the military says really killed their husbands, nor are they able to sue the manufacturers. She expects that both reports will criticize Ken's role in the crash.

As the months pass, she senses the Air Force wants to get the accident behind them. Ken's death is just an embarrassing episode, one they want to forget. But the service is also dragging its feet on modifying all the F-117 autopilots, and she worries about the other pilots still flying in Ken's squadron.

Two years later, another F-117 crashes at a Maryland air show, and this time TV cameras capture the pilot's narrow escape. Cathy Levens is contacted by the *CBS Evening News* and asked to tell her story. She decides she will go public in hopes of preventing further tragedies.

She informs CBS that she would like to visit the site of her husband's crash to place a wreath beside the crater on the Zuni reservation. She asks my opinion of making this gesture. I explain that such visits often provide the next of kin with psychological closure on their loss.

But nobody is prepared for what Cathy finds when she arrives at the Pueblo.

Tribal leaders greet her with great civility and escort her and the news crew to a special place in their headquarters building. Here, they show her the room that has been set aside as a memorial to her husband. Its walls are tastefully adorned with photographs and other memorabilia of Captain Levens. Some of these things Cathy has not seen for years. The Indians ask the CBS crew not to videotape this sacred place. They explain how they requested the materials from the military people who visited the reservation to recover the wreckage.

Cathy was deeply moved by the respect the Zunis afforded her husband. These Native Americans demonstrated their humanity by establishing a permanent memorial for the stranger whom they knew only in death. This kind of honor was something his own tribe failed to show for the warrior killed by their negligence.

7

Accepted Risk

It's dark as Specialist Robert Rogers boards the Black Hawk helicopter on the island of Cyprus. It's August 15, 1995, his twenty-fifth birthday. The soldier hopes to call his young wife, Candida, to celebrate after the mission.

He has only a year left to serve in the U.S. Army and can hardly wait to get out and enroll in college. But he also knows that is many months away, while in just a few minutes, his chopper will be over the Mediterranean racing toward friendly downtown Beirut.

This ruggedly handsome senior mechanic is actually serving as a "flight attendant" on the world's most dangerous airline. Moreover, he and his three comrades know just how risky military flying can be. Last year, eleven soldiers from his unit were blown out of the sky by friendly fire from two Air Force F-15s. What they don't know is that tonight, the threat is *aboard* their helicopter.

The Pentagon has, in effect, been running this air-taxi operation ever since the 1984 bombing of the American embassy in Beirut. The mission is called the Beirut Air Bridge because it provides our diplomats a safe link to the outside world. Being the last superpower does not mean much in that part of the world, where some factions like to shoot at all things American.

This is literally a fly-by-night operation. It involves piloting two helicopters in close formation, with their lights turned off, for one hundred fifty miles over water, in the dark. The choppers must also stay at very low altitudes to avoid radar detection.

All crew members wear special Night Vision Goggles (NVGs) during these flights. NVGs electronically amplify very dim light eminating from otherwise invisible objects. Because they help aviators to see in the dark, the devices are considered essential for such operations.

But for all their benefits, the devices do have some drawbacks. Everything appears in shades of green, as if viewed in daylight through very dark sunglasses. The heavy, binocular-like devices are rigidly attached to each crewman's flight helmet. NVGs have very narrow fields of view.[1] Since the NVGs are mounted on the helmets, the aviators have to constantly move their heads to scan large areas. The devices are also normally focused to see objects some distance outside the craft, rather than cockpit instruments and controls.

Because of the difficulties of flying with NVGs, Army regulations require that pilots constantly practice using these devices. To be considered "NVG current"—that is, legal to fly with such devices—an aviator must have flown for at least one hour using the goggles during the last forty-five calendar days.[2]

But the detachment commander has decided to send the copilot, Warrant Officer Donald Cunningham, on tonight's mission without the required recent NVG experience. In fact, this soldier has not flown with NVGs for the last 117 days.[3] Apparently, the commander expects him to become current with these devices on the way to Beirut.

This commander is not one who inspires confidence in his overworked troops. He is seen as too petty, and unwilling to listen to their complaints about safety issues.[4] A fortnight before, the pilot, Warrant Officer Michael Baker, jotted a prophetic note to his wife: "It is late. We did already fly, but could not go to Beirut. One helicopter broke down . . . now we have to do the whole thing tomorrow again. It's not any fun here. I believe that this commander is an idiot. He does not know what he is doing . . . I have a feeling that somebody will die soon. It is only a question of time."

The undesirable relationship with their commander is not the only thing bothering these soldiers. They are also unhappy that this assignment takes them away from their families, who are living in Germany. These deployments last for two months at a time. But they know such hardships are common for many troops in today's military.

This crew faces another, more immediate challenge tonight: Wearing NVGs complicates crew coordination, because you cannot readily see what the other crew members are doing. Furthermore, many of the Black Hawk's controls, including the two throttle levers, are located on the ceiling between the pilots. Since the left and right throttle knobs are identical in shape, it is difficult to tell them apart in the dark, even with NVGs.

To make matters worse, the Army, like most of the other services, has not thoroughly embraced Crew Resource Management (CRM) training. This in spite of the fact that such training has been shown to improve crew coordination in civil and military flying. CRM, in contrast, has become de rigueur for the airlines.

Tonight, this lack of training will be very costly for these four soldiers. Unbeknownst to them, things are beginning to unravel in this Black Hawk's engine compartment, located just a few feet over Rogers's head.

The ubiquitous UH-60 Black Hawk is the Pentagon's replacement for the obsolete UH-1 Huey of Vietnam fame. The U.S. Army received its first Black Hawks in 1978. They were powered by two fifteen-hundred-horsepower General Electric T-700 series gas turbine engines. These power plants were considered to be technological marvels, so much so that they were also installed in the Army's new helicopter gunship, the AH-64 Apache. But five years after they entered service, the engines began to fail unexpectedly.

Turbine engines are built with the precision of Swiss watches. The heart of the clockwork mechanism is the gas generator (GG). Inside this vessel, turbine rotors must spin at more than forty thousand revolutions per minute in temperatures reaching almost two thousand degrees Fahrenheit. The space between the tips of these whirling turbine blades and the stationary walls is only a fraction of an inch. This precise gap must be rigidly maintained. If the walls become distorted, airflow anomalies will cause the dozens of turbine blades to vibrate. These vibrations induce "metal fatigue" and drastically weaken the blades.

Fatigued turbine blades will eventually fail. Once the blades break off, these rapidly spinning components crash into each other and into the stationary parts. The entire engine then self-destructs in a matter of seconds. It quickly becomes a shuddering blowtorch, spitting red-hot metal and burning fuel from its exhaust pipe.

These types of failures in T-700 engines first began to occur in 1985. The Army and GE took another four years to develop a fix for the problem. It called for replacing the weakened blades and adding dampers to control vibrations. Unfortunately, the Army decided *not* to immediately recall the engines for modification.[5]

Instead, the service would continue to fly the unmodified helicopters until they were due back to the "depot" for regularly scheduled overhauls. These depots are government-operated factories where aircraft can receive major modifications and repairs. Completing the modifications this way would take several years to accomplish. Obviously, this looked like a good way to save money, but looks can be deceiving.

The Army's logic was apparently based on the fact that each helicopter has two engines. Headquarters decided that if one fails, the crew could just shut it down and limp back to base on the remaining engine. That was an interesting assumption, and in a perfect world, it would work just fine.

The Army even put out a message to let commanders and crew members know about the potential for such unexpected engine failures. It also reminded the troops to be prepared to use the proper engine shutdown procedures. It was sort of a "you all be careful now" memo. Unfortunately, retrofitting these defective engines would take years, and headquarters did not establish a system to tell people which aircraft had been fixed and which had not.

The situation is but another example of the Pentagon's cavalier approach to safety. If this same problem occurred in a civilian aircraft, the independent NTSB would probably generate an urgent recommendation insisting that the regulators, the FAA, issue an aeronautical directive (AD). This AD would probably require the aircraft operators, the airlines, to fix their aircraft as soon as the modification kits were available.

Unlike the military's approach, this civilian system emphasizes protecting passengers and crews. Obviously, all organizations have to try to balance costs with safety risks. Since military operations are innately more hazardous than typical civilian flying, one would think the military would place *more* rather than less emphasis on ensuring safety.

But as the men in Rogers's helicopter will soon discover, that simply is not true.

At 9:29 P.M., the two helicopters have been airborne for thirteen minutes. They are skimming five hundred feet above the waves at 160 miles per hour. Rogers is seated in the passenger compartment of the lead chopper. In the green world of his NVGs, he can see the dimly lit cockpit instruments, the waves racing by below, as well as the shoreline of Cyprus in the distance.

Everything seems okay at first. Then his mechanic's sixth sense begins to tell him something is not quite right. There is a strange noise coming from somewhere overhead. Before he can react, he hears a frightening radio call from the sister Black Hawk in trail. They see fire coming from Rogers's helicopter.[6]

Rogers looks upward out the right window and sees the bright glow of flames lapping back against the fuselage. He hears a rapidly decreasing squeal, the unmistakable sound of a turbine engine as it whines down.

Seconds later, the terrified soldiers are shouting into their microphones. Rogers's goggled eyes are focused on the glowing fireball to the right when he feels the craft veer sharply to the left—toward the seeming safety of the coast three miles away. He notices the pilots' hands groping for the overhead throttle controls. Rogers knows the pilots have just one shot at pulling the right throttle aft, into its "off" position.

This flier cannot believe his ears when he hears the sounds of the *second* engine quitting. He wonders what the hell is happening as the pilots curse their predicament. Because of the difficulties of looking upward with NVGs, somebody has mistakenly pulled the wrong throttle—the one that controlled the functioning engine—back into the cut-off position. Now the powerless rotorcraft is plunging toward the waves, and the doomed fliers know there is not enough time to restart the good engine.

Under such extreme stress, the human mind undergoes a phenomenon called "time dilation." Everything seems to be happening in slow motion. Rogers sees the backs of the two pilots' helmets as they try to look upwards at the ceiling controls, wondering how they killed the good left engine. In this state of suspended animation, Rogers can look across the cabin at his terrified fellow mechanic, Specialist Dale Wood. In what seems like an eternity, he can see the rotor blades striking the water, followed by the waves crashing through the windows. A dark death comes to Rogers and his three comrades as their bodies flail about the flooding cabin.

The tangled wreckage quickly sinks to the bottom of this foreign sea. America has lost a $10 million asset and four invaluable young men from its heartland. They include pilot Baker, who warned that somebody was going to die soon; copilot Cunningham, who never got to complete the one hour needed for his NVG currency; Specialist Wood, who could not believe what had happened; as well as Crew Chief Rogers, who will *not* be calling his wife this evening, nor going to college next year.

The "system" has claimed its latest victims. Within minutes, the second Black Hawk will begin to search in vain for survivors. Within hours, the next of kin will be notified. Within days, the military authorities will convene the first of their two standard in-house inquiries while rounding up the usual suspects, such as "pilot error." Within weeks, the Pentagon will begin to go public with its spin on what has happened.

The official investigation reveals that such failures of T-700 engines have occurred 150 times during the last six years. Nonetheless, the Army exonerates itself regarding the decision to delay repairing the engines. The service manages only a mild mea culpa by suggesting that perhaps it should *now* accelerate the overhaul schedule. Translation: Congress needs to give us more money because the taxpayers, not the manufacturer, have to pay for fixing the defectively designed T-700s.

The Army avoids acknowledging that senior officers should have been more diligent about identifying which aircraft had not yet been modified. Doing so would have allowed unit commanders and crews to avoid flying these particular helicopters on the most dangerous missions.

Headquarters then proudly informs the families that as a result of the investigation, five officers have been punished. It fails to mention that they are all mid-level personnel. These officers, of course, had nothing to do with the decision to knowingly operate a piece of defective equipment for years.

One of these junior officers will later claim he is being made a scapegoat for criticizing the practice of using unmodified helicopters on dangerous missions. Meanwhile, the Black Hawks used to transport commanders on routine missions reportedly *always* had the modified engines.[7] Furthermore, this junior officer knows that none of the senior military people involved will receive any punishment.

The officials, as expected, placed much of the blame on the pilots for shutting down the good engine. They did not mention the ergonomic problems inherent in trying to differentiate between two identical knobs on the ceiling while wearing NVGs. Nor do they acknowledge that their own tests show that, even in the benign environment of flight simulators, pilots selected the wrong lever one out of six times. Russian roulette odds! We do not *allow* soldiers to play Russian roulette with their revolvers, so why do we *force* them to play it with their helicopters?

What is more irksome, the Pentagon has for years labeled the process of intentionally forcing its fliers to use dangerous equipment as "accepted risk." They say as much in a letter sent to Rogers's relatives on September 26, 1996.[8] This bureaucratically worded tome describes the reasons for the Pentagon's lack of concern at the prospects of this kind of accident: "Since the aircraft are capable of single-engine flight . . . the risk assessment matrix normally used in Army aviation has categorized the hazards . . . at a 'medium' risk. This means an accident with marginal severity can be expected to occur frequently. . . . However, if the hazard is assessed against the total system considering the operational mission envelope of the aircraft, the potential exists for a catastrophic occurrence. The increased severity may result from an improper human performance to the root cause material failure."

This convoluted logic implies that, if or when such accidents occur, they are solely the fault of the inept crew. Does the Pentagon naïvely assume that humans should *always* perform perfectly? This blame-the-dead-guys approach understandably angers the next of kin.

As a final insult, the Army sends a group of briefers around to visit the families. These officers, headed by a colonel, will give them the Pentagon's version on what happened. These briefers systematically mislead the families. The Army claimed it had sent out twelve separate safety messages to all crew members before the accident; actually, only two had been issued at that time.[9] The Army claimed that unmodified helicopters had warning labels on their instrument panels —but such labels weren't used until after the crash.[10] Finally, the Army claimed that crews get engine-failure practice on a weekly basis; actually, it normally occurs only once or twice a year during simulator training.

What the Army briefers did not know was that the Rogers family had decided to secretly audiotape this shameful session. During the briefing, the Army officials told the victims' families that the failed turbine was part of the "accepted risk" of the job and that the fatal crash was due to "pilot error." The tape would later be turned over to the CBS *60 Minutes* producers. During an on-camera interview with Morley Safer, Robert Rogers's wife and parents suggested a different phrase—"*negligent homicide!*"[11]

Unfortunately, the types of problems illustrated by this tragic accident are all too common. What is more, the Pentagon has been sending its people aloft in dangerous equipment for decades—with predictable consequences.

8

Skeletons in the Closet

The terrible cost of the Pentagon's practice of putting people in jeopardy with dangerous equipment is not new. One of the more unusual crashes resulted from the exigencies of the Second World War. Interestingly, the crash occurred as part of an Army publicity stunt.

Shortly after Pearl Harbor, the Army discovered it was going to need lots of gliders. These simple aircraft were used to transport assault troops into enemy territory. The service decided that the untested, fifteen-place CG-4 should be the standard design.[1]

In March 1942, the Army signed contracts with eleven different companies for a total of 640 of this craft. These were "cost plus" contracts, meaning the government would pay whatever the manufacturers spent, plus a healthy profit.

Unfortunately, only a few of these companies had any experience at building aircraft. The names of some firms, such as the Ward Furniture Manufacturing Company, might have been a hint. The average price per glider varied widely, presumably due to some very steep learning curves. One company delivered dozens of gliders for only $14,891 a piece, while another firm produced a single glider for an astounding $1,741,809![2] But costs were not the only problem.

Several companies found building even these basic aircraft a challenge. Their personnel simply lacked the required technical skills, while their quality-control processes were nonexistent. Government inspectors finally began to worry. One firm, the Robertson Aircraft Company, was officially accused of gross mismanagement in May 1943.

The government's director of production, Lieutenant General William Knudsen, recommended canceling the contracts with four of the eleven firms, but Under Secretary of War Robert Patterson overruled the general. He demanded that all of the contracts, even those with poor performance, be continued.[3]

To keep the under secretary happy, the Army arranged a publicity stunt. It invited the mayor of St. Louis and several officials to take a ride in a hometown product—a Robertson-built CG-4. The flight was to take place at Lambert Field, Missouri, on August 1, 1943. During the demonstration flight, the glider suffered a catastrophic wing failure. It plunged to earth killing all ten passengers, including the mayor and several Robertson employees.

The subsequent investigation revealed that a faulty wing attachment fitting had failed. This component was manufactured by one of the subcontractors selected by the Robertson firm, the Gardner Metal Products Company of St. Louis. Ironically, this outfit was a former *casket* manufacturer!

This wartime subcontractor obviously did not understand aviation metallurgy. What was worse, the government neither checked this company's credentials, nor tested its products before putting people at risk. This sophisticated big-city mayor undoubtedly assumed that his country would not put his life in jeopardy.

Another accident claimed the lives of other trusting civilians. It occurred when 243 orphans were hastily loaded onto a giant USAF C-5 Galaxy transport[4] on April 4, 1975. Vietnam was collapsing under the communist onslaught, and Operation Baby Lift was supposed to be a humanitarian effort to evacuate these lucky infants to a new life in America.[5]

But several minutes after takeoff from Tan Son Nhut airport, the massive rear cargo ramp pressure doors suddenly blew open. Dozens of nurses and child care aids raced through the now depressurized cabin trying to calm the terrified kids. They were scared because they could not understand what had happened, but they were not the only terrified folks aboard.

On the flight deck, Captain Dennis Traynor soon realized he had a much bigger problem than this rapid decompression. His flight controls had jammed, so he now had to somehow maneuver the world's largest type of aircraft using engine power alone. He was hoping against hope that he could somehow get it back on the runway.

He tried steering this half-million-pound ark by increasing power temporarily to the engines on one side to turn and pulling power on all engines simultaneously to descend. But this was not something he was adequately trained to do, and large, slow oscillations soon developed as he approached the airport.

The terrified pilot had to crash-land the transport in the rice paddies one and one-half miles short of the runway. The fuel-laden craft shattered on impact, and only half of the 300-plus souls on board survived.[6] The Air Force later discovered a defective locking mechanism on the rear doors and modified the design.

Such problems are not limited to basic mechanical issues or to the exigencies of war. Sometimes manufacturers lack a technical understanding of other important fields, such as ergonomics. This is especially true when the government buys directly from the low bidder.

Ergonomics deals with the complexities of human capabilities and limitations. Some firms simply lack expertise in this field. Their "user-unfriendly" civilian products are at a disadvantage, because they do not sell as well as better-designed competitors' equipment.

Unfortunately, this is not a factor in military acquisition, because the people who select the equipment are usually not the troops who have to use it. Thus, it is not at all surprising to discover human factors engineering problems with military equipment. Tragically, such deficiencies are often uncovered only *after* a mishap occurs.

One such ergonomic problem dealt with the design of the modified fuel transfer panel on a KC-135 Stratotanker. This four-engine aircraft is the military version of the world's first successful jet transport, the Boeing 707. Its primary mission is to refuel other aircraft in flight, which vastly increases their range.

The Air Force ordered 732 KC-135s in 1956. Boeing employs a large human factors engineering staff, and their civil and military products normally reflect this emphasis on ergonomics. For instance, their engineers had carefully designed various KC-135 cockpit controls and displays. This equipment included the very important fuel transfer panel that was located between the pilots in front of their throttles.

Thousands of gallons of jet fuel were contained in various tanks located throughout the KC-135's wings and fuselage. This panel had several large gauges to display fuel quantity. It also employed large toggle switches to control fuel transfer pumps, along with large adjustable amber-colored lights to indicate when these pumps were turned on.

By all accounts, this was a user-friendly panel. It allowed the pilots to easily monitor and accurately control the aircraft's complex fuel system. This was vital in insuring that fuel was available for transfer to "receiver aircraft" as well as keeping the weight of the KC-135 properly balanced.

After these tankers had flown for several years, the Air Force decided to make a series of modifications. One involved redesigning the fuel transfer panel. A subcontractor replaced the large analog gauges with small digital readouts. The large switches were replaced with miniature ones. Furthermore, small fixed-intensity lights that showed which pumps were running were substituted for the Boeing-designed large, adjustable indicator lights. This new panel caused busy pilots to often overlook a pump running in an empty tank.

Crews were cautioned not to leave transfer pumps on once a tank was empty, and for good reason. These electrical devices are actually cooled and lubricated by the fuel they pump. Thus, running dry will eventually cause them to overheat. Hot electrical devices in empty fuel tanks have always been worrisome (more so after the 1996 explosion of the TWA Flight 800). After hundreds of hours of crews overlooking such dry-running pumps, these devices began to wear out.

There was always the potential that one of these worn pumps would ignite the explosive fuel vapors, but the service simply ignored this very real danger. "Accepted risk," the practice of routinely operating devices with known hazards, was at work again. These policies would cost the lives of more than one KC-135 crew.

On September 20, 1989, a KC-135 aircraft pulled into its parking space on the ramp at Eielson AFB in Alaska. Over the years, these pumps had been run dry countless times and were slowly grinding themselves to bits in the bowels of the aft fuselage fuel tank. It was then that this worn electromechanical device would self-destruct.

Before its engines were shut down, the jet burst into flames.[7] The overheated pumps had ignited the fumes in the aft fuselage tank. Two crew members, Master Sergeants William Malico and Cheryl Helgerman, were trapped in the conflagration.

Sometimes a problem starts off looking like "pilot error" or structural failure. It then turns out to be something very different, but *only* when somebody demands an in-depth investigation. Such was the case several years ago with a rash of Navy S-3 Viking accidents.

These compact, twin-engine, anti-submarine patrol planes were manufactured by Lockheed Aircraft Corporation. They often operated from aircraft carriers at night in marginal weather, because controlling the enemy submarine menace was a never-ending task.

The S-3s are normally flown by a pilot, with two naval flight officers and an enlisted sensor operator on board. All four crew stations are equipped with highly effective ejection seats. These rocket-propelled seats are one of the best safety devices in modern aircraft, because crew members can be rapidly lifted out of a disabled aircraft in most situations.

These upward firing seats work effectively in most cases—unless the aircraft has rolled over sideways or is rapidly descending toward the earth's surface. This causes problems because of the time needed to open the canopy, separate the crewman from the seat, and open his or her parachute—all of which happens automatically. At low altitudes, fractions of a second can literally mean the difference between life and death.

Several of these jets have mysteriously crashed after taking off from aircraft carriers, and most sink in deep water with no survivors. The Navy apparently felt these were just random cases of "pilot error." Spatial disorientation was the usual conclusion from these investigations. It seems dead S-3 crewmen tell no tales.

Then on October 7, 1989, another S-3 crashed. But this time, the enlisted crew member ejected safety. He said the jet rolled uncontrollably to the right shortly after being catapulted off the carrier's deck.[8] The pilot, Lieutenant Douglas Gray, had tried to right the craft, then exclaimed, "Oh my God! Eject! Eject! Eject!" The three officers were killed when their parachutes failed to open in time because the jet was rapidly rolling inverted as it crashed into the sea. The jet came to rest in ten thousand feet of water off the Virginia coast.

The Navy ignored the testimony of the enlisted crew member and initially refused to recover the wreckage. The pilots' widows eventually got a sympathetic congressman to force the service to bring up the wreckage. The Navy's investigation was inconclusive. The widows then hired expert safety investigators who ultimately discovered major problems with the aircraft's control system.

The next of kin knew it was virtually impossible to sue the government and very difficult to sue a government contractor. Nonetheless, the families hauled Lockheed into court in Atlanta. This looked like a "David versus Goliath" battle, especially since Lockheed had a massive plant just north of the city. But an unexpected revelation occurred when a Lockheed employee provided some startling evidence on the safety of their aircraft during this civil trial.

In an apparent gaffe, he quotes from a company report that describes an in-flight lateral control system problem that highlights an urgent, repeated, and an "as yet unresolved safety of flight problem." The Lockheed report also states: "This is the second documented lateral control system problem for the airplane since 1984. For some unknown reason the S-3 seems to be vulnerable to periodic loss of flight control effectiveness in flight."[9]

The expert witnesses for the families offer a potential explanation involving the design and testing of the aircraft's hydraulically operated flight control system. The court accepts this explanation and awards the families more than $4 million on March 31, 1995.

Shortly thereafter, I contacted a former associate who had become a senior Lockheed official. He revealed that there was another problem—the Navy's improper maintenance. The service had modified the original design during repeated overhauls. He quickly added that Lockheed lawyers could not bring this up in court and risk offending one of their best customers—the Navy. The company was simply trapped by the circumstances into "copping a plea" and paying off the families.

Sometimes the deficiencies ironically involve a piece of safety equipment. One such problem resulted in the crash of a T-2 Buckeye several years ago. Rockwell International manufactured this type aircraft. These twin-engine trainers have been operational since 1973, although the Navy has been planning to retire these weary jets for years. Budgetary and design problems with its replacement, the T-45, have meant the Navy's instructor pilots must continue using such obsolete equipment. Moreover, the Navy was not about to spend money updating these old jets.

This is evident to Lieutenant Mark Sharp from his T-2's fading orange and white paint as he begins the preflight inspection. He also notices the hydraulic fluid dripping off its fuselage onto the ramp at Oceana Naval Air Station, Virginia. The picture does not exactly inspire confidence, but this hardworking instructor expects July 23, 1994, will be just another tough day.

The T-2's hydraulic system is not Sharp's only concern. The student and instructor sit in separate cockpits and must communicate over an electronic intercom system. Being able to understand one another is obviously critical to safety. Unfortunately, this particular jet's intercom has been acting up.

Sharp also must worry about the bad weather that is moving in while he takes his student back to their training base in Mississippi. This particular rookie has been having problems. He dropped out of the program for personal reasons for five weeks. Now Sharp, who has a reputation as top-flight instructor, has been told to get him back up to speed.

Sharp needs to let this guy get as much "stick time" as possible. This means he must allow the student to do the takeoff during simulated instrument conditions. This is accomplished by putting the neophyte in the back cockpit under an opaque hood. The student is thus taught to rely solely on his cockpit instruments. The instructor, who sits in the front seat, acts as a lookout for traffic.

This is going to be a highly demanding maneuver, even for the best of pilots with a working intercom. Sharp is very concerned about the system, so he asks the flight-line maintenance people to fix it. They quickly replace a component and button up the jet. The flaps are then lowered into takeoff position to enhance the wing's lifting abilities. These aluminum appendages are critical to allowing the jet to stay airborne at the lower speeds encountered during takeoffs and landings.

While they taxi out to the active runway, the intercom becomes erratic—again. The student also becomes focused on a problem with his cockpit compass. Lieutenant Sharp insures the ejection seat control switch is in the desired position. If they have to eject, this system will protect his student by firing the rear ejection seat first.

As the jet accelerates down the runway, the student becomes confused. He instinctively pulls back on the control stick, launching the jet into the air. When it reaches 150 miles per hour, he realizes something is wrong. The flaps are retracting prematurely, and the wings are losing lift. Damn! Both men now realize that they are in very serious trouble.

Sharp takes control but is powerless to prevent the jet from slamming back onto the runway with its wheels retracted. Smoke and flames spurt from its damaged belly as it bounces momentarily back into the air. While the jet starts down a second time, Sharp sees that it is veering toward a clump of trees beside the runway. He reluctantly pulls the ejection handle. He knows that the T-2's antiquated seat is not as fast nor as powerful as the models found on newer Navy aircraft.

He watches in seeming slow motion as the canopy peels off, and he feels wind whipping around his helmet. On his windshield he sees the reflection of the bright orange glow as the rocket motor mounted on the student's seat carries that young aviator upward. Sharp worriedly watches the trees getting bigger in front of his windshield. Though only a split second, it seems like an eternity as he waits for his own seat to fire. Finally he feels it go, pressing his buttocks against the seat cushion as it flings him out of the craft. But by now Sharp and his underpowered seat are crashing through tree branches and foliage.

He will never see his student's chute open in the nick of time. But Sharp realizes that he is personally in a world of hurt, as things go from a fleeting green to a hazy black blur. He feels the tall weeds tear at his flight suit as his bones snap like so many branches.

It will be another twenty-four minutes before rescuers find his semiconscious body, still strapped in his battered ejection seat. The student survives with only superficial injuries, but life ebbs from Lieutenant Mark Sharp's traumatized body in a Norfolk hospital five hours and twenty minutes after he pulled the ejection handle.

While the official accident report will conclude that the student probably raised the flaps prematurely, it blames Sharp for the accident. It will say he rushed the takeoff and delayed making a timely decision to eject. It will *not* mention that if Sharp had another half-second he would have survived. Nor will it acknowledge that if he had been sitting on a newer type ejection seat, he would be alive, or that he is the twenty-eighth flier to die while using this obsolescent seat.

Lieutenant Sharp's father, Stan, graduated from the Naval Academy and spent his career in the service before earning a law degree. As a captain in the reserves, he is astounded by his service's indifference to the bigger issues that have cost his son's life. As a lawyer, he will become disgusted by the Navy's arrogant disregard for basic legal precepts by not acknowledging his request for "privileged" information.

Another T-2 ejection attempt will claim an additional victim several months later. This will convince Captain Sharp to mount a one-man crusade to get the Navy to retrofit modern ejection seats into its T-2s. Captain Sharp contacts me to discuss a strategy for doing this. His overtures will remind me of my earlier efforts to enhance the chances for crew members to successfully bail out of their disabled craft.

Military aircraft usually go in harm's way, none more so than the U.S. Air Force AC-130 Gunship. This is a highly modified version of the four-engine C-130 Hercules transport. Lockheed Aircraft Corporation originally designed this rugged aircraft to haul ninety paratroopers or twenty tons of military cargo into primitive airfields. Well over two thousand of these highly efficient turbo-props haul everything the troops need.

But some of these giant birds have also been modified for other missions. During the Vietnam War, LTV E-Systems Incorporated wins the contract to do one of the most interesting metamorphoses, but they are told all design work must be completed in ninety days.

The USAF discovered that lumbering transports could be converted to very effective weapons platforms for firing at ground targets. Mounting several machine guns and cannons, all pointing from the left side of the cavernous fuselage, makes such craft resemble Spanish galleons of a bygone era. These weapons are aimed simply by steeply banking to the left and flying in tight circles. Orbiting overhead, the Gunship can precisely pour thousands of rounds on a target, even when friendly troops are only a stone's throw from the enemy positions.

These craft are equipped with night-vision devices, illumination flares, armor plate, radar jamming systems, and have two important capabilities: they can stay on-station for hours, and they can carry lots of ammo. Their crew members just keep reloading the guns.

But these birds have one major limitation—they are large, slow craft and fly in endless circles. Thus, they are themselves easy targets, especially if the bad guys have heavy antiaircraft guns or guided missiles. Which is why in high-threat environments these craft normally fly only at night. Obviously, most Gunships are going to take hits, and some will be lost. Furthermore, these aircraft have a dozen or more of our gutsiest aviators on board, and they deserve a shot at surviving when the inevitable happens.

That's where I come into the picture, for I am in charge of human engineering and system safety on the first production AC-130s. It's 1968, the war is dragging on, and the Pentagon wants these birds pronto. I don't need a Ph.D. to figure out that getting twelve guys out of a tumbling transport isn't going to be easy. I study the engineering drawings and am taken aback.

The plan calls for everybody to put on chutes and saunter back to jump off the retractable ramp located under the tail. That's fine if the bird's willing to stay straight and level while you weave your way through a maze of guns, ammo cans, and expended shell casings. This will be a real challenge, especially for the several guys assigned to the guns in the forward fuselage, and for those on the flight deck. There's also the fact that the most dangerous item in the cabin, the highly explosive flare launcher, happens to be located on the aft ramp.

Ideally, you would give everyone on board an ejection seat, but that was impractical for several reasons. For instance, the gunners don't work sitting down, and trying to strap oneself into a complex ejection seat harness when the aircraft is tumbling would not be easy. The next best thing is to locate a bailout exit so that everyone can get to it quickly.

As I study various locations, the most practical seems to be the existing crew boarding door. This is a three-by-six-foot hole in the left forward fuselage at floor level. All that is needed is a storable "spoiler" located in front of the door. I consult with several experts on how this modification could be installed.

When deployed, this device would swing into the airstream and deflect the wind. These devices permit crew members to jump clear of the craft and are referred to as "manual bailout systems." KC-135 tankers have had a similar system for years.

After drawing up the plans, I visit my boss. He notes that nothing in the contract requires us to develop such a safety device. Besides, we are already running behind schedule. Technically, he is right, but I try unsuccessfully to convince him that we have an obligation to do so.

He finally announces that he won't permit such a spoiler on these aircraft, but he would agree to consider installing it as a "modification" once they are deployed. Translation: It's a good idea, but the company can make more money fixing a problem than by doing the right thing to start with. Our military-industrial complex is at work again.

I am not pleased, but he *is* the boss. I then try to privately discuss this shortcoming with an Air Force engineer who is reviewing the project. Like many of his comrades who I will later encounter, he is more interested in aircraft performance than safety. So the production AC-130s will go to war without my recommended manual bailout system. In fact, to this day, this critical safety device is still, in the language of the Pentagon, an "unfunded requirement."

As the years roll by, I will learn of the mounting death toll for this "unfunded requirement." Several AC-130s will go down in war and peace, killing dozens of America's most gallant warriors. Sometimes it gets really personal. Once, after I appeared on ABC's *Good Morning America*, the father of one of these victims telephoned me.

This distraught dad explained how his boy was the navigator on an AC-130. It was protecting a platoon of Marines who were in grave danger of being overrun during a nighttime firefight. After the sun came up, the gunship guys knew they were sitting ducks themselves, but they would not abandon the grunts on the ground. His boy's flaming AC-130 crashed into the Persian Gulf—and nobody could bail out.

Terms like "unfunded requirement" and "accepted risks" sound hollow to the parents of such victims. These unnecessary deaths should haunt all those who ignored my pleas, but they will not, so long as the Pentagon can sell the idea that these happenings are just the "price of doing business."

This AC-130 crew died because they could not use their parachutes to jump to safety. But sometimes the problem is even more egregious. For instance, those airmen who flew in the early Air Force T-3 Firefly trainers faced an almost unbelievable problem. The service had actually *removed* the parachutes from their aircraft.

Slingsby Aircraft in Britain manufactured these light planes. The Air Force chief of staff, General Merrill McPeak, had decided that student pilots should be better screened. He felt they needed to prove they could handle highly demanding "aerobatic" maneuvers such as loops, rolls, and spins. All this stunt flying is required for mastering military fighter tactics, but now it was to begin *before* students even entered formal jet-training.

The T-3 was designed as a civilian aerobatic trainer. This craft was unusual in that it was made primarily of fiberglass and plastic, rather than aluminum. It also had a reputation for being tricky to fly, especially when compared to the docile T-41, a version of the Cessna 172 light planes, which the Air Force had flown safely for thirty years.

McPeak had been a pilot for the Air Force aerobatic demonstration team, the famous Thunderbirds. He apparently placed great stock in stunt flying. The T-3 must have seemed the perfect vehicle for separating the "men from the boys." Never mind that these were basically just college kids facing some very scary flying.

Aerobatic training is considered to be so dangerous that the FAA requires that pilots always wear parachutes when engaged in these maneuvers.[10] But the Air Force insists it does not need to follow FAA regulations. When the Air Force was getting ready to order the aircraft, a colonel who knew I had worked in FAA headquarters contacted me.

He told me the service had tentatively decided to have the manufacturer remove the parachutes, and he wanted my views on the matter. I explained this was obviously a very bad idea for several reasons. If you do these maneuvers on a daily basis, sooner or later you are going to need to bail out. Besides, these folks were going to be sitting in a plastic aircraft surrounded by highly combustible aviation gas. Moreover, they would often be flying over rugged terrain, not suitable for making a forced landing. Yes, colonel, "chutes" could be a useful piece of T-3 equipment at times.

That was not the answer he wanted, so he did not bring it up again. I had assumed that cost cutting was the reason for this hair-brained idea. But I later heard that one general thought the "chutes" should go because students might become scared and jump out prematurely.

This reminded me of proverbial déjà vu all over again. During the First World War, allied pilots, unlike their German counterparts, were initially sent into combat without parachutes for similar reasons. Eighty years later, our leaders apparently still do not trust our troops to exercise good judgment.

The service also decided to order this piston-powered airplane with an oversized motor. A powerful 260-horsepower engine was required since half of the T-3 fleet was to be flown in the thin air of the high altitude at the Air Force Academy in Colorado. That required extensive modifications to this erstwhile off-the-shelf aircraft. The service then decided *not* to conduct comprehensive tests on the effects of these changes.

Another problem was the lack of light-plane experience among the Air Force Academy instructor pilots. Most of these bright young officers were experienced military jet flyers but had spent little or no time flying anything like the piston-powered T-3.

Piston engines are actually less reliable—and certainly more sensitive in terms of handling—than modern turbine power plants. Light aircraft are also like kites in that they are easily blown around by violent winds. Unfortunately, the academy also is located on the turbulent downwind side of the Rocky Mountains.

The final nail in the coffin was the service's decision *not* to provide a comprehensive training program for those instructors. It was as though the Air Force leadership saw the T-3 as just a big toy airplane. Students were supposed to receive approximately twenty-five hours of instruction in their curriculum. Instructors were often given only half that much instruction time before they began teaching their students.

There were other holes in this cursory instructor curriculum. For instance, spins were one very dangerous maneuver that didn't receive much emphasis. During these maneuvers, the airflow literally detaches from the wings, rendering the controls temporarily ineffective. The craft corkscrews earthward until the pilot carefully uses the control stick, rudder pedals, and throttle to coax the invisible wind-flow back onto the whirling wings. If all goes well, control is restored and the plane gracefully flies away. If not, the craft continues dropping like a lead leaf until it hits the ground.

The only other aircraft that Air Force pilots intentionally spin is the T-37 jet trainer. By contrast, instructor spin training in the T-37 is very comprehensive. Each instructor is literally shown all the ways things can go wrong while spinning the T-37. Interestingly, this craft has both parachutes and ejection seats. By contrast, the Air Force was adopting an almost cavalier approach for the T-3. Instructors were told only about *some* of its many spin idiosyncrasies.

The folly of this approach would come home to haunt us on the afternoon of February 22, 1995. Cadet Mark Dostal would intentionally put his T-3 into a spin, and his instructor would not be able to get the aircraft to recover. From their frantic cockpit viewpoint, both men would watch helplessly as the whirling world raced by in the last seconds of their short lives.

Six months later, two Firefly pilots in England would find themselves in a similar situation. After the Brits used parachutes to jump to safety, the Yanks had to rethink their no-chute policy. Parachutes would soon be reinstalled in these USAF aircraft. But a variety of other problems, ranging from brakes to the electrical system, began appearing.

As the months passed, the T-3's temperamental engines were constantly acting up. They would actually fail sixty-six times. Within two years, another cadet and instructor would needlessly die after their engine quit. A third pair of airmen would die when their out-of-control T-3 plunged to the ground while they were maneuvering to land. The Air Force would announce that their investigations had shown that all three of these fatal accidents were caused by a variety of unrelated pilot errors. However, this pitch was wearing a bit thin with the families and the public.

My phone would ring with stories from upset parents. I heard the academy was threatening to ground instructors who were too vocal about the T-3 problems. Meanwhile, cadets were being pressured into signing up for this *voluntary* course, "if they wanted to get promoted."

On January 12, 1998, *Time*'s Pulitzer Prize–winning reporter, Mark Thompson, broke this whole ugly story.[11] His journalistic instincts were alerted when the acting secretary of the Air Force did something interesting. He had belatedly ordered a "comprehensive review of the aircraft's purchase, testing, and operation."

Perhaps the best insight into this whole debacle was revealed by Thompson's interview with General McPeak. The former USAF top general unapologetically proclaimed, "Our mission is to train warrior pilots, not dentists to fly their families to Acapulco."[12]

More than a year later, the Air Force quietly scrapped the troubled T-3 program—after having wasted $46 million over eight painful years.[13] Interestingly, the service decided that it would instead send its prospective pilot candidates to civilian flight schools to earn private pilot licenses—just like those Acapulco-bound dentists.[14]

For three families, this move would offer little solace, and because of a strange coincidence, they would have to endure additional insult. The three dead T-3 instructors had previously flown the massive C-141 jet transports before receiving their Air Force Academy assignments. To the families of these three fallen aviators, General McPeak added a final insult by saying, "Maybe if you would have had three fighter pilots in there instead of three C-141 pilots, you wouldn't have had the same result."[15]

9

Abuse of Privilege

Not all of the services' difficulties are associated with new, untested designs. Some problems involve old equipment that should have been overhauled, updated, or replaced. These vintage machines require increased maintenance from experts. But that has become a problem as money gets tighter with the post–Cold War downsizing. Another problem is the burden imposed by organizational disruption. This was partly created by General McPeak's decision to "streamline" the service's time-tested aircraft maintenance system.

For decades, USAF maintenance consisted of three levels: flight line, back shop, and depot. In 1992, General McPeak announced a cost-cutting move. The back shops would be eliminated at most bases. These shops were where the specialists in various fields—such as hydraulics, electronics, and engines—worked. His idea was that the flight-line personnel would simply remove a defective part and send it back to the depot. Meanwhile, its replacement would soon arrive by overnight shipper. This chief of staff had a lot of radical ideas and did not appreciate any criticism of his pet projects.

His "just in time" maintenance system may have been theoretically more efficient, but it did not work well for several reasons. First, after the back shops were phased out, the specialists who really knew how to troubleshoot began disappearing from the bases. Unappreciated and angry, they left the service in droves. Rushed, inexperienced, neophyte mechanics, lacking specialized equipment or adequate supervision, now sometimes removed the wrong parts.[1]

Furthermore, the necessary replacement parts just are not there in sufficient numbers. Mechanics are thus forced to cannibalize parts from some aircraft just to keep others operational. All of this is occurring at a time when the need for transports, in particular, is dramatically increasing. Numerous times during the 1990s, President Clinton ordered personnel and equipment to be dispatched around the globe for open-ended "911 calls."

In today's squadrons, you will find weary equipment tended by worried mechanics. The HC-130[2] squadrons are some of the busiest. These four-engine transports are modified to support military rescue operations and are among the oldest Herky Birds still flying.

On the evening of November 22, 1996, eleven crew members, all based in Portland, Oregon, boarded their HC-130, call sign King-56.[3] These Air Force reservists had briefed for a routine training mission over the Pacific. Cruising at twenty-two thousand feet, things were uneventful for the first hour and twenty-four minutes. Aviation is often described as endless hours of total boredom punctuated by a few moments of stark terror.

When flying over water, everyone listens to the engines' vital signs. The crew member most involved with the care and feeding of the HC-130 is appropriately called the flight engineer. Seated between and slightly behind the two pilots, this sergeant manages to watch over the myriad switches, gauges, and warning lights.[4] His eyes constantly shift between his ceiling-mounted control panel and the engine gauges situated between the pilots' instrument panels. He knows this particular C-130 is older than many members of his squadron, with eleven thousand flight hours on its haggard airframe.

At 6:44 P.M., he spots something disturbing. The white needle on the two-inch-wide fuel flow gauge has begun to rotate counterclockwise. This shows that the number-one engine is drying up. He excitedly says, "Fuel flow to number one just went to shit!"[5] Now all the needles on that engine begin the roll back. Instantly, a dozen eyes stare at these small instruments while the unmistakable sound of a turbine engine winding down can be heard against the rumble of the three remaining engines.

Then, a minute later, before he can figure out why this engine is failing, he hears a second engine beginning to wind down. He cannot believe this is happening, but stoically announces, "We've lost fuel flow on, ah, number two."[6]

But before the crew can collectively analyze this complex emergency, the unthinkable occurs—the last two engines start to fail. As the remaining two motors fall silent, they instinctively turn the aircraft toward the illusory safety of the California coast, more than eighty miles away.

The pilot calls for the engine failure checklist, like a priest speaking to his parish. Disciplined fingers start walking through these voluminous documents. These dog-eared notebooks are their aeronautical "bibles" and tonight these are eleven true believers. They reverently begin their complex rituals. Switches are thrown, buttons pushed, knobs twisted. Checklist call-outs ring across the now silent, darkened flight deck.

However, nothing works tonight for this faithful but confused congregation as they clutch their personal flashlights like so many candles. What they do not know is that much vital information is *not* in these manuals. Without this critical data, they cannot extricate themselves from the grip of gravity. They spend the next several minutes making vain efforts to resuscitate the lifeless behemoth.

These gents soon decide they cannot save their aircraft. For sixteen long minutes, the powerless craft will fall through thick clouds toward the misnamed Pacific. The waiting waves grow ever closer in the windy darkness as the crewmen again turn to their checklists and manuals for guidance. Now they must focus on the best way of improving chances of their *own* salvation.

The pilot orders all crew members to don their anti-exposure suits. These waterproof, rubberized garments will permit them to survive for hours even in these frigid waters. They know they can walk to the back door and jump to safety with their parachutes.

But they are hesitant to do so for a couple of reasons. First, they do not have individual survival kits. Ironically, these safety devices were ordered months ago, but the kits just arrived at the unit and are still sitting on the ramp back in Portland. So much for just-in-time logistics.

There is a bigger reason for not bailing out: their flight manuals tell them not to do it. The manual tells them to ditch in the water. Ditching for them will mean making a powerless crash landing into choppy seas at night. Somehow this does not sound inviting. What their authoritative manuals do not mention is that no C-130 has *ever* ditched without fatalities.

The Hercules belly flops into the ten-foot-high swells and breaks apart. Sergeant Bobby Vogel, the radio operator, finds himself alone in the darkness like Jonah, who was belched from the bowels of a whale. For minutes he will hear screams, then hours of silence, till he is plucked from the waves by a Coast Guard helicopter. As the sole survivor, life will never be the same for this young citizen soldier. He knows his ten comrades lie on the sea bottom under a five-thousand-foot thick shroud of ocean.

The word is soon flashed across America. There is only one survivor of the decimated crew who themselves were in the rescue business. Ten deaths in a single military air crash is not very unusual, but normally the grief is spread around the nation. This crash will extract all its suffering from a single community.

A few weeks after the crash, a memorial service is held in the city of Portland. Three thousand people attend this solemn service. The crowd includes the families and friends, as well as good, patriotic folks from around the state. These people have just come to pay their last respects to their fallen neighbors. The mourners realize these "weekend warriors"[7] were making great personal sacrifices to help defend the country in these turbulent times.

But grief is not the only emotion running through this gathering, for they have heard stories that *all* the engines failed without warning. Furthermore, there is a rumor that this is not the first time such problems have occurred in a C-130. These people simply want to know *why* these airmen died.

But these civilians are apparently unaware that the Pentagon doesn't release such information—it's privileged. Soon the outraged families and the community are demanding answers, without much success.

Unfortunately for the Pentagon, these people are represented by a couple of newly elected senators who are not owned by the military establishment. Interestingly, one is named "Smith," like the Jimmy Stewart movie character who went to Washington. Gordon Smith and Ron Wyden are a couple of straight shooters who cannot understand why the Pentagon will not just answer their constituents' questions. That apparently was not part of their welcome-to-Washington training.

But there are a few other very determined Oregonians who are *not* prepared to go quietly into oblivion. They include three of the widows, Tawni Farrarini, Gayle Schott, and Sue McAuley. These soccer moms, an unlikely trio of truth seekers, decide to force the massive Department of Defense bureaucracy to answer a few questions about the King-56 crash.

The Pentagon quickly cranks up its "Maytag mafia" (so-called because these guys have more "spin cycles" than the fanciest washing machine). First, they sequester the Safety Investigation Board to insure that nothing leaks about the contents of the "real" inquiry.

Next they produce the Accident Investigation Board's report and its draftee president, Colonel Larry Landtroop. This confused colonel has thirty-five hundred hours flying the C-130, but like most board presidents, he has *never* investigated an accident before. His inadequate 456-page report concludes that the four engines failed because of "fuel starvation" for "unknown" reasons.[8] He is very courteous, although he cannot explain the mystery. This sad soul soon adds that he hopes that he never has to serve on another accident board.

The widows then decide they will take their questions to their late husbands' commander, Colonel Rick Davis. When they arrive at his office unexpectedly, he seems uncomfortable. The colonel then says, "Ladies, you've thirty minutes. Take your best shot."[9] These grieving widows are shocked when he explains the reason for his urgency—the colonel has horses waiting outside in a trailer. His priorities do not please the widows.

These women are understandably outraged as they leave this colonel's office, but not *just* because of his personal priorities. They also have friends and neighbors in the unit who are still flying in these dangerous crates, and they do not want other families to have to go through what they are now enduring. The Air Force later states that it sees no problems with this commander's attitude.[10]

The widows and families grow increasingly displeased with the service's handling of the investigation. These distraught people insist that they learn more from the press than from military officials. Furthermore, they cannot understand why the Air Force will not just tell them what is in the privileged safety report. Nor do they understand why the service is so reluctant to recover the wreckage. Then, too, there are persistent but uncorroborated stories about dozens of similar problems occurring to other C-130s. The Pentagon seems to be saying that it doesn't know why this crash occurred, but it does know it must be only an isolated problem. Thus, the case is closed.

Two other folks are also growing impatient with the Pentagon. Senators Smith and Wyden suggest that, because the Air Force apparently cannot figure out what caused the King-56 crash, perhaps the National Transportation Safety Board should be brought in to assist. The NTSB, of course, has a long history of solving complex air crashes. The Pentagon quickly but politely dismisses this suggestion as simply naïve. It also ignores other suggestions to release the contents of the safety report, to raise the wreckage, or to conduct an in-depth review of the C-130 engine problems.

The Pentagon is none too happy that the press has also begun to take note of this situation. The bureaucracy decides it's time to triple-team these pesky people. First, they use their large public affairs staff to get out their spin. Then they trot out their lawyers, who explain how it would *simply be illegal* to release this safety report to the NTSB.[11] We must follow the regulations, you know.

The third component of the counterattack is the Pentagon's idea of "safety speak." For instance, the Air Force chief of flight safety, Lieutenant Colonel Tom Farrier, soon offers some insightful remarks: "We give our boards the charter to explore all possibilities, to brainstorm, to say ' ... gee, maybe if we have all the crews put their left boots on their right feet, maybe the airplanes will fly better.'"[12] Farrier further suggests that the fact that there have been fifty-eight power-loss mishaps since 1987 "is not worrisome," considering the large size of the C-130 fleet.[13] There are probably a few folks in Oregon who would take umbrage with this statement.

These kinds of remarks also do not sit well with the two senators, who discover the Pentagon's Achilles' heel. The Defense Department, it seems, wants the Senate to quickly confirm the nomination of General Henry Shelton as the next chairman of the Joint Chiefs of Staff. This is the nation's highest military post, and they expect a rubber stamp on his nomination. Senators Wyden and Smith, however, announce that they are placing a hold on confirming this nomination *until* they get some answers to their safety questions.[14] This request gets instant attention. On September 11, 1997, the chairman of the Senate Armed Services Committee, the Honorable Strom Thurmond himself, calls the Pentagon.[15] The folks who work in this five-sided pagoda immediately see the merit in implementing all these erstwhile unworkable, naïve, and indeed illegal demands made by the Oregon senators.

The Pentagon invites the NTSB to read the safety report. It announces the undertaking of a "broad area review"—headed by a two-star general no less—to try to establish what is causing those "nonworrisome" engine failures. Furthermore, the Air Force will hire a contractor to help with the investigation and establish a toll-free phone line so crews can report any problems.[16]

Heck, they will even send a couple of friendly generals to Oregon to explain everything to the King-56 families. The senior officers make a brief appearance in Portland on October 3 to try to smooth some long-ruffled feathers.[17] Almost unnoticed is their offhand admission that there are major differences between the privileged safety report and the accident report that the families received. But not to worry, they say, we'll be back in about ninety days to explain everything—*trust* us.

On January 15, 1998, in an auditorium in Portland, the Air Force offers its mea culpa.[18] It seems its ninety-day broad area review has uncovered a few problems. A succession of contrite briefers will explain how they have actually uncovered *twenty-two major deficiencies.* There are also a total of seventy-one apparently "worrisome" incidents reported, rather than the fifty-eight "nonworrisome" occurrences mentioned earlier by the Pentagon safety expert.

As the briefers methodically go through the lists, the sobbing of family members overcome by grief periodically interrupts their words. These people are dumbstruck upon learning that there are so many problems with the C-130 fleet. Even more disconcerting is the fact their government could be so oblivious to these many safety deficiencies for so long. These simple, trusting Americans got a painful education on the Pentagon's priorities.

The twenty-two deficiencies ascribed to the C-130 fell into several categories. Eight of the most serious problems involved aircraft systems, such as old electrical wiring that had become defective. Another important aircraft deficiency was the limited number of channels on C-130 flight data recorders. These outdated "black boxes" had made it impossible to establish the status of many systems that may have caused the accident.

This revelation is especially disturbing to some because of an earlier pronouncement by the Air Force chief of safety, General Godsey. After the 1996 Ron Brown tragedy,[19] he said the service was able to adequately investigate that crash even though the aircraft lacked recorders altogether.[20] Independent safety experts are, of course, amazed at the naïveté illustrated by such contradictions.

Eight other deficiencies dealt with technical manuals. These disclosures were some of the hardest for the families to swallow. What the Air Force was saying was that those "bibles," which the crew members had tried to follow so religiously, did not contain some of the needed data or were simply wrong about other critical issues.

Most painful of all was the fact that the manuals told the pilots to ditch the airplane rather than have the crew parachute to safety.[21] It turns out, historically, that about 75 percent of people who stayed aboard those C-130s that ditched, died. By contrast, only 10 percent of those who parachuted from other aircraft over water died.[22] Many family members could hardly control their rage after learning these facts.

Other critical deficiencies identified included three maintenance inadequacies, such as the inability of personnel to troubleshoot critical components. These problems just might have been associated with the ill-advised cuts introduced by General McPeak.[23] Two other deficiencies involved training problems, including inadequacies with the all-important CRM programs. Such problems were associated with the Black Hawk friendly-fire accident described earlier.[24] The last of the twenty-two deficiencies involved the type of depot maintenance practices reported to have caused the Navy S-3 crash described earlier.[25] The service just does not know what modifications and/or parts are installed on a particular C-130.

The last segment of the Air Force broad area review presentation involved describing four possible scenarios, all of which involved pilot error. This led to some lively cross-examination from the widows in the audience. These women, it seems, had by now become sophisticated enough to point out inconsistencies in some of the briefers' assumptions.[26] The service ended by promising to recover critical components from the sunken wreckage, run more tests, and provide the King-56 families a follow-up briefing.

In addition, the commanding officer who did not have much time to talk with the widows asked to be reassigned. Colonel Davis claimed he had suffered too much nervous distress over this crash. The Air Force agreed and decided it was time for the colonel and his horses to go "adios."[27] He was appropriately transferred to a base in Texas. This pantheon of characters was further diminished with the 1997 retirement of the USAF chief of safety, Brigadier General Godsey.

Then, two years later, another key player on the King-56 investigation team also retired. Major General Bobby Floyd, who had skillfully led the broad area review, decided to seek civilian employment. Some civilians, however, remembered how he'd been instrumental in explaining that the crew, not the aircraft, was at fault. Thus, these civilians were surprised to learn that he was going to work for Lockheed Martin Corporation—the C-130 manufacturer. The Pentagon reassured them that this was *not* a conflict of interest.[28] Obviously, these civilians do not understand how this system works.

10

Unlearned Lessons

The media often ask me why military crew members continue to fly when they know they are at risk. The short answer is that they are simply dedicated to protecting this nation, even when it puts them at personal risk. The Portland C-130 crash reminded me of an earlier incident over a different ocean.

It involved a C-141 Starlifter, which is a four-engine jet transport, half again larger than the venerable Hercules. This "strategic airlifter" can transport heavy cargoes from the United States to trouble spots around the world. Several years ago, a C-141 suffered a four-engine "roll back," similar to the Portland C-130. This was also not the first time such problems had occurred in the C-141 fleet, although this particular aircraft was able to recover power and land safely.

I was sent to Europe as part of a team to investigate this incident. When the mechanics in Europe could not duplicate the failure on the ground, the Air Force ordered us to fly the aircraft back to the depot in Georgia for further tests. Needless to say, we were not eager to do this, but orders *are* orders.

I don't think it occurred to any of us to refuse to fly that night. It's just part of the job—you just salute smartly—or groan silently, in my case—and board the jet. I previously had been forced to make a crash landing in another plane that I was piloting, but this was the first time I ever *knowingly* flew in a dangerous aircraft.

Our jet's engine problems reoccurred over the North Atlantic. But the crew, anticipating such possibilities, quickly recovered power and landed safely. We were just lucky that night. After this up-close and personal encounter, I redoubled my criticism of the service's seeming indifference to taking unnecessary chances with its troops.

This did not exactly endear me to my bosses in the safety arena. Ironically, I did get a letter of commendation for this C-141 inquiry, from the incoming Air Force chief of staff, no less.[1] But this obviously was not enough to prevent the Air Force Safety Agency from firing me several weeks later. Seems these good ol' boys don't take kindly to anyone getting uppity.

Like the Hercules, the C-141s are old, and neither type of aircraft is equipped with state-of-the-art safety devices. One thing I always lobbied for was airline-type safety equipment, especially on troop-carrying aircraft. After all, unlike commercial passengers, our GIs can't decide for themselves which airline they want to fly after studying their safety records.

One of the problems facing all aircraft is the danger of midair collisions. Airline passengers are protected by the Traffic Collision-Avoidance System (TCAS). These onboard computerized devices have been required for many years to warn commercial pilots of potential collisions.

Such systems would also be especially useful for our military aircraft. This is because, in addition to sharing the crowded airspace over this country, they also fly in parts of the world where radar-assisted air traffic control is inadequate or nonexistent. Unfortunately, the Pentagon's vast fleet is exempt from having to comply with FAA regulations, and this has caused problems.

In my 1994 complaint, I mentioned that an Air Force jet came within three hundred feet of a 747 airliner over the Mediterranean. But the service ignored my plea. Two years later, the lack of safety equipment on the Air Force CT-43 transport that killed Ron Brown came to light. This *did* cause the service to at least acknowledge some of these deficiencies. But Congress and the Air Force have been slow to come up with the funds needed to install this vital equipment.

In 1998, this lack of safety equipment would cost the lives of nine crew members and twenty-four other people when their C-141 collided with another jet over the South Atlantic. The other jet was a Russian-made TU-154 airliner operated by the German military. The two aircraft were flying in a notoriously poor air traffic control environment, a fact that our Air Force was quick to point out in its news release. Neither jet had a collision avoidance system like TCAS installed, although this was not mentioned in the first news releases.

But reporters started asking why Air Force aircraft did not have a TCAS installed, as the service had promised to do after the Brown crash. The service spin-meisters quickly replied that this *particular* jet was so old that it was going to be retired in several years. Hence, they did not want to spend money on it.

They then produced a general who explained how the military didn't need TCAS systems because their pilots are trained "to always be looking outside."[2] That, of course, was a standard post-accident "pilot error" pronouncement. These masters of deception then added that the Russian-made jet lacked a "Western style" transponder, which is needed to be compatible with our collision avoidance systems.[3] That excuse deflected press criticism for a while.

Fortunately, when the media called me, I gave them the phone numbers of the people who had installed these compatible transponders years ago on this German-owned jet. The *Boston Globe* broke that story.[4] The Air Force was further embarrassed in that their aircraft was missing for twenty hours before any kind of search and rescue effort was mounted.

While the lack of TCAS on the ancient C-141 was embarrassing, it is even more surprising that its replacement, the C-17, was currently being delivered without TCAS installed. The Air Force is supposedly going to retrofit these new aircraft in a few years—if funds are available.

Why is it always that when it comes to safety, the folks who need it the most are the ones with the least interest in the subject? The DoD mind-set illustrates this axiom perfectly. Because military flying is known to be so dangerous, you would hope they would also want to have a lot of safety equipment. But that, unfortunately, is not true. The service's top fighter, the F-16, provides an excellent case in point.

The F-16 Fighting Falcons are today's frontline multi-role jets, which can attack ground targets or intercept other aircraft. The Lockheed Martin Company is still manufacturing these $30 million fighters more than a quarter century after they were first introduced. They have endured as the most versatile frontline fighter for friendly nations.

Tragically, dozens of these agile USAF jets have been accidentally flown into the ground. These frequent crashes occur when pilots lose track of where they are in relation to the terrain, especially at night. But this dangerous "spatial disorientation" phenomenon also occurs in broad daylight. Needless to say, it is almost always fatal.

Several years ago, one of America's most experienced fighter pilots was asked to head up an F-16 safety investigation board. The colonel knew that the destroyed Falcon had been dogfighting with another jet and was going "warp seven" straight down when it slammed into the ground. There was no radio call, no attempt to eject, and no evidence of mechanical malfunctions.

Even though this colonel was doing his first major crash investigation, this looked like an obvious case of spatial disorientation. But unlike so many board presidents, this guy was determined to prevent such accidents in the future. He had already found an embarrassing flaw in this command's training procedures, but he wanted to go the extra mile, so he called me at the safety agency.

I told him that Ground Proximity Warning Systems (GPWS) have been standard equipment on airliners since 1975. One of the world's top aviation safety experts, Jerry Lederer, long ago had documented how such devices had drastically reduced mishaps in commercial flying.[5] Moreover, the Air Force had recently developed an advanced GPWS designed for highly maneuverable fighter aircraft.

Fortunately, the flight test center at Edwards Air Force Base in California had already tested such a device. Installed on an F-16, it had been shown to provide automatic warnings to pilots during hundreds of test flights. I gave the colonel the test pilot's phone number. The colonel called me back to say how impressed he was with the system. But I knew it was now time to break his bubble.

His commanding general had been told about this system in several previous briefings on similar accidents. His general had always rejected the investigation board's recommendations to retrofit his jets with these safety devices. This particular colonel was an island of integrity in a sea of sycophancy. He was not afraid to risk the general's wrath to save some of his fellow fliers.

The colonel reported to the headquarters a day before the commander's briefing. He first informed the two-star general in charge of training about the deficiencies in his program. As expected, this general did not take the news well. The colonel's suggestion that training was a factor in this crash went over like the proverbial lead zeppelin. This general promised that he would take up this "preposterous" finding with the commander during the next day's briefing.

Bright and early the next day, this courageous colonel enters the lions' den. As the colonel comes to the finding dealing with training deficiencies, the two-star interrupts. He forcefully tells the four-star that this is a ridiculous conclusion. To everybody's surprise, the commander silences the two-star by saying that he agrees with the colonel—and wants to know just how fast the red-faced two-star can change his curriculum. The commanding general then turns to the colonel and tells him to continue.

The colonel takes a deep breath and says, "Sir, I know you have been told about these anti-clobber systems before. But you may want to hear my views on the merits of such systems. At only one hundred thousand dollars per jet, these new GPWS look highly cost effective."

At that point, the four-star interrupts: "You're right, I *have* heard about these systems before. But *no*, I don't want to go through this again!" The commander continues: "Obviously, there's something that you don't understand, *colonel*. We *could* have installed these systems for that price as the jets were being manufactured. But *now*, it would be far too expensive to bring the birds back to the factory and tear them apart to retrofit these systems. That would cost several times as much. So drop that recommendation, and skip to your next point."

This colonel knew that he could give up any aspirations of being promoted, but at least he could sleep well at night. He had given it his best shot. The commander's answer was not no, but *hell no!* Nonetheless, what the general said was actually correct. Modifying old jets to retrofit them with new systems *is* always much more expensive than building the systems into the aircraft in the first place.

More's the pity, because when the Air Force ordered its newest fighter, the F-22 Raptor, it lacked a GPWS system. Interestingly, these systems had just become cheaper by about 50 percent. They have even been improved, because they now utilize satellite navigation to enhance their effectiveness. Furthermore, the new Lockheed Martin–produced F-22s will cost several times the $30 million price tag of their F-16s. But the service still had not seen the advantage of buying state-of-the-art safety devices.[6]

Unfortunately, the lack of GPWS is not the only deficiency in the F-22. The Raptor is the next-generation stealth fighter and is supersonic. While most jets can make only short dashes at these speeds, the F-22 is actually designed to cruise at such speeds. That puts it at risk from a seemingly unlikely source—*birds.*

In fact, military planes literally collide with birds thousands of times each year. While the bird always loses, all too frequently the jet also crashes. This is because of the physics involved. Traveling at several hundred miles per hour, even a bird weighing only a few pounds packs a tremendous wallop. This is especially true if it hits the windshield.

I watched such things in 1969, when we tested prototype "bird-proof" windshields for the Cessna A-37 attack jets. A pneumatic launcher accelerated bird carcasses at the stationary jet. The impact looked and sounded like a hand grenade exploding. Some of our early windshield designs failed, allowing bird fragments to penetrate the cockpit with deadly force.

The Air Force should have already learned the folly of fielding a fighter without a bird-proof windshield. It initially ordered the supersonic F-111 without such protection. During its first decade, five of the jets crashed after birds penetrated their windshields. It was not cheap, but the service eventually retrofitted the entire F-111 fleet with new windshields in 1976. They never lost another F-111 to a bird collision after the modification.[7]

In the 1980s, Air Force jet fighters like the F-15 got new windshields that protect their crews from bird strikes at five hundred miles per hour—a smart move. But in the 1990s, the windshield of the brand-new, multi-jillion-dollar F-22 did not have anything like this level of protection. There is no excuse for putting our finest airmen in these super jets and sending them off to fly at these speeds without providing them with such basic protection.

The Air Force's other super-plane is the B-2 Stealth Bomber, designed by Northrop Aircraft. The taxpayers spent $2 billion for each of the twenty-one aircraft. This giant flying wing is so aerodynamically efficient that, with a couple of in-flight refuelings, it was able to bomb targets in Kosovo and Afghanistan from its base in Missouri. This awesome weapon has capabilities that pioneers such as Generals Mitchell and Arnold always dreamed of. Unfortunately, it also has some safety problems.

Earlier generations of jet bombers had up to six crew members, but the B-2 does everything with only two pilots aboard. These two individuals are kept very busy tending a digital flight deck that looks like a computer showroom. These pilots are highly dependent upon the craft's automated displays and control panels. This poses a major fatigue problem, because striking some targets from the U.S. requires them to work in the B-2's very cramped cockpit for over thirty hours straight.

It was not long before knowledgeable people became concerned about this aircraft's ergonomics. They had seen a copy of an unclassified draft report innocuously titled "Limited Assessment of B-2A Pilot-Vehicle Interface Effectiveness." This report was close-held for some very good reasons. But it was also apparently sent to an influential journal, *Inside the Air Force*. On December 13, 1996, the journal broke the story of the B-2's ergonomic deficiencies.[8]

The journal article states, "The cockpit of the B-2 bomber is only 'barely acceptable' due to dozens of deficiencies in its design that at times raise crew workload to dangerously high levels and create confusion in the cockpit that may further jeopardize aircrew safety . . . "[9] It describes how thirty-two of the ninety controls and displays assessed in the report were considered "unacceptable." Quoting the report, the article says, "Symbol usage is not consistent from one display to another, information common to different displays was formatted differently, [and] control mechanization was not consistent."

The article also quotes experts who conclude that " . . . the problems documented in the draft B-2 report are indicative of the low priority the Air Force gives to the human factor considerations in the development of weapon systems."[10] It also quotes unnamed experts who say that correcting the B-2 design problems will cost hundreds of millions of dollars. But this will be necessary to safeguard the $44 billion already spent on the program.

Another problem was the amount of testing being done on the jet. Congress passed a law in 1971 requiring that weapon systems be realistically tested *before* they were ordered into mass production.[11] But like many other things the Pentagon finds inconvenient, these requirements are simply ignored. This, of course, can have important safety implications during the service life of these weapon systems.

The Pentagon approach to safety has many inadequacies, but one of the most dangerous is that it also allows the various commands to ignore incidents that can later lead to accidents. These unreported events are ticking time bombs that often explode years later. One such event still haunts me.

Several years ago, two mechanics were servicing the oxygen system of an A-10 Thunderbolt II jet fighter. These systems contain super-cooled liquid oxygen, which is always very dangerous. The pressure vessel violently exploded without warning.

The concussion broke the jet almost in two, sending aluminum components flying though the air, badly injuring both men. This disaster was *not* reported to the Air Force Safety Agency as required by regulations. Presumably, somebody was trying to conceal the embarrassing accident from his or her superiors.

Weeks after the blast, a lieutenant colonel from the safety agency happened to be visiting this overseas base. By now the unit had surreptitiously obtained a "spare" A-10 from the storage facility at Davis Monthan AFB in the Arizona desert. The aircraft there are "mothballed" for their protection. "Unpickling" and flying this jet to this forward base cost the unit many thousands of dollars. Of course, taxpayers really pick up the tab. The commander of this squadron apparently told its mechanics to strip parts off this newly arrived jet to fix the wrecked aircraft.

Aside from the ethical issues, there are several obvious technical problems with doing this. First, the already overworked mechanics do not have enough time or personnel for such a major undertaking, considering that two of their number were laid up from injuries suffered in the explosion. Second, the mechanics lack the engineering expertise to rebuild a jet. Third, the base lacks the specialized tools—and especially the jigs—needed for such an elaborate undertaking.

Jigs are large steel fixtures used to hold the parts in exact alignment while they are riveted together. Without such equipment, the jet can end up dangerously "out of rig"—like a car whose frame has been bent in an accident. Such an aircraft will not handle the way the designers intended.

Aside from all these difficulties, there was the very real danger posed by *not* establishing the cause for the oxygen tank explosion. Concealing this accident might well allow a systemic problem with the aging system to go undetected. Thus, the problem might occur again with fatal results.

A few years later, an A-10 piloted by Captain Craig Buttons was the last aircraft in a three-ship formation approaching a bomb range near Davis Monthan AFB in Arizona. On April 2, 1997, his jet suddenly veered from the formation and disappeared. For almost two hours, the aircraft meandered eight hundred miles on a northeasterly course at low altitudes. No radio transmissions were heard. The A-10 eventually crashed at high speed into a thirteen-thousand-foot face of Gold Dust Peak in Colorado.[12]

It took the Air Force almost three weeks to even find the crash site, and more months of examining the wreckage to come to the conclusion that they could not explain what caused the crash. Their autopsy found no evidence of drugs, alcohol, or the AIDS virus. Various eyewitnesses on the ground suggested the craft seemed to be at least partially under the pilot's control by the way it was being flown shortly before impact.

Stories soon begin to emerge that Captain Buttons was upset that his parents had changed their religion and that he had had a "messy" breakup with his girlfriend. Another unsubstantiated story surfaced. It claimed he was a homosexual who had a falling out with a lover. Obviously, all these stories were used by the Air Force to publicly suggest the captain was suicidal.

But the evidence and innuendo were only circumstantial at best. Unfortunately for this suicide theory, nobody saw him say or do anything that alerted them to his supposed mental problems. Nor after months of medical and police-type investigations could the Pentagon's people come up with a suicide note. The service was determined to turn this incident into a criminal act. In late October, the military issued its conclusion to the press in two words: "spontaneous suicide."[13]

This was a rather self-serving conclusion, because the embarrassing crash became a "nonaccident." Thus this tragic event does not contribute to the service's all-important Class A mishap rate. Having investigated civilian and military crashes for decades, I have never run across such a bizarre set of claims. First, suicide is extremely rare in pilots. Second, there is almost always either a note, radio transmission, and/or other *compelling* evidence, none of which was present here.

I contacted a top official at the NTSB to ask what they would have concluded if Buttons had been flying in a civilian rather than a military aircraft. This expert, who had over twenty years with the board, quickly answered. With the evidence available here, the NTSB would not have concluded suicide. This highly professional organization would have described the evidence and pronounced: "cause undetermined."

I still wonder about another possible explanation. What if Captain Buttons's oxygen system had exploded unexpectedly, as had occurred on the ground a few years before? This would have left him dazed from the concussion and from a lack of oxygen. An injured, semiconscious, and disoriented pilot could easily be expected to fly in a manner consistent with the ground witnesses' observations in this case. *If* this happened, the military's system of covering up embarrassing mishaps claimed another victim, one whose reputation has been forever disgraced.

Incidentally, the squadron that had the earlier oxygen explosion was nominated for a top safety award several months after the unreported accident occurred. The Air Force Safety Agency—the blind watchdog—never demanded to know why the accident that their visiting lieutenant colonel had stumbled upon was not reported. Thus, the agency became part of the cover-up.

Unfortunately, this would not be the last unreported explosion aboard an A-10. A number of months before Captain Buttons's crash, an A-10's gun blew up unexpectedly. Though the massive 30-mm automatic cannon was located directly below the cockpit, the uninjured pilot safely landed the badly damaged jet at his overseas base.

Turns out another A-10 in his outfit had just suffered another unrelated accident. As with the earlier oxygen bottle explosion, the squadron had apparently decided not to report these two accidents. This may have been due to the fact that both occurrences appeared to be serious enough to qualify as Class A mishaps. Squadrons and their parent commands always like to report low rates for these major accidents, so they often intentionally misreport some accidents as mere "fender benders"—if they report them at all.

I had already been involuntarily removed from my safety responsibilities when I heard about these incidents. I was led to believe that the unit was probably hiding the jets until they could smuggle in parts to surreptitiously repair them—at which point these incidents would probably be reported belatedly as *minor* (read: non–Class A) accidents.

I therefore personally called the safety agency, which informed me unofficially that they had not heard about these incidents. Later on, I heard the unit had claimed they were just too busy to notify the safety agency about the incidents, even though this was a violation of regulations.

Moreover, unreported and uninvestigated incidents at this particular base would later contribute to a major disaster. This would in turn lead to an international flap over the safety of having Americans based in that country. The current "honor system" that allows military units, commands, and the three services to investigate themselves is highly dysfunctional because *every* accident offers valuable lessons that beg to be documented and disseminated to prevent their reoccurrence. Thus, the Department of Defense's many *unlearned lessons* are costly to our troops, taxpayers, and national pride.

11

Just Plane Fun

Unnecessary risk-taking has always been an integral part of the American military culture.[1] Indeed, it goes hand-in-glove with the Pentagon's traditional disdain for safety matters.

Some years ago, a military transport crew was eagerly taxiing out for takeoff when controllers gave them an unwelcome message. The crew was informed that they could not begin their cross-country flight because of weather and traffic problems along their route. If they were going to fly anytime soon, they would need to stay local, flying only in the vicinity of their base.

The crew began discussing its options. One pilot remarked that they had some time to kill. This prompted the other to suggest they should have some fun. Because low-level flying is always thrilling, they decided to launch on a local sightseeing flight. Unfortunately, they had not studied their maps to look for obstacles, as required by regulations.

This hop was illegal for a number of other reasons, and an enlisted crewman suggested that it was not such a good idea. These flying officers ignored his objection and pressed on. Minutes later, their aircraft collided with power lines with predictably tragic results.

The ensuing investigation quite correctly cited the pilots' poor judgment, but it ignored another more embarrassing fact. Military leaders often tacitly—and sometimes openly—encourage their pilots to bend or break the rules.

Navy Secretary John Lehman (himself a party-loving Navy flier) was once photographed congratulating Tom Cruise, star of the blockbuster movie *Top Gun*.[2] In the film, the Tom Cruise character flies the F-14 Tomcat at the Navy's elite fighter weapons school. Cruise's character repeatedly takes chances, such as buzzing an air traffic control tower. He enjoys being called dangerous and flies "at the edge." Unfortunately, the real Tomcat fliers would try to emulate this devil-may-care Hollywood image. The F-14 mishap rates would more than double in the years following this movie's release—in numerous not-so-great balls of fire, to borrow from the Jerry Lee Lewis song in the soundtrack.[3]

This 1986 movie made another impression that would also come back to haunt the Navy. It popularized a macho image for naval aviators, which somehow became twisted into a misogynist image. Many impressionable young fliers were carried away with the genre.

The movie's public-relations coup was doubly sweet, because it was used as a great source of ridicule toward the Navy fliers' arch rivals, Air Force pilots. Naval aviators have a unique bond involving mastering the dangerous art of landing on an aircraft carrier. This feat relies on using the aircraft's tail hook to skillfully snag one of four arresting wires stretched across the carrier deck.

Thus, the tail hook became the symbol for a profane annual frat-party-and-panty-raid-style bash sponsored by the Tailhook Association at the Las Vegas Hilton. Here, hundreds of inebriated Navy and Marine fliers would gather and encourage one another to perform increasingly immature acts during the week-long event. Women who happened to be handy became the willing or unwilling objects of crass sexual pranks. Secretary Lehman was said to enjoy watching these festivities.

In his brilliant book *Fall from Glory: The Men Who Sank the U.S. Navy*, author Gregory Vistica[4] describes a situation where two Air Force officers happen into a hotel suite during the Tailhook Association festivities. A naked woman is bumping and grinding to some provocative music. She stands astride a gent lying supine on the floor, taking in the view.

The Air Force pilots are soon asked if they know who the secretary of the navy is. Over the blaring music, these airmen apologize and confess they don't know his name. Their Navy host then points to the guy on the floor and says, "Well, there's our secretary of the navy right here."[5]

The 1991 Tailhook Association meeting was expected to be a blow-out for a couple of reasons. Many fliers were returning from the Gulf War with a chip on their shoulders. While they had helped achieve a brilliant victory, the Air Force had managed to garner most of the publicity, and therefore the glory. One major factor was that the Air Force had used its high-tech weapons to mesmerize the press.

Their affable commander, USAF Lieutenant General Charles A. Horner, provided nightly entertainment with pictures of smart bombs leveling buildings in Baghdad. Even the lowly Army trotted out videos of its Patriot missiles blowing Scuds from friendly skies, while General Schwarzkopf spun tales of his armor in action. By contrast, little was heard from the Navy except videos of cruise missile launches, which did not exactly hype the flier's role.

But by the spring of 1991, the whole world had changed. The Red Menace had disappeared, the stain of Vietnam was all but forgotten, and it was *great* to be a service*man* again. But women were becoming an increasingly important part of America's military and in fact had received a good deal of favorable press for their recent war work.

Leaders like Secretary Lehman, who retired a few years before, and the top-gun mentality had set the stage for a disaster in this "mother of all hooks." This time, the Tailhookers had groped a few of the wrong "gals."

One of the unappreciative gropees of 1991 was an accomplished naval aviator, Lieutenant Paula Coughlin. She also happened to be an admiral's aide. When she tried to discuss the matter with her boss, he ignored her, so she decided to file formal charges. Whistle-blower Cough-lin had no idea what she had started.

Dozens of other women came forward with complaints. The ladies were mad as hell and were not going to take it any longer. Scores of criminal investigations, Congressional hearings, and lawsuits would follow. These activities soon led to a scandal and disgrace, the likes of which would not occur again until Army drill sergeants were exposed as sexual predators at the Aberdeen Proving Grounds in 1997. Indeed, the years following the 1991 Tailhook gathering would profoundly change the whole military establishment.

But this was not the last time that disaster would result from the Navy pilots' mentality and bad judgment coupled with poor oversight. Dr. Robert Alkov's brilliant book, *Aviation Safety: The Human Factor*, describes how one Navy flier returned from the war to find that his unfaithful wife had run off with a superior officer.[6] This fighter pilot could not handle the news, so he turned to alcohol.

His flying had become so erratic that one of his fellow pilots sent an anonymous report to the commander of the Naval Safety Center, a two-star admiral. The admiral, sticking to the "chain of command" tradition, sent the letter back to the errant pilot's squadron commanding officer.

This officer, trying to get rid of this hot potato, attempted to transfer the pilot to another squadron, one operating a different fighter type, where he was not known.

His new squadron CO was unaware of his poor reputation. However, the CO had cautioned the pilot about his heavy social drinking, which the CO had observed firsthand. The CO also had to relieve the pilot from his duties as a department head due to incompetence.

This pilot soon got his new girlfriend pregnant. His debts mounted, and his stepson got into trouble with the law. His ex-wife had also refused him visiting privileges with their daughter and had garnisheed his wages.

Then he was passed over for promotion. This he blamed on his former superior, who just happened to be his ex-wife's boyfriend, who was now stationed at the Pentagon. Meanwhile, the pilots in his new squadron had become aware of his erratic flying and refused to go up with him. His new CO soon learned about these issues, but this superior officer received a short-notice transfer himself and did not adequately brief his own replacement on these serious problems.

The disturbed aviator had not completed checking out in the new type fighter when he requested permission to fly one to a distant airfield. His supposed purpose was to patch up hard feelings with an uncle. The squadron operations officer turned down his request for this unsupervised cross-country flight. The pilot then petitioned his brand-new softhearted CO, who authorized it.

When this pilot checked the weather at his proposed destination, he learned of an approaching snowstorm. Although aware that regulations prohibit flying into an area where snow is forecast, he filed a flight plan anyway and launched.

The pilot's visit went well, and he stayed up drinking in a bar with his uncle until the wee hours. Early the next morning, he phoned for a local weather briefing and learned that several inches of snow were possible. When he arrived at the civilian airfield, the snow was still falling and accumulating on his aircraft's wings.

But he has promised to have the jet back at the squadron that day, and time was now running out. So after quickly deicing the aircraft, he decided to depart without getting a weather update.

As his relatives watched, he taxied out. Accelerating down the runway, he yanked the jet's nose into an impressive, near vertical climb with afterburner roaring. Wagging his wings in a "bye-bye" gesture, he disappeared into the low overcast sky. Seconds later he become spatially disoriented. His out-of-control aircraft plunged back to earth, crashing several miles from the airport.

No mechanical problems were found in the wreckage, and his current and former COs were subsequently blamed for keeping a "failing aviator" on flying status. However, the admiral who was in charge of safety for the entire Navy was not mentioned in the investigation. This, even though he had been made aware of the pilot's erratic flying beforehand and had done little to stop it. Obviously, those misguided junior officers who wrote this accident report decided discretion was in order.

Unfortunately, these types of uncorrected problems would continue to plague the Navy. This pilot would not be the last fighter jock to attempt an air-show-style takeoff in bad weather with family members watching. Several years later, another naval aviator and his radar intercept officer tried this dangerous stunt from another civilian airport. Both died when their F-14 Tomcat crashed into a residential area. But this time, three people living near this airport also perished.

The new admiral in charge of safety for the entire Navy soon arrived on the scene. He had an important mission: *damage control*. He decided to attempt a radical maneuver himself. He actually tried to convince the press that the dead pilot's hare-brain maneuver was a legitimate type of military takeoff and added that the civilian tower controller had personally okayed it.

This senior spin-meister forgot to mention a small fact: this type of dangerous, air-show-style takeoff required specific authorization from both the air traffic controllers *and* the unit commander. The unit commander, hundreds of miles away, was unaware of the pilot's intentions. Another point that the admiral chose not to mention was that this pilot had just lost control and crashed another fighter several months prior to this accident. Nonetheless, his outfit had decided to put him back in the cockpit after that mishap.

The Navy ultimately admitted that his return to flying status had occurred because his was a very popular officer, though *not* apparently the best of aviators. Other radar intercept officers had reportedly complained about his shortcomings, to no avail.

The "three Ts mentality" (i.e., Top Gun, Tomcat, Tailhook) has also cost the Navy dearly in other situations. One of the most notorious cases involved another Tomcat pilot and radar intercept officer on a long cross-country flight. This crew had a college-boy prank in mind as they cruised in tight formation with another jet through the stratosphere.

At this altitude, the air is so thin that fliers will pass out in a matter of seconds without a pressurized cockpit and/or use of an oxygen mask. Unfortunately, pressurization systems in fighter cockpits are not as effective as those of airliners. Part of the problem involves the rubber seals around their big canopies that often leak. For that reason, fighter aviators are taught to always keep their helmet-mounted oxygen masks cinched tightly to their faces at high altitudes.

Less than an hour into the flight, both aviators in the second Tomcat remove their helmets and oxygen masks as they maneuver their jet abeam of the lead aircraft. Their smiling faces are showing as they both don their officer's caps and simultaneously render hand salutes. The crew in the lead Tomcat snaps their picture.

This joke photograph is probably intended for the officer's club wall back at their home base. Unfortunately, their grinning faces will never adorn that facility, for capturing this "Kodak moment" will prove deadly. It soon becomes apparent that the two unmasked fliers are unaware they are losing consciousness.

The crew of the lead Tomcat is powerless to warn their wingmen, whose earphones are in their two stowed helmets. Helplessly, they scream into their own oxygen mask microphones and painfully watch the other jet's nose slowly drop below the horizon. It soon begins to accelerate earthward and descends through several airways. Fortunately, it misses the airliners flying in the area. Eventually, the jet with its unconscious cargo impacts the desert at near supersonic speed.

Several months after this tragedy, I arrived at a nearby Air Force base to do some orientation flying. Base personnel who were familiar with the Tomcat wreckage and body recovery efforts told me something else shocking about this crash.

They suggested that the dead Tomcat crew was also going to disrobe and "moon" the gents in the lead jet. But these two guys apparently passed out before pulling off that part of the stunt. The Navy will later publicly dispute this mooning claim. They insist there is insufficient room in a fighter cockpit for a crew member to pull off his flight suit and expose his bare posterior. Other pilots will privately admit they have seen it done.

Like their Navy brethren, the Army has aviators who enjoy taking unnecessary risks. These hot dogs have also had their share of tragic displays of immaturity. One sadly memorable crash occurred near a picturesque resort during what was supposed to be a routine training mission.

Two Army fliers were taking a UH-1 Huey helicopter on an extended cross-country flight when they decided to land at a lakeside airport. They introduced themselves to a beautiful young woman who worked as a receptionist at the airport. They had soon persuaded her to go for a ride in their venerable helicopter. Never mind that carrying unauthorized passengers in a military aircraft is illegal.

It was not long before the three were winging their way over the lake. A low-altitude aerobatics show soon followed, which became a source of entertainment for many curious onlookers. This romantic interlude was soon interrupted when the helicopter's tail rotor dug into the water. The chopper's whirling main rotor blades immediately splashed down. The damaged Army craft soon rolled over and sank in twenty feet of water.

In the John Wayne movies, the soldiers always appear in the nick of time to rescue the damsel in distress. But this Hollywood image doesn't match reality. Our two crew members quickly released their own multiple-belt military harnesses and swam for shore. Not so the young lady who was trapped in the sunken wreckage. A nearby boat picked up these not-so-gallant fliers. Other would-be rescuers could not get to the female passenger's body for another twenty minutes.

Months later, a military court convicted the chopper pilot of violating flight regulations. I was later told by Army safety personnel that the passenger may not have been adequately briefed on how to release her complex safety belt mechanism.

The "guys in green" are not the only ones who like to show off to impressionable young women. While I was working as a military accident investigator, I encountered another case involving another service.

An older fighter pilot invited his young girlfriend out to the base to watch him take off. This guy had a reputation for being the life of the party at squadron social functions. He also was known for being a hot dog, and today he wanted to make an impressive departure for his lady companion's entertainment.

His "backseater" for this mission is an experienced navigator[7] who does not share the pilot's habit of taking unnecessary risks. As these two very different officers taxi their camouflaged F-4 Phantom warplane to the active runway, another vehicle is moving on the flight line.

This pickup truck is driving to the departure end of the runway. Its three occupants, unlike the jet's navigator, are aware that this pilot has a mini air show in mind. They even bring a video camera to catch it all on tape.

The vehicle halts at the edge of the runway just as the jet turns onto the runway and lights its afterburners. The roar and black smoke from the screaming twin engines are their cue that the show is about to begin. These people are crowded into the cab of this small truck. Two male airmen are seated next to the doors, while an enlisted lady who is *very* pregnant is sandwiched between them.

As the F-4 approaches flying speed, its pilot aggressively pulls back on the control stick. This jerks the jet's nose into the air as its powerful engines kick it momentarily skyward with more than thirty thousand pounds of thrust. But even this force is not sufficient to keep the heavy jet airborne.

An anxious backseater watches as one wing tip drops and begins scraping the ground. He instantly decides something must be wrong with the jet's controls. This experienced flier knows there's no time to discuss things in this situation, so he tugs on his ejection seat handle. A split second later, both aviators are being carried clear of the jet, because his ejection seat is set to also trigger the front seat in sequence.

The truck's occupants watch the jet crew eject and note that both guys get good chutes. These three GIs soon realize that the crewless jet is hurtling directly at their truck at warp speed. In terror, they try to abandon their doomed vehicle.

One of the men is able to scramble to safety, but the other and their pregnant companion are not so fortunate. They cannot escape from ground zero as the jet slams into the truck and incinerates them.

The wreckage is still smoldering when I am notified of the crash. A colonel from the unit soon comes to pay me a visit. This senior officer is obviously a friend of the reckless pilot. Apparently convinced that I am about to be assigned to this accident, he tries to sell me on the idea that this pilot is one of the best in the unit. Translation: The crash just had to have been caused by a mechanical failure.

I listen intently to his theories. But the colonel soon senses I am not very sympathetic to this convoluted logic. Nor am I willing to overlook the obvious issues involved in this crash. So he quickly decides to speak with my bosses. I am then informed I will *not* be working on this case. It is truly amazing how officers can pull together to protect a friend's reputation at the expense of the truth.

Another of these dramatic cases occurred when a well-liked officer was practicing for an air show in a B-52 Stratofortress. This eight-engine jet bomber was never intended to perform violent aerobatics. The massive jet is normally limited to only thirty degrees of bank. For air shows, pilots are allowed to increase this angle up to a sixty-degree maximum bank angle.

When the bomber base is told to put on an air show, a lieutenant colonel with a reputation for being a hot dog volunteers to fly the maneuvers. This guy is a very popular officer. He is also regarded as a "good stick," meaning that he is highly experienced and very skillful. But his judgment is another matter.

For years, this aviator pulled off a series of very dangerous stunts that senior officers just ignored. He seemed to pattern his aberrant flying behavior after a movie character who was supposed to be invulnerable to death.

This character was "Buzz" Rickson, a daring aircraft commander played by Steve McQueen in the movie *The War Lover*.[8] This World War II B-17 pilot performs unnecessarily dangerous flying feats to impress his crew, other aviators in his squadron, and his superiors.

But there is one difference. In the movie, his superiors are concerned with these antics and threaten McQueen's character with disciplinary action. Not so with our real-life "Buzz," who seems to be immune from criticism by the leadership at his base.

These stunts included sending his navigator into the bomb bay to videotape these weapons coming off their racks during a bomb run. This young man knows such unauthorized filming is obviously unnecessary and personally dangerous. Besides, he is aware there's a well-known military custom: crew members should be at their battle stations during activities like bomb runs.

But "Buzz" has decided he wants a home video of his bomb run instead. So the young navigator has to obey his wishes. That is because of another well-known military custom: subordinates must unquestioningly carry out their leader's orders during missions.

This young officer is the squadron's lead navigator, so he decides he should report this safety transgression to the unit's commanding officer. He makes a copy of the videotape and brings it to his CO—who turns out to be a friend and admirer of "Buzz." The navigator then encounters a not-so-well-publicized military custom: reporting safety problems is not conducive to career progression.

In a military unit, a commander has almost total authority over his or her people. The commander berates the young officer's actions. During this tirade, the CO tells him that he is no longer the lead navigator, but instead will be immediately reassigned to menial duties. When it comes to military safety, shooting messengers is an all too common practice.

"Buzz's" bomb-bay video was only one of this hot dog's many stunts. He was also known to intentionally make low passes on bomb ranges. Once, his copilot had to pull the control wheel back, and the jet still missed hitting the ground by only a few feet. "Buzz" broke out in sardonic laughter, revealing that he was playing a game of "chicken" with his crew. Only crew and their laundry will know just how scared they were. The pilot also was known to have put on a private air show for his daughter's baseball team during a game.

Furthermore, maintenance crews complained about having to repair the damaged B-52s, which he had overstressed. In addition, it was rumored that "Buzz" planned to do a barrel roll at the upcoming air show—because he expects to finish up his flying career soon after the event anyway. Some personnel at the base who hear about this tell their families *not* to be at the performance, just in case this hot dog tries to pull off this roll and loses control of the jet.

Some of the junior crew members were also becoming reluctant to continue flying with "Buzz." The wing commander should have called this lieutenant colonel on the carpet and chewed him out. Instead, a few senior officers decided they would fly with him themselves—to keep an eye on him. This proved to be a fatal mistake.

On the day of the air show practice, three senior officers show up to fly with "Buzz." During this practice, a tower controller tells him to "go around" because another aircraft is in the pattern. At slow speeds, only several hundred feet above the airfield, "Buzz" recklessly turns the B-52's control wheel to the left.

The three-hundred-thousand-plus-pound jet rolls over into a ninety-degree bank, which robs its wings of lift. The giant craft stalls out, and its nose swings toward the ground. The craft narrowly misses a USAF technical school and a nuclear weapons storage bunker.

In its vertical plunge, a wing clips a power line as the jet explodes into the dirt. The rapidity of the maneuver, the steep angle, and the low altitude conspire to deny "Buzz" and the other colonels time to eject. Several video cameras document this crash, and the tapes are replayed endlessly on national television.

Because this disaster had been seen by millions of taxpayers, the Pentagon could not just ignore it. Months later, one colonel who recently had taken over command at the base is singled out for a court-martial. Interestingly he knew little about "Buzz's" long-standing habits of ignoring safety, but he is convicted anyway. Sometimes even colonels can be scapegoats.

In my 1994 complaint, I note other similar crashes where the commanders were definitely aware of the hot dog's habits. But in these cases, the public was unaware of the accidents—so nothing happened to these culprits or their commanders. The lesson is clear: It's okay for your people to be hot dogs as long as the public does not hear about their screw-ups.

The "just don't get caught" attitude is well understood, even by junior jet jocks. This creates some temptations, especially when the service assigns training jets to tanker and bomber bases. The idea is to allow inexperienced Air Force copilots to use the jets to rapidly get additional hours by flying these relatively inexpensive aircraft.

This valuable program was sometimes loosely monitored. Unfortunately, a few such low-time fliers decided to take advantage of the situation to hotdog in these jets. These lieutenants and junior captains were full of youthful enthusiasm, but they knew military flight regulations—especially the one that prohibited flying over one's own family residence.

One of the saddest mishaps occurred when two young pilots decided to ignore such rules along with those against doing low-altitude aerobatics. They filed a false flight plan with their unit showing a different route, and then they landed at a civilian airport near one guy's hometown. They needed to wait for some cloudy weather to clear.

This whole community was delighted when this young man became an Air Force pilot. Furthermore, his parents had never actually seen him fly an airplane. While he was on the ground, he confided to the local air traffic controller that he and his companion were going to "buzz" his parent's house to have a little bit of fun. The pilot then called his relatives and asked them to round up their friends and neighbors.

Minutes later, his T-37 makes several low passes over the neighborhood. The neophyte aviator makes a low pass over the family homestead, so low that the nearby pine trees sway from the jet wash. He then pulls back on the control stick as the agile jet smartly climbs into a loop in a kind of aeronautical salute.

His parents are duly impressed as they watch from their front porch. His ex-Marine father is so moved that he wants to return his son's salute. The overconfident aviator then zooms low over the baseball diamond where, just a few years before, he had swung a bat. He enthusiastically swings the control stick rapidly left and right. This makes his jet's wings move up and down, waving to the folks on the ground who wave back.

Emboldened, he swings the jet back for another pass over the ballpark. This time he moves the controls too rapidly, even for this nimble craft to respond. As the airflow separates from the craft's wings, it violently corkscrews out of control. The gyrating jet impacts into a grove of trees. Horrified friends and family members rush to the burning wreckage in a vain attempt to assist the two dead fliers.

One can understand, but not excuse, the over-exuberance of the naïve junior officers. Not so, the behavior of generals and other senior commanders who sometimes set very bad examples by their reckless behavior. One well-known case involved a commander who bragged at the officers' club that his departure the next morning would be spectacular. All eyes were on his shiny jet as it taxied to the runway. The troops were not surprised when his jet began a barrel roll immediately after its wheels left the ground. The too-slow craft was then seen to depart controlled flight and crash before anyone could eject.

Because of such crashes, generals are supposed to fly only "under the supervision" of an instructor pilot. These instructors, who are often mere captains or majors, may have difficulty controlling the antics of a general who wants to show off.

Most generals and admirals know that flying jets is an expensive privilege extended to them solely because of their rank. And the majority of these leaders realize they have lost much of their flying skills, since they spend most of their time behind desks. These gents will usually listen to those junior officers assigned to fly with them. But others like to show off to everybody, including the young instructors who are responsible for keeping things safe. This makes for some awkward situations.

One incident involved a senior commander who had an executive version of the C-135 assigned for his personal use. This four-engine Boeing 707 airliner was not a toy. Unfortunately, this former fighter jock was used to flying solo and had a big ego. Furthermore, he made no secret of his disdain for transport pilots. Thus, getting his majesty to "straighten up and fly right" presented a real challenge for the instructor sitting in the copilot's seat.

The giant jet was returning from an overseas visit with the general's wife and their entourage in the passenger compartment. The general was flying the jet while his copilot/instructor, who was a major, handled the radios and talked with the controllers.

They were still at thirty-thousand-plus feet when an FAA controller told them to descend and cross a certain airways intersection at ten thousand feet. The copilot acknowledged the clearance as required by regulation. After a minute or so, the general had not reacted by starting down. Thus, the copilot tactfully mentions that they probably want to start their descent to comply with the controller's instructions.

The general does not even acknowledge his suggestion. This major is used to this kind of treatment and does not want to upset the general.

But he soon realizes they have to start down *soon* to cross the intersection at the ten-thousand-foot level. In these large transports, good pilots like to do things smoothly. Gradual, one-thousand-feet-per-minute descents are normal, because passengers are walking about back in the cabin.

The copilot is really getting nervous now, as he watches the navigational instruments indicating they are rapidly approaching the intersection—and the general has *still* not started down. So he decides to be more assertive, per his CRM training. He says, "General, sir, we really need to start descending *now.*"

Several seconds pass, and the general continues to be unresponsive, but the copilot notes an embryonic smile on the old man's lips. The major begins to really worry as he realizes it's now virtually impossible to follow the FAA clearance. He knows that he, not the general, will be blamed for the safety violation. He might lose his wings, or, more important, there might be other traffic at this altitude.

The copilot does not know what the hell the general is up to, but he decides to tell the controllers they cannot comply with the clearance and plead for mercy. As he starts to reach for the mike button mounted on the control wheel, the general goes into action. He shoves the control wheel forward while yanking the throttles back to idle. The general then quickly shoves out the wing spoilers, which kill the lift, just for good measure.

Now the jet's nose pitches downward violently as the transport plunges earthward. This is not what the Boeing engineers had in mind when they designed this aircraft. The major is terrified as his body is pushed upward against his shoulder harness straps. Loose objects migrate toward the ceiling under these "zero G" conditions. He tries to regain his composure as he watches the altimeter wildly unwind.

Just as they approach ten thousand feet, the general reverses everything, and the jet quickly returns to level flight. This occurs just as the navigational needles show they are crossing the intersection specified in the clearance. The hot dog general then chuckles, as if to say, now that's how *real* men fly. The angry major wants to say something, but before he can open his mouth, the cabin door slams open with a loud bang.

Both pilots swing around. Standing in the doorway is the general's wife, who is mad as the proverbial wet hen. In fact, her dress is soaked with liquid, and her fancy hairdo is drenched. Both men are speechless as she screams, "What *idiot* was flying this jet?" The major chokes back laughter as he realizes there *is* a God!

Perhaps William Shakespeare was right when he said, "The fault, dear Brutus, is not in our stars, but in ourselves . . . "[9] I would add, only if we allow this system to perpetuate.

PART
III

Tri-Service Tragedies

12

Unfriendly Fire

"Friendly fire" is the slang term for the unintentional shooting of your own troops while you think you are engaging the enemy. This often-fatal mistake is the most ghastly type of military accident. It is obviously the most *unfriendly* way to die on any battlefield. Such tragic incidents not only destroy vital equipment and the lives of cherished comrades, but they utterly demoralize the shooters as well as the surviving witnesses. Thus, the term is an oxymoron.

In the first four American "crusades" of the twentieth century (World War I, World War II, Korea, and Vietnam), it has been estimated that friendly fire—or "fratricide," as it is more properly called—accounted for 2 percent of the total casualties. This according to Lieutenant Colonel Charles Shrader, who did an official study of the problem.[1]

Other experts suggest that 2 percent is a rather low estimate.[2] But perhaps this fact should not be too surprising, given the reluctance of military personnel to report mishaps in general and especially those that are particularly embarrassing. Obviously, fratricide incidents are among the most embarrassing types of accidents. Another genuine factor is the difficulty of establishing what really happened in the midst of battle. The so-called fog of war is a very real limitation in documenting such events.

First, the enemy is not going to allow anyone to investigate the battlefield unmolested, certainly not while the fighting is still raging. That, of course, is the best time and place to begin documenting just what happéned. Second, the shooters may not know that they have hit "friendlies"—even after the fact. In the distance, demolished vehicles, be they friend or foe, may look pretty much alike. Last, if the unit receiving the friendly fire is wiped out, it may be impossible to establish just who did the shooting. Dead men, indeed, tell no tales.

Unfortunately, Shrader's study was done in 1982 and thus does not include data from America's fifth crusade, the Gulf War. This conflict was different in many ways. It was the first cyber-war, fought largely with electronic equipment, such as computers, satellites, laser-guided weapons, night-vision devices, robotics, and stealth technology.

The outcome was never in doubt, given the vastly superior technology possessed by the United States and its coalition allies, although nobody quite expected the quick, lopsided victory, nor the relatively few American combat deaths. Only 148 of our troops died during Desert Storm in the five-week air campaign and the four-day ground war with Iraq.

Another surprise was the dramatic increase in the percentage of those who were reportedly killed by friendly fire (35 of the 148 victims).[3] Many of those fratricide deaths reflect several factors including: new or untested technology, enhanced lethality of weapons, aggressive commanders, inadequate training, and poor ergonomics.

Often, in the heat of battle, commanders show their fallibility, and the grunts pay with their lives while their loved ones are left with haunting questions of why. Adding insult to injury, the Pentagon's system of self-investigation and *not* releasing the real reports insures that those questions will remain forever unanswered. Oftentimes the motivation for such secrecy is that the erring officer is a "favorite son" of a senior commander or, in some cases, actually a relative or an in-law. It seems that leaders don't want their protégés careers hurt by these unfortunate episodes.

Many times a hard-charging, mid-level combat commander just gets in over his head, becomes confused, fails to ask for help, and makes a poor decision.[4] The Pentagon's traditional lack of emphasis on safety insures the same type of problems continue to reoccur. One such incident involved the commander of an Army helicopter unit on a moonless evening during the Desert Storm conflict.

The AH-64 Apache is the Army's highly automated attack helicopter, designed to destroy enemy tanks with laser-guided missiles. It is equipped with a thermal viewing system that detects otherwise invisible heat from targets. This sophisticated "gunsight" allows the Apache's two crew members to have a virtual-reality view of the outside world in total darkness. Thus, its preferred operating environment is at night, when the enemy cannot see it coming.

This 180-mile-per-hour tank-buster soon gets its first 911 call of the Gulf War. The allies have been bombing Iraqi positions around the clock for three weeks in preparation for the coalition ground campaign. General Schwarzkopf now wants to know just what kind of fight his troops will be facing when the main land war begins.

He decides to task the U.S. 1st Infantry Division with probing the massive Iraqi defensive fortifications that run along the Kuwaiti border. The division then establishes "Task Force Iron," consisting of one thousand crack American soldiers. These troops have penetrated three miles into enemy territory along a twenty-mile front when their commander becomes concerned about a possible Iraqi ambush.

He knows elements of his force have engaged and destroyed one Iraqi armored vehicle on his right flank. But as night falls, his troops spot other enemy tanks dashing about behind the sand dunes in front of their lines. Suspecting an Iraqi trap, he sends an M-113 Armored Personnel Carrier and an M-2 Bradley Fighting Vehicle to secure that area and requests close air support.

The urgent call is received at the 11th Aviation Brigade Headquarters. Its commander, Lieutenant Colonel Ralph Hayles, has orders not to leave his command post to personally take part in combat flying. Unlike the Air Force and Navy, junior warrant officers do most Army flying, so senior commissioned officers are expected to direct the war fighting from rear areas. Colonel Hayles ignores these orders and jumps into the cockpit of the lead Apache.[5]

As the two helicopters approach the front lines shortly after midnight on March 17, a thirty-mile-per-hour crosswind has blown them slightly off course. When they contact the ground commander of Task Force Iron, he requests they destroy the hostile armored vehicles threatening his right flank. He is given the map grid coordinates of the location of these targets by radio.[6]

But Hayles is confused. His helicopter's onboard navigational computer contradicts the supposed location of the enemy armored vehicles. He tries to explain this to the people on the ground. He is reassured that the two targets in his thermal scope *must* be the enemy tanks. At first, he hesitates. He is then urged to "take 'em out"[7] by the task force commander.

Colonel Hayles selects his 30-mm automatic cannon. He aims at one of the vehicles and depresses the trigger. But the gun fires only a few rounds before jamming. The reluctant pilot selects the much more lethal laser-guided Hellfire missile system and locks it onto one of the unsuspecting targets. He continues to mentally question why his helicopter's navigational system disagrees with the target location data provided by the ground commander.

At that point he says, "Boy, I'm gonna tell ya, it's hard to pull this trigger . . . Back me up a little bit here . . . " Instead of helping this relatively inexperienced colonel figure out the problem, his copilot urges him to fire. Hayles depresses the trigger. The missile roars away as he mumbles, "I hope it's the enemy." In his scope, he sees the first target explode as the missile impacts.

His copilot then says: "Let's take out the second one. Let's go." Hayles quickly repeats the process by locking the laser guidance on the second target and squeezing the trigger. Again, his thermal display shows the vehicle explode as his missile finds its mark. He then sees two dazed survivors fleeing on foot and asks his wingman to fire on them.

But before the other helicopter can open fire, both chopper crews are told to cease fire because friendly vehicles have just been hit. Unfortunately, Hayles's concern about the location of his targets was well founded. He now knows he has almost certainly killed friendly troops. He then verbalizes this concern. "Roger, I was afraid of that. I was *really* afraid of that." Shortly after he lands, Lieutenant Colonel Hayles is relieved of command for disobeying no-fly orders. It seems this particular officer did not have friends in high places to cover up his mistake.

This has also been an inauspicious debut for the Apache. Its first ground-support kills in the Gulf War are two young Americans, Army Specialist Jeff Middletown and Private Bob Talley. On this moonless evening, six other soldiers are also wounded in the attack.

But the night is still young, and General Schwarzkopf's other troops are in a frenetic search to probe Iraqi desert defenses. Some of these soldiers come into peril as mechanized units dart around sand dunes in the trackless desert. They suddenly come upon each other while expecting the enemy.

Inexperienced young troops repeatedly have to make split-second, life-or-death decisions. In the darkness, friendly and enemy armor look very similar, and it is difficult for excited gunners to decide to take a second look and risk becoming casualties themselves. Incidentally, Hollywood did an excellent job of portraying this in the critically acclaimed movie *Courage Under Fire*.[8]

Many of these young troops are riding into battle tonight in America's latest cavalry weapon: the M-2 Bradley Fighting Vehicle. The taxpayers have spent $14 billion to develop and procure this weapon system, and the Army is eager to test its mettle.

This new armored scout is as big as a tank, equipped with a thermal sight, a 25-mm automatic cannon, and "TOW" antitank guided missiles. It is highly maneuverable and powered by a large turbine engine. But in spite of these high-tech features, this vehicle is a collection of compromises.

One of the most critical problems involves the Bradley's failure to pass "survivability" tests. This Army prizefighter has a glass jaw and can't take a punch. It explodes when hit, and the onboard fuel and ammo are threats to the soldiers riding in its troop compartment. Ironically, this vehicle was named after the heroic General Omar Bradley of World War II fame. He was known as the "GI's general" because he *always* took care of his troops.

The brass saw the videos of how this ersatz tank burst into flames when it was hit by gunfire during testing. The Pentagon also knows these tests were ordered by Congress. But when the vehicle failed to measure up, the military officials in charge simply ignored results and buried the data. That is until one officer became a whistle-blower.

The Pentagon, of course, fired the officer who went public to report these shortcomings. Colonel James G. Burton would later write a damning book, *Pentagon Wars*,[9] which describes the military's attempts to cover up the Bradley's problems. But all that is academic in February 1991, because the vehicles *are* in the inventory, and troops *are* headed into battle with a flawed design.

These deficiencies are not exactly comforting to the soldiers riding inside the Bradleys as they maneuver behind enemy lines tonight. One such soldier is Private Kevin Pollack from Tucson, Arizona.[10] When his vehicle encounters another tank in the darkness, a young officer panics and orders their gunner to open fire.

This gunner refuses, fearing they are targeting a friendly vehicle. Turns out the gunner is right. This encounter concerns Pollack, because he realizes that trigger-happy soldiers are everywhere, and his thin-skinned Bradley makes a big target. The apprehensive soldier will survive unscathed this evening, but he will not always be so fortunate.

Several days later, General Schwarzkopf decides it is time to hurl the coalition ground forces against Saddam's battered but still unbeaten army. Private Pollack is among the thousands of young American soldiers who salute smartly and mount their Bradleys. The troops expect the mother of all tank battles as the allied armored formations mass on the Saudi frontier.

By the evening of February 27, this major offensive has been raging for three days. In the hectic campaign, Pollack's unit of thirteen Bradleys has become lost. Shortly after midnight, his platoon commander orders their armored column to race across the desert and try to catch up with the main assault force. The Bradleys' turbine engines scream while their clanking tracks throw streams of sand upward, as if in protest.

In the distance, Pollack can see the night sky illuminated by multi-color explosions and tracers. The private looks around his Bradley's dimly lit troop compartment at nine other weary soldiers. He hopes that his platoon leader is going to halt, at least until they figure out who is involved in the firefight up ahead. Instead their commander directs them to creep ahead in single file, like so many moths drawn inexorably to the flames. This movement has not gone unnoticed.

Unbeknownst to Pollack and his comrades, other eyes are studying their stealthy procession from a distance. In the darkness, an American tank crew monitors these thirteen silhouettes as they slither along in the shadows. The tank crew soon decides they are watching a column of Iraqi reinforcements trying to sneak up on the ongoing battle.

These other Americans are seated inside an M-1 Abrams Main Battle Tank, which is an awesome killing machine. It is named after one of America's great military leaders, General Creighton Abrams, hero of the Battle of the Bulge in the Second World War and later the Army's chief of staff. Its primary weapon is a laser-aimed 120-mm cannon, which is powerful and deadly accurate.

The Abrams' gunner quickly places the cross hairs of his thermal gunsight on Private Pollack's Bradley and pulls the trigger. The massive projectile streaks across the desert floor at supersonic speed and rips into the Bradley's flimsy hull. The troop compartment immediately explodes into a conflagration, just as in the tests the Army conducted years before. The horrific concussion has dazed Pollack, who barely manages to scramble through an open hatch. But three of his comrades are dead or dying as flames consume the vehicle.

As this badly burned soldier lies on the sand beside the gutted hulk, he has no idea of the ordeal he is about to face. Private Kevin Pollack will soon lose the fingers of his right hand, and his charred body will ultimately require fifty-one painful operations. The Army will then discharge this disfigured private.

But the stoic former soldier will recover from his ordeal and ultimately rejoin some of his Gulf War colleagues when he finds employment in a homeless veterans shelter. His trial by fire has made him philosophical. He wonders why, on this first digital battlefield, the Army did not install an electronic system on its ground vehicles, as military aircraft have, to distinguish friend from foe.

This twenty-year-old does not blame the Abrams' gunner who pulled the trigger. Nor does he know an embarrassing statistic: that 77 *percent* of American armor vehicles destroyed or damaged in the Gulf War were hit by friendly fire.[11] But Private Pollack does know that he is grateful just to be alive. For he sometimes thinks of those who were less fortunate, those other GIs who came back from the Gulf in body bags.

One such soldier was a bright-eyed twenty-two-year-old kid from Nashville, Tennessee. Corporal Lance Fielder was a specialist with the 54th Engineering Battalion. On February 27, just hours after Pollack's accident, he will be killed in another inexcusable friendly-fire incident.[12]

Like the private, Fielder is part of the massive invasion of Iraq, although this corporal is not supposed to be in the actual battle. He is part of a convoy of vehicles hauling ammunition and other war supplies behind the front lines. But in this swirling battlefield, no one is really exactly sure where the front lines are.

Hours earlier, an ammunition transporter assigned to Fielder's unit had broken down. So he, three other soldiers, and their lieutenant, one Kevin Wessels, decide to stay with this vehicle. They are patiently waiting to be towed back to a secure area for repairs.

During the evening, dozens of other American supply trucks have passed within fifty feet of their position near an abandoned Iraqi airfield. So at 3 A.M., when these five soldiers spot armored vehicles approaching from the direction of American forces, they think they are about to be picked up. But they soon get an unpleasant surprise.

What they don't know is that the son-in-law of General Creighton Abrams is in command of the approaching armor unit of Abrams and Bradleys. The Third Armored Cavalry Squadron commander is a Lieutenant Colonel John Daly Jr. A dashing ex–West Pointer, he knows what kind of officers the Army likes to promote. This can-do officer has decided to aggressively attack the airfield, even though it is outside his assigned geographic area of responsibility.

One of Daly's subordinates is Captain Bo Friesen, who is a different breed of cat. And he is more than a little concerned by his boss's overeagerness to assault these suspected enemy positions. In the darkness, Friesen uses his thermal sight to scan the area around this abandoned airfield. He soon spots several unidentified troops and two vehicles up ahead.

Captain Friesen orders that warning shots be fired, thinking they are Iraqi soldiers and hoping to get them to surrender. Some of these shots hit an ammunition trailer, causing its contents to detonate. In the confusion, some people in his unit believe they are seeing returning fire from the target. Friesen's gunner fires a second burst, and he then orders a cease-fire. This thoughtful officer intends to let these vastly outgunned troops give up. But he soon learns that Colonel Daly has other ideas, as this overeager officer aggressively maneuvers his armored vehicles.

Meanwhile, the five startled GIs are crawling around in the sand after diving for cover. One sergeant has been hit in the leg. The shooting stops for a brief period, so Fielder bravely tries to go to his wounded comrade's assistance. But this selfless young corporal is soon cut down by a third sudden, unexpected burst of gunfire.

In agony, the wounded corporal crawls back to cover as more bullets rip into his chest. He then collapses on his stomach beside another comrade. The other soldier carefully rolls Fielder over as the corporal looks up and says "Oh, God!" and dies. Fielder's courage in trying to help a wounded buddy—and another man's stupidity—have cost him his life.

First Lieutenant Kevin Wessels, realizing his unit is in danger of being wiped out by friendly fire, musters courage above and beyond the call of duty. He fires a green flair into the night sky, hoping the additional light might convince the tank gunners they are firing at Americans.[13]

This young officer then turns on his flashlight, sticks his hands in the air, and bravely walks directly toward the incoming stream of bullets. As he approaches, the nearest Bradley gunner points a 50-caliber machine gun at his chest and says, "You better be an American." The courageous lieutenant's reply is X-rated, but decidedly American.[14]

A confused Colonel Daly then orders his troops to advance, only to discover that they have been shooting at "friendlies" all along. A saddened Captain Friesen was afraid of that. He is angry that Daly decided to have his tanks open up on the helpless foot soldiers with an unnecessary additional volley after he had called for a cease-fire.

Everybody knew these foot soldiers had nowhere to go. But Friesen distinctly remembers the colonel's voice on the radio screaming, "They're getting away! They're getting away!"[15] This was followed by a third machine gun burst, the *unfriendly* fire that killed Corporal Fielder.

Daly apparently thought they were not surrendering "fast enough." However, Friesen knows that even if they had been Iraqis, this action was unwarranted and probably illegal under the rules of war. Colonel Daly soon approaches Captain Friesen and suggests that they need to " ... keep this under our hat."[16]

This is just the beginning of a massive cover-up. A layer of lies, misrepresentations, threats, and bribes will be used in the coming months to try to prevent details of this tragic incident from becoming public. Perhaps even more disturbing, the Army will issue phony reprimands to those whose careers it wants to protect.[17]

Even more egregious, the service also targets convenient scapegoats to take the fall for this blunder, insuring that those most responsible will be spared from blame. The truth will eventually come out, but that will take years of determination on the part of Fielder's distraught parents, a major Congressional General Accounting Office investigation, and a sensational Senate hearing.

But that night, one deeply saddened Lieutenant Wessels surveyed the battle scene where Corporal Fielder's lifeless body once lay. In the bloody sand he found a crucifix on a chain. This silent knight had lost his cross.

As the lieutenant starts to retrieve it, Colonel Daly walks over to him and asks if he has ever been taught about the "fog of war." The colonel soon shifts the conversation to responsibility. The gist of this bizarre chat is that Wessels may have put his men in danger, and the colonel is not to blame for this incident.[18]

The military disinformation machine swings into action. Half a world away, the Army briefers contact Lance Fielder's parents in Tennessee the next day, February 28. These Army officers tell Ms. Deborah Shelton and Mr. Ron Fielder that their son has been killed in a firefight with Iraqi forces. This is the standard military "we regret to inform you" briefing, and these trusting citizens ask few questions.

Eight days later, these grieving parents watch as the Army lays their boy to rest with full military honors. The burial detail officer hands Lance's mother the American flag that has covered his coffin. Ironically, American guns then fire three noisy volleys—the same number that took his life. The bugler pays taps, but when the bereaved family asks for the details of Lance's death, they hear only silence.

Then at 3 A.M. on May 2, a ringing phone awakens a drowsy Ron Fielder. The voice at the other end says he was in Lance's unit when he was killed. This young soldier is calling from Saudi Arabia and adds: "The Army is lying to you. He was killed by an American unit." The soldier nervously says he cannot talk any longer but will come by and explain everything when he gets back to the States.

One hour later, Ron Fielder's phone rings again. He soon learns it's damage-control time, as Lance's former commander confirms the information given by the previous, unauthorized call. But this captain quickly adds that Lance will be posthumously getting an important medal—the Bronze Star with a "V" for valor.

The officer does not mention that several others will also be getting the coveted medal. These are the very people who killed Lance, including Colonel Daly. The written awards citations accompanying the medals intentionally contain inaccuracies and misrepresentations, suggesting the recipients had bravely battled enemy forces when, in fact, the *only* people that most of these guys fired upon were Americans.

That senior officers participated in this process is very telling. Awarding these highly prized, career-enhancing decorations under such conditions appears to have been deliberately done to insure the silence of those who participated in or witnessed this friendly-fire fiasco. Civilian cowards are often offered hush money, but the military employs something even more corrupting of its values. The awards might more accurately be labeled "hush medals."

To compound their frustrations, Lance Fielder's parents later learn that *all* the families of friendly-fire victims were given notification letters at exactly 3 P.M. on the same day, August 12, 1991. Fielder's parents will later testify they felt this well-coordinated tactic was designed to overwhelm the media and to prevent in-depth coverage of the many individual tragedies.[19] Now, Fielder's folks know that something is very wrong, and they want answers.

The Army soon announces it is going to have its own people do a thorough investigation into these very troubling *potential* problems. Military internal affairs inquiries are often just another type of damage-control mechanism. The Fielder family would soon learn that this is especially true when these problems are particularly embarrassing, or if they involve high-level people.

The Army suggests the medals should be rescinded but contradicts itself by concluding that there was *nothing* really wrong with the claims made to award those medals. When Ms. Shelton decides to inquire herself about the status of the reprimands that were supposedly meted out to the officers responsible for her son's death, she apparently strikes a nerve. She is told: "Quite frankly, madam, this is a military matter and none of your concern."[20]

How dare these pesky civilians question the integrity our military establishment! Hell, we even posthumously promoted her boy to sergeant. Some people just have no sense of gratitude.

Deborah Shelton soon decides it is time to contact her senator to plead for someone outside the Pentagon to investigate this entire matter. It is not long before the newly elected but powerful Senator Fred Thompson takes an interest in this very emotional and seemingly egregious situation.

Senator Thompson is a sophisticated legislator, wise beyond his tenure. He served with distinction years ago as a senior counsel on the Watergate hearings. America knows his stentorian voice from his many character roles in the movies. But he is not acting when he volunteers to help examine this issue. This man who has sniffed out conspiracies before knows that what is needed first is a thorough, objective documentation of the facts.

The General Accounting Office (GAO) then launches a very comprehensive investigation into this whole matter. The topic will eventually get on the docket of the Senate's powerful Permanent Subcommittee on Investigations. Insiders regard this panel as the "soul of the Senate." Furthermore, it is chaired by one of the nation's most courageous, non-partisan, and fair-minded legislators, the unassuming but diligent senior senator from Delaware, Bill Roth.

Another quiet legend of the Senate learns about the upcoming hearing and offers to participate. This fellow has a longstanding reputation for ferreting out governmental abuses. He is none other than the gravelly voiced senator from Iowa, Charles Grassley. His homespun wisdom is anathema to those who live inside the Washington beltway and believe they are all-knowing. When this person speaks, the people know it comes from the heart—and the heartland.

Ms. Shelton can hardly wait as her day in court draws near. Others are also becoming interested as the hearing date approaches. News leaks abound that this is going to be a *very* interesting session. It seems the mainstream press is beginning to wise up to the military's post-Vietnam style of managing their reporting: well-orchestrated briefings, controlled press pool tours, and pre-selected video clips. This was the steady diet that *real* reporters found less palatable than the MREs (Meals Ready to Eat) rations that they had to endure during this war. Now it appears that they and the public may get a chance to see a different side of that high-tech conflict.

Meanwhile, across the Potomac, the Pentagon goes to "DefCon One"[21] alert status as they review the draft GAO report. They know this document will soon be *openly* discussed in the Senate hearing chambers before all those reporters and cameras. The military establishment was less fearful of Saddam Hussein than of this forthcoming truth-telling session. This well-entrenched bureaucracy knows it has been outmaneuvered by one resourceful mother who is about to finally get her hearing on what really killed her boy.

Members of the Pentagon's well-voiced damage control team quickly prepare themselves. First, they can try to take some of the credit for *helping* get the terrible truth out, although that's a bit of a stretch for all but the most gullible. More important, their many friends on the Hill can no doubt be persuaded that this is simply a one-time aberration, and these "green hawks" are likely to want to send the Pentagon more money to develop technology to fix these problems. Incidentally, did we mention we are planning to do some of the work in your district, Mr. Congressman?

But no one in the "puzzle palace" is quite prepared for what is about to happen as Senator Roth gavels the hearing open on June 29, 1995. The witnesses seated in the stately mahogany-paneled hearing room include GAO investigators, senior Army officials, Fielder's distraught parents, as well as a few somber officers who were the key participants in the battle that fateful evening over four years ago. What was it that Dr. Martin Luther King Jr. used to say about "justice delayed?"

These warriors include a pair of individuals who are not in uniform today, *Mister* Bo Friesen and *Mister* Kevin Wessels. The audience will soon hear how the former captain who issued the cease-fire that should have prevented Fielder's death received a letter of reprimand for his actions that night. He chose to leave the service. Former Lieutenant Wessels, who risked his own life trying to save his men by walking into the line of fire, also received a letter of admonishment and chose to leave the service. Not since the My Lai Massacre has the Army so ignored one of its *true* heroes, who risked his own life to save others.

The third warrior present is Lieutenant Colonel John Daly, who ordered the attack that killed Corporal Fielder. This understandably nervous officer is still in his highly decorated uniform.

The senators make their opening remarks. Roth openly disputes the validity of the Army's claim that Wessels indirectly contributed to this tragic accident. He also questions why recommendations for medals for bravery were so quickly issued, and why some officers were promoted despite evidence of wrongdoing.

The articulate senator remarks, "Our role here today is to determine the truth. Above all else, this country owes the family of Sergeant Fielder, and all the families who suffer the loss of a son or daughter in military service, the absolute truth. This is the very bedrock of integrity within our military system."[22]

The microphone is then passed to Senator Thompson, whose clarion comments scope the purpose of these proceedings. He notes it is not the intent of this subcommittee to try to second-guess what our military decision makers do in the heat of combat. He quickly adds, however, that the facts uncovered so far "cry out for us to make an inquiry into this case." He then adds, "I hope that this investigation will result in a stronger United States Army."[23]

Senator Grassley then speaks, and, as always, he pulls no punches. "To me, this appears to be a case of organized lying . . . I see reverse accountability . . . where the culprits get rewards and promotions, and the heroes get punished. Too often that is the way the Pentagon does things . . ."[24] He then reminds everyone how this tragedy was not unique. Trigger-happy officers have disgraced us before, when Air Force pilots fired on two Army Black Hawks over Iraq. He finally laments: " . . . the military seems unable to deal with these accidents in an honest and forthright manner . . ."[25]

The senator's laments would foreshadow the general dissatisfaction with the lame explanations offered by senior Army officials during the daylong hearings. The Army, however, did act decisively in one matter: Colonel Daly's coveted bronze star was revoked the next day. And in the years since, the Army has begun to examine technological fixes to overcome friendly-fire problems. These efforts have included testing computerized "battlefield combat identification systems," which will theoretically allow gunners to determine if a potential target vehicle is friendly.[26]

First Lt. Laura Piper, an Air Force intelligence analyst, was a passenger in the U.S. Army Black Hawk helicopter shot down over Iraq by friendly fire, April 14, 1994. *Joan Piper*

Military personnel inspect the Black Hawk wreckage. The author was removed from the investigation when he refused to go along with the cover-up of the friendly-fire incident. *U.S. Air Force*

Orville Wright's plane at Ft. Myer the day of the U.S. Army's first test flight, September 3, 1908. Orville Wright is sitting on the right with passenger Lt. Tom Selfridge on the left. This aircraft suffered a propeller fracture after takeoff and crashed near Arlington National Cemetery. *National Archives*

Minutes after the crash, Lieutenant Selfridge is placed on a stretcher. His head wounds proved to be fatal. Selfridge became the world's first aircraft accident fatality. *National Archives*

During World War II, the B-24 *Lady Be Good* became lost over the Mediterranean at night and crashed in the middle of the Sahara Desert. All aboard died, and the wreckage was not found until 1959. As in thousands of other war-zone accidents, the crewmen's deaths were improperly counted as "battle deaths." *National Archives*

One of the eight servicemen killed during Operation Desert One, the aborted rescue attempt of U.S. hostages in Iran in 1980, lies dead in the foreground. A Navy H-53 helicopter collided with an Air Force C-130 during a nighttime sandstorm at the secret refueling base. *Associated Press*

In 1975, mechanical problems caused this U.S. Air Force C-5 to crash near Saigon. Half of the more than three hundred Vietnamese orphans and crew aboard the plane died in the crash. *U.S. Air Force*

Maj. Ken Levens shows the family his F-117 stealth fighter's cockpit. The author warned the Department of Defense about ergonomic problems with the F-117's cockpit, but the deficiencies were not corrected. These deficiencies resulted in the F-117 crash that killed Major Levens in 1995. *Cathy Levens*

Air Force cadet Mark Dostal and his instructor were killed in 1995 when Dostal's T-3 trainer (pictured here) spun into the ground. Prior to this crash, the Air Force removed parachutes from these aircraft. *Shirley Dostal*

Army crew chief Robert Rogers stands beside his Black Hawk helicopter unaware that its right engine is defective. The Army knows that the power plants in these helicopters have failed 150 times before, but they have delayed fixing the problem. Not long after this photo was taken, Rodgers and three others were killed when the right engine failed and they crashed into the Mediterranean. *Allen Rogers*

Navy instructor pilot Lt. Mark Sharp stands beside his T-2. When his student botches a take-off, both men eject. Sharp will die because of the plane's obsolescent ejection seat. He is the twenty-seventh victim of this problem, but he won't be the last. *Stan Sharp*

Army Black Hawk gunner Tony Bass was killed in the 1994 friendly-fire incident over Iraq. His father, Cleon, resigned his Air Force commission after suspecting a cover-up in the investigation. *Cleon E. Bass, Sr.*

Army corporal Lance Fielder was killed by friendly fire during the Gulf War. During Senate hearings, Fielder's parents learned how the Army had covered up the mishap. *Deborah S. Harris*

An M-2 Bradley Fighting Vehicle. During the Gulf War, 77 percent of all U.S. armored vehicles damaged or destroyed were hit by friendly fire. The Bradleys, in particular, tended to explode because the on-board fuel and ammunition were not properly protected from hostile fire. *Department of Defense*

A B-52 pilot known for his reckless flying, but still permitted to fly, loses control of his bomber and crashes, narrowly missing a school and a nuclear weapons storage facility. *U.S. Air Force*

An F-16 caused a horrendous accident at Pope Air Force Base in North Carolina after colliding with a C-130 cargo plane. The F-16 glanced off the C-130, crashed into the ramp, and exploded in a giant fireball. The F-16 pilots ejected in time, but the jet's flaming wreckage engulfed two parked C-141 transports (one pictured here), as well as hundreds of nearby Army paratroopers. One hundred GIs were injured, and twenty-four others died. *U.S. Air Force*

Lt. Kara Hultgreen, the Navy's first female fighter pilot, standing beside an A-6 jet, a type that she had successfully flown from land bases for years. *Gloria Ferniz/San Antonio Express News*

Hultgreen crashed into the ocean when a defective engine valve failed while she was attempting to land an F-14 on an aircraft carrier. In the photo, the wreckage of her jet is on a salvage barge. *U.S. Navy*

Commerce Secretary Ron Brown (second from right) standing in front of the Air Force CT-43 jet that would crash and take his life in the former Yugoslavia in 1996. This aircraft (a military version of the Boeing 737) lacked modern navigation and safety devices. Also, the pilots on this mission had not received required Crew Resource Management training. *Associated Press*

Secretary Brown's plane hit the side of a mountain near Dubrovnik while landing in bad weather, killing all 35 people aboard. The accident report admits that crew training deficiencies were a factor in the crash. *Associated Press*

T. Sgt. Thomas Mueller was a talented F-15 mechanic. He and another Air Force sergeant were working on an F-15 control system when they incorrectly connected two identical-looking control rods. This design-induced error caused a fatal accident. The service was determined to convict the two hapless sergeants of negligent homicide, but a distraught Mueller took his own life. *Peter Mueller*

Navy gunners mate Clayton Hartwig pictured with cannon shells for the 16-inch guns aboard the battleship *Iowa*. When poor maintenance, defective gunpowder, and a host of other problems caused the *Iowa*'s massive gun turret explosion, the Navy tried to use Hartwig as a scapegoat. Further investigation produced extensive evidence to the contrary. *Kathy Hartwig-Kubicina*

Capt. Amy Svoboda was the Air Force's first female fighter pilot to die. She is seen standing beside her A-10, which had been modified for night attack missions. But the Air Force had not installed modified cockpit lights for use with night-vision goggles. This unmodified instrument panel, which was difficult to read while wearing the goggles, contributed to her becoming spatially disoriented during a night mission. She crashed, and the accident report blamed the mishap on pilot error. *Sharon Svoboda*

The USS *Vincennes* enters port. In 1988, this highly automated guided missile cruiser's crew was engaged in a battle with several gunboats in the Persian Gulf. The captain became confused when an aircraft approached his ship, and his crew failed to relay critical radar information. The *Vincennes* accidentally shot down an Iranian Airbus airliner, killing 290 Islamic pilgrims. *U.S. Navy*

A nuclear sub performs a rapid surfacing maneuver. U.S. submarines have sunk three civilian ships while surfacing, most recently when the USS *Greeneville* collided with the Japanese fishing vessel *Ehime Maru*. *U.S. Navy*

Marines parachute from a V-22 Osprey. The Marine Corps desperately wants to buy a fleet of these tiltrotor aircraft to replace many of its helicopters. The V-22 is expensive and mechanically complex. It is fast, too, but it suffers from a number of problems, including dangerous aerodynamic idiosyncrasies, high maintenance requirements, hydraulic system problems, and software glitches. *U.S. Navy*

The first of four V-22 crashes that have claimed a total of thirty lives. In this case, a wiring problem in the aircraft's flight-control system caused the test pilot to loose control. Deficiencies in the aircraft design and testing eventually caused the Pentagon to rethink the program's viability. *CBS 60 Minutes*

Evidence suggests that American troops were exposed to potentially deadly biological and chemical agents during the Gulf War when Iraqi munitions stockpiles were destroyed. Some of the military's protective suits were defective, while some troops were not wearing protective gear at all. Thousands of Gulf War veterans have reported health problems that may be linked to this exposure. *Department of Defense*

Pvt. William Leland III (left) on his way to a parachute jump. Private Leland was killed on a training mission when his parachute failed to open. Just hours before his fatal jump, President Clinton told military leaders that reducing the number of personnel killed in mishaps must become a priority. *William Leland II*

13

One of the Boys

Tuesday, October 25, 1994, will be a watershed day for military safety. The sun is shining on stately brick residences with their manicured lawns at Fort Myer, in northern Virginia. Here, not far from Arlington National Cemetery, the Army provides living quarters for the Pentagon's top officers. These homes are also less than a mile from the spot where Lieutenant Tom Selfridge crashed decades earlier.

The lieutenant's accident occurred when a propulsion failure threw his aircraft out of control. On the other side of the republic, another young aviator will perish this afternoon in a similar fashion. Like Tom Selfridge's tragic death, this accident also will be a first. Today's victim is another young lieutenant who will soon join Selfridge in Arlington and in footnotes of history books. Today's accident will claim the life of America's first *female* fighter pilot.

This day is also a very special occasion for one of the living residents of this historic post. In front of his bedroom mirror, the Air Force chief of staff smiles with pride as he dons his new, deep blue, service dress uniform. His wrinkled grin is understandable, because General Merrill McPeak has personally designed this expensive uniform.

It replaces the more traditional Air Force "service dress blues," and this officer, for one, is delighted with the suit's fetching appearance. Of course, every member of his service has to replace his or her wardrobe, but that is a small price to pay for serving under such a visionary leader. Besides, much of the expense will be covered by the taxpayers.

These new outfits will look great at the general's retirement. That ceremony will be held this afternoon at nearby Andrews AFB in Maryland. There, flags will fly, bands will play, and the assembled troops wearing those new uniforms will breathe a collective sigh of relief with McPeak's departure. During his three-year tenure, this general has certainly been a controversial figure. Underpaid troops having to buy new wardrobes are the least of this service's worries.

Under McPeak, the mishap rate has dramatically increased.[1] No one is sure how the Air Force is going to pay for his "composite wing"[2] idea, and expert maintainers are departing in droves after he decimated their career field.[3] Meanwhile he has gladly agreed to support America's ever-growing number of commitments. He has even canned a phrase for this effort: "Global power, global reach."

Our general was also never one to withhold his views on important aviation issues. For instance, he has suggested that women should *not* be allowed to fly combat aircraft. But he has had less to say about that topic since President Clinton picked a woman to serve as secretary of the Air Force. This new boss apparently does not share the general's view on that issue, and neither does Congress, which lifted the ban on women in combat in 1993.

One mile away from the general's quarters, a white truck is pulling up to a massive five-sided limestone building. A postal worker will haul several gray bags marked "U.S. Mail" to its busy post office. In one bag, there are two overstuffed Priority Mail envelopes from Albuquerque, New Mexico.

These parcels are addressed to Pentagon offices of Secretary of Defense William Perry and Secretary of the Air Force Sheila Widnall. The arrival of these envelopes with my whistle-blowing information has been timed to ensure this less than popular general will have already departed his post—going quietly into the sunset, and hopefully, oblivion.

These packages contain information on the many unnecessary mishaps that happened on McPeak's watch. His predecessor had to be fired for inappropriate remarks about bombing Saddam Hussein's mistress. Thus, I felt it prudent to wait for this day, because the Air Force, with its thousands of hardworking troops, did not deserve another black eye for its leadership problems. Furthermore, a lame-duck chief of staff focusing on trying to refute such charges could actually put these folks at risk in such perilous times.[4]

Three thousand miles away, in the bowels of the aircraft carrier USS *Abraham Lincoln*, Lieutenant Kara Hultgreen is donning her greenish-gray flight suit. This majestic gray warship is cruising fifty miles off the coast, near San Diego, California. The young lady feels that October 25 is just going to be another exciting day of honing her skills as a naval aviator. She is looking forward to soon completing her carrier qualifications and deploying as America's first female fighter pilot.

Many of her male shipmates, however, share McPeak's views on female aviators. They see her as a token figure rushed through some of the world's most dangerous flight training, simply as a public-relations gesture. To them she is just part of the Navy damage-control package designed to silence critics. Many of these officers believe she would not be allowed into this last bastion of male supremacy if it were not for the Tailhook Association debacle three years ago.

Furthermore, some members of her squadron would not mind one bit if something happened and she washed out of the program. These hotel hooligans have not given up; they've just gone underground—into the Abe's wardrooms and workspaces. But everyone aboard this vessel also knows the Navy brass would like her to finish with flying colors. It's widely rumored that they want to beat the Air Force in graduating the first female fighter pilot.

The always-jocular lieutenant just wants to be one of the boys and fly jets for her country, nothing more. This young woman knows she is a symbol for all who believe she should have the freedom to follow that dream. But she is a little naïve about the whisper campaign raging below the decks of this ship whose namesake was assassinated because he stood for freedom.

Hultgreen confidently dons her white helmet, carefully tucking in her curly, windblown auburn hair as she steps onto the Abe's vast flight deck. This lady is convinced that she has earned the right to be here. She's paid her dues by three years of flying the Navy's more docile A-6 fighter-bomber from shore bases. Now it's her turn to check out in its super-fighter, the F-14.

This lady is all business today as she examines her Tomcat. This sleek aircraft was designed to fly and fight more than twice the speed of sound while spitting guided missiles at enemy aircraft. Its Sunday punch is the thirteen-foot-long Phoenix missile, which can destroy enemy aircraft at a range of sixty miles. Two pairs of these deadly weapons are normally mounted flush on pallets along the underside of the fuselage. Such firepower makes this bird of prey the ultimate fighter. But its design is unique in other ways.

The F-14 has twin afterburner-equipped engines that produce more than twenty thousand pounds of thrust apiece. But these power plants are *not* located directly beside each other as they are on other jets. Instead they are ten feet apart, embedded on the edges of its wide fuselage. The craft's giant wings are also unusual because they fold aft for supersonic flight but are swung forward during takeoffs and landings.

Its highly sophisticated radar and missile control systems also require a second person, who sits several feet behind the pilot. This other vital crew member is called a radar intercept officer (RIO). These two people must closely coordinate their respective tasks to safely fly this demanding jet. At no time is this more critical than during a landing aboard the carrier, for this aircraft is the largest fighter currently used by the U.S. military. Hultgreen has remarked that flying the F-14 is like "dancing with an elephant."[5]

She begins looking across the deck for F-14 number 03, which she will be flying today. She soon spots her jet by the black numbers painted on each of the bird's dull gray twin tails. She notes it's equipped with the standard fuselage drop tanks, which contain additional fuel for its thirsty engines. But as the lieutenant continues her preflight inspection of jet number 03, she discovers this is *not* a standard Tomcat.

She carefully examines a Rube Goldberg contraption hanging under her jet's belly, just behind the nose wheel. This location is where the two forward Phoenix missiles normally ride. These sleek missiles are mounted flush against the fuselage to minimize the airflow disruption. The idea is to limit the size of protuberances, which always generate performance-robbing "parasitic drag."

The ungainly looking apparatus is actually two sets of bomb racks designed to allow the Tomcat to drop bombs as a secondary mission. She notes this decidedly un-aerodynamic collection of struts, brackets, and braces protruding into the slipstream must hurt performance.

She remembers the relatively few F-14s that have these ungainly racks are disparagingly called Bombcats. Although there is no ordnance on 03's racks, for some reason she has been assigned to fly *this* particular jet today. The lieutenant has little time to think about this as she and her RIO board the craft.

She is glad to be flying with one of the squadron's sharpest RIOs today. Lieutenant Matthew Klimish has previously helped other pilots check out in Tomcats, and he is often assigned to fly with VIP pilots who visit the squadron. At 2 P.M. they are catapulted into the salty Pacific air to begin their training sortie. One hour later they return to the boat and enter the landing pattern.

Everything goes smoothly as pilot Hultgreen and RIO Klimish pass downwind abeam of the ship. They zoom past on the left side of the massive vessel traveling in the opposite direction. Their F-14's wings are in the forward position, and its landing gear, flaps, and tail hook are all down. The jet is thus "properly configured" for landing as she checks in with the landing signal officers (LSOs).

These flying officers are positioned on the aft left (or "port side") corner of the carrier deck. LSOs carefully watch every aspect of each approach and landing. It is their job to help talk aviators down by advising them of errors or deviations. They also grade every landing. There is very little margin for error in this business.

As the F-14 crosses directly behind the Abe's stern, Hultgreen holds the control stick to the left and the fifty-four-thousand-pound fighter responds by banking in that direction. During this sweeping left arc, Klimish reminds Hultgreen about her speed: "You're five knots fast."[6] While this is only six miles per hour too fast, she eases the jet's twin throttles back to slow down the craft.

An almost imperceptible "pop" is heard as the jet continues its left turn. But what neither crew member realizes is that the jet's left engine has a critical valve that is sticking. This malfunction will later figure in the accident chain. Meanwhile, Hultgreen has slowed the jet, and Klimish calmly announces she's "on speed."

But another problem soon appears when Lieutenant Hultgreen realizes her turn is not steep enough. Distracted, she has somehow allowed the jet to overshoot its intended course. Now she has to quickly get it headed back toward the ship.

She then commits a rookie error in trying to increase her turn rate by pushing on the left rudder pedal rather than by increasing the bank angle to the left with the control stick. Basically this causes the jet's nose to move left and forces it to "yaw" or skid sideways through the air. This is a *very* dangerous move at low speeds.

When any aircraft starts to yaw, even slightly, it is literally flying through the air crooked. This disrupts the airflow, which is forced to travel across the fuselage and other structures. As a consequence, parasitic drag increases immensely. It's like riding the brakes on a car. The RIO from his backseat cannot tell what is causing the problem but calmly informs the pilot of what needs to happen. "We're ten knots slow, let's get some power on the jet!"

Hultgreen immediately starts to add power, but now there is another *major* problem. The stuck valve, coupled with yawed condition, has disrupted the smooth flow of air into the left engine. Now the massive bomb racks, which hang down in front of this downwind engine's air scoop, are disrupting the airflow into the ailing left power plant.

Aerodynamically, it is choking and not producing the full power needed to balance the twenty thousand pounds of thrust coming from the right engine ten feet away, which by now is in afterburner. As Mr. Wright and Lieutenant Selfridge first discovered eight decades ago at Fort Myer, any propulsion imbalance at low speeds can quickly lead to a loss of control.

Hultgreen now slams her right foot all the way forward on that rudder pedal while she simultaneously rolls the jet wings-level with a quick right stick movement. Now, directly in front of her windshield lies the eighty-thousand-ton "iron island" looming larger by the second.

But in her understandable excitement, she has also violated another cardinal rule when she allows the nose of her jet to begin rising high above the horizon. She is supposed to keep it at a lower "angle of attack" to allow the massive jet to accelerate quickly. Time to salvage this situation rapidly expires.

The LSOs watch this sequence unfold and quickly respond by transmitting the code word "Wave-off!" This is verbal shorthand saying: "Don't try to land, but go around now!" This command is repeated and followed by a series of others: "Raise your gear ... power ... power ... power ... " and finally, "*eject, EJECT!*"[7] But the command is to no avail, because the F-14 has begun a violent wing over and is headed for the water. Lieutenant Hultgreen's elephant has lost its footing.

"Dumbo's" death dance has begun, and Lieutenant Klimish isn't going to wait to see how it ends. This backseater's keen survival instinct tells him there is barely enough time to escape. He yanks the yellow-and-black handle on his ejection seat. This rocket-powered seat responds a nanosecond later.

The RIO's ejection seat begins to clear the dying jet just as the F-14's left roll angle reaches 90 degrees and its nose has dropped to 10 degrees below the horizon. The aircraft is now only sixty-five feet above the waves. Klimish's parachute will snap open just before he hits the water.

The jet's dual-sequenced ejection mechanism has been selected earlier, so the pilot's seat will automatically be fired exactly four-tenths of a second later. But even this brief interval is too long. By the time Hultgreen's seat has fired, the jet has rolled to more than 110 degrees. It's now in a 25-degree nose-down attitude and a mere fifty-five feet above the water.

Lieutenant Kara Hultgreen's dreams of becoming the Navy's first female fighter pilot will end at one minute past 3 P.M. when she hits the water at 160 miles per hour. While her crew mate will be quickly rescued by helicopter, her lifeless body and her jet will slowly drift downward in a kind of submerged ballet.

They both come to rest in thirty-eight hundred feet of water less than three hundred feet apart. The pregnant pachyderm has landed upright on its three landing gears. Also touching the sandy ocean floor are its extended tail hook and the bomb rack protuberance hanging from its belly. Hultgreen is still strapped into her ejection seat, her chute unopened.

By then, the sun is setting over that limestone building on the Potomac as taps ring out across the tombstones' long shadows in Arlington. Tom Selfridge does not know it yet, but he'll soon have another companion in death, another lieutenant no less. In any case, this terrible Tuesday will prove to be a pivotal day for the Pentagon's concept of safety.

Before her body reaches the ocean floor, phones are ringing in San Diego, Norfolk, and Washington with the news of the accident.

Now the brass will *really* have to scramble to manage the story of this mishap. By tomorrow morning, the detractors will no doubt start with the "I told you so's." The Pentagon spokespersons will have to portray this as a horrible, one-time problem. It has nothing to do with the brass' ideals on gender integration or any other decisions made by one of their untouchables.

Over the months, facts and rumors began to trickle out from the usually twin military investigations. The spin that the Navy brass wants to put out on the crash is this: The late Lieutenant Hultgreen was an excellent aviator who was just one of the boys, going through the standard checkout when, wouldn't you know it, she happened to get a jet with a bad motor valve. What a shame. We just did not have enough money to fix these old F-14 engines—end of story. Oh, by the way, did you catch the great funeral we gave her at Arlington? PR guys are very convincing—when the public doesn't have all the facts.

Of course, the insiders knew this was largely window dressing. But it did point to one very *real* problem—the lack of funds to properly maintain the service's aging military aircraft fleet. Unreliable engines were certainly at the forefront of this problem, and the Navy had known about the bad valves for some time.

In fact, there was another problem in that the first of the Tomcats were terribly underpowered. The Navy would have really liked to install bigger engines on the F-14A models while updating the bird's outdated electronics. But the service was broke. It had squandered most of its aircraft budget trying to buy a new stealth bomber, the soon to be infamous A-12.

The *Washington Post* would later do an article calling that aircraft "The Ultimate Stealth Plane,"[8] because it will cost the taxpayers billions and nobody is ever going to see it. The debacle surrounding the A-12 project suggests that military fraud, incompetence, and cover-ups are not limited to their mishap investigations.

The problem was this: The A-12 was too expensive, overweight, and behind schedule, but few people knew this except the auditors who were threatened in order to keep their mouths closed. So when the Cold War ended, then Defense Secretary Dick Cheney announced he would be reviewing all major aircraft acquisition programs, with an eye to canceling those that were unneeded or troubled.

What happened next was one of the most disgraceful episodes in the annals of the Pentagon. The *Post* article cites an IG report in which the former secretary of navy was accused of concealing the A-12 problems.

Up to one thousand of these jets were scheduled to be produced by the low bidders—a consortium of McDonnell Douglas and General Dynamics. "Low" is a relative term here, because the contract was expected to cost almost $100 *billion*. These companies have also been less than fully forthcoming about the jet's growing list of problems.

But when two DoD analysts, Tom Hafer and Debbie D'Angelo, noted the program was in trouble, their bosses were unhappy with these whistle-blowers, to say the least. Their civil service careers were in real jeopardy for their doing the right thing. This was and is standard DoD treatment for speaking up, as the pioneer whistle-blower, Ernest Fitzgerald, points out in his fascinating book *The Pentagonists*.[9]

The work of these in-house auditors indicated the jet was five thousand pounds overweight, two years behind schedule, and the program was $500 million over budget, to date. Their enterprising bosses then refused to let the report go forward to Secretary Cheney. The secretary was so unhappy with these and other shenanigans[10] that he would later cancel the program on January 5, 1991.

The contractors would in turn challenge the legality of his actions and win multibillion-dollar judgments against the government—hence the title of the brilliant *Washington Post* piece.[11] But the immediate trouble for the Navy was that their *other* bomber program, updating the A-6, had been canceled earlier. This was done to come up with the funds for the now defunct A-12.

Translation: Because the Navy no longer has a long-range bombing platform, it must cede this vital deep-strike mission to McPeak's Air Force. There was *no way* that would happen, because this capability was a major justification for keeping the carriers afloat in the post–Cold War era.

So, the Navy brass quickly hatched another backup to the backup plan. The big but not too powerful F-14 fighter would now become a bomber by *simply* adding a few bomb racks. Voilà! Now we have a dual-role fighter, in Pentagon parlance. That was how those pesky racks ended up on Hultgreen's jet.

But the story does not end there. It was not long before those sailors who shared McPeak's views on women in combat leaked a copy of the privileged safety report to the *Navy Times*.[12] The editors of this insider newspaper then put it on the Internet. This safety report was much more enlightening than its sister document, the accident report, which was all the public is ever supposed to see.

The simplistic "it was just a stuck engine valve" theory, central to the accident report, seemed entirely inadequate next to the detailed explanation documented by the "real" investigation and described in the safety report. The latter document, which was never supposed to be seen outside official circles, also blamed Hultgreen's performance.

Of course, bashing her was the underlying incentive for those who would risk their careers, not to mention jail, just to release this privileged report. So, as usual, the Navy brass got more egg on its collective face. But the real problem was not so much what was *in* this report as what was *excluded* from the document.

Mark Thompson wrote a *Time* magazine article about my military safety crusade in May 1995.[13] Shortly afterwards I got a call from reporter Ron Lewis, who writes for the *Air Forces Monthly* magazine and had just done an article on the Hultgreen accident.[14] In a former life he was also a military weapons technician who worked on bomb racks. He asks if I have seen the Navy photo of her F-14 Bombcat wreckage lying on its back dockside at San Diego.

I reply that I have not, but the leaked safety report did not mention anything about the bomb racks being installed on the jet. How interesting, because if present, these drag-producing devices obviously would be a factor in any yawing-type situation. I quickly review the leaked safety report to confirm my recollection. Yes, here's the page where the DoD lists "property destroyed or damaged": One F-14A and its two drop tanks.[15] No mention of any bomb racks.

Three days later, copies of the official Navy photos arrive at my home. As I view these photos of the modified F-14, I cannot believe my eyes. What a piece of junk. Ron Lewis used to work on such equipment, and clearly this was the worst case of a makeshift modification either of us had encountered in our military careers.[16] This meticulous investigative reporter was right about his facts.

Obviously, leaving this information out of the report was no accident. But I wondered just how much the Navy knew about the performance effects of these racks, especially when the bird was in a yawing situation. Even more baffling was the issue of why the Navy didn't even let its own people know about this problem. I, of course, had previously seen many public denials of such things, but this was a rather extraordinary effort at deception. The Navy was obviously *very* sensitive about something. But what?

Two theories came to mind: Perhaps the Navy was so embarrassed by the crash that they didn't want even any internal discussion of how this unsafe design contributed to her death. That's one possibility, but there was another more plausible one that involved the perennial problem of interservice rivalry. Because the Air Force also gets courtesy copies of the Navy safety reports, this rival service would know the Bombcat was not a safe—and therefore not a viable—weapon system.

Armed with such embarrassing documentation, some Machiavellian general, perhaps one who was pushing USAF composite wings as an alternative to aircraft carriers, might just leak this embarrassing information to Congress—a Congress which, incidentally, had just been assured that the F-14 was on its way to becoming an exceptional bombing platform.[17] I decided to suspend judgment until I could get more information on this sad possibility.

I used to teach CRM courses at the Naval Air Test Center at Patuxent River, Maryland, so I inquired with them about whether these racks were adequately tested on the F-14. Bingo! I was told that funding limitations resulted in only abbreviated testing. This was just what I was afraid of.

Unfortunately, such shortcuts are not that unusual. Military modifications to earlier, previously tested aircraft designs nowadays get only minimal evaluations due to funding limitations. This would not be the first time such shortcuts have caused crashes. I remember how the Air Force lost a jet equipped with inadequately tested and modified fuel tanks a few years before.

When I spoke with other people familiar with the early Bombcat's weapons drops and flight tests, I learn some more disturbing things. They felt these jets were much less stable and would buffet (i.e., shake violently) at times with the racks installed. They also said things like "You really have to *respect* these Bombcats," meaning the jet was potentially dangerous.

Another interesting problem was the bomb racks' location. Drag created by these unstreamlined protuberances was well forward on the fuselage. This meant that once the jet started to yaw to the left, the massive drag would rapidly pull its nose leftward in an ever-accelerating manner. The racks' location also disrupted airflow to that engine, reducing its thrust and exacerbating the violent left roll rate. This made the four-tenths of a second difference between Hultgreen's and her RIO's ejection times critical—literally the difference between life and death. Again, this was probably not something the Navy wanted blabbed around.

The bottom line was that the Bombcat was obviously trickier to fly than the standard jet. So that fact inescapably leads to another very ugly question. Why was a rookie like Hultgreen, who had not even completed full carrier qualification, assigned to fly such a jet? This obviously was *not* something the Navy wanted to go into, even in an internal, official-use-only, privileged document.

But this just illustrates a *real* problem for the Navy. Did someone *intentionally* give her this tricky jet in hopes that she would not successfully qualify? There is some circumstantial evidence suggesting this might be the case. There were obviously people who resented her presence.

Some evidence comes from the treatment received by the only other female fighter pilot in Hultgreen's unit. Lieutenant Carey Lohrenz had her flight records stolen by a male officer in her unit who sent them to an organization known for lobbying against women in combat.[18] Even after she had successfully completed the F-14 program, she was removed from Navy flying status. Her commander had decided she was unsafe, while a popular male aviator who'd had a recent crash was immediately returned to flight status, only to be killed in another accident. A Navy IG investigation noted that Lohrenz had been the victim of widespread harassment.

All this suggests that Kara Hultgreen's death was even more tragic than most people realized. But the Navy, investigating itself, did not want to come clean with the American people. She did not just die because of a stuck engine valve, nor because she was incompetent. She died because a complex set of problems that included the Pentagon's policies, funding shortfalls, dishonest contractors, and, just perhaps, some Machiavellian stunts by misguided squadron mates. No one should rest until the whole truth is told about the lady's untimely demise on a black Tuesday.[19]

But she won't be the last female fighter pilot to lose her life because of problems such as poor equipment, high-level intrigue, bad executive decisions, or funding problems. Captain Amy Svoboda died when her A-10 crashed into the Arizona desert during a bombing run on the night of Tuesday, May 27, 1997. She was the first female Air Force fighter pilot to die in a crash. As expected, the service soon announced that "pilot error" was responsible. Like the Navy's investigation of Hultgreen, this investigation also conveniently overlooked some important facts.

The A-10 Thunderbolt II is a purpose-built ground attack jet. Unlike the sleek F-14, this aircraft is designed to fly low, slow, and close to the ground. It's a "mud fighter" with a large, rapid-firing 30-mm cannon in its nose. Two jet engines, sans afterburners, protrude from the back of its slab-sided fuselage. This craft also has heavy titanium armor plate protecting its single-place cockpit and is designed to be highly maneuverable. As a result, it can duke it out with enemy tanks.

The self-effacing folks who fly the A-10 call it the Warthog, for this is one ugly beast. Because this aircraft is not glamorous, the Air Force brass has never taken any interest in the jet. This disinterest would have costly safety consequences.

For instance, the A-10 is the only currently operational jet fighter that does not have a two-place trainer version. That can cause *big* problems for pilots checking out, because there is literally no instructor in the backseat to quickly anticipate and correct dangerous mistakes. The Air Force's earlier decision to skip buying two-seat A-10s now forces the squadrons to come up with "work arounds" for training rookies.

The squadrons have to have the instructor pilot fly in another A-10 "chasing" his student's jet. He must literally try to correct student errors by talking with him on the radio. Obviously, having to fly two jets is very expensive and inefficient, because the students often make mistakes, so missions have to be repeated. But more important, it is simply *unsafe*.

This situation also means that a flight simulator is *absolutely* vital to safely learn to fly the A-10. When investigating a 1988 A-10 crash, I spent a lot of time "flying" the simulator, because there is no two-place jet. As an aviation psychologist, I had to try to visualize what may have caused the pilot to err. While I was finishing my investigation, I heard the simulator was soon going to be retired.

I learned that it was part of the brass' plan to get rid of the A-10. After all, if you eliminate the simulator, the training program will soon follow. Logically, you cannot check out people in a modern jet without a simulator or two-place aircraft. But there was another component to the plan to ditch this unglamorous workhorse.

The Air Staff, the Pentagon generals who run this service, had arranged for a "fly-off" between the sleek F-16 and the stodgy A-10. This drill would conclude that the F-16 was better than the A-10 for close support missions. But an insider who participated in the study informed me how the ground rules were definitely rigged to insure that the F-16 would win.[20] This was just what the brass wanted to hear.

But before the Pentagon could phase out the Warthog, Saddam Hussein made his move into Kuwait. Now there was a desert full of hostile tanks, so in the eleventh hour, they called for Cinderella in armor plate. The titanium slipper fit perfectly as the A-10 destroyed hundreds of Iraqi tanks. Videos of their burned-out hulls littering the desert appeared nightly on TV.

Suddenly this ugly bird was the belle of the ball. That created a bit of a PR problem for the generals who had decided earlier to junk the Warthog. So they reluctantly give her a reprieve. But now there was no money to buy another simulator or to build a few two-seater jets to insure the safety of those rookies who would soon be assigned to fly this jet.

Enter Captain Amy Svoboda, who also just wants to be one of the boys. After graduating from the Air Force Academy and instructing others in T-37 training jets for several years, she has paid her dues. She is now eager to master the techniques needed to fly the A-10. This captain is very adroit at handling jets.[21] The fact that she is a world-class volleyball player may have something to do with her excellent hand-eye coordination.

She will need every bit of these skills, for the Air Force has now decided to have its A-10 pilots wear Night Vision Goggles. NVGs, of course, make the jet more deadly after dark because the pilot can spot many hidden targets. The Pentagon likes to claim it now "owns the night." But these devices can also increase pilot workload. Depth perception and peripheral vision are also definitely limited when using NVGs. These factors decrease the margin of safety in such operations. Furthermore, as noted earlier, a pilot's NVG skills quickly deteriorate when not flying with them regularly.

By May 27, 1997, Captain Svoboda had been away from flying for a few weeks.[22] Without a two-place trainer or simulator, she will have to get "re-current" the hard way—by flying the jet solo. In addition, for this evening's mission she will be wearing NVGs, and it's been forty-five days since she's been tested in their use.

Tonight she's planning to drop five-hundred-pound bombs on a range west of Tucson, Arizona. Illumination flares are supposed to be available to help her identify her targets. They also provide a relatively fixed reference when maneuvering at night.

But there is another problem tonight. Her jet's cockpit lighting system has not been fully modified for use with NVGs. Normally, customized NVG-compatible lightbulbs are installed inside each cockpit instrument. These modifications are needed because glare from the standard instrument lights is too bright and will simply wash out the supersensitive goggles, effectively blinding the pilot.

The Air Force logistics system, which is still reeling from McPeak's organizational experiments and continued cutbacks, is supposed to supply this modified equipment to A-10 squadrons. This expense is simply the *down payment* for "owning the night," as the Pentagon likes to say. But these costly modifications run thousands of dollars per jet.

So instead, the service issues less expensive filters, which are Velcroed over the glass faces of cockpit instruments. But these "cheapo" filters do not work well with one critical instrument, the Attitude Director Indicator.[23] Thus, pilots with these jerry-rigged instruments have to fly with their cockpit lights dimmed, increasing their chances of succumbing to spatial disorientation.

The Air Force is aware of these dangers, because another pilot had to eject from his A-10 more than a year ago after he became disoriented using NVGs in an unmodified cockpit. The service also knows that the Army and Navy, who started using NVG years earlier, have suffered dozen of crashes. But the Air Force ignores these problems and presses on with its A-10 NVG program.

Unfortunately, Captain Svoboda is assigned to a jet that does not have NVG lighting installed on all cockpit instruments. As an Air Force Academy cadet, she majored in human factors engineering, so she knows this is a very dangerous configuration from an ergonomics standpoint, for it drastically increases the probability of her misreading a critical display tonight.

As the mission progresses, she and her wingman take turns diving at the targets while other jets drop illumination flares. On her final bomb run, after "pickling" her weapons, she begins to pull up and rolls to the right to avoid a simulated enemy threat. Captain Svoboda is also eager to see how she did, and the young lady overbanks the jet. A quick peek over her shoulder will reveal how close her bombs came to hitting the target.

This is a mistake, because turning one's head rapidly while wearing NVGs can be disorienting, especially if the peek turns into a stare, because the illumination flares have gone out. Captain Svoboda does not realize it, but she has allowed her A-10 to roll inverted, and she is now headed downward at fifteen degrees.

Another pilot, sensing Svoboda is disorientated, radios for her to "check dive angle."[24] Unaware that she is actually upside down, Svoboda instinctively pulls back on the control stick, intending to climb. This reaction quickly swings her jet's nose further downward. Seconds later, her aircraft explodes as it slams into the darkened desert. She becomes the forty-fifth Warthog pilot to die in a crash.

Captain Svoboda knew this was a dangerous mission but did not appreciate just how much the Air Force had compromised her safety. The links on this safety chain stretch all the way back to the Pentagon, but the service's in-house investigations will look only at her errors. This lady saluted smartly, trusted the system, and launched into the night, never to see the dawn again. Like Lieutenant Hultgreen, she was headed for the history books, an honor she would have gladly forgone.

A certain senior officer who thought women should not be flying fighters might say this distaff duet died in accidents because they were not very skillful. I would remind him that America's ace of aces, Major Richard Bong, also died in an accident. So even a *man* skillful enough to shoot down forty enemy aircraft can become an accident victim. Hultgreen might find it interesting that Bong died almost half a century earlier when his P-80 engine failed on August 6, 1945.[25] No, general, the ladies were in good company, and it was the *system* that took their lives.

14

Anchors Awry

At sea, the captain has always been regarded as the lord and master of his vessel. He is an all-powerful commander whose word is final. Nowhere is the tradition of *not* questioning the skipper's decisions more prevalent than in safety matters. These commanders are aware of the sea's unforgiving nature, so they should be very conscientious about safety. Unfortunately, that is not always the case. Furthermore, when a tragic accident does occur in the air or aboard a vessel, the term used to describe submarine operations applies to all naval arenas—the "silent service."

The egregious problems associated with Kara Hultgreen's fatal mishap were gender related, but unfortunately, such situations are all too common. When it comes to accidental death, the Navy has become an equal opportunity employer. This code of silence insures that the same kinds of nautical disasters will continue to occur. Several classic catastrophes alone have caused hundreds of deaths.

One such event occurred late in the evening of January 25, 1987, aboard the super carrier USS *Nimitz* as she cruised off the coast of unfriendly Libya.[1] During the Cold War, the U.S. kept tabs on the Soviet vessels sailing in waters around "Gadhafi-land." Ever since our fleet was caught unprepared at Pearl Harbor, America has decided to constantly spy on potential adversaries. To do this special "elint" (i.e., electronic intelligence), aircraft were stationed aboard aircraft carriers operating in foreign waters.

At 7 P.M., a gray-colored EA-3 Skywarrior covered with antennas of every description is catapulted into a pitch-black Mediterranean sky.[2] This massive aircraft is crammed full of electronic eavesdropping equipment. The back-end crew consists of a navigator and five electronic specialists, including linguists who speak Arabic and Russian. At the controls of this flying listening post is an inexperienced young pilot. The young man is very apprehensive, not about tonight's mission, but about the landing he must make in a few hours. And for good reason.

At eighty-two thousand pounds fully loaded, the EA-3 is as big as a bomber and accordingly is nicknamed the Whale by those who have to fly her. In fact, this twin-engine aircraft is one of the largest carrier-based jets. The EA-3 is therefore arguably the most difficult type aircraft to land aboard the "boat." Furthermore, flying around in circles while your crew eavesdrops on the bad guys is not very glamorous. It has been said that no pilot has "ever" volunteered for a Whale assignment.

As noted earlier, all carrier landings are exciting, even under the best of conditions. When the Navy studied heart rates of its flyers during the Vietnam War, it learned something interesting. Pilot heart rates were actually higher when they were landing aboard the carrier than when they were under fire in combat.[3]

Stress and the resulting anxiety are always present during carrier landings, but this anxiety is understandably elevated when flying in larger jets. Furthermore, stress is always much higher during night carrier landings. Many experts feel that landing a Whale on the carrier at night is probably the most demanding thing asked of aviators. Not surprisingly, the EA-3's mishap rate was twice that of other Navy jets.[4]

Amazingly, because the Navy cannot get experienced flyers to volunteer, it has decided to draft neophytes. This practice is not unlike the old nautical practice of "press ganging"—kidnapping people from the waterfront when a sailing ship was shorthanded. Thus, these "nuggets," so-called because of their shiny new gold wings, go right from flight school to this most dangerous of assignments. As mentioned earlier, safety obviously is *not* a priority for the fleet.

No one knows this better than Lieutenant Alan Levine, who is at the Whale's controls tonight. But he is also aware of something else. Although he finished near the top of his class in flight school, he has never mastered the very considerable techniques needed to smoothly land this slippery fish.

Because of these deficiencies, he had been grounded when he was previously stationed aboard the USS *Kennedy*. But the fleet desperately needs "Whale drivers," so this pilot has been returned to flying status. Now, the senior officers aboard the *Nimitz* are going to make a man out of him—whatever it takes.

At 10:40 P.M., Levine makes his first landing attempt. He peers at the dim lights on the carrier's gently pitching deck and heads for her stern. The ship is doing almost thirty miles per hour, and he has to catch one of four steel cables stretched across this miniature airport. The landing signal officers (LSOs) stationed at the edge of the deck are in radio contact, and they know all about this lieutenant's problems. He repeatedly makes approaches that are too high, too fast, and overpowered.

As a consequence, instead of slamming the jet's wheels firmly on the deck and letting the tail hook catch a wire, he tends to let the jet drift over the wires and gently touch down in the area beyond. Instead of pulling a wire out while coming to a screeching halt, the jet rapidly "bolts" back into the air as the pilot pushes up the throttles and goes around for another attempt at landing. Such missed landings are called "bolters," and every pilot does one occasionally.

His second landing attempt ends the same way. At 10:55, he does another bolter on his third attempt. On top of everything, Levine's fuel supply is beginning to get low. He reports he is down to four thousand pounds of fuel. His pucker factor is off the scale.

When I flew as a Navy psychologist, I often spoke with instructor pilots and LSOs, as well as their skippers. They told me you rarely pushed a pilot beyond three landing attempts. The reason was obvious; the pilot's flying abilities were most likely going to decrease with further attempts.

He or she just becomes more erratic. They may even panic and try to dive for the deck and hit the back of the ship instead. These experts said that after three bolters at the boat, you try to send them "back to the beach." Translation: Unless you are in the middle of the ocean, just let them go back and land at a regular airport and try again tomorrow. These operators were describing something that psychologists often study, the relationship between stress and human performance.

The shrinks call this phenomenon the "Yerkes-Dodson Law."[5] This is a bell-shaped curve depicting this important relationship. It shows that for a given task, as stress or arousal increases, performance also increases—up to a point. But performance eventually peaks at the optimal level of stress. After this, as stress further increases, it just *reduces* performance. Laymen have a term for this part of the curve—panic.

At this point, the EA-3's fuel situation is such that it would be prudent to have Levine top off from one of two tankers that were theoretically kept ready for just such contingencies. To rendezvous with a tanker for an aerial refueling is not exactly a walk in the park, but hopefully it will at least take his mind off his landing problems for a few minutes.

Unfortunately, the first tanker's hose mechanism jams, so Levine can't get his gas from this guy. The officers aboard the *Nimitz* now order the backup tanker to be launched. But they soon discover that somebody on the deck crew has failed to get the jet ready. Unfortunately, it is located in the middle of a flight deck parking jam. Thus, it cannot be repositioned to the catapult in time to get to our fuel-challenged EA-3.

Everyone is getting seriously concerned. The *Nimitz*'s senior officer directs that Levine attempt a fourth and then fifth landing. It is now 11:12, and his fuel is down to nineteen hundred pounds. Seems the Whale's thirsty engines are sucking up the kerosene like a pig at the slop trough. At this point, the commander decides it's time to take drastic action.

He orders a rarely used "crash barricade" to be installed across the carrier's deck. This emergency device resembles a tennis net on steroids. It is supposed to be twenty feet high once erected. As the name suggests, it is designed to insure that a disabled aircraft will be caught in the nylon netting as it rolls underneath the towering top-cable.

The installation process is only supposed to take a few minutes. But shortly after he orders the barricade erected, the senior officer is told about another problem. The deck crew cannot find a critical part needed to hold the top cable in the fully extended position. Without this missing fitting, the barricade is only twelve and a half feet tall, and the Whale's massive nose is nearly that high. And that assumes Levine can get his nose wheel quickly planted on the deck, something he has struggled with all evening.

The officer in charge decides to tell the pilot only that there is a "delay problem" with the barricade. Thus, the pilot is not aware he has only a two-foot margin to successfully hit this sagging net. The commander apparently does not want to further upset the already rattled lieutenant.

Meanwhile, Levine has been thinking. He sees the rescue helicopter hovering beside the *Nimitz*. Experts tell me that when this type jet gets down to less than one thousand pounds of fuel, the crew is normally *ordered* to abandon their aircraft. Levine is down to eight hundred pounds of fumes when he requests permission to initiate bailout procedures. There is a tone of desperation in his voice.

He does not have to wait long for his answer. "Negative, negative. You *will* land your plane on the ship,"[6] comes the order from the *Nimitz* commander. This young pilot's flight suit is soaked with perspiration as he hears these dreaded words. As a naval officer, he has to obey these orders.

Now the die is cast as a mortified Lieutenant Alan Levine makes his final approach. Just like his five other attempts tonight, he's high and hot. The LSOs at first try to calmly talk him down. But as they realize he is not responding, they also begin to panic, while repeatedly shouting the command for him to "cut." This term is a directive. It means, "Pull your throttles all the way back to idle, and pray you catch a wire."

In the darkness, the giant gray jet swoops across the ship's stern, and its elevated nose overrides the sagging barrier. The Whale instantly cuts the steel cable running across the top of the nylon netting. Its nose gear is bent backwards. The seventy-two-thousand-pound craft then crushes this flimsy barricade under its massive belly like a vengeful Moby-Dick stomping Captain Ahab.

After the jet breaks through the net, Levine is just another passenger as he helplessly mashes the toe brakes located on top of each of his rudder pedals. The wounded Whale then races down the length of the ship's steel deck trailing a shower of sparks as its aluminum underbelly grinds away. This spectacular rending of the lower fuselage and its antennae begin decelerating the jet.

By the time the damaged jet reaches the front of the deck, it has slowed to a crawl. So as the Whale's nose drops over the ship's bow, its tail pivots upward. The aircraft then plunges sixty feet into the dark waters. And like mythical Moby-Dick, she soon breaches the surface while dozens of stunned sailors watch in amazement from the *Nimitz* decks.

The sailor with the best view is Jeff Wiget, who is the rescue special-ist aboard the chopper that has been standing by during this airborne ordeal. This eager skin diver has been in his wet suit ever since the problems began. He now positions himself in the chopper's open door, waiting for the orders to jump.

He watches the EA-3 floating beside the *Nimitz*. The fuselage is all but submerged with its vertical fin sticking high out of the water. The rescue helicopter is hovering forty feet overhead, illuminating the hulk with its powerful spotlight. The eerie picture looks like a scene out of the movie *Jaws*, except this fish is not moving.

As the minutes go by, Wiget scans the water for signs of life. He knows there are undoubtedly several badly injured sailors in the partially submerged fuselage. Wiget has been trained to rescue people in just such situations and cannot wait to jump into the water.

But his boss, the helicopter aircraft commander, won't let him go to work. Incredibly, the *Nimitz*'s top officer is telling him *not* to let his crew members go to the aid of the downed airmen.[7] Wiget cannot believe his ears, but the point becomes moot because fewer than ten minutes later, the Whale and its human cargo slip beneath the waves.

It is headed for the bottom of the Mediterranean two miles below while the *Nimitz* sails away from the area with a crew saddened by this tragic loss of their shipmates. Explaining the preventable catastrophe *should* have been a major concern for those senior officers who bungled this situation. But they are not worried—for good reason. This is the "silent service," and nobody important is going to hear about this eve-ning's errors. Or so they think.

In fact, three days will pass before the families are even notified that their loved ones were "lost at sea." Sounds like their kids were "mis-placed in the Med." Months will pass before the Navy releases its *official* accident report. As usual, it blames the crash on "pilot error." A fallen knight's silence is ensured. Furthermore, it describes the chain of worker-bee errors and material problems that contributed to this tragic accident.

However, it is intentionally vague about the mistakes by the top officers. Several important issues are not really addressed, for obvious reasons. Questions like: Why did the Navy put inexperienced aviators in these hard-to-fly jets? Why wasn't Levine sent back to land at an airport after his first few bolters? Why was the crew not allowed to bail out? Why were the rescuers not allowed to approach the floating aircraft?[8]

Such questions, of course, involve issues the Navy is not willing to investigate, because the answers would hurt the career of one of its untouchables. I was told that the officer who was in charge that night had friends in high places. This captain made sure the heads of this underlings rolled for their errors, but no one held him accountable for his flawed decision making. In fact, he was soon promoted to admiral.

Normally, that is where stories like this one would end. But the Navy has video cameras that are designed to record everything that happens on its carrier flight decks. Like the Rodney King situation, there is nothing like a good video to get things rolling. Fortunately, somebody with a lot of courage and integrity smuggled the tapes of the crash sequence off of the *Nimitz* and sent them to a reporter.

Kristina Rebelo writes for the well-known television show *Hard Copy*. She was so shocked at what she saw that she called me, as well as the families of the seven victims. This show aired the graphic crash videos several times to a national audience in February 1995. The message was unmistakable—the Navy is not telling the whole truth about this disaster.

Then on October 1, 1995, Arnold Abrams did a comprehensive piece for Alan Levine's hometown newspaper, the *Sunday Newsday*[9] on Long Island, New York. This article involved interviews with witnesses, such as would-be rescuer Seaman Wiget, and relatives of the hapless victims. Their passionate words cry out for answers. After all, they have had to endure years of knowing there was some kind of cover-up going on.

The navigator's wife, Lyn Callender, said of the official accident report, "It was a waste of paper, obviously intended to get everyone off the hook."[10] The pilot's mother remarked that "It was so wrong for them to say Alan was responsible for the deaths of six other men."[11] She opined that the families just want the "truth."[12] But their pleas were in vain, for nobody in the Navy was about to criticize one of their new admirals or the system, which protects people like him. But I tell the families that as bad as this cover-up is, I have actually seen worse.

Certainly one of the worst cases involved an incident on April 19, 1989, aboard the battleship *Iowa*, which was taking part in a gunnery exercise. It had been forty-six years since this battlewagon narrowly escaped an accidental torpedoing during another gunnery exercise. That time, she happened to have a few important visitors on board—she was transporting the president and the entire joint chiefs of staff to the Tehran Conference.[13]

On this day in 1989, there are no real dignitaries on board, just one visiting admiral and hundreds of hardworking sailors. But not all these grunts will be around when the ship's bugler plays taps this evening, for something will go terribly wrong in her number-two gun turret as this historic ship steams three hundred miles north of Puerto Rico.

The USS *Iowa* is getting old: her design is a relic of World War II, and some of her ammunition dates back to before the Korean War. Meanwhile, her people are mostly youngsters from the Reagan military buildup era. These are patriotic kids who heard the "It's not just a career, it's an adventure" recruiting pitch and signed on to fight the Evil Empire, or at least keep it at bay. Actually, the Soviets do not have much to fear from this vessel. It is better suited to practicing gunboat diplomacy against troublesome Third World opponents.

In fact, many experts think the *Iowa*—and the other three dreadnoughts that President Reagan and Navy Secretary Lehman have brought out of mothballs—is largely symbolic, a $2 billion investment to signal that the American military is back from the abyss of Vietnam and ready to take on all comers.

While it has some modern weapons, such as cruise missiles, this vessel's trademark weapons are her nine mighty sixteen-inch cannons. These unique guns are mounted three to a turret, with two turrets forward and one aft. The huge weapons are capable of hurling a twenty-seven-hundred-pound projectile more than twenty miles with pinpoint accuracy.

These guns are also unique in another way: the projectile is separate from the propellant. This propellant comes from up to six individual 110-pound cloth gun-powder bags. These bags are loaded into the breech after the projectile is pushed up into the giant gun's barrel. A large hydraulic piston is used to push both the projectile and powder bags into the gun's breech. This piston is controlled by a sailor seated in the so-called gun room, who must carefully "ram" these items into the barrel.

Obviously, this is a very delicate and dangerous procedure. Everything needs to be in good working order to safely operate these massive weapons, which are closely surrounded by an attentive crew and encased in a heavily armored compartment. But as the *Iowa* prepares to fire her guns, not everything is shipshape. Gregory Vistica, in his classic exposé, *Fall from Glory,* describes some of the problems.[14]

The crew is afraid of the ship's ancient electrical system, so they have installed smaller lightbulbs in the gun turrets to keep from blowing fuses. Hydraulic-fluid leaks go unreported for years. Most disturbing of all, the ship's gun-loading system has been known to rip open the cloth ammunition bags and spill the gunpowder.

Other problems are human in nature.[15] It supposedly takes 118 sailors to operate each massive gun turret, but the number-two battery today is short thirty-seven people. Some training records are also missing, so nobody is sure who is fully qualified to do what. Furthermore, most of these fellows are inexperienced, and a few have marginal performance ratings.

One exception is a very well-qualified sailor who is assigned to the top level of this turret, Gunner's Mate Clayton Hartwig. This young man is the "gun captain" and normally stands beside the center cannon. Hartwig has been in the service for six years and aboard the *Iowa* for three of those years.

This sailor is a clean-cut, highly motivated chap who is following in his father's footsteps—another gunner's mate. But he is a little different from most other young sailors. He does not drink or chase women when on shore leave. In fact, he has developed a close friendship with another young sailor, Kendall Truitt, who is assigned to this same turret four levels below, in the ammunition magazine.

Shortly after 9:50 A.M., powder bags are brought up from the storage magazine. They arrive by special elevator to the top level in the turret, the gun room. The left and right cannons are promptly loaded, but there is some difficulty with the center weapon. Seconds pass and a sailor speaking on the intercom says, "I have a problem here. I'm not ready yet."[16]

The next thing heard is the sound of a blast as it rips through the turret's upper levels. This "problem" will literally explode in the faces of these sailors this morning. It will also cause "secondary explosions" all over the Navy.

Many people have questioned the need and cost-effectiveness of continuing to operate these giant vessels. But the Navy brass seems determined to keep these weapon systems afloat. Thus, some plausible explanation must be offered to the public and Congress for this explosion—preferably one that does not address the current problems of these ships.

"What" happened soon became obvious: the powder bags had somehow ignited before the breech of this cannon was closed. Thus, the uncontained explosion, concussion, and fire had blasted through the upper levels of turret number two. This violent explosion with its searing heat had crushed bulkheads while ripping through the hatches connecting various floors of this heavily armored compartment. In the top levels of this nautical Dante's inferno, forty-seven sailors died instantly.

Fire and smoke poured from all the openings in this turret as firefighters sprayed hundreds of gallons of water into the battered and blistered gun battery. Those gallant lads had tried to rescue their injured shipmates from this holocaust, but they also knew they must prevent the ammunition in the magazine, four levels down, from exploding and destroying the whole vessel.

While describing *what* happened was fairly obvious, establishing precisely *why* this blast occurred would be harder. This endeavor should have been a top priority for the Navy, but right from the get-go there were difficulties. First, everyone who had witnessed the "problem" in the gun room was dead. The powerful blast and subsequent fire had also destroyed much of the evidence. Then the firefighters had hosed overboard other potential evidence by washing down the previously burning gun room.

On April 20, the day after the tragic explosion, the Navy announced it was going to investigate itself. It offered the standard pledge of a full and complete investigation. Per the military mishap inquiry protocols, it then assigned a trusted officer to head the investigation.

One Rear Admiral Richard Milligan was given this task. He had experience at commanding a battleship but *not* in conducting a sophisticated accident inquiry. The admiral immediately authorized a complete cleanup of the turret, destroying other critical evidence. This type of mistake was often made by those untrained in the vital techniques of mishap investigation.

That same day, other naval officers drove to the Hartwig home in Cleveland, Ohio. They were there to tell his parents their son was missing and presumed dead. That would not be the last Navy visit to this residence, for officers would soon return, this time to ransack Hartwig's bedroom. These trusting family members had no clue as to what was going on.

The Navy believed Hartwig was a homosexual. It seems the Navy heard Gunner's Mate Hartwig had taken out a $101,000 Navy life insurance policy and named his buddy, Truitt, as the beneficiary.[17] Somehow the Navy concluded that Hartwig *must* have intentionally sabotaged the gunpowder to cause the accident. The service believed Hartwig's psychotic act was precipitated by Truitt's announcement that he was getting married.

Since the Navy also believed homosexuals are mentally unstable, they concluded that Hartwig decided to kill himself and everybody else in the turret, including Truitt, and probably sink the ship. But Truitt survived the explosion and denied any such relationship. Moreover, no suicide note was found, nor a letter home, nor anything else to confirm this bizarre theory. But that did not stop these determined Navy sleuths.

They even concluded that Hartwig had surreptitiously placed a detonator between the powder bags, presumably without anyone else in the gun house seeing him. These clever Navy investigators even *thought* they had detected minuscule traces of foreign substances in the powder residue, which *could* be the remains of this imaginary detonator. Of course, a jillion folks and things were in the compartment before and after the explosion. But that fact did not seem to bother these guys.

But the Navy was sticking to its guns, so to speak, although many insiders were waving the caution flag on this theory. And rightly so, because this evidence was very thin—even for the minimal standards used in military investigations.

There was another problem with this theory. Gunner's Mate Hartwig's body was reportedly *not* found in the gun room, but rather on the deck one level below.[18] The body was also *not* completely charred like everything else in the gun room. Ergo, he was *not* near the powder when he was supposed to have sabotaged it.

Furthermore, an officer assisting with this investigation told me something very interesting. When the Armed Forces Institute of Pathology was getting ready to autopsy the victims, a very senior admiral tried to intervene. He ordered that these postmortem examinations be stopped, because this was a "criminal investigation." Obviously, the admiral did not want these medical examiners to look too closely at Hartwig's body. Fortunately, this courageous medical officer ignored the admiral and performed the required medical procedures.

So *how* did a suicidal homosexual manage to place the detonator between the powder bags when he was not even in the compartment at the time? The short answer was, it did not matter, because the only taste test that this story had to pass was that of the Navy's brass. And they could not be too particular then.

But for other reasons, this theory was just too good to challenge. Hartwig was the perfect scapegoat. He was dead, so he could not protest in a court-martial proceeding. Furthermore, he was only a low-ranking sailor with no connections, just one of those dangerous "queers" who always caused problems in military organizations. It would be another five years before President Clinton would demand an end to harassment of military homosexuals with his "Don't ask, don't tell" policy. Best of all, the Navy's beloved battlewagons were safe, as long as they weeded out *those* kinds of guys.

On September 7, 1989, the Navy announced its findings: Gunner's Mate Clayton Hartwig had *intentionally* caused the explosion, probably because he was despondent over a failed homosexual relationship. End of story. The admirals naïvely thought everything would end when they issued their official report.

But the Hartwig family was incensed and got their fire-breathing congresswoman, Mary Rose Oakar, involved. She and others in Congress were not at all convinced the Navy's self-serving conclusions should go unchallenged. These representatives demanded a *truly* independent inquiry.

Their demands led to a study by the world-renowned Sandia National Laboratories in Albuquerque, New Mexico. This organization had studied high explosives as detonators for nuclear weapons for decades. Their experts could not find traces of the detonator that the Navy investigators had supposedly identified. Instead, they conducted their own tests and proved that excessive pressure *could* ignite the propellant packaged in cloth powder bags.

Thus, accidentally over-ramming the powder bags was a very logical explanation, one that the Navy had ignored. The Congressional General Accounting Officer (GAO) also became involved with this issue. On August 29, 1991, the *Washington Times*[19] quoted the GAO as stating that this was a "previously unrecognized safety problem." But perhaps the best quote came from Congresswoman Oakar: "If the Navy has a shred of honor left, it must do the right thing and admit this was a tragic accident and apologize to the Hartwig family."[20]

After the GAO and Sandia Laboratories reports came out, the Navy was in a bad public-relations bind. Their earlier assertion that Hartwig had "most probably" caused the blast no longer held water.

So the chief of naval operations, Admiral Kelso, held a press conference on October 17, 1991, to admit that they may have been mistaken in blaming Hartwig in their first investigation. The Navy's senior admiral then admitted that the service was now not sure what caused the explosion. However, he stopped short of making a formal apology for all the pain they had inflicted on this sailor's family.[21]

But there was one more piece of evidence, which I was told was being withheld by the Navy. Those cloth bags containing the gunpowder required special storage in temperature- and humidity-controlled warehouses. Otherwise, the chemical composition of the gunpowder would change, making it more susceptible to impact detonation, such as by over-ramming. But such storage facilities were expensive.

These requirements were well known to Navy munitions experts. But what was not revealed was that the old powder aboard the *Iowa* that day might not have been properly stored. I was informed that an admiral had overruled a civilian munitions specialist who demanded *all* such powder be properly warehoused. Apparently the admiral wanted to save money and thought he knew more about such things than his expert. This admiral was not the last senior naval officer to overestimate his own knowledge.

15

High-Tech Holocausts

The Navy's problems do not always involve young men operating old equipment. Sometimes the highly lethal technology is so advanced that *it* is dangerous, often because the service has not taken the time to warn the sailors how things can go terribly wrong. Then, too, sometimes the Navy picks and promotes an excessively zealous commander who really does not understand the technology.

That occurred in 1988 when one of the Navy's newest warships, a guided missile cruiser, was sent to the Persian Gulf. The skipper who the Navy put in command of the ship mistakenly thought he knew exactly what he was doing. His errors in judgment and the "fog of war" would lead to the deaths of hundreds of people and disgrace for the Navy and the nation.

His name was Captain Will Rogers. With his prematurely gray hair and weathered facial features, he resembled his namesake, the laid-back comedian of the 1930s who said, "I never met a man I didn't like." But that is where the similarities ended.

Captain Rogers was a hard charger, the kind of officer the Navy likes to promote. He could not wait to take his ship into harm's way, to confront the Iranians.[1] Like most of his contemporaries, Rogers could still remember how they had desecrated the bodies of the dead Americans after the Desert One fiasco eight years before.[2]

Now the Iranians were at it again. This time they had the gall to challenge the United States Navy to a shootout in Iranian territorial waters during the Iran-Iraq War. The Iranians had laid mines that had badly damaged two American warships. They also had attacked unarmed merchant vessels, which the United States had pledged to protect. Now intelligence reports were suggesting they had something up their sleeves on the day before the Fourth of July.

Captain Rogers commands the USS *Vincennes*, a ship at the other end of the technology spectrum from the Second World War battleship *Iowa*. His ship is crammed from stem to stern with the latest gadgets. It bristles with radar, computers, helicopters, missiles, and automated deck cannons. Its state-of-the-art Aegis electronic brain is named for the magical shield used by the Greek god Zeus. It permits the ship to simultaneously track hundreds of aircraft, missiles, submarines, and surface ships. Because of its heavy reliance on computers, some have dubbed this ship Robocruiser.[3]

Unlike the *Iowa*, which is best suited to engage Third World adversaries, the *Vincennes* is tailor-made to counter the Soviet armada. This superior American technology is expected to allow our sailors to defeat their Russian counterparts on the high seas. Sailors have been paraphrasing a popular beer commercial. "Yes Ivan, this boat's for you."

Unfortunately, this super-cruiser is headed into the confined waters of the Persian Gulf. The Iranian adversary uses hit-and-run tactics with a fleet of small speedboats on this hazy inland sea crisscrossed by commercial shipping and airline traffic. Their tiny vessels are crewed largely by youths armed only with handheld rocket launchers, machine guns—and revolutionary fervor.

But the U.S. Navy, despite its billion-dollar automated warship, will ultimately have to rely on the judgment of commanders like Captain Rogers to make critical, split-second, life-and-death decisions. His duty station is the Combat Information Center (CIC), which is located two floors below the bridge. This is where the arcane electronic data come together and must be deciphered by sometimes-fallible human beings.

The CIC is just a windowless control room. It looks like a video arcade, with more computer screens and people than you can shake a mouse at. Captain Rogers will have three problems when his cruiser steams at flank speed into harm's way: 1) information overload, which will be overwhelming at decision time; 2) poor ergonomics, resulting in some critical pieces of data not being on his computer screens; and 3) the lack of CRM training, for when push comes to shove, this group of specialists will not function as a team.

At 6:33 A.M., Captain Rogers is shaving in his cabin when he gets some exciting news. Another warship, the frigate USS *Montgomery*, has radioed that she has been engaged with thirteen Iranian speedboats. These Revolutionary Guard craft have been menacing a Pakistani merchant vessel near the critical Straits of Hormuz. But now, they've turned toward the American warship, a move out of character for the young disciples of the Ayatollah, who prefer to pick on unarmed merchantmen at night.

The *Montgomery* is forty miles away as Rogers orders "all ahead flank."[4] The *Vincennes*'s four 80,000-horsepower gas-turbine engines whine in protest as they shove the eight-thousand-ton vessel through the tepid waters at more than thirty miles per hour. The officer aboard the Joint Task Force Middle East (JTFME) flagship hundreds of miles away has just authorized this move by radio.

This delights Rogers, who does not want to miss out on the big event. He immediately launches one of his H-60 Seahawk helicopters (the naval version of the Black Hawk) to scout ahead. At 8:18 A.M., Rogers orders his crew to general quarters. This preparation for battle is justified, because his helicopter is reporting the Iranians are now threatening a German merchant ship.

But before the *Vincennes* arrives on scene, an Omani patrol vessel chases the small Iranian boats away. By 8:40 A.M., the JTFME flagship guys are directing the *Vincennes* to leave the area immediately. Obviously, these headquarters wimps want to reduce the level of confrontation.

Rogers is not happy with the new orders. His crew laughs when they hear their skipper sarcastically protest this directive with headquarters. "You want me to do *what?*"[5] While Rogers brings his ship about as ordered, he leaves his helicopter in this hot area to shadow the Iranian speedboats.

The crew of the *Vincennes* soon has bigger fish to fry, as an Iranian P-3 Orion patrol bomber appears on their radarscopes at 9:09. This four-engine aircraft is equipped with deadly Harpoon missiles. The U.S. sold these aircraft to the Shah of Iran, along with F-4 Phantoms and F-14 Tomcat fighters in more congenial times.

Unlike the lightly armed speedboats, these aerial weapons represent a *real* threat to American warships. The *Vincennes*'s crew knows this as they contact the P-3 by radio to warn him not to come within fifty miles of their ship—or else.

The "or else" is the explicit threat to blow him out of the sky with the ship's supersonic Standard SM-2 antiaircraft missiles. The Iranian P-3 crew promptly acknowledges that they understand and will keep their distance. At least these Iranian flyboys know what kind of Navy they are up against.

It is not long before Rogers's attention is diverted back to the speedboats. It seems his Seahawk helicopter has followed Khomeini's kids as they head their boats back to Iranian territorial waters empty-handed. The chopper's Rules Of Engagement (ROEs) require it to stay four miles from the boats.

But when the H-60 pilot closes to within two miles, he provokes the young Revolutionary Guards into taking a few potshots at his minimally armed chopper. At 9:15 he radios the *Vincennes:* "We're taking fire. Executing evasion."[6] This, of course, means that the warship will *have to* come to the aid of its defenseless chopper.

That does not exactly displease Captain Rogers, who barks out commands, "General quarters . . . Full power."[7] In the sterile, darkened Combat Information Center, the men can hear the sounds of battle preparation: boots running across steel decks, watertight doors being slammed shut, the whine of the turbine engines as they spool up.

At 9:40, the quartermaster informs Captain Rogers that they have just crossed the Iranian territorial waters twelve-mile limit. The captain knows they are now technically in violation of international law, but he is unconcerned because he is in a hot-pursuit situation. What are the Iranians going to do, complain to the UN?

Two minutes later, the harried speedboats reverse course and head for the *Vincennes.* Big mistake! Remember, it's the Iranians who are always accusing the Americans of acting like "cowboys." While this is not exactly *Roy* Rogers they're messing with, this particular cowboy does have a pair of guns at the ready—two rapid-firing five-inch automatic cannons.

Captain Rogers has both the Iranian boats and JTFME flagship guys *just* where he wants them. He now "asks" headquarters for "permission" to open fire. These senior officers have no choice but to concur with the on-scene commander when he says the enemy boats are showing "hostile intent." The headquarters types also place the nearby *Montgomery* under Rogers's control for the impending sea battle. This captain has not fired a shot, but the battle is already going his way.

At 9:43, Rogers orders both American warships to start blazing away with their automatic five-inch guns at the small craft. The maneuverable speedboats make difficult targets, and they are also shooting back. Two Revolutionary Guard boats are quickly blown out of the water as Rogers hears incoming bullets bouncing off the sides of his ship.

As the speedboats' helmsmen maneuver to throw off the Americans' aim, another Iranian is also maneuvering. He is Captain Mohsen Rezaian, who is the senior pilot on Iran Air Flight 655. At 9:45, he has just steered his Airbus 300 airliner onto the runway at the Bandar Abbas airport. This airport is fifty-five miles from this ongoing sea battle and is used by both commercial airlines and the Iranian military. In fact, the Iranians have moved F-14s to this airdrome in recent weeks.

Captain Rezaian is in a hurry. He is concerned with trying to make up time because he is running twenty-seven minutes behind his scheduled departure. As usual, he switches his radar transponder on when he taxis the wide-body transport onto the runway.

This giant airliner has 290 souls on board, including sixty-five children, as it climbs out over the hazy Persian Gulf. Captain Rezaian keeps his radios set to frequencies to talk with the Iranian controllers. He is steering his airliner to Amber 59, a civilian airway that crosses the Persian Gulf. This pilot has no way of knowing that Captain Rogers just happens to be maneuvering his warship directly below this same invisible airway. And right now, the sea captain is getting very busy as he is engaged in a gun battle with several armed speedboats.

At 9:47, the powerful radar aboard the *Vincennes* picks up the Airbus transponder as it leaves the runway. Because Iranian fighter planes, including F-14s, are also based at the Bandar Abbas airport, the target is electronically labeled "unknown, assumed enemy."[8] This despite the fact that its transponder is squawking a *civilian* mode. After all, setting a military aircraft's transponder to a civilian mode could be a trick to sneak up on our warships. The airliner is then given an electronic tag that appears on the computer screens in the ship's CIC.

Meanwhile, in the *Vincennes*'s CIC, Captain Rogers overhears crew members discussing other aerial tracks, including another potential fighter track. But before he can sort out all the aircraft information, our cowboy captain is told about another problem. At 9:50, his forward gun has jammed right in the middle of this shootout.

Rogers immediately orders a full-rudder turn to allow his aft gun to have a clear shot at the enemy boats. This vigorous turn causes the massive ship to heel over. Manuals, charts, and other loose objects are thrown off tables as standing sailors grab onto their computer consoles to avoid losing their footing. In a matter of seconds, Rogers hears the reassuring sound of the aft gun mount blasting away at the enemy. In the CIC, Captain Rogers can literally smell the gun smoke as it is drawn into the ship's air-conditioning vents.

The excitement level in the CIC has climbed off the Yerkes-Dodson scale. Captain Rogers soon learns that the aircraft that departed Bandar Abbas airport four minutes earlier is now only thirty-two miles from his ship and closing fast. The ship's radio operators repeatedly transmit warnings: "Unidentified aircraft . . . you are approaching a U.S. naval warship . . . You are standing into danger . . . Request you alter course immediately . . . "[9] But this target continues to bear down on Robocruiser.

At 9:51, Rogers contacts the JTFME flagship to inform headquarters that he believes an Iranian F-14 is approaching his ship. Furthermore, he intends to shoot it down if it gets closer than twenty-three miles. Headquarters concurs but requests that the radio warnings continue to be given.

These warnings continue to be broadcast on emergency frequencies. The ship's company does not realize that the airliner's radios are set to different frequencies. The Aegis radar continues to show the target closing on the *Vincennes*. As the blip crosses the twenty-three-mile point, Captain Rogers hesitates.

At 9:52, instead of launching his missiles, he directs the target be "illuminated" by a beam from the ship's powerful fire-control radar. Fighters always have radar-warning receivers. Such systems tell their pilots when they are about to be hit by an antiaircraft missile so they can immediately take evasive action. Thus, *if* this is a fighter, it should turn.

All eyes in the CIC are on the computer screens as everyone realizes the target is *not* turning. But other possibilities race through the minds of those trapped in this steel and silicon box. What if he's a "Khomeini kamikaze" intent on crashing into the Great Satan's warship—like the suicidal truck driver who took out all those Marines in their Beirut barracks back in 1983?

Meanwhile, some officers in the CIC have begun to wonder about *another* possibility. What if this target is a "comair"—that is, a commercial airliner? They have been searching their schedules but do not see anything listed for this departure time at Bandar Abbas.

That is because this airliner is almost a half-hour late. One officer speaks up and verbalizes his fears: "Possible comair."[10] Hearing this, Captain Rogers gestures with his arm to *silence* him. The crew knows better than to bring this issue up again. The Navy has not yet discovered the value of CRM for sailors.

This captain has also been listening to other background conversations over the CIC's many channels. One involves a discussion about a descending fighter plane. He does not realize that these sailors are describing *another* track. This was a U.S. Navy fighter more than a hundred miles away that the Aegis computer has momentarily confused with Rogers's incoming target. Furthermore, Rogers's screen, unlike regular air traffic controller displays, does not show him the target's altitude. This is a major ergonomics deficiency—but what do you want for a billion bucks?

At 9:53, the worried captain hears another sailor musing aloud: "Goddamn it, he's getting close."[11] Captain Will Rogers reluctantly realizes time has run out, and he knows that somebody is going to die. He decides it is *not* going to be his sailors.

His fingers nervously grasp the overhead key that allows the missiles to be fired. He quickly rotates it to authorize the launches. A missile system controller sees the fire-authorization light illuminate on his console, but he pauses and asks for verbal confirmation before attacking this target. The word quickly comes back: "Yes."[12]

At 9:54, two Standard SM-2 antiaircraft missiles scream off their rails on the forward deck of the *Vincennes*. Their glowing solid-rocket motors quickly accelerate the deadly weapons to supersonic speeds. In seconds they will disappear into the hazy sky overhead trailing white smoke.

Ten miles away, Captain Rezaian is giving a routine position report as his Airbus climbs toward its intended cruising altitude of fourteen thousand feet. The tower tells him, "Have a nice day,"[13] and he responds, "Thank you, good day."[14] Seconds later, shrapnel from the cruiser's missiles rips through the giant jet.

The aircraft will break up as it plunges toward the Persian Gulf. A video camera crew aboard the *Vincennes* captures this distant dot falling from the sky as Robocruiser informs headquarters that it has destroyed the "F-14." Phones soon ring in the Pentagon. People are jubilant that the Iranians have been taught an important lesson.

But within hours, the magnitude of the tragedy is uncovered when Flight 655 does not arrive at its destination. The horrific news is flashed across the globe in the days that follow. TV networks are soon broadcasting pictures of floating bodies of men, women, and children. Their clothes have been literally blown off by the windblast during their two-mile fall. Their naked bodies are tied together beside the speedboats.

When the Iranians soon announce that the "Great Satan" has murdered 290 innocent Islamic pilgrims, the Pentagon spin-meisters have to work fast to counter the adverse publicity. This situation is especially embarrassing because America had been so critical of the Soviets for accidentally downing Korean Airlines Flight 007, a Boeing 747, several years before. Now the bloody shoe is on the other foot.

First, the Pentagon decides that the shoot-down was actually legitimate, because Captain Rezaian and the Iranians deliberately flew over an ongoing sea battle. Our military spokesmen suggest the Iranians were irresponsible and deserve criticism for putting all those passengers at risk. The Pentagon also initially suggests the accident occurred in international waters, when they know the *Vincennes* was actually in Iranian territorial waters.

Though some inside and outside the service thought Captain Rogers had been unnecessarily aggressive in pursuing the speedboats, there never was any serious consideration of blaming him for the shoot-down. Even if he was confused in firing on the aircraft, he was only protecting his troops, and that shall always be the *first* responsibility of any commander.

Besides, the Pentagon disciplined another Navy captain the previous year who *failed* to act quickly enough during an aircraft attack in the

Persian Gulf. His destroyer, the USS *Stark,* was accidentally hit by two Iraqi air-launched cruise missiles, and thirty-seven sailors died.[15] The Iraqi fighter pilot mistook the American warship for an enemy vessel during the Iran-Iraq War.

Furthermore, the Navy learned many years ago that scapegoating a senior officer can backfire. Captain Charles McVay III was the skipper of the cruiser USS *Indianapolis* that transported one of the first atom bombs to the West Pacific during World War II. On the return voyage, his ship was torpedoed and quickly sank. Several hundred sailors were drowned or eaten by sharks. The Navy had not adequately warned McVay about enemy submarine activity along his route and did not launch a timely rescue effort. But after the war, they decided that he would make a good scapegoat to deflect public outrage over the tragedy. The service soon court-martialed and hounded this wrongfully disgraced senior naval officer who later took his own life.[16] Public outrage over this shameful episode resulted in McVay being recently exonerated of these charges.[17]

So when the *Vincennes* returns to port, the Pentagon awards Captain Rogers the Legion of Merit, and the rest of the crewmen get lesser medals. America then apologizes for the accident and offers to pay compensation for the victims. Iran declines, because it has a different kind of "payment" in mind.

On December 21, 1988, America is caught off guard when Arab terrorists retaliate. Another airliner is climbing to cruising altitude with 258 passengers and crew when a bomb goes off in the Boeing 747's luggage compartment. Many experts believe that blowing up Pan Am Flight 103 over Lockerbie, Scotland, was a direct retaliation for the downing of Iran Air Flight 655.[18]

But the Arab fundamentalists also have something a little more personal in mind for Captain Rogers. On March 10, 1989, a pipe bomb explodes in the family van as his wife, Sharon, drives to work. This California schoolteacher narrowly escapes.[19]

Overly zealous skippers do not always cause the Navy's high-tech problems. Sometimes they involve inadequate testing of dangerous equipment. When a trusting commander was not informed of one such potential hazard, disaster ensued.

This problem was described in two recent publications. *Blind Man's Bluff*[20] is a fascinating book that discusses the exploits of our submarine forces during the Cold War. But it also reveals certain disturbing information about the loss of the USS *Scorpion*. This sleek nuclear attack sub suddenly sank on May 22, 1968, in the mid-Atlantic with all ninety-nine officers and crewmen.

The Navy withheld many details about this tragedy, and at times even seemed to encourage rumors that the Soviets may have somehow been involved in the sinking—for good reason. The Navy's negligence may have been the *real* cause of the tragedy.

Modern subs are equipped with homing torpedoes, but these "smart" weapons are not without their problems. Submariners know that the torpedo's electrical motors can occasionally start up *spontaneously*, while the weapon is inside the sub's closed torpedo tubes.

When this type of "torpedo emergency" occurs, the captain must quickly maneuver his boat to periscope depth to visually ensure that no other vessel is in the line of fire and then release the berserk "fish."[21]

But there was a more dangerous problem with such weapons, one the Navy apparently did not want to discuss with its sub crews. Some of the powerful electrical batteries used in such torpedoes were defective. These devices could burst into flames and explode without warning. The resulting blast could, in turn, actually ignite the torpedo's warhead. This was a far more deadly scenario, one that would require a different type of emergency response: immediately surface, evacuate the torpedo room, and prepare to abandon ship.

The *Blind Man's Bluff* authors describe how the Navy had been ignoring its own regulations on mandatory testing of these batteries.[22] Furthermore, the service apparently did not want to "alarm" its crews by warning them about this more dire kind of problem.

Evidence presented in this book as well as a recent *Proceedings* magazine article, "Real Story of Scorpion?" by Captain C.A.K. McDonald, suggests a deadly battery-induced explosion probably occurred aboard that submarine.[23] The *Scorpion*'s skipper, Commander Francis Slattery, thinking he had a runaway torpedo motor, took the countermeasures needed to deal with this less dangerous emergency—with fatal consequences. The captain's actions were understandable. Not so the brass's failure to protect its sailors from such potentially deadly equipment.

The failure of the Navy Department to do its homework became a death sentence for the *Scorpion*'s trusting crew. Based on recently declassified information, Captain McDonald's brilliant article described the likely scenario for the final minutes in the lives of this group of now silent knights.

As the skipper brought his boat to periscope depth, the burning torpedo warhead exploded, flooding the forward hull. The lucky nearby sailors died instantly from the blast. For their shipmates, death would not be as quick. They raced to shut watertight doors throughout the sub.

With her forward hull compartments flooded, the *Scorpion* foundered and began her headlong plunge toward the bottom. Her remaining crewmen were now locked in their sealed compartments. They soon realized that they were trapped.

For ninety-one seconds, these terrified sailors could hear their shipmates' screams as steel compartments throughout the ship collapsed under the ever-increasing sea-water pressures. The *Scorpion*'s lifeless imploded hull finally came to rest in eleven thousand feet of water—a high-tech trash pile with ninety-nine men who never returned from patrol.

Three years later, Congress passed Public Law 92-156. This and subsequent legislation was designed to insure that the services would conduct realistic "operational tests" of weapon systems and their components *before* putting troops at risk. This process should have prevented tragedies like the loss of the *Scorpion*.

But thirty years later, the "system" is still broken. The Navy has refused to perform shock tests on all components of its newest type attack sub, the three-billion-dollar *Seawolf*. These supposedly required tests were designed to insure that all components would survive the stresses of most underwater explosions. The Navy apparently had diverted some of its testing funds to other uses. Such decisions continue to place those who volunteer to go in harm's way at exceptional risk.[24]

PART
IV

Wild Blue Yonder

16

Chariot of Fire

Military air traffic control has always been a challenging endeavor. Nobody knows this better than Staff Sergeant Chris Cross as he surveys the congested skies from his control tower. He carefully watches as several nimble jets circle overhead like so many chariots lapping each other in the coliseum. But what this controller does not realize is that he is currently part of an organizational experiment, one that will soon explode before his very eyes. For the sergeant's commanding general has come up with an impractical idea, and the men and women at this air base are just so many guinea pigs.

Shortly after assuming command in 1990, the new Air Force chief of staff, General Merrill McPeak, proudly announced one of his pet projects, "composite wings." This plan involves stationing several very different types of aircraft together at the same base. This concept had serious operational and safety problems, but nobody wanted to criticize the general's brainchild.

McPeak was convinced that such units had several innate advantages. The personnel from different weapons systems would better understand each other's tactics by working together constantly. But the biggest advantage claimed for composite wings was that this varied group of aircraft could be deployed to overseas trouble spots as a "package." These smallish units theoretically would contain everything needed to project airpower.

Organizationally, they would resemble the groups of flying squadrons aboard the Navy's aircraft carriers, which deploy together on cruises. In essence, an Air Force composite wing would be a kind of land-based aircraft carrier. What is more, it was argued that they could be deployed to far-flung places faster than any carrier and be ready to fight almost as soon as they landed. This sounded good on paper, but this also assumed the State Department could negotiate landing rights from a friendly neighbor in the region.

Such outfits looked tailor-made for dealing with problems of the "new world order." After all, it's said that when a foreign contingency occurs today, the president always asks, "Where is the nearest carrier?" Once these Air Force units were operational, he might say, "Let's send a composite wing instead."

That, of course, would counter one of the main advantages touted by the Navy's friends in Congress. Thus, many people were suspicious that the real mission of composite wings was to enhance the Air Force's ability to compete with the Navy for scarce funds.

There were, however, a couple of problems with composite wings. First, establishing such units and relocating large amounts of equipment and personnel would be very costly. Even more expensive was the need to duplicate highly specialized equipment at so many dispersed locations. A composite wing with several types of aircraft would need a much greater variety of tools and spare parts than a conventional wing with only one type aircraft. Thus, composite wings were inefficient because they ignored the "economies of scale"—something that McPeak, who had an undergraduate degree in economics, apparently chose to ignore.

Another obvious extra cost was the requirement to have specialized maintenance training for each weapon system. However, the general might have believed that his other bright idea, "two level maintenance," would do away with many of the real maintenance specialists at all wings, composite or conventional. You can't argue with that logic. But there were other troops, such as air traffic controllers, who also needed specialized training to work at the new wings.

All these facts suggest that the idea of composite wings flew in the face of the prevailing fiscal realities. Moreover, General McPeak and his advisors knew vital resources were becoming increasingly scarce. He decided to forge ahead anyway, apparently determined to make his legacy a changed Air Force.

This general did not take kindly to criticism, although he often paid lip service to total quality management (TQM) principles. Like CRM, these concepts encouraged empowerment of subordinates and participative management styles. The general's critics used to quip that he thought TQM really meant "To Quote McPeak." Thus, his staff and subordinates knew better than to call his composite wing "baby" ugly. Obviously, no one was going to try to convince him that these wings vastly complicated both logistics and training, especially at small bases.

Perhaps the best example of such problems occurred at Pope Air Force Base in North Carolina. This base had the misfortune of being selected as one of the prototype composite wings. Here, sleek single-engine F-16 fighters with their afterburners roaring were brought in to fly in a confined air traffic space with lumbering four-engine C-130 transports as well as the twin-engine, low-and-slow A-10 ground attack jets.

There were several other unique problems with establishing such an experiment at this particular airdrome. First, it had only a single, short runway, while most air bases have long multiple runways. One reason that Pope AFB was selected was that the Army's only remaining parachute division, the famed 82nd Airborne, was located at nearby Fort Bragg. Thus, the paratrooper cargo for the C-130s was close by. The bad news was that the Army had an airfield, parachute drop zones, as well as artillery and gunnery ranges in the adjacent airspace. This restricted the directions in which these diverse types of aircraft could fly.

Another problem was that the F-16 is only a single-engine aircraft. Because jet engines occasionally fail, their pilots must practice making "simulated engine-out" approaches. The F-16 doesn't glide very well, so each pilot must know what it looks and feels like to get the jet back onto the runway after an engine has flamed out.

They do this by pulling the throttle back to idle, pointing the nose toward the runway, and hoping they don't run out of airspeed, altitude, and ideas all at the same time. This simulated flameout or "SFO" maneuver is always exciting for both pilots and controllers. In fact, there are a couple of different types of SFO approaches. The most demanding is the dreaded "straight in SFO," where the jet is farthest from the runway. As the name implies, the pilot just tries to stretch the glide to hopefully make it to the runway.

In such a maneuver, the controllers, if they can spot the jet at all, see only a dot in the distance. It's coming straight for them at a couple hundred miles per hour. Normally the controllers know when the pilot is going to practice this maneuver. Thus, they have time to ensure that other air traffic is out of his way *before* this guy comes sailing into their traffic pattern. The name of the game is to always anticipate this dangerous maneuver ahead of time.

There are two pieces of technology that could help the controllers at Pope. The first is radar, which is installed in their tower cab. Unfortunately, the rotating radar antenna hits the "target" only once every several seconds. So if the target exceeds a certain speed (approximately 290 miles per hour), the scope goes into its "auto-coast" mode. The device is saying: "This guy is going so fast, I'm only guessing where he is." Once this happens, the Air Force procedures forbid using this radar data for separating traffic.

The other device is a control tower visual simulator. This device permits neophyte controllers to efficiently hone their skills without putting aircraft at risk. It's often said that the "sim," not the tower, is where you want to learn from your rookie mistakes. Over the years, simulators have become standard devices for teaching commercial and military pilots.

In recent years, the FAA purchased these devices for training their controllers. When I worked for that organization, it was obvious controllers had a lot of clout. They were viewed as a national resource, one worth investing in the best training equipment to support. Besides, they had a tough union.

Military controllers, in contrast, are *just* enlisted folks. They are on the bottom of the priority lists. Consequently, the Air Force has decided it cannot afford luxuries like control tower visual simulators for these people.

Air safety always depends on people following procedures so they can anticipate what the other guy is going to do next. This is called being "predictable." In so-called visual conditions, controllers need to tell fliers where other traffic is so the pilots can see and avoid hitting these planes. All pilots know certain well-established flying rules.

Thus, in good weather, the controller will "call the traffic." This involves telling pilots where the other aircraft is relative to their own position. The pilots should then acknowledge that they see the other traffic, usually with the proverbial "tally ho" response. Once this sequence occurs, it is the responsibility of the faster craft's pilots to maintain visual contact with, and to maneuver clear of, the slower plane—if necessary.

The controllers will obviously help if they see a "conflict" (i.e., a potential collision). But once the traffic is identified to fliers, the primary collision avoidance responsibility normally lies with the "pilot in command" of the overtaking aircraft. Of course, restricted airspace—such as artillery ranges and civilian air traffic in the vicinity of Pope—add to the challenge for aviators at this particular base.

All these limitations also cause myriad headaches for the air traffic controllers. These are the folks who somehow must orchestrate this aerial ballet. They are absolutely vital to safety, but they rarely get the respect that they so richly deserve.

One such controller was Sergeant Cross. He was assigned as the Pope control tower "watch supervisor" for the afternoon of March 23, 1994. As he walked up the several flights of stairs to reach his glass perch, he knew that his responsibilities would include overseeing the training of two apprentice controllers. These two rookies have been struggling to master the complexities of controlling traffic in this less than optimal situation. At least one, the most junior, has had real problems—especially since the fighters arrived at Pope.

Chris Cross is in many ways emblematic of the techno-warriors today's military so desperately needs. The sergeant was the top graduate from military air traffic controller school and was the distinguished graduate in his class at the Noncommissioned Officers Academy. In his spare time he is completing a masters degree in hopes of getting an Air Force commission in the near future.

Cross and a number of senior controllers at Pope have become increasingly concerned with their ignorance of procedures for dealing with the F-16s. They have requested permission to drive a USAF staff car to another air base where F-16s have been located for years.

They want to spend a few days studying how controllers there handled these slippery jets. They are particularly interested in observing the demanding straight-in SFOs. Thus, they would better understand the techniques needed to manage traffic at Pope. Their request is turned down, supposedly because of a shortage of funds.

This money-saving decision would prove very expensive a few weeks later, because when Cross's crew reports for its afternoon shift, neither the sergeant nor his understudies have seen a straight-in SFO. In a little more than an hour, that will change. But March 23, 1994, will prove to be a day of unimaginable horror for the troops at both military bases that straddle the city of Fayetteville, because a controller's worst nightmare—a midair collision over a populated area—will occur before Sergeant Cross can intervene.

As the sergeant drives to work, it's high noon. He sees the crowded flight line. Dozens of diminutive A-10 and F-16 fighters are dwarfed by the huge C-130 and C-141 transports parked on the ramp. Also nearby are five hundred camouflage-clad soldiers milling around in the parachute staging area. It's a typical day in "Fayette-nam," as the natives sometimes call the Pope-Bragg military complex, because it's reminiscent of an earlier war zone. These soldiers are standing in formation or lining up to board the waiting transports.

Most will soon be airborne, en route to the several nearby parachute drop zones. An hour from now, the lucky ones will be safely jumping out of the rear doors of their cargo compartments. The unlucky ones will still be standing by on this ramp, like commuters waiting their turn to board an aerial conveyer belt.

About the time that Cross and his crew are climbing the stairs of the control tower, a captain departs Pope in an F-16. This sleek, two-tone, mako-gray chariot roars into the humid air, its afterburner streaming a cone of fire. An excited young officer is a passenger in the craft's rear cockpit. The two aviators are headed for the bombing range but will soon be returning to Pope.

The passenger has just completed flight training but does not have an assignment yet. He is getting an orientation ride—his first time in the highly maneuverable F-16. The captain will be showing the neophyte pilot how *real* men do SFOs. This promises to be a roller-coaster ride without the rails.

A thrilling hour quickly passes for our two fliers. As the F-16 returns to the Pope Air Force Base area, the pilot contacts Fayetteville

Approach. This is the FAA control facility that feeds traffic to the Pope tower. The captain tells the civilian controller that he wants to do a straight-in SFO at the air base.

Because this maneuver is so demanding, there is a written procedure requiring the FAA controller to contact the Pope tower with this information—well before the jet penetrates the base's control zone. This is normally done by a telephone call. But this busy civilian controller is working other traffic, so she ignores the requirement and clears the speedy jet into Pope airspace.

The first time the Pope controllers hear about the inbound F-16 doing a straight-in SFO is when the pilot announces his presence. By then, he is only nine miles out. This causes more than a little anxiety in the tower, but they clear him for the approach anyway. They also tell the F-16 about the C-130 closest to him. They expect the F-16 will be over their runway in a few short minutes, and they already have two C-130s who are also getting ready to land.

This, of course, is the type of challenge that controllers are supposed to handle. The two junior controllers try to come up with a plan to "de-conflict" this traffic. That is where judgment comes in. They somehow have to sequence the two lumbering transports with this fast mover—not an easy task. Sergeant Cross begins to be concerned as he watches his understudies trying to cope with this situation. But he also knows he can't be too quick to intervene, or they will never learn what to do.

Initially the two junior controllers think they will have both C-130s maneuver around the traffic pattern long enough to allow the faster F-16 to land first. The most junior controller then mistakenly uses the call sign of a third C-130, which has already landed, when addressing the nearest C-130. The pilots of this airborne C-130 naturally ignore these commands because they assume the controller is talking to another aircraft. Both junior controllers are becoming more confused, until the plane with that call sign informs them he has already landed.

By the time these two embarrassed controllers get the call-sign snafu straightened out, their close-in C-130 crew has already made a routine ninety-degree turn toward the runway. The pilot will shortly be making another ninety-degree turn to line up with the runway for landing. Now the two junior controllers decide to change their previous game plan and try to sandwich the F-16 between the close-in C-130 and the other more distant C-130.

But they soon realize that there isn't enough time for the close-in transport to land and clear the runway with the faster jet inbound. The more experienced junior controller who's helping train his teammate then intervenes. He tells this slow-moving C-130 that he can only make a low approach instead of actually landing, which would take more time. Cross anxiously watches his charges and keeps trying to spot the inbound jet.

None of the other controllers has seen the jet. They have been looking but not in the right places, because aircraft, during final approach, normally fly about a three-degree angle with the horizon. Having never seen a jet make an SFO approach, they're not sure how high above the horizon to look.

What is more, the jet pilot has *not* recently radioed his position, because so many other folks are talking on the frequency. But there is another, more critical problem, one related to the way the F-16 pilot is doing this particular SFO. These demanding and potentially dangerous maneuvers are supposed to be flown in a *very* prescribed manner, which is described in detail in the aircraft flight manual (called a "dash-one").

He should be flying at approximately 250 miles per hour, but his speed is actually well over 330 miles per hour. While this is no doubt providing a very thrilling ride for the young officer in the backseat, our captain has lost track of his current position. The F-16 pilot's actions also violate one of the basic rules of airmanship, because he now has become "unpredictable."

Furthermore, when he radios the Pope tower to give a current position, he is actually miles closer than he believes. The controllers therefore think the slow-moving C-130 will have time to depart the approach end of runway before the F-16 arrives there. But the fighter pilot's unexpectedly fast SFO, coupled with erroneous positioned reports, results in a situation that nobody in the control tower anticipates.

One of Sergeant Cross's controllers advises the F-16 pilot that the C-130 in front of him is "short final on the go."[1] Every pilot knows that this means the transport is very close to the approach end of the runway, and its crew has added power to do a "go around." This indicates that the C-130 is low, but it's not going to be landing.

The F-16 pilot gives a routine-sounding radio call: "Three green . . . low approach."[2] This verbal shorthand declares he has checked that all three wheels are down, and he is going to make a low pass over the runway, rather than touching down. The casual tone of his voice lulls the controllers into thinking everything is okay. They breathe a collective sigh of relief. They believe surely this guy must have spotted the much larger transport, even if they cannot yet see his small jet.

His calm radio demeanor belies the fact that he is allowing his craft to overtake the C-130 like a bat out of hell. The F-16's nose is also blocking him from seeing the camouflaged cargo plane. What's more, he has made no effort to maneuver the jet so he can better spot the transport. The gleeful ambience of this sunny afternoon's flight will soon change to one of panic.

By the time the F-16 pilot gets the critical message about the C-130's location, he's almost on top of it. Several hundred feet above the runway, he begins to level off in preparation for a low pass. As this jet jock pulls back on the craft's control stick with his right hand, the giant transport suddenly appears in his windshield. He does not have enough time to avoid the impending collision. Boom!

The F-16's forward fuselage smashes into the right side of C-130's tail and continues forward to clip the back of its right wing. The fighter pilot instinctively slams the throttle forward with his left hand as the jet's afterburner lights with a second boom. He cannot believe his eyes as his damaged jet shoots past the battered transport.

The sound and sight of this impact has not gone unnoticed. A thousand eyes focus on the unfolding aerial drama. One pair of eyes belongs to another pilot who sees the collision from the cockpit of his C-130 sitting on the ground. He excitedly keys his mike and transmits, in a directive tone of voice: "Eject! Eject! Get out of there! Get out of there!"[3]

The F-16 pilots instinctively yank their ejection seat handles and are launched from the tandem cockpits of their damaged fighter. These modern gladiators unceremoniously depart their flaming chariot.

Directly in front of the suddenly vacant jet are more than five hundred soldiers in the parachute staging area, along with a handful of Air Force personnel in several parked transports. The F-16 accelerates to more than 350 miles per hour, its afterburner spewing fire. The troops must feel helpless as the jet rockets toward them.

The jet slams into the concrete ramp and skids into two giant C-141s. The fighter's fuel tanks rupture, throwing fuel high into the air. Sparks will soon light this kerosene cloud. The fighter's burning airframe shatters into a thousand fragments as it spreads carnage across this cement no-man's land. This zone of death will spread into the grassy knoll and the clump of pine trees adjacent to the flight line. This shower of burning shrapnel instantly engulfs dozens of helpless troops.

The controllers hit the crash alarm button in the control tower cab, but nobody has to tell the nearby fire trucks that they are needed. The men in the tower have the best and the worst view of the crash scene, for they have to watch dozens of people aflame before their eyes. But they also witness feats of heroism as paratroopers run into the flames to rescue burning comrades.

The controllers quickly clear the C-130 badly damaged in the collision to return for what turns out to be an uneventful landing. In an instant, three aircraft have been destroyed. More important, twenty-four paratroopers are dead or dying, while another hundred have been grievously injured, most with incredibly painful burns.

One of the victims is a thirty-year-old paratrooper, Staff Sergeant Michael Kelley, who has burns over 70 percent of his body. As the medics haul him away, they know he has a slim chance of surviving. The rule of thumb for estimating the probability of dying from burns is your age plus the percentage of the body surface burned. Mathematically he's a dead man, but this guy is determined to beat the odds and live.

The controllers helplessly watch the scores of ambulances shuttle casualties to hospitals. It never occurs to these three young men in the tower cab that the troops on the ramp will not be the only victims of this tragic afternoon's events. But that will soon become painfully obvious.

Within hours, the service will begin putting together its two standard investigating boards to examine this crash. The Air Combat Command in Langley, Virginia, will control both of these inquiries. The safety investigation theoretically should establish precisely why the mishap happened. Meanwhile, the accident investigation is supposed to objectively identify who should be held accountable for this occurrence.

It is important to understand what goes on in the collective psyche of such investigating boards. Because of the magnitude of the losses and the publicity in this case, both of these inquiries will be highly politicized efforts. These inquiries will be designed primarily to protect the careers of the important folks. The three grunts who happened to be on duty in the control tower are expendable in this power game.

In spite of prodding by people like myself and several well-meaning members of both boards of inquiry, their efforts will soon turn into the familiar blame game. But there are unique problems in this particular situation, because the voting members of these boards know there are certain highly relevant issues that they cannot go into. These areas deal with the obvious mistakes made by their bosses. The resulting problems were definitely links in the so-called accident chain.

Some of these areas included the chief of staff's brainchild, the composite wing concept—but no one is for ending his or her career by bringing up that fundamental problem. This hot potato has become even more incendiary because of a General Accounting Office report. This watchdog agency issued a 1993 report pointing out the flaws with the composite wing concept.[4] So, obviously, this issue is going to be off limits.

Then, too, these two boards could have delved into establishing just who decided to locate a composite wing at this *particularly* inappropriate base, with its many limitations regarding airspace and runways. The likely culprits for such decisions were the commander or senior staffers at the Air Combat Command, but because these gents were the convening authorities for both investigations, it was unlikely that anyone was going to vote to examine such problems. The fact that these draftee investigators hold day jobs working for this same command just might have influenced their thinking.

Well, how about the examining of the lack of training for the air traffic controllers, or the flawed procedures for handling straight-in SFOs? Investigating these issues thoroughly would probably expose the Pope wing commander or his staff to serious criticism. The presidents of both these investigation boards are his contemporaries. So these fellow wing commander (or wing commander wannabes) are not very eager to cast any stones. Glass houses, you know. After all, next year it might be his turn to investigate a crash at *your* base.

Then there is always the young pilot who showed a considerable lack of judgment in performing the maneuver in this manner. Why not? Isn't "pilot error" one of the favorite board findings?

Because the board presidents of such investigations are normally aviators who fly the same aircraft as the mishap pilot, they are sometimes inclined to empathize with aviators from that flying community. After all, they may have even pulled such stunts themselves. Apparently, these board presidents may not have been interested in hanging this pilot.

There would soon be another reason for not playing up the culpability of a hot-dog pilot—the embarrassing B-52 crash a few months later that was caught on video and played repeatedly on national TV. This accident was reported to have involved just such a hot-dog pilot. These kinds of unfortunate happenings are not good for an organization's public image. We cannot have the public hearing that there are *two* such guys flying for the Air Force.

Okay, that just leaves the controllers. These are three enlisted guys who happened to be on duty when the mishap occurred. They are just grunts who have no one with any power to defend them. Thus, they are easy targets for scapegoating. This is perhaps the most virulent problem associated with such misguided investigations. I often refer to this sick practice as "scapegrunting."

Actually, I hear about one board member who is balking at blaming these controllers. This individual is brand-new to the process and can't believe they are really going to take this shameful course of action. The officer asks to privately speak with one of the veteran investigators from the safety agency, Mr. George Burton.[5] He is a highly respected civilian expert who is often assigned to consult in specialized areas on these investigations.

This consultant explains to the concerned officer that this is how the system works, but as a "voting member" of the board, one can always issue a minority report. The officer already knows that if you decide to undertake such a drastic action, you should be prepared to resign from the service, because your career is over anyway. Understandably, the need for self-preservation wins out in the end. No minority report will come from this investigation.

The days and weeks after the crash are hard for Sergeant Cross, who follows the sad events occurring at the twin military bases—the flags at half-staff, the funerals, the memorial services with taps being played for the fallen members of the 82nd Airborne, the newspaper stories of soldiers like Staff Sergeant Michael Kelley fighting to survive his terrible burn injuries.

All this would be disturbing enough, but Cross and the other two controllers are immediately decertified. This just means they cannot control traffic pending the outcome of the accident investigation. He is told that this is simply a precaution. He is assigned to do paperwork downstairs. He feels this is pretty standard stuff, so it does not bother him too much.

Then Sergeant Cross hears that the F-16 pilot, who he felt was responsible for the crash, is immediately returned to flying status. In fact, Cross actually helps him file flight-plan paperwork several days after the crash. Cross becomes suspicious when a senior sergeant in his unit tips him off. The pilot has a "guardian angel," a senior officer who is going to protect this captain's career.

Sergeant Cross, feeling he has done nothing wrong, is eager to tell his story to investigators. When he is introduced to the senior sergeant who is going to interview him for the board, he is relieved because the guy is also wearing an air traffic controller badge on his uniform. Surely this man will understand the impossible situation he was faced with that fateful afternoon. But that is not exactly what the Air Force has in mind.

It isn't long before Cross realizes that this "inquisitor" is not interested in hearing his explanations. This guy starts by asking several "when did you stop beating you wife?" style questions. He demands to know why Cross did not follow a number of air traffic control procedures that are no longer in effect. Before Cross can answer, the interviewer interrupts. He asks why Cross did not use his radarscope. Cross realizes that being a controller himself, the investigator has to know the answer to that ridiculous question.

But Cross starts to explain the obvious: The jet was traveling so fast that his scope went into the auto-coast mode, and controllers are prohibited from relying on such data. Again the investigator interrupts with another question before Cross can complete his explanation. This process continues for what seems like hours. It is now obvious to the soon-to-be former sergeant what is happening. He is at once shocked, angry, and scared.

A few weeks later, he is informed that he has been found responsible for the accident, along with his most senior understudy. His commander informs him that the Air Force, however, is willing to be *reasonable*. They are just going to give him an "Article 15, non-judicial punishment."

Translation: He's being offered a one-time good deal. If he will agree to accept the punishment ascribed by his commander, he will not be court-martialed, although the Article 15 could involve large fines and demotions. Once again the sergeant is shocked, angry, and scared.

Sergeant Cross decides to contact a civilian lawyer. He could then ask for a court-martial to beat this bogus rap and clear his good name. But he soon learns that if he goes the court-martial route, the Air Force is prepared to indict him on twenty-four counts of negligent homicide, one hundred counts of inflicting grievous bodily injury, five hundred counts of reckless endangerment, several counts of careless destruction of government property, and so forth.

If convicted on all counts, the sergeant could theoretically be serving time until the *twenty-second* century. Maybe, with good behavior, he could be out in time to celebrate the tricentennial. Then he finds out that the civilian lawyer fees will cost him several years' worth of sergeant's pay. In short, he's caught between the devil and the deep pockets of the big blue machine.

He reluctantly takes the Article 15 and is busted down to senior airman and fined eight hundred dollars. He is also barred from controlling traffic. Shortly afterwards, he decides to ask for an inspector-general investigation of this crash to hopefully clear his good name. Obviously, the former sergeant has not had much experience with military inspectors general.

In contrast to Sergeant Cross, the F-16 pilot has not been treated too badly. Not only is he back in the cockpit again, but this remarkable young man has also just been selected as junior officer of the quarter for Pope Air Force Base. Within months he will be recommended for promotion to major. Maybe the old sergeant was right about the captain having a guardian angel.

Several months after the Pope accident, an important general from the Pentagon is visiting the Air Force Safety Agency. Naturally, the other senior personnel and I are asked to meet with him. I am the lone civilian among a covey of colonels in the commander's conference room when this general arrives. It is not long before the general brings up this matter of the Pope investigation and the fact that the controller has had the gall to demand an IG investigation. He asks for our opinions on the quality of these investigations.

As always, I wait for the assembly of officers to give their views, but there is only dead silence. After clearing my throat, I say, "General, none of us were assigned to the Pope investigations. However, I would urge that you talk with Mr. George Burton. I believe he has some strong views on this topic." Needless to say, the general never contacted Mr. Burton.

In the months and years after these tragic events, a number of good and bad things will transpire. The procedures for the Pope controllers will be hastily rewritten. Straight-in SFOs will be banned throughout the Air Force for a year. General McPeak will retire with full honors in 1994. He will head for Oregon to enjoy a generous retirement pension.

Airman Cross will be prevented from returning to his beloved control tower for three years. He will have to also contend with constant harassment from his commanders, especially after the national media discovers his plight. One officer, however, will come up with what passes for a peace offering in such cases. He suggests that if Cross admits he killed the twenty-four paratroopers, apologizes for his unprofessional conduct, and stops talking to the press, the general just *might* let him go back to controlling traffic.

Staff Sergeant Michael Kelley, after dozens of painful surgical procedures and months of laborious physical therapy, will recover, only to be forced to leave the Army in 1995. Although he will always be badly disfigured, he is looking ahead to becoming a history teacher. He also starts to write a book about his struggle.[6]

In 1996, the Pope-based F-16s will be quietly slipped out of town. In 1997, a new chief of staff will tell Congress that composite wings are being "scrapped."[7] That year, with prodding from the press, the DoD inspector general will finally direct that a new accident investigation be undertaken. This will actually be the first time in history that has happened. Late that year, Cross will contact me to say that he really is not expecting much from the latest inquiry. Unfortunately, the Air Force, unlike some of its fighter jocks, will remain predictable.

This third investigation will basically say the pilot used poor judgment, but it will *not* exonerate the controllers. Acclaimed reporter Philip Shenon of the *New York Times* will pen a story with the headline "Pilot

Also Blamed for Air Force Crash,"[8] but unfortunately, the piece will only appear on page seven. Most of the media all but ignores this story—not exactly the vindication that Cross had hoped for.

Late in 1997, this disappointed former sergeant will be offered a chance to resign from the Air Force—without any retirement benefits. He quickly accepts the offer to become *Mr.* Cross and gets on with his life. As Walter Cronkite used to say when signing off, "And so it goes."

17

The Bell Tolls for Thee

It's a beautiful spring day in 1985 as we trundle past the gleaming airliners on the ramp at Washington National Airport. From my overstuffed passenger seat, I enviously stare at the two pilots several feet ahead of me. I can hardly wait to change places with the copilot to begin my checkout in this executive jet.

Today, we are the only occupants of the Learjet. This type aircraft is regarded as the hottest executive jet, and for good reason. The legendary craft was originally designed as a fighter plane for the Swiss Air Force. But an enterprising American, Bill Lear, bought the design, added a passenger cabin, and voilà, behold an executive jet that can transport several passengers in cramped luxury at fighter speeds.

The fighter heritage is reflected by the set of large fuel tanks mounted on each wing tip. These "tip tanks" resemble napalm bombs, adding to the fighter motif. Furthermore, the Learjet, with small wings optimal for slicing through the stratosphere, flies like a fighter plane. It has a deserved reputation for being tricky to handle, especially at slow speeds during takeoffs and landings. I know this from investigating Learjet crashes. But all seems serene as we taxi along the becalmed Potomac this morning.

205

When we roll onto the active runway, the copilot acknowledges the controller's takeoff clearance while the pilot smoothly pushes the twin throttles forward. The roar from the jet's engines increases, and we are collectively pushed back into our seats by the compact bird's quick acceleration. The concrete begins to race by now. Rubber skid marks from a thousand previous landings become a black blur. Scant seconds later, the copilot calmly announces "Rotate" in a professional monotone when the jet accelerates through the so-called rotation speed. The pilot dutifully responds by pulling back on the control wheel, raising the plane's sleek nose skyward.

Suddenly, the reverie is shattered when the pilot shouts, "Abort! Abort!" He adroitly yanks the throttles back into the reverse position and then stomps on the tops of both rudder pedals, engaging the wheel brakes. The engines roar in compliance as the bird begins to decelerate. The copilot keys his mike and informs the controllers, "We're aborting!" The overheated brakes squeal in protest. My heart races when I notice the Potomac looming ever larger outside the windshield as we race inexorably toward the end of the runway. But we soon slow to a crawl, and the jet anticlimactically swings onto the last taxiway exit.

The pilot turns in his seat to tell the copilot and myself that we had a major fuel imbalance problem. As the jet began to lift off, he felt the left wing was too heavy. He then explains that we must have left the cross-feed valve open. This valve is located in the fuel lines connecting the left and right side fuel tanks. When the jet was parked on the inclined ramp overnight, fuel simply ran from the up-hill tank into the lower tip tank.

We had somehow overlooked the large difference between the fuel quantities in these tip tanks during our preflight inspection, which could have been fatal had we actually become airborne. I soon realized that we had cheated death because there is not sufficient force available at low speeds to right the jet—even with full rotation of the control wheel.

The laws of aerodynamics come into play. The ailerons, located on the trailing edge of the wings, just cannot deflect enough wind to lift up the heavy wing. The amount of force these control surfaces can generate depends on the quantity of air molecules in the slipstream flowing around these flap-like devices. Thus, at low speeds, there is no way they can overcome a massive weight imbalance.

Once again I am reminded of the fundamental truism that flying is always a delicate balancing act. Only the prompt, well-coordinated actions by this experienced crew had saved our lives today.

A decade later, another Learjet would depart from another Washington airport carrying a highly decorated general and a senior Pentagon official, but these two distinguished passengers would not be so fortunate. They will be trapped by a series of problems that are indicative of the compromises that permeate today's military.

On the afternoon of April 17, 1995, their C-21, which is the military's designation for the Learjet, will leave Washington's Andrews Air Force Base. In less than two hours, these two important leaders, four other passengers, and the two pilots will perish during a botched emergency landing, for this aircraft has a vexing malfunction that totally confuses its inexperienced crew.

At the controls is a very concerned first lieutenant, Paul Bowers. He is unhappy because the aircraft's complex fuel system has been acting erratic on the inbound flight. For some reason the fuel control panel seems to have a mind of its own, and it keeps pumping extra fuel into the left tip tank. When he arrived at Andrews earlier that day, he initially hoped the maintenance guys would have a spare fuel panel to permit a quick swap.

Bowers does not know it, but the problem is not in the panel per se, but is actually being caused be one of the jet's fuel pumps. Its electrical relay has jammed, so this device keeps running, even when its toggle switch on the fuel panel is placed in the "off" position. The weight of the unwanted fuel going into the left tank has upset the delicate lateral balance of the Learjet, requiring Bowers to constantly compensate.

After arriving at Andrews, the conscientious lieutenant asked the maintenance contractor to fix the fuel panel but was told that it would take too much time. Besides, "spares" (that is, spare parts such as fuel panels and relays) are in short supply throughout the Air Force. Instead of properly troubleshooting the jet's fuel system, one of the contractor's mechanics shows the lieutenant how he might be able to "trick" the system by quickly flipping the suspect toggle switch.

As with the ill-fated ValuJet Airlines, much of today's military maintenance is contracted out to the lowest bidder. The lieutenant decides he will have to live with this "fix" and hope somebody can figure out what is really wrong once they get back home. The reality is that there are no spares, no time, and no whining allowed.

Bowers, a handsome twenty-seven-year-old bachelor, wants to make a career of the Air Force and knows these facts of life all too well. Besides, he's a native Texan and a can-do guy who was just selected as his base's outstanding pilot.

Today has already been a typically long one for the lieutenant. It began at 4:15 A.M. when he reported to his squadron at Randolph AFB in Texas. Bowers was scheduled for a fifteen-plus-hour duty day, but things have been running late as usual, and this bright young man knows the name of the game is to move the mission and don't bother complaining, 'cause nobody's listening in today's overworked military.

Lieutenant Bowers has spent almost nine hundred hours flying the C-21 since he won his wings two years ago, but he has less than eleven hundred total flight hours. To fly as a "pilot in command" for a commercial Learjet operator, FAA regulations require that one have an Airline Transport Pilot license. Earning this license takes an absolute minimum of fifteen hundred hours, and most civilian pilots have many more hours before they get this rating. Bowers would not be able to qualify, but the Air Force is not required to follow FAA regulations on minimum crew flight time. Thus, the safety of the military's most senior personnel is often in the hands of some of its least experienced flyers.

Bowers's copilot, Captain Paul Carey, has not been much help in trying to figure out the fuel system problem. This officer has more total flight time—more than twenty-two hundred hours—but most of his flying has been in T-38 trainers and C-130 transports. Carey actually has even less time than Bowers in Learjets, with just over six hundred hours.

Both of these relatively inexperienced pilots keep referring to the procedures in their Air Force checklists and flight manuals, trying to figure out why the fuel panel won't do what they want. That, of course, is *exactly* what the service trains its pilots to do, and these good soldiers are just following procedures. What they do not know is that their trusted texts are wrong. The answer to their problem is very simple—just pull the malfunctioning fuel pump's circuit breaker. But this critical piece of information is *not* to be found in their Air Force documents.

Ironically, the proper procedures for dealing with this type of fuel imbalance problem *are* clearly stated in the current FAA-approved manuals and checklists used by civilian Learjet pilots. This is because the NTSB aggressively investigates civilian crashes and incidents. It then issues recommendations to the FAA, which in turn usually issues aeronautical directives requiring changes to the flight manuals of commercial operators. The manufacturers and the operators are also usually very diligent about reporting service difficulties to the FAA. In the civilian world, which places a higher priority on safety, word gets around much more quickly than in our military.

The specific disconnect here was that these procedures were not known when the Learjet was first delivered to the military in 1984. And over the years, the Air Force has simply not updated its manuals with this critical information. Furthermore, by law, the Air Force is not required to follow FAA regulations on flight manual updates. Besides, it costs money to keep revising these documents, so a command decision was made to forego purchasing updates from the manufacturer.

All of these factors place a great burden on the rank and file—guys like Bowers and Carey, who are constantly caught in no-win situations. As they reluctantly file their flight plan at Andrews, they know they dare not inconvenience their distinguished passengers by canceling the mission. Seated in their passenger compartment are none other than the Air Force Assistant Secretary for Acquisition Clark G. Fiester and Major General Glenn A. Profitt II, the director of plans and operations for the Air Education and Training Command. The latter just happens to be their boss, and both VIPs want to get to Randolph AFB in Texas pronto.

Furthermore, these pilots know that Mr. Fiester is not just *any* assistant secretary from the Pentagon, he is also a "friend of Bill's"—Perry that is. Defense Secretary Perry had persuaded his longtime friend to come out of retirement to take this demanding post.[1] In fact, Fiester has been one of Perry's closest colleagues since they worked together at Penn State University thirty-eight years ago. This distinguished-looking, gray-haired engineer is truly one of the nation's top experts in the field of electronics. But the energetic sixty-one-year-old will be dealing with other issues on this mission.

He is on his way to Texas to give a pep talk on one of the Pentagon's pet projects, acquisition reform. This is the Pentagon's master program to save billions by streamlining purchasing policies and doing things like buying commercial, off-the-shelf items rather than customized items built to military specifications, such as the widely criticized nine-hundred-dollar toilet seat. Obviously, this program is a top priority for the Pentagon, which is quickly discovering the realities have changed since the "fall of the wall." But Fiester has another, somewhat less pleasant lecture to hear when he's down Texas way.

He has to get up to speed on human factors. Fiester plans to meet with the Air Force's top human factors engineering officer to see what can be done to ameliorate the myriad of ergonomic problems identified by my 1994 whistle-blowing complaint.

This has become a must-do meeting after the Air Force discovered that the DoD inspector general has also independently come to the same conclusions regarding widespread problems in the service's ergonomic efforts. The scathing executive summary of the IG report states on page 1: "Program managers did not adequately address human systems integration during the acquisition process."[2]

Fiester does not know it, but the scheduled briefer just happens to be a confidant of mine. This colonel was delighted that I had filed my complaint, although this "unindicted co-conspirator" could not publicly acknowledge his complicity. He is also an outspoken fighter pilot who has literally seen these ergonomic deficiencies kill some of his colleagues.

He intends to bend this assistant secretary's ear, big time. The colonel hopes to convince this kingpin that he needs to radically overhaul the current Air Force approach. This will insure that such problems do not go uncorrected during the acquisition process. Fiester, being a conscientious and sophisticated senior bureaucrat, would no doubt have listened attentively and launched a program to fix these deficiencies.

Thus, more than the lives of the eight occupants are at stake as this Learjet departs Andrews and swings southwestward to chase the sun across the old Confederacy. Its two weary pilots have requested a route that will get them home as quickly as possible. They plan to rapidly climb to thirty-nine thousand feet, passing north of Atlanta, Georgia, as they streak toward the Lone Star State.

From his passenger seat, General Profitt glances at his watch as the gleaming blue and white C-21 breaks ground at 4:38 P.M. He is eager to get home. This highly experienced pilot would rather be holding the controls himself, but he knows he has to let his young subordinates do the flying today, for his duties on this flight lie in the back, with this most distinguished Pentagon PAX.[3]

General Profitt is a command pilot with over six thousand flying hours and five hundred combat missions. This highly decorated officer, with seven Distinguished Flying Crosses and thirty Air Medals, was entrusted with coordinating the electronic warfare campaign in the Gulf War. These efforts blindsided Saddam Hussein's forces and paved the way for a quick coalition victory. With his closely cropped fighter pilot haircut and a chest covered with "combat confetti," he looks the part of the aging warrior.

I first met this distinguished officer two years before when he requested a briefing on Crew Resource Management (CRM). He had just assumed his current position and knew he had to get the most out of every training dollar. I was warned that he liked to ask tough questions, so I was glad to hear that Lieutenant Colonel John Nance would be part of this briefing. Nance, an Air Force reservist, is also an internationally known safety expert. From his many appearances on national television, Nance had developed a persuasive style that was bound to help persuade Profitt to support CRM training.

What neither of us knew was that Profitt had an interesting sense of humor. When Reservist Nance introduced himself, the general mentioned he was currently sleeping with a beautiful lieutenant colonel in the reserves. He then waited for the room to recoil in disbelief at what he had just admitted. The general, with a sheepish grin, quickly explained that she was his wife. After that humorous start, the briefing went well, and Profitt became a strong advocate for CRM training in subsequent months.

General Profitt just happens to be in Washington on April 17, 1995, for an unrelated purpose. But for protocol reasons, he is expected to personally escort this important visitor to his command. Profitt is also looking forward to returning to Randolph and the arms of his beautiful wife. Besides, he wants to discuss some training issues with Fiester, such as CRM. The general has tried desperately to obtain the best courses for his troops, but he has not always been successful.

Profitt, a highly experienced pilot himself, has extensively studied CRM techniques, because he recognizes their value. Unfortunately, the two men in the Learjet's cockpit this afternoon have neither the general's experience nor his familiarity with this important type of training. Their limitations will be become painfully evident before the day is out, for these young pilots will soon discover the gremlins in their fuel system are still alive and well as they approach Atlanta airspace.

Bowers is flying with one eye on the fuel gauges when he says, "I don't know, it's like we have multiple problems . . . this is highly weird."[4] Carey notes that they have an eight-hundred-pound imbalance. At 6:56 P.M., they decide to radio the FAA Atlanta air traffic control center. They inform the controllers that they are having problems getting fuel out of one of their wing-tip tanks. The pilots ask permission to jettison some fuel so they can get the jet balanced.

Bowers and Carey then request a direct route to Maxwell Air Force Base, located outside of Montgomery, Alabama. There they might be able to get somebody to fix their jet's malfunctioning fuel system. They estimate they are only twenty-eight minutes from the safety of the large runway at this military base. Two minutes later, the controller in the Atlanta center clears them to proceed to Maxwell.

One minute later, the controller authorizes them to jettison fuel after the increasingly nervous Learjet crew radios that they " . . . just need to even out the wings. . . . we got a pretty good imbalance going." They then open the valves on both wing-tip tanks and begin to dump fuel overboard until they are empty. This leaves the crew with another problem, because the jet has only limited fuel capacity in its other small fuel cells. Now they have to worry about running completely out of gas.

They then get permission to start descending from thirty-nine thousand feet. Meanwhile, the two befuddled pilots get distracted trying to radio Maxwell to insure the base knows there are two very distinguished passengers on board. But our aviators soon realize that the small in-wing tanks are now becoming unbalanced as fuel is rapidly being transferred from the right wing tank into the recently emptied left tip tank. Furthermore, their right engine is being fed from the right wing tank, which will soon be sucked dry. Now they realize things are *really* going to get dicey.

Several more agonizing minutes pass before our overstressed fliers inform the Atlanta controller that they need to get to Maxwell as quickly as possible. A few minutes later, these pilots are growing desperate as they radio that they need to land at the "*closest* piece of pavement" because they are "not going to have engines shortly."

At 7:15 P.M., the controller tells them that the Alexander City airport is twelve miles ahead at "twelve to one o'clock." This is aviation lingo for, "It's almost straight off your nose, just a little to the right." This small airport has no control tower or emergency equipment, but it does have forty-four hundred feet of asphalt, and this has to sound like salvation to our desperate duo. They radio that they want to land at Alexander City. The pilots request that the controller " . . . clear everybody out of our way" as they pull power back and shove their nose over to dive at this airfield.

As these two young men struggle with the mental gymnastics of getting this unwieldy jet to the small airport, gravity becomes their enemy. The weight of the fuel in their left wing is making it difficult to keep the jet upright. An adrenaline high has clouded their judgment as they rush to get the jet on this runway.

At first, they try to land on the south runway. They then decide to line up for a left downwind approach to the north runway. This decision will force them to try to make two 90-degree left turns. In the middle of this confusion, Bowers gives control of the jet to Carey. Unfortunately, Carey, who is in the right-hand pilot seat, cannot see the runway, because it is off to the left side of their flight path.

As they swing to the left, they start arguing about when to extend the landing gear and flaps to configure the jet for landing. Doing these required things will also slow the jet down, which in turn will decrease the effectiveness of the ailerons. Furthermore, the fuel imbalance has now become so bad that Carey must use both hands on the control wheel just to steer the jet. He thus has to ask Bowers to manipulate the throttles.

Concerned about the low fuel, they initially decide to throttle back both engines but then decide to push up the left engine power setting to counteract the effects of the fuel imbalance, which is trying to pull their left wing down. The resulting asymmetrical thrust in turn causes the jet's nose to swing to the right.

They then start pushing on the left rudder pedal to balance the forces and stop the rightward turn. Meanwhile, their eyes become riveted on one particular instrument, the turn-and-slip indicator, to the exclusion of other vital indications.

This instrument shows if the craft is in balance and which rudder pedal needs to be depressed. The two harried aviators soon start arguing about which pedal should be pushed and how much. One pilot depresses the left rudder as the other opposes him by stomping on the right pedal.[5] Bowers then shouts, "Step on the rudder!" as Carey shouts back, "*Paul, no! Paul! Paul, don't!*"

In this cauldron of confusion, the jet overshoots the runway and drifts downward as it travels three miles to the northeast, just a few hundred feet above the terrain. The aircraft suddenly shudders, and the young pilots watch in disbelief while their world literally turns upside down. When the craft rolls rapidly to the left, both pilots slam their control wheels to the right in a futile effort to cheat death.

But the tumbling jet crashes inverted into a forest. Its airframe disintegrates as sixty-foot-tall trees fall like tenpins. The remaining fuel from its ruptured tanks explodes in a blinding flash. These quiet Alabama woods are transformed into hell's half-acre as the eight victims instantly perish.

The clock on Secretary Perry's wall back in Washington says it's 7:22 P.M., but it will be several hours before he gets word of his lifelong friend's demise. This, of course, won't be the first time the secretary has received news of a tragic military crash. Such calls are never easy, but this time it is *truly* personal.

What is worst, only a year will pass before this tragic scene repeats itself when another senior colleague of Perry's will board one of his jets, only to die in a fiasco. This sensitive cabinet officer is destined to become a Faustian character haunted by his poor bargain, for William J. Perry is caught up in having to repeatedly defend the devilish system that has robbed him of cherished comrades.

Three months after the Learjet crash, the Air Force released its official accident report. It concluded that improper rudder inputs in conjunction with overly aggressive asymmetrical power application had caused the jet to depart controlled flight. But there was another factor that contributed to this tragedy: the crew members' lack of exposure to CRM principles.[6]

Furthermore, this cockpit confusion and breakdown in crew coordination had to be obvious to at least one victim, who then realized this was going to be his *last* mission. From his passenger seat, General Profitt watched helplessly as his young crew caused the once nimble Learjet to gyrate wildly and plunge into the trees. While this prominent American hero always knew that he might be killed in combat, he never expected to die in such a manifestly preventable accident.[7]

The general's battered corpse is soon removed from the wreckage. More than eighteen months have passed since this stoic officer wrote to the USAF chief of safety to request assistance in developing a CRM program for his fliers. In his letter of September 21, 1993, General Profitt said, "I am convinced Dr. Diehl's unique knowledge and experience will save the Air Force time, resources, and lives. I hope we can continue to use his expertise . . . "[8]

Unfortunately, my superiors at the safety agency did not share Profitt's views. Thinking this letter was just another case of Diehl upsetting a general with his alarmist rhetoric, these safety officials ignored his plea. For Glenn Profitt, Hemingway was indeed right—sometimes the bell *does* toll for you.

18

Cheating Life

President Clinton said of his favorite cabinet officer, " . . . Ron Brown walked, he ran and flew through life."[1] But this vibrant flight through life was in peril as his jet began its approach to the war-torn airport at Dubrovnik, Croatia. Secretary of Commerce Ronald H. Brown, the high priest of capitalism, was bringing an entourage of experts to help restore this ravaged land.

In aviation, when we take chances and get away with it, we say we are "cheating death." But on April 3, 1996, the Air Force would tragically end up *"cheating life."* Ron Brown and his thirty-four companions would never land, for this approach was the last link in a long chain of unfortunate events.

The Pentagon's "airline" has always been a collection of compromises. Because transporting passengers is not a primary military mission, they take more shortcuts than a ValuJet[2] comptroller. Nowhere is this more evident than in post–Cold War Europe.

Here, the new world disorder has forced the U.S. Air Forces Europe (USAFE) to accept a host of unexpected challenges. But this command was often denied the necessary resources. The military's most basic rule is, "The mission is first everything else is second," while its next most basic rule is, "No complaining about the first rule." Unfortunately, this mentality would set the stage for disaster.

The young pilots of Ron Brown's CT-43 (the military version of the Boeing 737 airliner) are intimately familiar with both rules as their jet (call sign IFO 21) penetrates the rain-soaked clouds. Captains Tim Schafer and Ashley Davis also know this is going to be a very tricky approach—at best. But to divert to their alternate destination without at least trying to land would be unthinkable, because they have been ordered to take this most distinguished visitor and his entourage on this mission. Schafer and Davis know all too well that even questioning the safety of such a mission could be hazardous to their careers. They have witnessed such an object lesson recently.

Their boss, Lieutenant Colonel James Albright, commander of the 76th Airlift Squadron (AS), had discovered this the hard way five days earlier. He had articulated the potential dangers of such missions and was summarily fired! It seems that Albright's boss, the commander of the 86th Airlift Wing (AW), concluded he was not a "team player."[3] For the men and women of this command, the message was clear—speaking up to protect your passengers and fellow crew members has its costs.

Colonel Albright had good reasons for speaking up. His unit and its people were being routinely directed to operate unsafely for a variety of reasons. For starters, their flying environment was treacherous. They operated in the congested European airspace. Their air traffic control procedures were sometimes subtly different from those back in the States, and some controllers were not that friendly. Then there was the language problem. Since the Second World War ended, international law has required all radio communications to be in English. But not everybody has mastered this second tongue. In addition, European weather was notoriously poor much of the time.

If that wasn't bad enough, now they must fly into the former Soviet Union and its Eastern-bloc satellites—as well as the war zone in the erstwhile Yugoslavia. This presents a major problem, because like their civilian airline counterparts, USAFE transports should land only at inspected and approved airports.

USAFE is required by regulation to inspect such airports and to provide a list of approved airports for its crew, but the command has not done this and has asked for a "waiver" (that is, permission to ignore this requirement).[4] The Pentagon has turned them down, but nobody seems to be voicing any concerns about such safety compromises—except Albright.

In such a stressful operating environment, Crew Resource Management training is vital. There was no mention of this command's CRM deficiencies in its previous major accident investigation, the 1994 shootdown of Black Hawk helicopters. However, there is now a regulation, Air Force Instruction (AFI) number 36-4322, which requires all commands to provide such training to the flight crews. Unfortunately, USAFE has also ignored this regulation.

The flight crew of IFO 21 also had problems with their maps. Our military fliers normally rely on aeronautical maps and charts produced by the U.S. government. Most airline pilots the world over use products sold by a private company, Jeppesen Sanderson, Inc. These "Jepps," as they are called, basically depict the same information as their government-issue counterparts. Airlines use Jepps because they are easier to read. This is especially true for the small, five-by-eight-inch maps called "approach plates" that are used during landing.[5] This flight was using the Jepps, instead of the usual military maps, because they are the only maps available for places like Dubrovnik.

Military crew members need to be trained on subtle differences between the two types of maps. This is something else the command failed to do.[6] But there is another, even more basic problem with military fliers using Jepps. Unlike the U.S. government, which actually gathers the survey data and does the calculations on which its maps are based, Jepps just use the information that is supplied by the host country.

Tragically, the Croatian government has miscalculated an important piece of information on the Dubrovnik airport map. The so-called minimum descent altitude (or MDA) is too low by several hundred feet. This critical cartographic inaccuracy, when combined with even a small navigational error—namely, a slight deviation left of the proper course—can put an unsuspecting aircraft into the nearby mountains. Had USAFE properly surveyed this airport, it may have detected the Croatian government's blunder.

Another major problem for flight IFO 21 is that, in bad weather, the *only* kind of instrument procedure available at the Dubrovnik airport is an outdated nondirectional beacon (NDB) approach. This type of approach was common fifty years ago but has all but disappeared from modern airline or military operations—for a number of good reasons. They are not very accurate in providing lateral course guidance, and they provide *no* vertical guidance. Hence, they are classified as "nonprecision" approach procedures. The accuracy of the cockpit instruments, called automatic direction finders (ADFs) that are used for such approaches are also known to be adversely affected by weather phenomena such as thunderstorms and even the static electricity that aircraft pick up during flight.

NDB approaches are known to be extremely difficult to fly. They require pilots to constantly monitor their ADF instrument readings and quickly do several types of arcane calculations while making simultaneous control inputs. The result is a very high mental workload, which drastically increases the probability of a critical error.

But an even larger problem is the fact that this particular NDB approach requires *two* ADF receivers be installed in the cockpit.[7] One receiver must stay tuned to the first frequency, which will be used by the pilots to establish the aircraft's course (119 degrees) over the ground. The second receiver is simultaneously tuned to the second beacon frequency, which tells the pilots when they have arrived at the so-called missed approach point. This is where the instrument landing procedure ends. There the crew must decide if they can see the airport to land. If not, they must break off the landing and go around. Unfortunately, the CT-43, the flagship of the 86th Airlift Wing, has only a *single* ADF receiver. Thus, it is illegal for the Air Force to even send the aircraft to this airport in poor weather. This glaring deficiency will make it difficult for the craft to land safely.

But Captains Schafer and Davis know that as military "crew dogs," they will be expected to shut up, salute smartly, and *make* it happen, for they have no union, no ombudsman—and no way of getting out of this dangerous dilemma. Interestingly, when it comes to military aviation, the more senior the passengers, the more the pressure and the *less* the safety. This dangerously demented equation has trapped these two young men.

Even under the best of circumstances, this would be a very difficult mission. Aviation safety expert and author John Nance has popularized the concept of "margin of safety." This outfit has been operating on the edge for a long time, and today this margin continues to shrink for a variety of additional reasons.

The crew has had to cope with four mission changes in as many days. Copilot Schafer had his sleep interrupted repeatedly the night before. Things had not gone well on the previous flight to Tuzla. They were running behind schedule because their passengers had arrived late. While inbound to Tuzla, the crew had to be reminded by the controllers that they were well left of the final approach course. The Tuzla controllers used their radar to detect this dangerous deviation, but there is no radar installed at Dubrovnik. On top of everything else, the Dubrovnik weather is supposed to be marginal.

On their final flight from Tuzla to Dubrovnik, things go from bad to worse. The pilots mistakenly begin flying this leg on the *wrong* airway. Such errors are more common for fatigued and overstressed fliers. Fortunately, the controllers also catch this embarrassing gaffe, but the crew falls fifteen minutes behind schedule while correcting its navigational error. They also know the U.S. ambassador and the prime minister are waiting on the ground at Dubrovnik to meet the commerce secretary and their other distinguished passengers.

What is worse, the Dubrovnik weather has continued to deteriorate. The clouds are descending, and there are significant crosswinds and rain. The cloud ceiling is now only five hundred feet above the airport. This altitude is more than one thousand feet below the lowest level to which the pilots can legally descend, the so-called MDA. Because the ceiling is so low, if this were a civilian airline flight, regulations would prohibit the crew from even attempting this non-precision approach. But Captains Davis and Schafer don't have that out.

With such a distinguished passenger on board, these military fliers also know they must at least *try* to see if they can find the airport—even in this soup. The major danger here is the rugged mountains that lie just north of the airport, especially with the crosswinds blowing them in that direction. Furthermore, the crew cannot see this dangerous terrain today because of the dense clouds and rain. To avoid such hazards, they are totally dependent on their aircraft's minimal instruments and their unfamiliar maps.

The Dubrovnik tower clears them to the first radio beacon (which is ironically called the "final approach fix"). Their "pucker factor" is already off the scale when another pilot, who landed at the airport an hour earlier, gets on the radio. He wants to describe how *bad* the weather is and adds to their burden by reminding them about the important people impatiently waiting on the ramp. Such radio chatter can be very distracting at times like this.

Pilot Davis, who is flying, allows his speed to get one hundred miles per hour too fast, as the CT-43 screams over the first beacon. Furthermore, he has *not* configured his craft for landing by properly extending the wing flaps and landing gear. To make matters worse, he is on the *wrong* course. He is nine critical degrees left of the proper track and heading directly toward the towering mountains just north of his intended flight path. But this is difficult for him to discern in the clouds with his craft's limited instruments. In the parlance of aviators, he has succumbed to one of the deadliest of sins—he has lost "situational awareness."

The only person who can salvage this predicament is the man in the right-hand cockpit seat, copilot Schafer. But he is so fatigued that he has not adequately challenged any of these deviations. And like Davis, he is *very* confused. He also has lost his situational awareness while trying to interpret the constantly drifting instrument needles. Like his aircraft commander, he cannot figure out their position in relation to the airport.

Now, as they near the "missed approach point," they have recovered somewhat, although the pilots do not have the required second radio receiver to know where they are. Aviators have a sixth sense, however, which often tells them when an unseen danger is very near. Davis has pulled back on the control wheel and throttles, and the big Boeing has dutifully slowed down and leveled off.

The jet's windshield wipers beat out a steady tattoo in a vain attempt to clear the rain splattering against the ship's windshield. Schafer's weary eyes have been occasionally peering outside into the clouds, hoping against hope to catch a glimpse of the airport. His eyes flick back to the cockpit instruments and then to his maps.

But the jet has already overshot the missed approach point by a mile and drifted two miles off course. Now both pilots are thinking it's about time to make an apologetic PA announcement to say that they could not find the airport. But before anyone can key a microphone, the craft's Ground Proximity Warning Systems scream "WOOP, WOOP, PULL UP!"

Davis instinctively yanks back on the control wheel and firewalls the throttles—to no avail. Newton's second law of physics dictates that a hundred-thousand-pound craft cannot respond that quickly—as its inertia carries it into the jagged rocks. Before anyone can scream, the aluminum cocoon shatters itself across the desolate ridge.

Captains Davis and Schafer, Secretary Brown, and the thirty-one others die mercifully quick deaths. But for one technical sergeant who is seated in the aft cabin, death takes a while longer. A search and rescue team does not reach her for several agony-filled hours. They rush this young military flight attendant down the slope, but they cannot get her battered body to medical assistance in time to save her life.

The crash of USAF flight IFO 21 posed a particular problem for the Pentagon because it dramatically refocused attention on so many of the problems that I had tried in vain to bring to the attention of the secretary of defense eighteen months earlier. He and his handlers had moved with glacial slowness to even acknowledge these widespread problems. This time one of the victims was a fellow cabinet officer.

For me, perhaps the most interesting note in the Air Force's self-serving accident report was a passage of three almost parenthetical sentences.[8] "Additionally, HQ USAFE operations staff had not implemented the Cockpit/Crew Resource Management (CRM) Program required by AFI 36-2243. The 76 AS had recently developed a squadron CRM program that the mishap pilots had not yet attended. Tenets taught in the resource management program are designed to help crews avoid mishaps like the one experienced by IFO 21 . . . by improving skills for managing workload, aircrew decision making, and enhancing situational awareness."

Two years had passed since the twenty-six people died when USAFE fighters shot down the Black Hawk helicopters. I had specifically tried to point out the importance of CRM to this command then, but they unceremoniously removed me from that investigation. Now Secretary Brown and thirty-four others had to die to get this command to even acknowledge the value of such training. However, as expected, their seven-thousand-page report contained no criticism of the Pentagon, the air staff, or the safety agency for their roles in delaying and derailing this vital training.[9]

Ironically, in the December 1993 issue of the *USAF Flying Safety* magazine, I wrote an article titled "Crew 'Recourse' Management."[10] It explained that perhaps this was a better name for CRM training because, when everything else goes wrong, such training is the crew's last "recourse" to prevent the mishap. Sadly, Davis and Schafer had not received such instruction, and the service's shortcuts had ended up cheating them out of life.

A strange and tragic epilogue would follow the erection of their tombstones. Enlightened safety professionals always advocate proactive prevention measures. But some organizations, such as the Pentagon, tend to wait until after a major catastrophe has occurred before even considering safety enhancements. These types of reactive measures are sometimes call "tombstone mandates."

Secretary Brown's accident led to several such mandates, because it was hard, even for the Pentagon, to ignore this much embarrassing evidence. After all, Mrs. Clinton and Chelsea, not to mention the secretary of defense himself, had all ridden on board that particular aircraft only weeks before this crash. Furthermore, there was little the DoD could do to conceal most of the equipment, training, and management deficiencies manifested by this tragedy.

The national media was understandably having a field day. The Pentagon gang, ever mindful of its public image, announced a number of fixes. Most were worthwhile and long overdue, but some amused the insiders.

Case in point: The media had blasted the Pentagon because its crews were still using dangerously obsolete NDBs for instrument landings. This was especially embarrassing since the DoD already owned and operated a multibillion-dollar, super-accurate, satellite-based navigation system.

This technology is called the Global Positioning System (GPS). Modern aircraft often have receivers that depict GPS-based navigational information *directly* on their cockpit instrument panels. These revolutionary displays provide airmen with very accurate and easy to interpret data.

In a knee-jerk response to this criticism, Secretary Perry announced that the Pentagon would immediately purchase *handheld* GPS receivers and issue them to all military pilots who fly passenger jets. Good damage control is one of the Pentagon's fortes. But no one apparently told Secretary Perry that the CT-43 unit *already* had these devices for its pilots—*prior* to the crash. These handheld units were used to calibrate other aircraft navigational receivers while on the ground.

Unfortunately, these handheld units were not useful as an instrument landing aid for jets, since both pilots already have their hands full during landings. In fact, people assigned to that unit have said that using such devices would actually *decrease* safety. In spite of this, the Pentagon spent millions to purchase handheld GPS receivers and even more money training crews in their use.[11]

Disgusted military fliers were forced to go along with this charade, although there were a few interesting remarks. It seems the FAA requires the manufacturers to print a warning of the side of these receivers: "This device is not legal for use during instrument approaches." This was a source of classroom humor, because the Ron Brown botched instrument approach *was* the rationale for purchasing these units. Furthermore, the DoD was just wasting the time of these busy crews with such useless training. Of course, *nobody* was going to bring such facts to the secretary's attention now that his spin-meisters had decided this was *the* quick remedy for such accidents.

The bigger problem was that the misinformed secretary did not push for the implementation of *real* solutions to such problems. This situation continued to haunt military safety. For instance, in the wake of the Ron Brown crash, Congress recommended that a host of modern safety devices be installed on military transports.[12] Mr. Perry's subordinates did little to comply with this legislation, and as a result, more young men and women would soon be cheated out of life.

19

Accountability Run Amok

As a devout Christian, Technical Sergeant Thomas Mueller knows what he is about to do is a mortal sin. His heavily calloused fingers nervously fondle the pistol. He says a prayer in the hope that he's going to a better place, for this master mechanic has already done a tour in hell—courtesy of the institution he has faithfully served for eighteen years.

Earlier, Mueller typed a letter to the widow of one Major Donald Lowry. The sergeant has asked her to forgive him for his role in her husband's untimely death. Mueller desperately wants her to understand that he was *not* negligent while repairing the major's jet.

This troubled airman now hears the strident voices in the distance. They belong to the military posse demanding his surrender. Like a cornered animal, he knows time has run out. In desperation, the sergeant raises the weapon to his head. He simply cannot stand the torment any longer. He squeezes the trigger.

Ironically, the sergeant's death was the by-product of a bungled military plan to improve its image. Early in 1995, the service launched a highly publicized quest for "accountability." But unlike its recruiting motto, "Aim high," this effort is not going to point any fingers upward—at its top leaders. Instead, the initiative will focus its fury on a couple of hardworking enlisted troops.

Mueller and another sergeant became the unwilling posterboys for this misguided campaign. They alone were to be court-martialed for a unique mistake. The military contended that their criminally negligent behavior had caused a pilot's death. Thus, they must be held accountable as a matter of principle.

This simplistic logic ignored a number of embarrassing issues—issues that dealt with things not under the purview of the accused—but the Air Force leaders did not intend to be confused with such facts. To protect themselves from criticism, they literally spent a million dollars to insure these sergeants would be convicted.

Mueller and his "partner in crime," Technical Sergeant William Turner Campbell, had unintentionally cross-connected two identical-looking control rods on Major Lowry's jet. On May 17, 1995, these mechanics struggled to correctly align the components that were located in a small, dark compartment in the bowels of the F-15. They even used a flashlight and mirror to try to inspect their work. When they finished, the aircraft was worked on by other mechanics. It was then rolled into a hangar at Spangdahlem Air Base in western Germany. The stage was set for disaster, which would occur thirteen days later.

But this disaster really began decades ago in St. Louis, Missouri, on the drawing boards of the McDonnell Douglas Company. Their designers began sketching what would become a premier air superiority jet. Ergonomics textbooks warn designers to avoid using the same size connectors on such rods.[1] The potential for inadvertently misattaching two identical fasteners is obvious.

Such poorly designed equipment is an accident waiting to happen. Moreover, this incident at Spangdahlem was not the first time F-15 mechanics had made this same "design induced" mistake. But the Air Force chose to ignore the problem, so its troops simply did not get the word about this particular pitfall.

Equipment design problems can wreak havoc with the overworked mechanics in the post–Cold War Air Force. These patriotic men and women are expected to make up the shortfalls in America's overcommitted and underfunded military. They struggle around the clock on the far-flung flight lines and maintenance hangars just to keep an aging fleet of jets airworthy. Twelve-hour workdays and parts shortages are commonplace.[2] Yet these technicians know that there is no margin for error in handling delicate aircraft components. Unfortunately, this particular ergonomic deficiency is concealed in the Eagle's most critical system—its flight controls.

With these rods cross-connected, the ailerons (located at wing tips) and the elevators (on the tail) do not move in the proper directions when the pilot moves his control stick. Pilots the world over always perform a control check before taking off. During this ritual, the pilot moves the stick in a certain pattern while peering at the control surfaces to see if they respond in the proper direction. Air Force pilots are actually required to do two such checks while nearby mechanics watch attentively. When doing both preflight checks, the doomed pilot and two of the accused sergeants' fellow mechanics will somehow overlook these vital cues.

On the morning of May 30, 1995, Major Lowry taxies the F-15 onto the runway for takeoff. He pushes the two throttles all the way forward with his left hand, engaging the afterburners. The dull gray F-15 quickly accelerates with an ear-splitting roar. With this right hand, Lowry pulls back on the control stick, but the jet's nose refuses to rise. At 250 miles per hour, he pulls back on the stick a second time.

Instead of pointing its nose skyward, the errant Eagle rolls over violently. It barrels off the runway and skids through the grass. Shredding itself into a thousand pieces, it kills Lowry before he has a chance to eject. Black smoke billows from the wreckage as sirens wail, and rumors and grief quickly spread across the base.

These are tough times for the stoic men and women of Spangdahlem Air Base. One year ago, two of their F-15 pilots shot down the Army Black Hawk helicopters over Iraq. But this time death has come to one of their own, and on their very doorstep. In this summer of their discontent, things would soon get worse—at least for a couple of their comrades.

The glare of public ridicule again focused on Air Force safety inadequacies. Captain Wang, the radar officer who was expected to take the fall for the Black Hawk shoot-downs, has been acquitted. This surprising court-martial verdict soon caused problems for Air Force leaders. The families of the twenty-six Black Hawk victims were understandably livid that no one was being held "accountable" for that tragedy.

The Air Force was also being widely criticized, because the Spangdahlem-based pilots who did the actual shooting had earlier gotten off scot-free. Moreover, the press and Congress soon joined in this chorus. Thus, the era of "accountability" was about to dawn, and crap always rolls downhill, as the saying goes. This time, the two mechanics are at the bottom of that hill.

From his lofty perch in the Pentagon, it must have appeared to the Air Force chief of staff, General Ronald Fogleman, that *something* was wrong at Spangdahlem. Perhaps its commander, Major General Charles Heflebower,[3] had not gotten the word about Fogleman's new accountability campaign. Fogleman wanted everybody to get with the program, and Heflebower soon threw the book at his two hapless mechanics.

Mueller and Campbell were going to be charged with negligent homicide plus a few counts of dereliction of duty—just for good measure. Basically, their conviction would only involve convincing the members of a military jury of their guilt. This should have been easy since jurors are handpicked by the commander's people to be sympathetic to his viewpoint. But there were several major problems with making these particular charges stick—and Heflebower's legal advisor had cautioned him about certain issues.[4]

First, this control system was so poorly designed that even the best mechanics could not spot when the two identical-looking control rods had been reversed. Furthermore, the evidence clearly suggested that the accused had conscientiously tried to insure that these rods were properly aligned. Obviously, the defendants could logically argue that the service had bought another dangerous piece of equipment and then forced its people to contend with the shortcomings.

Second, there were problems with the guidance provided in their maintenance manuals. The language used did not clearly state whether Mueller and Campbell actually needed to physically verify if the control surfaces really moved as advertised after reconnecting the rods. Their manual stated that this check is required *if* you repair *or* adjust the control system. These sergeants had done neither. They just disconnected the rods so other mechanics could work on an adjacent fuel tank. When the other technicians were finished, the accused then reattached these rods.

Then there was the problem with the training. Obviously, the Air Force had done little to educate its mechanics about this potentially catastrophic problem. Mueller and Campbell swore that nothing in their training told them the rods were easily interchangeable. Other mechanics quickly confirmed this fact to the prosecution.

Moreover, this design deficiency had caused previous incidents in 1986 and in 1991, when sharp-eyed mechanics and pilots who noticed the misaligned control surfaces before takeoff had averted disaster. Investigations into these two near accidents, as well as the current crash, had been critical of the Air Force for not modifying the rods to preclude them from ever again being accidentally cross-connected.[5]

These investigations had also pointed out that the Air Force Safety Agency had failed miserably in its responsibility to get the word out to the mechanics. However, its reports were "privileged," and therefore these sergeants could not even see the documents, much less use such information in their defense. The sergeants' lawyers asked the secretary of the Air Force for permission to examine the reports, but she refused their request.

Last, his own legal advisors had informed General Heflebower that, while Mueller and Campbell could be shown to have messed up these delicate procedures, several other people were in better positions to have easily detected the control surface misalignment problems. Heflebower was also told that one of the charges against the sergeants—that they had not correctly filled out the paperwork—might be viewed as "petty." But the general knew that in the military justice system, the commander holds *all* the cards.

Thus, he dismissed this advice and ordered his legal staff to proceed with the full action. Heflebower thereby released his legal pit bulls on these two devastated GIs. This pair blamed themselves for the major's death, but they could not fathom why they were being hounded for what was just an honest, albeit tragic, mistake. They began wondering how far the service was prepared to go to obtain convictions. It soon became obvious that the prosecutors would do whatever was necessary to break them.

These jet mechanics were quickly transferred to the motor pool to wash and repair cars. Fellow mechanics reported attempts by prosecution lawyers to coerce them into saying Mueller and Campbell were careless, inept, and so forth. Enlisted troops who had tried to resist were verbally threatened. One key witness said the prosecutors would " . . . cut me off at the knees . . . " if he testified for the mechanics.[6]

The mind games never ended. Before the accident happened, Mueller was getting ready to ship out. His household goods and furniture had already been packed up and removed to a warehouse. Now the Air Force refused to return these items, putting an intentional hardship on his family. The Air Force thus insured that the "sins" of the father were visited upon Mueller's sons. The judge soon issued a gag order on everyone, essentially isolating the two sergeants from their former colleagues, the very people who could have provided psychological support for the besieged pair.

To some, the prosecution team also seemed to take a perverse pleasure in breaking these guys. For example, "somebody" left the pilot's autopsy photos on Mueller's desk, where he could not miss seeing them. Viewing these full-color, eight-by-ten-inch enlargements of the victim's mutilated corpse left an indelible mark on his psyche. Mueller became increasingly distraught after looking at these gory pictures. He told Campbell, who had avoided viewing these photos, that he could never close his eyes again without seeing the bloody images.

The Air Force establishment had targeted these two sergeants with laser precision, but the mechanics had a few important allies, including the popular *Air Force Times* weekly newspaper. This widely read insider journal had been reporting on my campaign to improve military safety.[7] The *Times* soon heard about the sergeants' plight and began covering their story. The paper published their appeals for information that might be related to the F-15 control problems. The brass was furious and determined to stop this end run.

I saw the stories and knew I had to become involved again—just as I had done before when the service had targeted Captain Jim Wang[8] and Sergeant Chris Cross.[9] Besides, I knew an important fact about this case, one that needed to be brought out.

In 1993, the U.S. Air Forces Europe (USAFE) command had used some of my Crew Resource Management training materials at one of their F-15 units. The program reduced maintenance errors similar to the one Mueller and Campbell had made by a whopping 64 percent. But like so many good ideas, this kind of training was never implemented.

Because this information showed that the Air Force had botched another chance to prevent Major Lowry's accident, I mailed the vital information to the sergeants. I sent the packages on January 19, 1996, so that they would arrive in time to be used during their military grand jury proceedings. When I did not hear from either man, I began to wonder what had occurred. A few weeks later, the ugly truth came out when I received a call from Mueller's attorney, Captain Melissa Hagen.

She explained that the Air Force Office of Special Investigation (i.e., their "secret police") had been tipped off. Apparently they had been warned that I, a known whistle-blower, was trying to help the accused sergeants. Thus, the gendarmes claimed that when my sealed envelopes had arrived in the Spangdahlem mailroom, they were already torn open. How convenient. These officials were, of course, concerned that I was supplying "privileged" information to the accused, a criminal offense.

So naturally they confiscated the envelopes and promptly turned this vital information over to the presiding judges. These officers of the court in turn concealed my data from the defense attorneys until *after* the military grand jury had indicted the sergeants. Such tactics were reminiscent of those used by Hitler's gestapo. I asked Captain Hagen if this constituted a denial of due process. This young attorney emphatically replied "yes!"

This was not going to be a trial, but a "legal lynching." Things were going from bad to worse in the months that followed as the prosecutors tightened the noose. Mueller's parents called to thank me for trying to come to their boy's aid. As the trial approached, I heard that the prosecution was bringing in dozens of witnesses from as far away as Japan, while the sergeants were limited to a handful of character witnesses. The prosecutors even tried to get Major Lowry's family to testify against the mechanics but were rebuffed when his family asked for leniency instead.

On September 9, 1996, I wrote Defense Secretary Perry to complain about the lack of due process in this trial, but to no avail. Three weeks later, on October 3, 1996, as his trial began, Thomas Mueller got up early. He took out his 22-caliber derringer and departed from his unfurnished home. When he did not appear in court, the Air Force immediately declared him a *deserter* and organized a manhunt.

Unbeknownst to Thomas, his father, Peter, had just arrived from the States. Peter tried to join in the search because everybody knew Thomas had a weapon and was depressed. But Air Force officials managed to keep Peter at bay as they combed the sergeant's favorite haunts—the forests located on the base perimeter. As the posse approached, Thomas put the gun to his head. Bang!

In a split second, this once peaceful German woods turned into a mob scene. The sergeant's pursuers, after hearing the shot, rushed toward a hunting blind, a crude wooden structure. They immediately found his grievously injured body. But the sound of this shot would soon travel beyond these bucolic woodlands.

Mueller's mother, Heidi, called me the next day with the tragic news. In my profession, one becomes used to discussing death dispassionately, but I nevertheless broke down in tears. Hearing this grieving lady say that Peter would be bringing their son's body home to Florida for burial was just too much. I knew Peter was a German-born lawyer who had once actually worked for the United States Air Force. He was also the one who suggested the young Mueller join up. Now this remorseful father would be taking a final journey with his boy.

As word spread across Spangdahlem and throughout the Air Force, the rank-and-file became outraged. Many folks spoke their minds in an unmilitary fashion, creating a "disturbance in the force." Documents, including privileged reports that Mueller had been denied access to in life, mysteriously appeared at his residence. His family was shocked to see what information the Air Force had withheld.

The media was also hearing about these strange and tragic events. Several news organizations were showing an interest in the story. With a CNN camera team reportedly heading to Spangdahlem, the officials had had enough. The Air Force, which once proudly claimed it had never been turned back in combat over wartime Germany, was now in full retreat. These leaders just wanted to cut their losses. So they quickly offered to drop all charges against Sergeant Campbell, provided he accept an immediate discharge. The befuddled GI agreed and left the Air Force, forgoing the pension benefits he had earned.

Obviously, exonerating Campbell was awkward for these officials. But things would become even more unpleasant for the service spinmeisters. The glare of public ridicule over this mishandled case forced them into another distasteful, albeit insincere, pronouncement. The Air Force reluctantly stated that they were considering filing charges against a senior prosecutor, presumably for withholding my mail and other potential offenses.

On October 18, 1996, a deputy under secretary of defense replied to my letter of September 7, saying they would look into my "allegation" of denial of due process. I was dumbstruck by this belated response. All I could think of was that Bill Perry had missed *another* opportunity to do the right thing. While the secretary had never met this faceless GI, as a cabinet officer he still had a duty to protect him from such abuses.

On December 20, 1996, CNN interviewed me in an attempt to put this bizarre tragedy in context. Lou Waters hosted this thirteen-minute broadcast. I simply explained that the accident and the prosecution of Mueller were graphic evidence of the military's widespread safety problems. Furthermore, the organization seemed be in a constant state of denial. That contention would prove prophetic as new events unfolded.

On December 30, 1996, an *Air Force Times* editorial[10] called for the chief of staff to apologize to the sergeants' families for this obvious miscarriage of justice. Instead, an incensed General Fogleman suggested on January 20, 1997,[11] that Sergeant Mueller may have shot himself because a former supervisor was going to testify he *had* known about the control rod problems. Other Pentagon spokespersons quickly distanced themselves from this statement, suggesting the general may have *overstated* the case.

On February 21, 1997, Peter Mueller called me to say that a senior prosecutor was actually going to be investigated for her alleged offenses. No one really expected that anything would come of this sham inquiry. Obviously, the service would not dare try to punish her, because she could easily point the finger at those higher-ups who may have encouraged her to "get the sergeants." So nobody was surprised when the Air Force later sheepishly declared that it had cleared its erstwhile prosecutor of any wrongdoing.[12]

Almost a year had passed since a despondent Sergeant Mueller shot himself. Early in the evening of March 28, 1998, I got another call from his dad. Peter's voice had the tone of a man who has just had a great burden lifted from his shoulders. He joyfully declared the Military Board of Review and Corrections had just made a surprising ruling.[13]

This important panel had announced the Air Force had acted improperly when it charged Peter's son with negligent homicide. This board's conclusions were certainly definitive and so critical of the military hierarchy that they reportedly had to be rewritten and toned down.

The surprisingly candid edict from an obscure military auditing organization seemed like a small concession. But this pronouncement did at least officially clear Thomas Mueller's good name. Thus, the long-tormented airman could finally rest in peace. Now his family could try to get on with their shattered lives.

By contrast, I dared not relent. It had been more than three years since I had filed my whistle-blowing complaint, and little had happened to reform this dysfunctional dynamo. Indeed, the mechanism that crushed Mueller whirled on, unabated and unabashed. His death certificate said the sergeant died from a self-inflicted gunshot wound, but he was really another victim of the military's bungling approach to safety.

Thus, I *had* to continue the fight to reform this process before it claimed additional victims. But how? After all, the Department of Defense is literally the most powerful organization on the planet. What's more, this entrenched bureaucracy had so far proven itself immune to criticism. Was I just kidding myself about this seemingly quixotic quest? I began to contemplate the disturbing events of the last few years.

PART
V

After the Whistle

20

Pandora's Five-Sided Box

My "complaint" package had arrived at the Pentagon on October 25, 1994, to a reception of contemptuous silence. Several weeks later I was invited to Washington to discuss my "allegations" and not so politely informed that I had just opened Pandora's box. These smug Potomac power brokers knew that they had everything on their side—except the truth.

So they apparently decided just to "slow roll" the whole process, because most people in that city have short memories when it comes to things like whistle-blowers. These DoD "experts" would just have to study my claims and recommendations to death—so to speak. The days and years that followed would not be pleasant. I would be forced to watch insult heaped upon injury as the Pentagon continued with business as usual while other servicemen and women died.

Dedicated GIs like Tom Mueller had joined the cavalcade of the fallen, which included outstanding junior officers like Laura Piper. Indeed, all ranks were represented in this grim procession, from promising cadets like Mark Dostal to highly decorated generals such as Glenn Profitt. Occasionally, the dysfunctional system even reached up and claimed VIPs like Secretary Ron Brown. But nothing much had really changed except the names of the victims.

It got so I dreaded answering the phone for fear of having someone else tearfully describe to me how his or her loved one had perished and how the service would not tell them the truth about the accident. The newspapers also contained disturbing information on the latest rash of military crashes. Pentagon spokespersons would often suggest they could find "no common thread" to these recent mishaps—as if that non-explanation somehow made things okay.

Another disturbing phenomenon was the increasingly frequent description of a variety of unexplained illnesses befalling a growing number of Gulf War veterans. There seemed to be a strong parallel between the military's rampant safety problems and its handling of these disturbing medical issues. The Defense Department PR establishment quickly replied that their experts had concluded there was no *real* problem, just delayed stress reaction to combat.

But what I dreaded the most were the ubiquitous television news programs with their around-the-clock coverage. I hesitated to turn on my set for fear of having to view another military accident scene. Sometimes it really got personal because it involved people and units with which I had worked.

Such was the case the morning of September 4, 1998. Half awake, I flipped on the tube. The matter-of-fact TV commentator's voice said, "Officials at Nellis Air Force Base in Nevada announced that two of the their H-60 Pave Hawk[1] rescue helicopters crashed last night. All twelve crewmen aboard the rotorcraft were killed in the mishap."

"Damn it, not again!" I screamed back at the glowing screen. For I knew these guys surely had to include some of my former students. My phone soon rang. A friend was inquiring if I had caught the piece. "Yeah, I saw it. No, I don't know who was aboard. Thanks for calling."

As I hung up, my mind flashed back to another call four years before—from a young captain at that base. He started describing the multitude of problems facing the crew members assigned to fly rescue missions. This very sincere-sounding young officer calmly laid out the situation.

There simply were not enough choppers or crews to meet the numerous requests for their services. Supporting America's far-flung military commitments was already taking its toll. Spare parts were in short supply, while the rough operating conditions just accelerated maintenance problems of these mechanically complex machines. Furthermore, the senior leaders of the Air Force were mainly ex-fighter jocks who had little understanding—much less respect for—helicopter crew members. Hence the disparaging moniker "rotor-heads."

This conscientious officer was obviously concerned about his fellow airmen who had to make do in this dangerous operating environment. Furthermore, he had just been placed in charge of putting together the curriculum for the Air Combat Rescue School. He had heard about my successful training programs on safety, human factors, and CRM, and he wanted to know if I would come and teach a course on those topics. He knew that such a course might literally be the difference between life and death, especially for some of his less experienced comrades.

The captain had apparently heard that my lectures were well received because I always stressed pragmatic "rules and tools" that aviators could incorporate into their daily flying routines. Some of these concepts I had picked up during decades of personal flying. Other ideas I had encountered while investigating dozens of accidents. Still others I discovered during my human factors research and aircraft design work. But I had gleaned much just from *listening* to aviators discuss close calls that had happened to them. The most gratifying aspect of this process was when they called back, often years after getting the training, to describe how using my techniques had saved their lives.

I explained to the eager captain that I would be glad to help out. But not everyone at the safety agency wanted me talking with the troops. One senior officer often tried to prevent me from accepting these requests. So I simply told the captain that he would have to have his commander, the school commandant, *demand* my services—by name. The junior officer took my hint and arranged for a very forceful request to come from his superior. The ploy worked, and I was on my way to Nellis. There, I would soon discover that the captain had not exaggerated the dangers facing the dedicated fliers whose motto was "That Others Might Live."

Looking at the audience, I could see all the signs on their faces—chronic fatigue from months of overwork. Many had been deployed to austere "forward areas" for more than 120 days during the past year. When some flier went down, they launched, regardless of the weather or other problems. After weeks of such missions, they returned to Nellis physically and mentally drained. They then had to play catch-up by performing a myriad of other "collateral duties" (i.e., the things they missed while deployed). Their "can do" spirit was all that was keeping them going.

The stress in their voices reflected the fact that most had been continuously operating in a very dangerous and uncomfortable environment—flying in noisy, wind-whipped helicopter cabins, often in turbulent air. Many missions required flying only a few hundred feet above water, or worse yet, over rugged terrain in all kinds of weather. Crew coordination and communication were always critical, and the poor quality of their interphone systems was another problem with which they had to contend.

But perhaps the look in their eyes was most revealing, for the worst aspect of their mission was the night tactics involving the use of night vision goggles (NVGs). These helmet-mounted "binoculars" required squinting into a surreal, shades-of-green world for hours on end. Their stoic eyes revealed another cost of conducting such operations.

The night I arrived at Nellis, my young captain host had insisted on meeting with me for dinner. I thought maybe he was just being circumspect and observing the rules of protocol. After all, as a GS-15 civilian, I was technically equal in rank to a full colonel. But when he handed me a recent chopper crash report, I knew he had a more important reason for the dinner invitation. He did not want me to be blindsided the next morning.

He said, "You had better read this, because the students will undoubtedly ask you about this accident and why the investigation was so badly screwed up." Indeed, I had heard about this report. It was obviously something that senior officials did not want discussed.

The report intentionally focused on the usual "pilot error" babble while totally ignoring several important facts that reflected on the poor decisions of the top generals. In reality, the mishap was caused by cost-cutting actions taken by these senior officers. Their miscalculations had cost the lives of several young fliers and the loss of a multimillion-dollar piece of equipment.

These commanders had closed the helicopter detachments at a number of forward installations. This meant that new pilots arriving at these bases had no experienced helicopter aviators "to show them the ropes" on flying in the local area. The buildings, electrical power poles, and lookout towers around these forward bases were *camouflaged*. But the inexperienced visiting pilots had not been adequately warned about such hazards to low-flying rotorcraft.

Furthermore, the young men were apparently sent aloft on an overcast night when the clouds were blocking any moon or starlight from reaching the terrain or other obstacles. Thus, their NVGs were useless in spotting these camouflaged structures. The report did not include this relevant data. It was obvious to anybody who understood the issues that the report was a cover-up.

This jibed with what I had been told by a couple of conscientious colleagues. These insiders confided the report was so ridiculous that several of the officers in their military safety center had courageously refused to sign off on it. In fact, officials at that center had to go all the way to the Pentagon to find an officer with a low enough IQ (that's *integrity* quotient) to put his signature on the flawed report.

My young host was right. The students in my class soon brought up the bogus investigation and demanded to know how officials could promulgate such reports. When I told them how I recently had been fired for complaining about just such problems, the class gave me a standing ovation. Obviously, they appreciated that *somebody* cared enough to take a stand for the little guys.

More important, they paid close attention to what I had to say. I tried to lay out the precepts that would help keep them alive, even when leadership, mission tasking, equipment design, maintenance, and weather were lousy. In fact, I quipped that perhaps CRM should actually stand for Crew *Recourse* Management—"Because it's *your* last recourse when everything else has gone to hell. Just try to follow these procedures and remember, you can break the chain of events that would otherwise lead to an accident." They listened intently and took copious notes.

But I would teach only two classes at this institution. The Air Combat Rescue School would eventually be absorbed into the Weapons School. This was the Air Force's version of "Top Gun," the flagship training program of the newly established Air Combat Command. The former commandant and my host went on to other assignments, and my candid remarks may not have been politically correct enough for the new management.

I heard through the grapevine that the operating tempo continued unabated, but when many of the old heads in the rescue business retired, inexperienced fliers who needed this training even more usually replaced them. But unfortunately, they would not get my CRM information.

In fact, the Air Combat Command decided that it would order a command-wide CRM program, sort of a "one size fits all" philosophy, which would soon come a cropper. In 1994, that command issued a poorly written Request For Proposal (RFP), and I would soon be drawn into an attempt to improve the quality of this multimillion-dollar misguided effort.

My phone rang several times as soon as the document was published. CRM experts working for contractors who had been in the business for years could not believe their eyes. The RFP was so naïvely written, they could not figure out what the command wanted in these vital courses. They asked me to call headquarters of the Air Combat Command and try to fix the problem.

When I contacted the officer who had written the flawed RFP and tried to tactfully explain some of the problems with this document, he became incensed. "How dare *you* speak with *my* contractors. Who the hell are you to meddle in my acquisition effort? No, I do not want your advice!" he added as he slammed down the phone. His biggest concern seemed to be that rewriting might upset his general who had initiated the flawed effort. Obviously, this misguided officer knew where his priorities lay.

Thus, those rotor-heads trapped in fighter-pilot-land would just have to make do with whatever they got. I knew this was a *statistical death sentence*, for it was not a question of *if* accidents would occur because of these problems—just *when*. Unfortunately, their margin for safety was getting thinner as time wore on.

This fact becomes painfully obvious when two H-60s lift off the Nellis ramp on the evening of September 3, 1998. Both choppers turn northward and head toward the Pint-Water Mountains. As the bright lights of Las Vegas disappear behind them in the distance, the crew members do not realize just how badly the deck is stacked against them.

This flight was briefed as a low altitude, NVG formation flight, and light precipitation was falling over the rugged terrain. When they departed at 8:35 P.M., the dozen weary crew members aboard the choppers all knew this was going to be a long and very demanding evening at best. Furthermore, several of the crewmen were simply not up to the rigorous demands of this kind of flying.

The military culture, however, forced these gung-ho guys into the air without a safety net. Training, proficiency, and leadership problems had become rampant—but nobody in authority wanted to hear any whining. Months later, an *Air Force Times* article[2] would summarize the situation: "Among the crew members were a pilot with a weak performance record, an airman who likely would not have been on the training mission had supervisors been aware of problems in his training, one airman under medical orders not to fly and another who was supposed to have been off flight duty, a second lieutenant who had not been properly cleared for the mission, and a senior noncommissioned officer filling a position for which he was not qualified."

The squadron's very able second-in-command is personally leading this two-ship formation tonight: Lieutenant Colonel William Milton is seated in the left seat of the lead bird. A conscientious copilot, Captain Karl Youngblood, sits beside this veteran chopper pilot. This eager young officer has been tasked with planning the mission, although he does not have the minimum requirements to be fully combat ready. But the weakest link in the chain sits in the cockpit of the second H-60. In its left seat is an inexperienced aviator who has had difficulties his entire flying career.

Captain Philip Miller had finished near the bottom of his undergraduate pilot training class. Following the custom of the Air Force, he had been assigned to fly the less glamorous but more demanding helicopters. While checking out in helicopters, he failed in several key phases. His problems continued into his H-60 flying career. During a recent annual check ride, his examiner had to intervene four times.

What is worse, Captain Miller has flown only seventy-four hours during the last fifteen months. This is well below the amount of recent flight experience required to maintain *any kind* of reasonable proficiency. Tonight, this struggling young aviator is in over his head—but he has to fly. Besides, he is just one of twenty inexperienced copilots clogging the squadron's training roster, although the unit is supposed to have only eleven neophytes.

The H-60s have been airborne for a little over an hour when the lead chopper abruptly turns to the right. This jinking maneuver simulates reacting to an enemy threat, an imaginary missile shot. These types of simulations are designed to make such training exercises more realistic, but they also increase aircrew workload. Both choppers are now only a couple of hundred feet above the desert, traveling at more than a hundred miles per hour in the darkness.

Captain Miller is trying to join up with the lead chopper so they can fly in tight two-ship formation. He must carefully maneuver his craft alongside of the lead chopper while the pilot to his right pretends to make a radio call for imaginary fighters to retaliate against the simulated missile battery that just "fired" at their flight.

This inexperienced flier stares through his left cockpit window using his NVGs. Suddenly he starts drifting in toward lead. His NVGs, with their shades-of-green, out-of-focus images, just do not provide this struggling aviator with the critical cues he needs to judge distance in the darkness. Before he can react, his rotor blade slices into the right side of lead's cockpit.

It's all over in a split second as both out-of-control helicopters barrel roll violently to the left and shatter into a thousand pieces across the desert floor. The once vibrant human cargo of these two H-60s will become intertwined with tangled wreckage. Molten aluminum and blood run down the gentle sloping sands as twin fireballs rise into the Nevada sky.

Several hours later, Nellis officials will contact the loved ones of these men. Devastated by the news, these next of kin will begin to ask one question, *Why?* These family members are just the latest victims of the military's safety negligence, but unlike the dead fliers, *their* agonies won't end in an instant.

These newest victims do not realize that it has been more than four years since two other H-60s went down in another desert, half a world away. And the next of kin from that catastrophe in northern Iraq *still* have never been told what happened. Watching how our military establishment used its power to evade responsibility, which added to the agonies of those earlier victims, has not been pleasant.

21

Damage Control

A year after launching my 1994 one-man attempted coup to reform military safety, I heard Lieutenant Laura Piper's mother, Joan, wanted to speak with me. I had seen news photos of this lady at her daughter's funeral. She knew I had been fired from that friendly-fire investigation and needed to discuss the incident that had claimed her daughter's life.

As I dialed her number, I remembered how difficult it had always been to speak with the next of kin. Mutual friends had mentioned Joan was an elementary school teacher and her husband, Danny, was a retired Air Force colonel. As soon as she spoke, I was struck by this articulate woman's passion for the truth and by her frustration with the "system."

Mrs. Piper soon began detailing the government's abuses as well as the problems she and other next of kin were facing. Immediately after the accident, the Pentagon announced it was offering one hundred thousand dollars compensation to the families of the *foreign* victims. But the government would not be paying compensation to the relatives of our troops because the Feres Doctrine prohibits such redress.

Then there was the matter of the medals. American troops who are seriously injured in combat are awarded the Purple Heart. For those who are killed in action, the next of kin are always given this coveted medal

245

posthumously. But the supreme sacrifice has to be the result of *enemy* action. The Pentagon decided that even though their loved ones died in a war zone, accidents would not count.

The government would reverse itself on this issue, but the action just added insult to injury, for belatedly releasing the medals had forced the families to bury their fallen warriors with not-so-full military honors.[1]

But such affronts to decency paled in comparison to the fundamental issue, *Why?* The families, in their endless grief and growing outrage, had attracted the interest of the press and a few members of Congress. These people were growing a little suspicious of some strange goings-on.

First, the service immediately gave immunity from prosecution to the man who led the attack, Captain Wickson. They then brought his wingman, Lieutenant Colonel May, up on charges. Not surprisingly, the charges against May were soon dropped.[2]

Next, they briefly considered going after a major aboard the AWACS radar plane. After all, he was supposed to be in charge of coordinating things in the airspace. But they soon dropped the charges against him and decided instead to focus their search on another culprit. Perhaps a low-ranking radar observer aboard the AWACS would do. This would provide a perfect "scapegrunt."

The military justice experts decided to hold the craft's so-called senior weapons director solely responsible—one Captain Jim Wang. With the massive resources of the Air Force arrayed against this lone GI, this would surely be an open-and-shut case.

Thus, the Pentagon could let everyone—the irate families, pesky Congresspersons, and the noisy press focus all their disgust on this one young man's actions. According to this scheme, his gross dereliction of duty *obviously* had caused this accident. And now he would have to stand before the military bar of justice solo.

But it was also patently obvious to anyone reading the newspapers that the "management" of the complex combat zone operations over northern Iraq was completely flawed. Interestingly, the services never really investigated the actions, or rather inactions, of the complacent senior officers who were supposed to be running the show.

One of the more intriguing calls I received was from a major who had flown with one of these senior officers. He had known this particular colonel from a previous assignment. This colonel was now one of the officers who managed the complex and ever-changing rules of engagement in the no-fly zone. The major claimed this reckless senior officer had personally caused another mishap earlier in his career.

But the major said he was barred from testifying to that fact during that earlier safety investigation. This senior officer's career had been therefore protected, and he advanced through the ranks. This reckless colonel-to-be reportedly used to equip, "Rules are for fools." Apparently he had not learned anything over the years.

I soon read that the military grand jury had decided to throw the book at Captain Wang. He was being charged with three counts of dereliction of duty. I could not believe my eyes when I read the "specifications" against the captain. Amazingly, they were essentially the first three items in the core curriculum of the new Air Force CRM training program.[3]

The problem was that Wang had *not* received this training, a fact the prosecution apparently did not know. Unfortunately, this CRM course only became mandatory nine weeks *after* the shoot-down, when the secretary of the Air Force signed a directive requiring this training for all aircrew members.

The Air Combat Command and its predecessor, the Tactical Air Command, had dropped the ball by not mandating the course earlier. I was in the room in 1990 when the fateful decision was made, which is apparently why I was unceremoniously removed from the Black Hawk shoot-down investigation in 1994.

The Air Force proudly announced that Captain Wang's trial would take place in June 1995 at Tinker Air Force Base near Oklahoma City. Because Wang was assigned to a unit in the Eighth Air Force, they were in charge of his court-martial. The always-efficient gears of military justice quickly began to grind.

I soon contacted Wang's military lawyer, an energetic Major Gerald Williams, and informed him of the facts relating to his client's lack of training. I did not have to explain the significance of this oversight to this feisty defense attorney. He quickly asked me to send him a copy of the specific CRM regulation.

A few days later, he called back to inquire if I would appear as a defense witness at Wang's trial. I agreed, even though I felt that might cause problems for my relationships with people like Joan Piper. In recent months, she and several relatives of other shoot-down victims had called me repeatedly. They wanted to inform me of their so-far fruitless efforts to obtain answers and some level of accountability from the military.

Some of these folks were becoming increasingly disenchanted with the military establishment. One such individual was Captain Cleon Bass. He had enlisted in the Air Force eighteen years earlier and eventually had earned a commission. When his son Cornelius had asked about joining the Army, Cleon and his wife, Connie, had encouraged him to sign up. After all, they felt the service was one institution in which a young African-American could find opportunity and justice.

Unfortunately, twenty-two-year-old Army Specialist Cornelius Bass was assigned to that fateful helicopter flight over Iraq. Captain Bass was forced to witness the military machinations after his boy's death. This formerly gung-ho officer soon decided he could no longer wear the once cherished uniform of the United States. He resigned his commission and retired before completing his twenty-year hitch.

I had to carefully explain to the Bass and Piper families that, while I felt Captain Wang's confusion had certainly contributed to the deaths of their kids, the service's approach to safety was the *real* culprit. Intellectually, they understood these issues, and yet they still emotionally felt that Wang was partly responsible for the tragic sequence of events. But they also knew that it was important for me to appear as a defense witness at the forthcoming trial to tell this larger story.

However, this was not to be, as I soon learned when Wang's attorney called me. Major Williams seemed upset as he related how the military judge had denied his motion to have me testify. I remembered how much the military's justice system resembles its cozy accident investigation system.

Seems the prosecutors, judges, and, in turn, the list of jurors are all basically selected by the convening authority. This was the military organization that had the problem in the first place. No potential conflict of interest there, of course. Not surprisingly, the conviction rate in court-martial proceedings normally runs about 95 percent[4]—and our young captain was facing a "hanging jury."

Then Major Williams added that the judge felt that Wang already had too many people testifying. Furthermore, the convening command, the Eighth Air Force, supposedly could not afford to pay the expenses of so many defense witnesses.

More than a little angry, I informed this attorney that I would write to the commanding general and offer to appear at the trial at my own expense. I would point out that my appearance was necessary to insure Captain Wang would receive "due process." Major Williams wished me luck but was not very optimistic.

Some of my former associates still working at the Air Force Safety Agency heard what I was up to. They knew what was going on and provided me with some interesting data. This information revealed the hypocrisy of the leadership of the Eighth Air Force, as well as that of their own organization.

Largely because of the adverse publicity including my 1994 complaint, the Air Force chief of staff had set a goal of dramatically reducing the Class A mishap rate. My old boss, the Air Force chief of safety, General Godsey, was to lead this effort. The leadership of the Eighth Air Force and all the other generals were aware of this edict.

On May 5, 1995, an Eighth Air Force B-52 suffered a catastrophic engine failure and limped back to base. After it landed, investigators began examining the badly damaged aircraft. They discovered that both the number-three and number-four engines had exploded. Fragments from these disintegrating power plants had penetrated various other aircraft structures. The craft's rear fuselage and tail were very badly damaged.

Basically, Class A mishaps are those involving death or material damages in excess of $1 million.[5] It was obvious that this aircraft would cost several million to repair, and officials at the Eighth Air Force were informed of these unpleasant facts.

Apparently, they did not like what they heard and may have suggested that some creative accounting be employed to get the *officially* reported costs below that magic million-dollar figure. This sort of teamwork would help the command's image, of course.

I was told that the dutiful wizards went to work to make it happen. Basically they arranged to "obtain" a tail section from another surplus B-52 for "free." They then discovered some other cost savings. The two destroyed engines were written up as only "damaged" and therefore "repairable."[6] This bit of subterfuge alone "saved" the command 83 percent of the almost $900,000 list price of each power plant.

Generals appreciate troops who understand what they want—even if it involves bending the rules a bit. One can just imagine how this situation was reported to the Eight Air Force leaders. "Guess what generals? That B-52 incident turned out not to be a Class A after all. Besides, the taxpayers are picking up the tab, and who's going to question our mishap report? Certainly not the 'good old boys' at the safety agency. After all, they want to show a Class A mishap rate reduction. So we're all on the same team, just trying to do what the chief of staff wants." Unfortunately, war is not the only place where truth is the first casualty.

Ironically, this subterfuge was being perpetrated at the very time when these same officials were dragging Captain Wang before the bar of justice. Furthermore, these "repairable" engine fragments were to be shipped back to logistic facilities at Tinker Air Force Base. Thus, this scrap metal would practically have to be hauled past the building where Wang was being tried. So much for accountability. Not surprisingly, the Eighth Air Force also declined my offer to testify at my own expense. So much for due process.

By the time I heard back from the Eighth Air Force leadership about my offer, Wang's trial was about to get under way. When I told his attorney that I wouldn't be allowed to testify, the major and I discussed another way of getting the facts before the jury. The judge had not sequestered the jurors, and one Oklahoma City television station was covering the trial in great detail. After all, Wang and the others on the AWACS were hometown boys stationed at nearby Tinker.

This local NBC affiliate (KFOR) had done a series on the background and the issues in this notorious trial. They also had been including a several-minute spot each evening describing its latest developments. The jury members were known to be watching this program nightly—apparently curious about what the media was saying about this inflammatory case.

I called the station to inform them of these hidden issues. They asked me to make an appearance on the nightly news. In several minutes I explained the significance of the missing CRM training and its relationship to the three charges against the young captain. The plea was essentially, "If the charges don't fit, then you've got to acquit." Mission accomplished, for on June 20, 1995, this jury acquitted Jim Wang on all counts.[7]

I later spoke with friends of the victims who had followed the trial closely. They said that after learning about the whole situation with which Wang had had to contend, they too would have voted for acquittal. But that obviously meant that the Air Force was officially holding *nobody* accountable for this disaster.

Not surprisingly, families of the victims were devastated, and several soon turned to the chairman of the Senate's Permanent Subcommittee on Investigations (PSI), one William Roth. This very senior legislator was not afraid of demanding answers from the services. After all, this committee had just finished investigating another friendly-fire accident and cover-up involving the death of Army Corporal Fielder.[8]

The victims' families and I soon got word that the PSI would investigate the Black Hawk fratricide incident. This was the tentative plan: As with the Fielder inquiry, the committee staff would begin a very detailed investigation. They could also employ the considerable resources of the General Accounting Office (GAO). The plan was to gather and analyze factual data and then issue subpoenas to key players. Finally, this Senate subcommittee would hold public hearings and try to force the truth to light.

That was the plan. But the Pentagon had some other ideas. They simply did not intend to cooperate. After all, opening this Pandora's box might expose some of its top officers. Furthermore, the guys in the five-sided limestone bunker had had a lot of practice in dealing with unfriendly legislators and their staff investigators.

As the months went by, I heard repeatedly from GAO staffers and the PSI chief investigator, Mr. Eric Thorson.[9] I gladly provided all the evidence I had on the tragic incident. These dedicated sleuths had worked hard to gather information from many other witnesses. Being good investigators, however, they could not ethically tell me what else they had learned. But I sensed they were making good progress.

Finally, I got a call from an individual familiar with the Senate's activities. In his monotone voice he said, "I thought you should know that they have finished the first phase of their investigation. Senator Roth is prepared to go forth with the PSI hearings, so federal marshals may soon be sent to the Department of Defense to serve subpoenas on four senior officers involved with the shoot-down.

Wow! That night I called the next-of-kin families, who were delighted that the wheels of justice finally seemed to be turning. But their joy would be short-lived, for the Pentagon just ignored the subpoenas, arguing that such actions were invalid—a comment the Senate staff found ludicrous. The Department of Defense spokespersons further claimed that this whole process could lead to an undermining of public confidence in the military justice system.

The Pentagon lawyers knew they were on flimsy legal ground with this kind of argument. After all, this Senate Permanent Subcommittee on Investigations *had* an oversight role. But the Pentagon knew they had to do something to buy time, because having these four officers testify under oath in a public hearing would undoubtedly expose the cover-up. That was what had happened in the Fielder case—who, after all, was killed by a former chief of staff's son-in-law. Who knew how high the malfeasance might go this time?

The biggest concern of Pentagon lawyers had to be that one of these four officers would tell the Senate that Air Force Chief of Staff McPeak had indeed tampered with the court-martial of the two F-15 pilots. Such interference is a serious crime under military law. It was widely rumored that the tempestuous general, himself an F-15 pilot, did not want these guys prosecuted.[10]

But Pentagon officials also knew that they had one thing on their side—time. All they had to do was stonewall long enough. Senator Roth, who had almost single-handedly championed this cause, would be resigning as PSI chairman. After this session of Congress adjourned, Roth was moving up to head the full Finance Committee.

There he would have his hands full and would no longer have the authority to pursue this matter. The Pentagon officials knew that a new chairman would take time to come up to speed. More important, the new guy might not be as eager to pursue this contentious matter with the Defense Department, given its many loyal supporters in Congress.

It worked. The Pentagon engaged in legal maneuvers until the session ended, and the subpoenas died. Now they just had to dodge one more bullet—the GAO report. The next of kin waited patiently for GAO to issue its findings.

This report was finally made public in November 1997.[11] Deprived of critical witness testimony, its basic conclusions were not surprising.

The report found that the accident investigation met its basic objectives but was not complete because the investigation did not assess relevant information available to it. In fact, the GAO had identified *130 flaws* in the DoD accident report.[12] But these were relatively minor problems, not the nefarious conspiracy the families and others suspected.

The bottom line was the GAO could document *no conclusive* evidence of a cover-up or improper influence by high-ranking officers. This report was disappointing to the families, to say the least. But it did contain one bombshell that was a knife to the hearts of these long-suffering folks.

The GAO may have uncovered *why* the two F-15 pilots were so eager to fire at their hastily identified helicopter targets. Their scheduled patrol of the no-fly zone was about to end, and they were going to be replaced by a flight of two F-16s. The GAO had inadvertently discovered one of the bitterest intra-service rivalries in recent memory.

The F-15 Eagle is arguably the best-dedicated air-to-air fighter in the world. As its lofty name implies, it is supposed to be at the top of the pecking order in the Air Force. The much smaller F-16 Falcon also has to perform less glamorous ground-attack missions. Thus, "Eagle drivers" have always looked down on those pilots who fly the smaller "lawn darts," as they call the F-16s.

This rivalry got ugly in the early eighties when an F-15 pilot was rumored to have been caught engaging in a homosexual act with his mechanic.[13] After this widely discussed incident, F-16 pilots loved to torment their haughty counterparts. Typical barbs included notes left on base bulletin boards: "The Eagle driver who lost his *pink* flight gloves can pick them up at the front desk."

But this rivalry was really heating up in the months preceding the fratricide incident, because the F-16s had scored *all* the recent air combat kills over Iraq and Bosnia. Knowing this, the Eagle drivers undoubtedly wanted to get back into the game—with disastrous consequences.

So the families would be treated to one final insult. Not only would nobody ever be held accountable for their loved ones' deaths, but the final link in the chain of events that led to the catastrophe may have involved a ridiculous fighter jock rivalry gone overboard.

The military apparently did not believe in punishing people for such "understandable" mistakes—boys will be boys. In contrast, it would try to crush anybody who complained about safety problems. I would actually see many despicable examples of this unwritten policy after filing my whistle-blowing package.

As a result of my complaint, the service found its safety programs being studied by a number of outside organizations and ad hoc committees. They knew they somehow had to control what their service members and civil servants might say to these inquiries. The leadership was prepared to play hardball with those who might be potential collaborators.

One of the ad hoc committees that looked into Air Force safety problems was the so-called blue ribbon panel. They soon decided to commission a survey that would supposedly document how officers who had served on mishap investigations felt about such things as inappropriate pressure from superior officers. This sounded like a good idea until I learned *what* organization they selected to conduct the survey—the Air Force Military Personnel Center.[14] That was the organization that controlled all USAF career assignments.

Former investigators were understandably afraid to answer the questions candidly, for fear of retaliation. Soon some of them contacted me. They felt that answering the survey questions honestly might adversely effect their getting desirable assignments in the future. Those personnel guys could potentially send you to Iceland for your next tour if they didn't like some of your answers.

Civil servants are supposed to be protected from illegal pressures, but the Air Force also has ways to influence their behavior. One example of such untoward pressure occurred in the midst of these inquiries, which were being conducted by the blue ribbon panel, GAO, DoD inspector general, Defense Science Board, and others. This led to one of the more proactive cases of "damage control."

I learned about this incident from phone calls by a number of former associates who still worked in the safety agency. They said the general who was then chief of safety had just held a meeting where he announced that he was "contemplating" making some major cuts in his civilian workforce. It seems he did not feel that he had enough flexibility in controlling their behavior. They would be replaced by a like number of military personnel. The civilians obviously got the message, and few were willing to volunteer anything to these investigators—lest it get back to the general.

Generals certainly have many interesting ways of controlling GIs. One is to revoke already earned promotions. All they have to do is call the personnel center and "redline" the officer. The usual explanation is that the military has "lost confidence" in their subordinate's skills, leadership, or attitude.

One such case involved a captain who had already been selected for promotion to major. This young officer told me he felt he might be redlined. He had been assigned to investigate a fire that had occurred aboard an AWACS. The August 3, 1995, fire had badly damaged the multimillion-dollar radar antenna as well as much of the craft's radome structure.

The problem was that the generals in the command that had the accident—and who were running the investigation—apparently did not want it reported as a Class A mishap. Basically, the captain and the other more senior officers on the safety investigation board were being told to reduce the cost of the damage to get under the magic million-dollar limit. This would have to involve some illegal subterfuges.

The toughest trick was coming up with another antenna for free. The only spare AWACS antenna is stored in the so-called War Reserve Spares Kit. As the name implies, this vital equipment is supposed to be moved as a package to a war zone. Obviously, the *only* time kit components are to be used is to support those forward deployed troops during a conflict.

But these senior officers apparently decided their little cover-up was more important and ordered this vital antenna surreptitiously removed. They then directed that the radome's aluminum structure, which was destroyed in the fire, be written up as non-accident "metal fatigue." Finally, they used a ridiculously low figure of $16 per man-hour to estimate repair cost. Collectively these subterfuges reduced the *reported* cost of this incident below the million-dollar figure.

The gutsy young captain had vigorously objected and understandably felt his promotion was in danger of being redlined because of his stance. In the end, he caved in and signed this bogus report, knowing that further debate was useless. But he was still concerned that these senior officers might retaliate.

I would personally learn that generals can be very vindictive with people who are too candid on safety issues. I was informed that my name had been submitted to be a consultant to the prestigious Defense Science Board panel studying military aviation safety. But before I could participate, a general who knew about my whistle-blowing demanded that I be barred from this study. Such retaliation is supposed to be illegal, but nobody ever seems to get in trouble for doing it.

In fact, this de facto DoD policy of *encouraging* retaliation against whistle-blowers has been around for years. The best-known case involved a civil servant named A. Ernest Fitzgerald, who blew the whistle on massive cost overruns in the USAF C-5 transport program. The Nixon administration officials and the generals constantly harassed him. Fitzgerald fought back and eventually won a small measure of reform as detailed in his book, *The Pentagonists*.[15]

Interestingly, the GAO recently completed a massive study of waste, fraud, and abuse in the various government departments. They concluded that the DoD was the organization with the worst problems. The GAO also noted that the DoD's hostile climate toward whistle-blowers has contributed to its long-term problems.[16]

Another more important problem with the DoD is its reluctance to seriously examine problems identified by whistle-blowers. I feared this might be happening as I spoke with personnel in the inspector general's office. Several other officers who had courageously offered to testify about these military safety problems quickly confirmed these fears. I remember getting a call from a former Air Force officer who was a mishap investigator.

After being interviewed, he called to ask if the person who interviewed him was *really* an IG investigator. This lieutenant colonel described how this investigator seemed to be trying to put words into his mouth. "He kept suggesting that there was *another* potential explanation, other than Diehl's, which was the *real* cause of a particular accident. He did not seem interested in talking about the data that supported your allegations, only discussing other, farfetched explanations."

Still other key witnesses told me they were never contacted. Four such individuals were recently retired senior officers from the Air Force Safety Center. These officers included a well-known flight surgeon, one very experienced military lawyer, an officer who had directed their safety training programs, and another who was formerly in charge of preparing all statistical reports for the organization.

I asked these individuals to put their views in writing and send them to me. The letters were addressed to the White House, and I forwarded them en masse. The president's staff reportedly sent them to the Pentagon for action. These letters all vouched for the fundamental problems that I had identified in my complaint, but none of these people were *ever* interviewed by the IG. Obviously, these DoD investigators must have realized they could not explain away these very critical statements from such highly credible witnesses.

For example, Lieutenant Colonel Jim Miholick was assigned to the safety center for a total of thirteen years and retired after serving as chief of its data analysis branch. This unit prepared all Air Force mishap statistical reports including those furnished to the DoD and Congress. In this officer's September 2, 1996, letter he states:[17] "Sir, I am aware of Dr. Diehl's activities and concerns about the state of our military safety programs and wholeheartedly agree with his recommendation for correcting their deficiencies. I, too, have personally observed or been involved in inadequate investigations, intentional cover-ups, and the 'creative classification' of accidents (mishaps) to artificially lower the reported accident rates."

When the DoD inspector general staff finished its thirty-month-long investigation, the results were widely quoted by the military press. For instance, headlines in the *Air Force Times* proclaimed, "Accident-Probe Mismanagement Charges Rejected."[18] The magazine described how my allegations of mismanagement and cover-up could not be substantiated. Obviously, Lieutenant Colonel Miholick must have been working in an Air Force Safety Agency on a different planet.

Interestingly, this same article did note the IG had concluded that I had raised some "valid points" in several areas. They included undue command influence, inappropriate accident cost accounting procedures, illegal use of hypnosis, insufficient training, and poor equipment design. So maybe my efforts were not totally in vain.

The article also quoted at least one happy camper, General Godsey, who stated that Diehl was " . . . not credible and should not be considered as such in future issues he may raise."[19] Apparently, the important awards I have won, my couple decades of experience, and my doctorate in the field do not count for much in this general's mind.

Speaking of credibility, I once suggested a question to a reporter on his way to interview the Air Force chief of safety: "General, how many accidents did you personally investigate *before* becoming chief of safety?" I was genuinely curious to hear the answer. Irritated by the reporter's query, the general reportedly declined to answer the question. According to the reporter, the general instead retorted that the interview was about to end.

For generals, controlling pesky reporters is almost as easy as intimidating junior officers. These people, however, occasionally fight back.

Such was the case with one of the officers assigned to investigate Cadet Mark Dostal's crash at the Air Force Academy. The young student pilot and his instructor were killed when their T-3 spun to the ground during an aerobatics-training mission.[20] Remember, since the service had removed the parachutes from these aircraft, the men had no chance to bail out.

As a result of my complaint, the blue ribbon panel made several recommendations. One was that an officer from the safety center be assigned as a voting member to each Class A safety investigation board.[21] That way, there would supposedly be at least one safety expert on every inquiry.

But that idea could backfire if the safety center officer had the courage to argue with the others on the board. Remember, those other people are all from the major command that had the accident. Thus, they have a vested interest in pleasing their commander, who assigned them to run the investigation.

I spoke with one lieutenant colonel from the safety center shortly after he returned from investigating Dostal's mishap. This brilliant officer was known to be one of the most knowledgeable safety experts assigned to the center, but he was also one of the most outspoken. That latter trait can be a real liability in the military safety business.

He had pleaded with the board to look beyond the usual babble about things like "pilot error." The T-3 program was assigned to the Air Education and Training Command (AETC), and the other members of the board felt that such a radical idea would not fly with their generals. But they philosophically agreed with this real safety expert's views.

So they allowed him to write up his ideas on the *underlying* factors that had caused this mishap, but they could not allow such information to appear in the main body of their report. They eventually decided that his thoughts should be hidden in "Tab Z," in the back of the thick document—where nobody would notice it.

In the end, this lieutenant colonel wrote a very detailed analysis describing how various problems had contributed to the mishap.[22] Its logical treatment stood in sharp contrast to the simplistic explanations offered elsewhere in the report.

Everything was fine until a senior general at AETC headquarters happened to read "Tab Z." He found the safety center expert's exposé, which of course contradicted much of the official information in the main body of the report. This general obviously was not pleased with this situation and may have forcefully expressed his concerns.

Back at the safety center, our lieutenant colonel soon was informed of the general's displeasure by a supervisor. Actually, he was threatened with an undesirable "no-notice transfer" if he continued to push his own "agenda." This brave investigator then replied that he might have to file an inspector general complaint—like Dr. Diehl had just done. Another complaint, of course, was not something these officials could handle right then with all of the ongoing outside scrutiny. After all, they had been trying to suggest that Diehl was only a not-credible, disgruntled employee.

In the end, this diligent lieutenant colonel got a good tongue-lashing, stressing his "immaturity." This hardworking investigator had merely tried to do his job. More significantly, these safety officials ignored the important ideas in his analysis.

That was unfortunate, because in the months that followed, two more cadets and their instructors would ride T-3s to their deaths. Thus, with top cover from the Pentagon, the Air Force's dysfunctional policies rolled on unchanged, and four more young men paid with their lives. Damage control gone amok!

The last years of the twentieth century revealed a host of problems with the military safety programs. Unfortunately, those in leadership positions often seemed more concerned with public relations and protecting their own careers than in organizational reform. They were committed to stifling criticism rather than listening to those who could articulate methods of enhancing safety.

22

A Plethora of Plagues

President Clinton must have felt like a biblical Egyptian leader at times, for his White House years were plagued by persistent safety problems. The Black Hawk fratricide incident was only a harbinger of things to come. Some disasters, like the one that claimed his close friend, Commerce Secretary Brown, would bring tears to his eyes. Such occurrences might have reminded this modern-day Pharaoh that there would be no respite—*unless* he fixed the underlying problems. Unfortunately, nobody in the Pentagon wanted to play Moses and tell him how to accomplish this.

Interestingly, Bill Clinton's own child had flown on the very same poorly equipped military transport only weeks before it crashed, killing Ron Brown. The secretary's catastrophic accident was soon followed by several incidents involving other people close to the White House. In fact, history almost repeated itself when a military version of the Boeing 707 jetliner carried Mr. Brown's replacement, Secretary Mickey Kantor, to Japan.[1] Mr. Kantor and part of his entourage had to remain in Japan on business while the venerable VC-137 returned to the U.S. with the rest of the passengers.

Over the Pacific, this four-engine jet developed a "problem" and had to make an emergency landing in the Philippines. As it taxied up to the Manila terminal, witnesses noticed something was obviously wrong with this well-known aircraft. Smoke billowed from the open windows and doors of this gleaming blue-and-white craft with "The United States of America" emblazoned across its fuselage. A stuck engine valve had overheated the plastic air-conditioning duct works. These melting materials had produced the smoke. Interestingly, the plane was en route to pick up the vice president.[2]

Within several months, two different types of presidential support helicopters would crash.[3] Four crew members died when a brand-new Marine H-53, still undergoing tests, crashed at its factory in Connecticut.[4] Weeks later the president made a campaign stop in Florida. An H-46 accompanying him clipped a lamp pole at an Orlando airport.[5] Fortunately, the crew members of this USMC chopper were able to scramble to safety before it burst into flames.

Another eight airmen perished along with one of Mr. Clinton's Secret Service agents when their USAF C-130 slammed into a mountain after taking off from Jackson Hole, Wyoming.[6] This rather inexperienced crew was assigned the mission of transporting a presidential support vehicle to New York City, where the president had gone to celebrate his birthday. Unfortunately, their craft was not equipped with a GPWS,[7] nor had all of the flight crew received CRM[8] training.

Then there was the incident over Ireland on May 27, 1997, where Air Force One had to take evasive action to avoid a near midair collision with a UPS cargo jet. Clinton's VC-25, a modified Boeing 747 aircraft, had all the latest safety devices, including TCAS,[9] which provided the critical warning to his crew.[10] But other military aircraft are still not so well equipped. Such deficiencies have persisted for years. This in spite of the fact that Congress, after hearing about the lack of navigation and safety devices aboard Ron Brown's jet, had urged the Pentagon to quickly bring its fleet up to U.S. airline standards.

But not everything is as safe as it should be, even for the president. I would discover this during a 1994 visit to the 89th Airlift Wing. That unit flies Air Force One and other VIP support aircraft out of Andrews AFB near Washington. I taught a special CRM course to flight crews assigned there and was shocked to learn about some of their problems.

For instance, because of funding limitations, their "flight attendants," even on presidential missions, had not always received annual hands-on training in using safety equipment, such as the emergency evacuation slides. Interestingly, even cut-rate airlines were required by the FAA to provide such recurrent training to their cabin crews. I reported these problems to my superiors at the Air Force Safety Agency, but no one apparently wanted to take any actions that might be critical of this elite unit.

By 1997, because of the rash of recent crashes, the president demanded a study into the safety of military passenger aircraft. The Pentagon promptly turned to a favorite trustee to review this situation. Retired Vice Admiral Don Engen[11] had just finished chairing the Air Force blue ribbon safety panel two years earlier.

As in that previous study, he found very little that needed fixing, just a little tweaking—for there were *certainly* no major systemic problems.[12] In this new study, the admiral even calculated that the mishap rates for such military passenger aircraft operations were statistically better than those for the airlines using similar equipment.

But a sharp-eyed member of Congress, Bob Livingstone, who just happened to be the chairman of the House Appropriations Committee, wanted another, perhaps *more* independent, look at the issue. A member of his committee's research staff contacted me and requested that I perform a review of these issues.[13] I quickly agreed to help.

I soon discovered *why* the U.S. DoD safety record looked so good compared to that of the "airlines." The Engen statistics reflected the accident rates for *all* the world's civilian airlines flying a particular type of jet. I thought it would be more appropriate to compare our military aircraft rates with those of the U.S. airlines flying this same type aircraft. To be fair, this U.S. airline data should include both their domestic and overseas flying.

The reason for Engen's optimistic finding was that almost 80 percent of airline accidents occur to Third World airlines, which operate many of the same U.S.-made jets.[14] So when compared to the Third World airlines, the DoD's safety record does not look too shabby. But when I recalculated the numbers for various types of aircraft using only U.S. airline data, the DoD averaged about five times as many crashes per flying hour.

Thus, my comprehensive report to Congress[15] came to somewhat different conclusions than had the "independent" Pentagon study. My analysis suggested more sweeping changes in equipment, procedures, and training were needed—especially the urgent retrofitting of airline-type safety devices on all military passenger aircraft.

But airplane crashes were not the only military safety problems facing the president as the century drew to a close. The services also had many problems on terra firma. Occasionally, these incidents were merely embarrassing. Such was the case on September 21, 1998, when the Japanese defense minister and his staff were invited to visit the Pentagon.[16]

All was in readiness for this important diplomatic occasion. As their be-flagged limousine approached the familiar building, a barrier unexpectedly sprang up. This massive steel device was supposed to provide an instant roadblock to halt potential terrorist vehicles. Unfortunately, it was underneath the diplomats' car. It unceremoniously slammed into the vehicle, tossing the terrified statesmen into the air. Embarrassed administration officials soon visited the victims in their Washington hospital beds.[17] Interestingly, a Pentagon senior official remarked that another barrier had previously impacted the underside of Defense Secretary Perry's car.

Sometimes these incidents were more than just embarrassing. Tragically, this same type barrier would claim the life of a retired reservist at MacDill AFB near Tampa on February 18, 2000. A three-foot barrier popped up under her car as she drove into a lot on the base, smashing the windshield and causing both air bags to deploy. She died at the scene.

Accidental death more often rains from the skies. Such was the case during the 1999 NATO bombing campaign designed to persuade Serbian president Slobodan Milosevic to end his war against Kosovo. There were twenty "collateral damage" incidents during the brief air campaign where errant bombs or missiles accidentally hit civilian bystanders.[18]

The worst of these occurred as Milosevic was beginning to talk about withdrawing his troops. On May 7, an Air Force B-2 Stealth Bomber dropped its satellite-guided bombs on the Chinese embassy in downtown Belgrade.[19] Three people died instantly, while twenty-seven others were wounded. Concussions from this incident would reverberate around the world.

The high-tech weapons had hit their aim points, but outdated maps had mistakenly depicted that particular building as the location of the Serbian arms agency headquarters. The Chinese had actually been in this building for more than a year.

Although one unnamed CIA analyst was eventually blamed for the mistake and fired,[20] other causes were soon revealed. These underlying reasons for the targeting errors were even more disturbing.

A former CIA analyst, Patrick Eddington,[21] pointed out that in 1996 Congress directed his agency to turn over its imagery component to the Pentagon National Imagery and Mapping Agency. He noted that there subsequently was a loss of coordination between the CIA and DoD on critical issues. Furthermore, this was neither the first nor last time such problems have caused fatal accidents.[22]

Such explanations did not sit well with everyone. The president would write to his Chinese counterpart trying to explain the mishap.[23] In spite of Mr. Clinton's very public mea culpa, several riots soon erupted as Chinese citizens attacked and damaged the American embassy in Beijing. Other riots soon occurred across the planet. An embarrassed America would later offer to pay $4.5 million to compensate the Chinese bombing victims.[24] The U.S. would ultimately offer the Chinese government another $28 million in reparations for its mistake.[25]

On April 19, 1999, a similar tragedy occurred when an F/A-18 fighter-bomber dropped two 500-pound bombs on the Navy's Vieques Island target range. This island off Puerto Rico is only fifty-two square miles but has a population of more than nine thousand people who are more than a little nervous about living so close to live ordnance releases.

These two bombs missed their target and exploded beside a watchtower, killing one civilian guard and wounding three others. The next day, the angry residents of Vieques marched through the streets in protest. The governor of Puerto Rico soon wrote to President Clinton asking him to stop all bombing practices on the island. This incident also became a catalyst for those island dissidents who wanted Puerto Rican independence from the U.S.[26]

Besides wayward bombs, the administration was also being asked about the rash of accidents involving, of all things, defective U.S. Army trucks. Basically, that service operated two classes of these mundane vehicles: the post–Vietnam-era trucks like the M939 and the much newer FMTV, Family of Medium Tactical Vehicles.

The older type vehicles seemed to be having a hard time avoiding highway accidents. These workhorses apparently were more comfortable trundling along off-road in the mud, where their lack of such safety features as antiskid brakes and radial tires did not matter much. But at highway speeds, young soldiers were having a hard time avoiding crashes.[27]

The newer Army trucks, the FMTVs, were having a different kind of problem.[28] Their drive shafts were vibrating so badly that they could break loose from the engines, drop down, and become lodged in the ground, flipping the truck over.

Perhaps the Army should have expected such problems, since this was the first military truck that Stewart & Stevenson had ever manufactured. Being new to the business, they apparently overlooked a few basic automotive engineering principles. What do you want for $16 billion?

Between the problems with these types of old and new trucks, the Army had killed more than one hundred GIs and seriously injured hundreds more.[29] Not surprisingly, some members of Congress were beginning to demand answers. After all, this isn't exactly rocket science.

However, rocket science was another department that was causing fits for the American military. The Air Force's largest launch vehicle, the mighty Titan IV super-rocket, was having problems hurling military satellites into orbit. By now the United States armed forces had become highly dependent on such space-based assets.

On August 12, 1998, a Titan IV pitched over and exploded forty-one seconds after lifting off from Cape Canaveral. At first, the Air Force tried to conduct its usual "privileged" mishap investigation. Sorry fellow rocketeers, but we just can't share the info about this failure with you civilians. There was an ensuing furor from the entire commercial space launcher industry, and the service was forced to release all information on this mysterious accident. The Air Force spent $45 million investigating the incident, and after seven months, it concluded that faulty wiring and poor quality control caused an electrical short, which resulted in a guidance system malfunction.[30]

The next two USAF Titan IV launches did not fare much better. But the mishaps, on April 9, 1999, and May 30, 1999, were apparently caused by somewhat different problems. The upper stage engines of both rockets shut off prematurely. Thus, they failed to place their satellite payloads in acceptable orbits.[31]

Then, a week after the latest Titan failure, a thunderstorm passed close to the Cape. Workmen had to temporarily abandon preparations to launch a military global position system satellite mounted on top of a Delta II rocket. When these technicians returned, they discovered water had somehow gotten *inside* the satellite.[32]

Mother Nature can be cruel at times. But the bottom line was the American taxpayers were out $3 billion for these fiascoes. Plus, our troops were denied the use of vital communications, navigation, and reconnaissance satellites needed to prosecute the Serbian campaign—and our enemies knew it.

But as bad as such accidents are, sometimes the scariest thing is a minor mishap that could, but for the grace of God, have been a major catastrophe. One such incident occurred on the evening of February 4, 1999.[33] The U.S. Navy destroyer *Arthur W. Radford* was steaming at just over seventeen miles per hour. She was making steady circles to the left around a buoy outside the busy entrance to the Chesapeake Bay. The visibility was clear, and the sea reflected gentle four-foot swells at 12:40 A.M.

On the bridge of this compact, six-thousand-ton warship, its relatively inexperienced crew members were focused on calibrating electronic instruments.[34] No one paid much attention to the large blip appearing on their radarscope. This blip belonged to the *Saudi Riyadh*, a container ship that was entering the bay. She was holding a steady course and speed of twenty miles per hour.

Meanwhile, on the bridge of this massive 27,700-ton merchant ship, its third officer watched the smaller blip, which seemed to be turning away from his freighter's intended course as they approached. The *Saudi Riyadh* had twice tried to make radio contact with the strange-acting smaller vessel on the standard VHF frequency. Then the increasingly concerned third officer radioed on the emergency channel for mariners, "Ship on my port bow. Please keep clear of me."[35] There was no reply.

As the freighter approached the buoy, this mysterious target kept changing headings and now appeared to be on a collision course. This large merchantman was unable to avoid hitting the smaller warship. The starboard side of the destroyer's bow hit the port side of the much larger freighter, leaving a thirty-foot-long gash in the larger ship's hull.

The destroyer bounced off the side of the freighter like a beach ball off a brick wall. It, of course, faired much worse than the massive freighter—largely because of the laws of physics. Even this glancing blow partly crushed the warship's forward hull structure, bending its keel. There was a gaping hole, twenty feet deep, which extended from the warship's main deck to below its waterline. The ship's forward five-inch cannon turret was even knocked off its mounts, but miraculously only one sailor was injured. The destroyer crew did not realize how badly they were hit until they arrived dockside.

The Navy soon announced that it had relieved the *Radford's* captain of his command.[36] The brass simply ignored things like the reduced training given to its seamen and service-wide personnel shortages that had forced this skipper to sail without a full crew complement. But these admirals knew that the repairs to the two ships would cost many millions of dollars, so not surprisingly, they insisted their vessel had the right of way. More important, everyone now realized just how close the Navy had come to a truly catastrophic incident, one that could have easily claimed the lives of a couple of hundred sailors. The Navy spent $45 million to repair the damage and then decommissioned the ship.

As if the bad publicity on this mishap weren't enough, the media had to dredge up information on a few of the Navy's *other* accidents that it would rather forget. On the tenth anniversary of the infamous 1989 battleship *Iowa* gun-turret explosion that killed forty-seven sailors, CBS's *60 Minutes* aired an updated episode. This piece described new damning evidence in the Navy's clumsy attempt to deflect criticism from its bad gunpowder, poor leadership, inadequate training, personnel shortages, and decrepit maintenance—by blaming the mishap on a suicidal homosexual sailor. This piece was based largely on a new book on the subject, *A Glimpse of Hell*, by Charles C. Thompson II.[37]

Another interesting book on this topic appeared about the same time, *Explosion Aboard the Battleship Iowa*.[38] A Sandia Laboratory scientist who participated in the investigation, one Richard L. Schwoebel, authored this candid work. Surprisingly, the Naval Institute Press published it. The latter is largely controlled by the Navy Department. Apparently, they still have "a few good men" aboard.

But the integrity of the Navy brass didn't always shine. Another egregious problem with the Navy's traditional approach to safety and accountability was revealed during the NBC airing of *Mutiny*, in 1999. This program was based on a 1989 book, *The Port Chicago Mutiny*, by Robert L. Allen.[39] This book described the worst stateside military accident during the Second World War and then explained why the ensuing "mutiny" had occurred.

Port Chicago was a major ammunition-loading facility near San Francisco. It was destroyed along with two freighters by a powerful blast on July 17, 1944, which was felt as far away as Nevada. After the blast, survivors were forced to search the debris for bodies of their comrades. Three hundred and twenty people had died, two-thirds of whom were sailors assigned to the all-black loading crews.[40]

Both the book and the TV program explained how, in the racially segregated Navy of that era, untrained "Negro" sailors were assigned to these dangerous duties. White junior officers supervised these loading gangs. But neither these officers nor the men were properly instructed on safety procedures. For instance, the troops were not instructed on how to handle a recently introduced type of highly unstable explosive, "torpex."

Furthermore, as the need to feed the Pacific war's ammunition requirements increased, Navy leaders pressured these officers to reduce loading times. They, in turn, pitted their respective loading crews against one another in loading contests. Of course, this was one "game" where a fumble could be deadly.

After the accident, the Navy investigation focused blame on the black sailors—adding insult to injury. Understandably, scores of the African-American survivors refused to return to their duties on the ammo docks. Many offered to volunteer for combat assignments, but the Navy brass was certainly not going to listen to uppity "colored" troops.

These black sailors were promptly court-martialed for mutiny—and convicted. The ringleaders received long jail sentences. Military justice was just as swift in those days. A few years after the war, most of the mutineers were quietly released for time served and given dishonorable discharges.

More than five decades later, one of only two surviving ringleaders asked the president for a pardon. Freddie Meeks, a dying old veteran, wanted the president to admit he was a victim of the rampant racism of that era. Military officials promptly urged Mr. Clinton not to get involved.[41] But, just before Christmas 1999, the president granted Meeks's request.[42] However, everyone should remember that the Navy's unsafe practices were the *real* culprit. If there were no accidents, there would be no need for scapegoats of *any* color.

Another contemporary public relations fiasco involved the low-flying U.S. Marine Corps EA-6 jet that hit gondola wires stretched across a picturesque Italian valley. Twenty civilians from five different European countries died on February 3, 1998, when their cable car plunged more than 350 feet to the ground near the resort of Cavalese. The crewmen were able to fly their badly damaged radar-jamming jet back to base, where they made an emergency landing.

This mishap caused the administration great consternation because the crew was stationed at Aviano Air Base. This Italian base was vital to conducting an air campaign over nearby Yugoslavia. U.S. officials at the base had authorized these four young Marine captains to make a low-altitude training flight. This type of fun mission was often used as a reward for a job well done. In this case, the pilot had completed his six-month tour and was headed back to the States.

The Italian press was particularly brutal after hearing that the crew was flying the jet too fast, too low, and was off course for much of this training sortie. None of the other crew members had challenged their pilot's obviously dangerous flying.

The Italian press had already called the crew "Rambos."[43] When it was learned that a video camera was involved and that the tape was missing, things really got ugly. This suggested these fliers were just fooling around, making home movies and putting civilians at risk. Partly because of the adverse publicity, the U.S. government would eventually pay the families of the twenty victims a total of almost $40 million.[44]

The Marines are part of the Department of the Navy, and this was not the only time that organization paid dearly for ignoring the need for thorough CRM training. On January 29, 1996, a Navy F-14 pilot decided to do an aggressive "air show" type of takeoff in front of his parents in Nashville. His navigator apparently did not object to the dangerous maneuver. They lost control as the jet entered low clouds and crashed into a nearby neighborhood, killing themselves and three civilians.

Weeks later, Navy officials testified before Congress that CRM was a factor in the crash. They promised that the service would update and enhance its CRM training programs for the Navy and Marine crews.[45] But this was not done in a timely manner, as evidenced by the gondola collision, and everyone was trying to protect their own careers from the ugly consequences of this high-profile accident.

More than one year after this tragedy, the Marines brought the pilot, Captain Richard Ashby, to trial. The military jury eventually acquitted him of the twenty counts of negligent homicide, even though he acknowledged to flying aggressively. He and his navigator would later be convicted of obstruction of justice for hiding their cockpit videotape. Captain Ashby seemed to personify the typical "rogue pilot" described in Tony Kern's acclaimed book, *A Darker Shade of Blue*.[46]

But not all the blame could be placed at this pilot's feet. Besides the lack of CRM training for him and his crew, his maps did not depict the location of the cables, his radar altimeter may not have been working properly, and there had been confusion over whether the minimal permitted flying altitude was one thousand or two thousand feet above the terrain.

Furthermore, Captain Ashby was a "character created by central casting" in that he epitomized the risk-taking military aviator. After all, the Pentagon helped cultivate the image by providing support for popular movies like *Top Gun*, and, more recently, *The Flight of the Intruder*. The latter depicted the lead character laughing aloud while doing low-altitude aerobatics through mountain valleys in an A-6. Ashby was just playing the character role assigned to him.

Of course, senior Marine leaders played their respective roles—also from the movies. In this case, they all pretended to be surprised to learn that one of their officers would take such chances. This character role came right out of the classic film *Casablanca*. For not unlike the French prefect Renault, who *suddenly* discovered that gambling was going on at Rick's Café, these officers pretended to be shocked at such happenings.

Playacting aside, the geopolitical implications of this mishap were enormous. This was evident after Ashby's verdict was announced on March 5, 1999. Italian Prime Minister Massimo D'Alema was on a state visit to the White House. He very publicly vented his displeasure as the cameras rolled. This display forced an embarrassed president to respond that the United States would take full responsibility for the accident.[47] By now, this apologizing drill must have become noisome to our commander in chief.

23

Ill Wind

As painful as trying to explain away such preventable accidents is for the president, it pales in comparison to trying to justify the Pentagon's actions regarding the so-called Gulf War Syndrome. To some extent, the very label "accident" seems to imply an unforeseeable, one-time occurrence. The same cannot be said for the many complex actions of the Defense Department in this far more nefarious arena.

This medical debacle involves literally tens of thousands of troops, many with very painful and often debilitating medical problems that may linger for years. Their torture could be captured on camera, and the public knows that something must be done to help these men and women who went into harm's way for this nation.[1]

From the outset, the Gulf War Theater was a caldron of potential health threats, and America had rushed almost seven hundred thousand of our finest young people into this environment. They were facing a remorseless enemy, known to have a massive arsenal of chemical and biological agents. Ironically, U.S. firms supplied much of the technology for these weapons of mass destruction when Iraq was viewed as an ally. Saddam Hussein had openly used poison gas against the Iranians and dissident Kurds living in Iraq.

This would not be the first time our GIs had faced such horrific threats; their grandfathers had to contend with German gas attacks during the Great War. But not-so-veiled threats of U.S. nuclear retaliation apparently dissuaded the Iraqis from openly using such deadly weapons in this conflict.

Ironically, it would be the American aerial bombing of the Iraqi weapon warehouses during the war, followed by the demolition of their abandoned ammunition dumps after the war, which let the genie out of the bottle. Thousands of our troops downwind of these destroyed facilities would be exposed without warning to low-level poison gas.[2]

But there was another threat that few people in the U.S. military establishment had even considered. Many American tanks and aircraft were equipped with a weapon never before used on a battlefield—high velocity cannons firing depleted uranium (DU) rounds. These super high-density "magic bullets" would cut through the thickest enemy armor.

The only problem with these projectiles was that they vaporized on impact, throwing a fine mist of uranium (U-238) particles into the air—which would soon fall back to earth. American ground troops and vehicles would eventually plow through this nuclear dust bowl as they raced across desert battlefields.

Officials did little to warn our GIs about such potential dangers. Later on, in the euphoria of victory, many troops were allowed to crawl around destroyed enemy vehicles exposing themselves to these toxins. Others were assigned to bare-handedly refurbish dozens of U.S. vehicles hit by friendly fire. Interestingly, these damaged vehicles were later hauled to the radioactive dumps.[3]

Furthermore, the thousands of tons of DU scattered across the region would present a major environmental problem, because the radioactive half-life of U-238 is four and one-half *billion* years. The military's head-in-the-sand philosophy would later come back to haunt the Pentagon when other nations, such as Japan, discovered we had used such weapons on bombing ranges in their countries. Administration officials had to scramble to offer apologies.[4]

Then, too, there was a very ancient threat, one that had lain quiescently underground for eons in this region. The entire battlefield sat astride one of the world's largest oil fields. When the retreating Iraqis torched thousands of Kuwaiti oil wells, millions of tons of pollution would be carried into the stratosphere. These black billowing clouds marched across the sky. American troops breathed the acrid fumes for days as they were thrust into this "darkness at noon" scene.

Last, there were potential self-inflicted wounds from the experimental drugs that officials had hastily decided to use on our troops. Their thinking was that inoculating these troops with such agents could offer some protection against deadly toxins they might soon encounter on the battlefield.

For instance, pyridostigmine bromide (PB) pills were given to 250,000 troops, supposedly to counteract the effects of chemical weapons.[5] It has even been argued that some troops were secretly inoculated with an untested, specially modified Anthrax vaccine.[6] Such actions violated both U.S. Federal Drug Administration law and the Nuremberg Accords, which prohibit nonconsensual drug experiments on humans.[7] But the Pentagon had long been in the habit of ignoring such niceties, as revealed in a recent book describing how unsuspecting American civilians were injected with radioactive plutonium.[8]

In the months and years that followed the war, the hidden costs were beginning to emerge in military clinics and VA hospitals across this nation. Thousands of servicemen and women reported a disturbing list of ailments. Their diverse illnesses include: mysterious infections, gastrointestinal problems, muscular-skeletal complaints, low-grade fevers, painful headaches, chronic fatigue, memory loss, and cancers.

Even more disturbing to these vets was the Pentagon's reaction to this epidemic. At first, Department of Defense officials just seemed to ignore these illnesses. But when reports of such problems continued to mount, the Pentagon decided to take formal action. Its well-coordinated efforts fell into the now-familiar categories—the five "*Ds*": deny, demand, delay, destroy, and disparage.

First, *deny* there is any *real* problem. It's all in their heads. "You know, it's just delayed stress syndrome, which occurs with many troops after every war." Then *demand* that the Pentagon *alone* must be allowed to handle such problems. After all, they're *our* people, and *we* certainly can be trusted to have their best interests at heart. Next, *delay* the inevitable by promising to do a *very* thorough review of these matters. This, of course, will take years. Many folks will die off; most of their spouses will remarry and hopefully lose interest in this controversy.

When those tactics did not silence the victims, their families, the media, or Congress, it was time to nuke 'em: *destroy* or conceal any evidence that might reveal culpability. Perhaps the most inane example was the missing logs of chemical agent detection reports. The official explanation was almost laughable. Sorry, a computer glitch has erased those electronic records, and the backup paper copies have also disappeared. The fact that duplicate copies of both types of logs were maintained in the U.S. as well as in Saudi Arabia certainly made this explanation sound ludicrous.[9]

And finally there was that last favorite tactic of those in power: *disparage* the data, theories, pleas, and especially the reputations of anyone disagreeing with the military's stance. The Pentagon defenders would be dealing with two classes of troublemakers—outsiders and insiders—and they had effective methods for handling both groups.

For outsiders, the military can just argue that they don't have their facts straight. Or better yet, they don't understand the *real* situation, because they have not seen all of our privileged information that we can't release for national security reasons—of course. Then the military can simply ignore their requests for data and their complaints. What can they do, since we hold all the cards anyway?

This time-tested tactic, however, does not work well with those who are organizational insiders. But there are even more effective methods for dealing with such dissidents. Insiders who demonstrate that they cannot be trusted should be isolated or, better yet, punished. If they so much as breathe a word of this, these clowns must be forcefully reminded just *who* they work for and *what* happens to employees when they do not keep their mouths shut. Jobs can be abolished, grants canceled, budgets cut, and undesirable transfers arranged.

For instance, after much criticism, the Pentagon eventually discovered something interesting. One conscientious officer, who just may have suspected an embryonic cover-up was under way, kept a copy of some of the missing chemical logs in his home. The DoD IG immediately announced that they were conducting a *criminal* investigation into this officer's actions.[10]

Moreover, the Pentagon has also been known to denounce its own contractors when they come to the "wrong" conclusions. Such was the case after they hired the prestigious Miter Corporation in 1996 to do a classified study of potential chemical weapons use in the Gulf War.

Miter's experts thought they had uncovered "compelling" evidence that Marines were exposed to poison gas land mines. But the Pentagon denounced this $2.5 million study as "sloppy" and a "wild goose chase." Of course, such pronouncements can eliminate an organization from receiving future work.[11]

The Pentagon's many well-paid, loyal experts and public relations staffers were gainfully employed to harass both classes of troublemakers. This "Pentagon Praetorian guard," as always, tried to hide behind the flag by constantly reminding everybody of the overriding "national security issues." However, in spite of their concerted efforts, the scheme would eventually begin to unravel. Their attempts to control this situation failed for several reasons.

The media, Congress, and the American people had a collection of painful memories. It was hard to forget the Pentagon's earlier episodes of "protecting" the safety and health of its personnel. Discredited programs like the military's LSD experiments during the Cold War on unwitting soldiers were not very reassuring. And who could ever forget those old newsreels showing unprotected troops marching across nuclear test sites as mushroom clouds billowed overhead? Of course, these same clouds soon spread radiation for hundreds of miles, exposing the general population to fallout. These troops and civilians, the so-called downwinders, later developed health problems. People soon began recalling how the military establishment had tried to stonewall, vigorously denying such occurrences were dangerous, or, when cornered, reminding everyone that such risks, while regrettable, were necessary for national security.

Against this growing chorus of criticism, the White House established an independent panel of experts to examine the highly complex and emotionally charged issues. The Presidential Advisory Committee on Gulf War Veteran's Illness, a respected twelve-member panel, would have the very daunting task of sorting out cause and effect.[12] Large numbers of patients had been exposed to a myriad of potentially deadly agents at various times. The challenge was to scientifically correlate exposures with the ensuing illnesses using classic epidemiological techniques.[13]

They would have to tackle one of history's most complex public health puzzles, one in which many pieces were missing, partly because of the lack of previous research on issues such as low-level exposure to poison gas, and partly due to the "fog of war"—including the military's poor record keeping.

But many folks also suspected that somebody just might be stone-walling. The Pentagon was not very pleased with a truly independent review into deficiencies in protecting its troops. Thus, it did not offer the panel much real assistance. Besides, like a bunch of mischievous choirboys, they claimed to be very busy with their own in-house inquiries on the topic.

By the fall of 1996, things were beginning to wind down. After months of arduous investigations and contentious hearings, this highly frustrated presidential panel was about to issue its findings. They had been unable to establish credible scientific evidence between cause and effect for this diverse set of toxins and illnesses. Furthermore, some of these problems seemed to be related to postwar stress. Besides, they could not definitively document their chief suspect, widespread exposure to low levels of poison gas. The Pentagon was almost off the hook, when the bombshell hit.[14]

Actually it was a couple thousand bombshells, stored at the munitions dump called Khamisiyah. This vast ammo dump, located 110 miles north of the Saudi border, was captured intact as allied troops overran occupied Kuwait. The CIA had warned the Pentagon about Khamisiyah as a likely location of such dreaded weapons. U.S. field commanders in the theater passed this data on to some units, but not to the Thirty-seventh Combat Engineering Battalion.[15] That unit was assigned the tricky task of destroying this large complex of bunkers, pits, and warehouses a few days after the cease-fire.

Another problem was that the Iraqis, unlike the allies, did not use special symbols to distinguish deadly chemical weapons from standard bombs, rockets, and artillery shells. Furthermore, few GIs could read Arabic. As a result, these troops were unaware that thousands of rounds containing deadly sarin and mustard gas were concealed among the countless tons of enemy munitions. These troops followed orders by setting demolition charges and evacuating the area.

From March 3 to 10, 1991, massive detonations rocked the area like man-made earthquakes. The huge blasts sent tons of debris mixed with deadly chemicals into the stratosphere. There, the prevailing winds carried it over one hundred thousand unsuspecting American GIs. Numerous chemical alarms went off downwind,[16] but headquarters personnel assured the troops that these must just be false alarms, probably caused by things like the smoke from all the burning oil wells. They did, however, record the information in headquarters chemical-weapons logbooks—which would someday disappear.[17]

Within weeks of the cease-fire, Iraqi officials would confess some important information to the American officers. They identified exactly where Iraqi troops had stored their chemical weapons at Khamisiyah. Within months of the cease-fire, UN weapons inspectors visited these facilities and examined the physical evidence.[18] They confirmed Khamisiyah was a chemical weapon site and sent a report to the U.S. Department of Defense.

The Pentagon had had all of this information—the chemical logs, Iraqi confessions, UN inspectors report—as well as data on other chemical-weapons stores bombed during the war. Furthermore, they had control over such information for years as the presidential committee began its investigation. But somehow *nobody* thought to offer this data to the panel.

Other people, realizing that tens of thousands of sick American veterans were in constant agony, came forward with more disturbing data. Two Central Intelligence Agency employees decided to become whistle-blowers. This husband-and-wife team, Patrick and Robin Eddington, were determined to reveal the truth.

They disclosed key data on the collusion between the Pentagon and the CIA on a wide variety of issues including known chemical weapons locations as well as deficiencies in U.S. chemical detectors and personnel protective equipment. Patrick, himself an officer in the Army reserve, later published a comprehensive exposé, *Gassed in the Gulf,*[19] describing the situation. Perhaps the saddest statement in Eddington's book was that " . . . a new generation of veterans have come to understand that the government that they fought for is now their worst enemy."

As more and more evidence emerged, the Presidential Advisory Committee on Gulf War Veteran's Illnesses wanted to look deeper into several issues, including the "missing" Pentagon data. The Defense Department, sensing problems ahead, had already announced it would drastically expand its work to get to the bottom of the Gulf War illness phenomena.[20]

Translation: We're really going to try harder, largely by throwing a lot more taxpayer money at this effort. This new funding amounted to $12 million. Interestingly, the Pentagon also found $184,500 to hire an outside public relations firm to help them spin away the stench created by their earlier bungled efforts.[21]

On January 8, 1997, President Clinton announced he was extending the panel's charter for several additional months to insure an independent overview of this ongoing Pentagon investigation.[22] The panel's chairwoman, Dr. Joyce Lashof, said, "We hope these initiatives can begin to restore public confidence in the government's investigation of possible incidents of chemical agent exposure."[23]

Other folks were less confident in the Pentagon's sincerity, including members of powerful committees in both the Senate and House, which had ongoing investigations into the Gulf illness matter. Many of their comments were highly critical of the Pentagon.

For instance, the chairman of the Veterans Affairs Committee, Senator Arlen Specter, described the explanation given for missing chemical logs as " . . . just incomprehensible."[24] Senator John D. Rockefeller IV said, " . . . the Pentagon has squandered the trust of the American people."[25] Former Senate staff investigator James Tuite III contended, " . . . there was a conspiracy to destroy documents related to the Gulf War."[26]

Members of the House Government Reform Subcommittee were no less critical. Their chairman, Congressman Christopher Shays, said the delay in releasing information was " . . . a deliberate deception of Congress, and an unconscionable withholding of information (from Gulf vets)."[27] He noted the Pentagon had failed to account for battlefield hazards, and their postwar investigations were conducted " . . . with a tin ear, a cold heart, and a very closed mind."[28]

Congressman Edolphus Town added, "If we learn nothing else from the Gulf War, accountability cannot be abandoned."[29] America's commander in the war zone, General Norman Schwarzkopf, would eventually lament that reports of his troops' illnesses were " . . . handled rather 'cavalierly' . . . "[30] As usual, Defense Secretary Perry defended the Pentagon's role by stating that no chemical warfare agents " . . . were in the theater, much less used, during the war."[31] Worse than these words of regret and denial was evidence that GIs were actually directed *not* to don protective gear when chemical alerts sounded.[32]

Another problem with such gear emerged years later when it was revealed that some of the protective suits made by one particular company had defects. These suits were supposed to be airtight but were discovered to have a variety of problems including holes and stitching irregularities which might result in the death of users in a contaminated environment. Officials from this company, Istratex, which had first produced the suits in 1989, were later prosecuted for fraud and conspiracy.[33]

More surprising was the fact that the Defense Department had not discovered these problems until 1996. Furthermore, they had not removed the defective suits or shared this information with troops for five years. The official reasons for these actions were even more shocking—they might have to issue the defective suits to troops headed for potential action in Bosnia.[34]

This would not be the last time that the Pentagon would be embarrassed by revelations about failing to protect its troops. Shortly after the terrorist attacks on September 11, 2001, thousands of American sailors were headed for the waters off the coast of Afghanistan. Weeks later, as the fleet launched airstrikes, stateside headlines started describing anthrax-infected letters in the U.S. mail. This led to widespread discussions about the dangers of biological and chemical attacks, which must have concerned the sailors because of loved ones back home.

Then stories began appearing about biological and chemical agent tests that the U.S. Navy had conducted on sailors in the 1960s.[35] Low-flying aircraft made passes over vessels enveloping them in clouds of dangerous agents while unprotected sailors huddled below deck. The Navy wanted to know if the ships' ventilation systems alone offered adequate protection from these airborne agents.

Years later, some of these sailors began showing up at veterans hospitals with complaints ranging from chronic respiratory problems to cancer. But the Defense Department refused to discuss these long-secret tests. After years of pressure by Congress and the Department of Veterans Affairs, the Pentagon finally admitted that the tests had taken place and confirmed that thousands of sailors were involved. The former CIA analyst, Patrick Eddington, who later became the associate director of the Vietnam Veterans of America, said that his organization " . . . was 'appalled' that the experiments were ever conducted and that it took 40 years for the Pentagon to acknowledge them."[36] Perhaps spurred by such criticism, the Pentagon recently admitted that those troops who served in the Gulf War were almost twice as likely as others to contract the fatal neurological illness amyotrophic lateral sclerosis (Lou Gehrig's disease).[37]

Such revelations opened old wounds because of an earlier situation, the infamous Agent Orange matter. Chemical defoliant was sprayed over millions of acres of jungle in Vietnam. This was intended to better reveal potential enemy targets and ambush points, especially those along strategic roads and waterways and those near American bases.

Ironically, this issue was not really resolved until the Gulf War era, when the government and the chemical companies were forced to admit that dioxin in Agent Orange could cause a host of medical problems. These giant companies, responding to a class action suit, finally offered to compensate the victims—the troops who had come in contact with this herbicide and developed cancers as well as other illnesses.[38] But even this small measure of justice had taken many years.

One of the terrible ironies related to Agent Orange involved a senior commander and his beloved son. Admiral Elmo Zumwalt Jr. later became chief of naval operations. Based on assurances he had received that this chemical was harmless to humans, he ordered its widespread use during the Vietnam Conflict. Sprayed areas included those where his son, Lt. Elmo Zumwalt III, was a patrol boat commander.

In their book, *My Father, My Son*,[39] they explained how they suspected a father's ill-advised decision contributed to his son's cancer and even to the severe learning disability of his grandson. Sadly, Lieutenant Zumwalt died of cancer in 1988 at age forty-two.

In a situation reminiscent of the Zumwalt Agent Orange Tragedy, a recent Department of Veterans Affairs study reported that children of Gulf War veterans are over twice as likely to be born with birth defects as those of other vets.[40] Thus, it seems the sacrifices of the fathers continue to be visited on the sons.

Renowned CBS commentator Mike Wallace said on the television program *The Twentieth Century*: "In turning its back on the victims of Agent Orange and the Gulf War Syndrome, the Pentagon only deepened the chasm of mistrust that divided it from the civilian community it is pledged to serve.[41]

PART
VI

Righteous Remedies

24

Walls of Shame

On June 12, 1987, Ronald Reagan went to Berlin on a mission. His epic plea, " . . . Mr. Gorbachev, tear down this wall . . . ," still echoes across history. That ugly structure had prolonged the mistrust between the West and the Soviets. The removal of this shameful symbol of absolute power two years later began a long-overdue healing process.

The time has now come to dismantle another wall, one running through the very soul of this nation. Americans should ask the president to join with Congress in removing the procedural barriers shielding the Pentagon from accountability on safety and health issues. This would do more than anything else to protect those who so selflessly serve the republic.

A dozen years after Ronald Reagan's plea, another student of history visited Germany. On May 5, 1999, Bill Clinton addressed the troops stationed at Spangdahlem Air Base. These men and women were providing support for the Kosovo campaign. Just hours before, he had learned of the war's first American casualties. Two Army pilots died when their AH-64 Apache helicopter crashed during a night training mission. A somber commander in chief looked across the throngs of camouflage-clad troops. President Clinton reminded them how dangerous such operations can be and thanked them for their service and sacrifice.[1]

Ironically, Serbia would sue for peace several weeks later without killing a *single* American GI. But within weeks of the cease-fire, five more U.S. soldiers would die in Kosovo mishaps—three in traffic crashes, one from an accidental gunshot wound, and another from electrocution.[2] These events followed a sadly familiar pattern—the reality that America now loses many more service members in accidents than it does in combat.

If the president had asked the Pentagon about this amazing statistic, he would undoubtedly have heard some of its standard mantras: " . . . military operations are innately dangerous," " . . . these are acceptable losses," " . . . accidents are the price of doing business," " . . . we don't have as many accidents as we used to," and so forth.

However, if Clinton had asked one of his predecessors that same question, he might have learned something different, for an earlier president knew a well-kept "military secret." Jimmy Carter was a former naval officer who was also a nuclear engineer. As such, he could have told Clinton something remarkable. For more than half a century, no American GI had *ever* been killed by nuclear weapons in an accident. So why is it that the *most* dangerous weapons seemed to be the *safest?* The answer is obvious, but achieving this miracle took a concerted effort.

First, the reason for this perfect record was that everybody *demanded* elaborate safeguards be taken to insure that an accidental nuclear detonation would be virtually impossible. Second, the leaders in Congress and in the executive branch always provided adequate funding to achieve this lofty goal. The government then systematically undertook a complex effort to accomplish this task. Although not as glamorous, the success of this program ranks with that of the Manhattan and Apollo Projects. But few people have examined the details of this fascinating story.

From the get-go, officials decided to establish a world-class technical facility to serve as a focal point for this work. They chose a site near Albuquerque. This central New Mexico location would be close to nuclear weapons production facilities at Los Alamos as well as to the only USAF atomic bomber wing, the famed 509th, at Roswell, New Mexico. President Harry Truman, who *knew* where the buck stopped, immediately asked the renowned Bell Labs to manage this enterprise. It would soon come to be named Sandia National Laboratories after a nearby mountain chain.

Here, some of the best minds in the nation were quietly assembled. Top experts in the cutting-edge fields of electronics, materials science, system safety, and human factors labored to solve complex technical issues. The government, through the Defense Department and the Atomic Energy Commission, funded their work. These interdisciplinary teams of specialists methodically pushed back the frontiers of knowledge, often inventing new concepts as they went.

The vital work went on for decades driven by twin demons, the specter of falling behind the "evil empire" in this deadly arms race, and the unthinkable—an accidental detonation. For perhaps the first time on this scale, nothing was overlooked or assumed regarding safety. There had to be multiple safeguards, redundancy, and defense in depth—a systems approach to everything.

The "fail-safe" concept was born. It simply meant that if a minor component, subsystem, or even a major system failed, design features or procedural safeguards would prevent a chain reaction from causing an unintended detonation. Every possible contingency was supposed to be anticipated. It was as if everything was a giant electrical wiring network, with each component protected by a circuit breaker. Interestingly, the term "fail-safe" became a household word only when Hollywood produced a movie by the same name in 1964.[3]

Because most accidents involve human errors, Sandia Laboratories' experts closely examined all potential human failure modes, as well as suitable countermeasures. Their scientists developed many innovations, such as detailed probability tables describing the frequency of errors. These tables even contained error data on such mundane tasks as over-tightening a screw.

Simultaneously, other military human factors laboratories were established or expanded across the country. Some of these research facilities dated back to the Second World War and before. But now there was an even greater sense of urgency to the work, for the cost of this new equipment was becoming astronomical, and the consequences of failure much more troubling. Fortunately, a great many of these innovations also spilled over to non-nuclear military equipment applications, which helped reduce their mishap rates over the years.

Much of what these laboratories did was to help engineers and designers better understand ergonomic issues. They attempted to document human capabilities and limitations, and thereby improve the safety and effectiveness of America's vast arsenal of weapon systems—many of which would soon carry a nuclear punch. This vital research examined issues such as the best way to design a crew station to optimize operator performance. This work was often challenging for the men and women faced with solving such riddles.

For instance, cockpits of many fighter planes were already cramped—and now the human factors specialists had to figure out the best location for still *another* weapons control panel. These experts looked at the literature on ergonomics, built mock-ups, and tested alternative layouts with actual pilots. After interviewing the test subjects, scoring questionnaire responses, and examining reaction times and error statistics—they froze the design. But this research did not focus exclusively on the machine, or even the so-called man-machine interface. Much of the work dealt with the purely human side of the equation.

For instance, they looked at how to select the "best" individuals with the knowledge, skills, and temperaments for certain jobs such as pilot, electronics technician, or air traffic controller. After selection, these troops then had to be trained for their particular positions. Because most of these training courses lasted for months, they were very expensive. Many were also highly dangerous. The experts had to decide how this training could be improved with things like flight simulators, programmed texts, or computer-based instruction facilities.

These diverse research efforts also dealt with "biological barriers" —physiological factors such as human noise tolerance. How loud could a control room be without degrading the performance of a warship's crew? Other research efforts examined organizational management issues, including how to develop better methods of controlling factors such as fatigue through optimal work-rest schedules for personnel assigned to missile silos.

Much of the information would eventually find its way into civilian products, from apparel to automobiles to the processes used in factories and offices across the land. This government-funded research paid the American people handsome dividends and helped maintain our status as a world leader in technical innovation. Such widely acclaimed work also made some of these research centers famous.

Arguably, the best known was the Air Force Laboratory at Wright-Patterson Air Force Base in Dayton, Ohio. This facility continues to develop important innovations that facilitate improving the state of the art in the field. For example, the lab was instrumental in establishing the Crew System Ergonomics Human Systems Information Analysis Center (CSERIAC) (although the name has recently been changed to the Human Systems Integration Analysis Center).[4]

As these names suggest, the center synthesizes countless research and development databases into something useful to the designers. This massive clearinghouse allows users throughout the world to quickly obtain information on vital human factors questions without having to reinvent the wheel.

Other military human factors programs have successfully tackled different problems. One stellar example was the U.S. Army's so-called MANPRINT program. This strange acronym is derived from MANpower, PeRsonnel, and INTegration. This program was actually *forced* on that service in the early 1980s after several of its new weapons systems failed to measure up. The reason for these failures was that no one was looking at the human element while the equipment was being designed.

Although the contractor's highly trained engineers and technicians could operate and fix the equipment in the factory, the average GI had problems doing these things at night, in the mud, and under combat conditions. In some cases, it just took too much training time or too many troops to maintain. What's more, Congress was getting tired of coughing up money to constantly fix these problems.

The Army modified its whole acquisition process to insure that new weapons systems would work for the average soldier under real-world conditions. The contractor had to demonstrate that it had included critical human factors considerations in designing its product. This involved meeting strenuous requirements in seven different areas: ergonomics, systems safety, manpower, personnel, training, health hazards, and personnel survivability. From its location in the Pentagon, the MANPRINT program also made the management of many large corporations sensitive to the reality that they needed to do their human factors homework to win Army contracts.

This program was a boon to improving the Army's equipment, although there were a few weapons, such as the Bradley Fighting Vehicle, that were purchased in spite of these deficiencies. There, the problem involved extraordinary pressure *not* to conduct proper operational testing, which would have revealed such flaws. Sometimes, well-connected special interest groups can overwhelm even the best of programs—to the detriment of the taxpayer and the common soldier.

Another way of improving safety involved the need to *grow* a group of in-house ergonomics experts, people who wear the uniform and who can not only talk the talk, but also walk the walk. In the 1960s, the Navy realized that flying jets from aircraft carriers was going to present some unique safety challenges, so they established a cadre of "aerospace research psychologists." This unique program still operates today from Pensacola Naval Air Station in Florida.

The group consists of dozens of eager, physically fit young men and women who have earned doctorates in experimental psychology and who want to get a commission and fly jets. They go through an abbreviated naval aviator orientation program and solo in the primary training aircraft. After getting "wings of gold,"[5] they are assigned to various military laboratories and training facilities. These valuable people provide a unique perspective because they understand both the operational environment and the science of ergonomics.

With the exception of the CSERIAC data clearinghouse, these individual cutting-edge Air Force, Army, and Navy programs never became DoD-wide efforts. This was due largely to interservice rivalry. But one major innovation adopted by all three services was the concept of "system safety."

This endeavor employs a complex collection of methodologies that analyze hazards and control risks. Its current incarnation is military standard number 882D. Basically, the system safety concept sprang out of the realization that there had to be a procedure for understanding the myriad of ways complex equipment can fail, as well as structured methods of controlling the effects of such occurrences.

It is a discipline that relies on a host of procedures to accomplish this. A widely used technique is the "failure-mode-and-effect analysis," which in turn employs "fault trees" to depict how each event in a chain occurs—so called because the various sequential contingencies, when plotted, resemble the branches of a tree.

A very simple example might depict how a fire could occur in a cargo compartment. For a fire to occur, fuel, oxygen, and an ignition source must all be present. The analysis would systematically examine all the ways this could happen. To compute the probability of the problem occurring, the analyst would combine the individual probability of occurrence for each branch of the tree.

Another fundamental tenet in this discipline describes the ideal approach to preventing mishaps, the "safety order of precedence." Taxonomy depicts, in hierarchical order, the most desirable countermeasures: First, try to eliminate the hazards or risks. Second, consider incorporating built-in safety features. Third, examine the efficacy of providing warning devices. Fourth, if all else fails, establish procedural safeguards. Obviously, economic and/or operational issues may preclude selecting the most desirable types of countermeasures, those at the top of this hierarchy. But despite this reality, the concept provides a very useful philosophy to help manage risks.

All the progressive concepts described above would not have evolved as quickly without the funding and support of the Department of Defense. Now for the *bad* news. Unfortunately, these programs represent isolated pockets of excellence submerged in a sea of indifference. Furthermore, many of the important military programs are facing cutbacks for budgetary reasons, or worse, because of a lack of advocacy by some leaders.

A couple of examples come to mind. An Air Force B-1 crashed in 1998 when all four engines quit after the crew tried to shut down one engine because of a fire warning.[6] A simple electrical short occurred where all four engine-control wires came together. This is a classic systems safety no-no—a "single point failure."

Then there is the Air Force's newest fighter, the F-22 Raptor, which was designed without any kind of modern ground collision avoidance system, a major cause of military crashes.[7] Both the B-1 and the F-22 cost around $200 million each, and there will be more losses. But the Air Force Material Command and Air Force Safety Center recently decided to save a few bucks by drastically downsizing their respective system safety groups.

There is a common thread that runs through most such organizational shortcomings. Simply put, the senior leadership in the Pentagon—those who hold the real power—traditionally have had little interest in, much less an understanding of, the subject of system safety.

Most of these officials usually only pay lip service to safety and health issues. They react rather than anticipate. They seem to prefer engaging in *damage* control, rather than *danger* control. And there are some understandable reasons for such behavior.

Remember, they know that when something goes wrong, they normally will face only in-house investigations. These quick-and-dirty inquiries are conducted by their own subordinates, amateurs who are part of a "good old boys" network. Besides, the embarrassing information will never be released outside of the DoD because it's considered "privileged." Then the Feres Doctrine will insure that there cannot be any embarrassing lawsuits. No wonder most of these leaders have lacked a long-term vision. As Proverbs 29:18 says, "Where there is no vision, the people perish. . . . "

By contrast, when the Pentagon is *told* to accomplish something, *and* the Congress provides ample funds, they *will* make it happen, big time. One rather interesting example was the DoD air carrier analysis system, which in some ways parallels the Pentagon's approach to nuclear weapons safety.

For decades, the DoD contracted with airlines to haul its troops and cargo when they did not have the capacity to use their own transports. Up through 1985, the Pentagon simply put out bids to move groups of troops and stacks of stuff from point X to point Y. These contracts went to the lowest bidder, the only stipulation being that the airline had to hold an FAA certificate.

Unfortunately, some fly-by-night charter airlines knew how to bend the rules. Every few years or so, one of these "cockroach corner" operators would crash, but nobody paid much attention. After all, safety records of these unknown civilian outfits were no worse than those of military transport units. Besides, it is not like the dead GIs could sue. The Feres Doctrine also protected these companies as long as they met the minimal government requirements in the contract.

But this system would change because of a single event. On December 12, 1985, one of these operators, Arrow Air, was bringing a load of 248

U.S. Army special forces troops back from the Middle East. It looked like these GIs would make it back home to Fort Campbell, Kentucky, just in time for the holidays.

Their aging DC-8 had landed to refuel at Gander Airport in New-foundland, Canada. After attempting to take off into snow showers, the heavily laden airliner crashed and burned. One of its engines failed to develop full power, and the crew had not spent enough money to get the aircraft properly deiced. Everybody on board perished.[8]

Ronald Reagan openly wept as he addressed the families at their Fort Campbell memorial service. After holding hearings, Congress and the administration quickly agreed that this system *had* to change. Funds were provided almost immediately to allow the Air Force to build a system to inspect and monitor the safety and financial condition of any airline bidding on military charters.

The FAA hurriedly trained a group of military pilots and maintain-ers on airline practices. These experts were assigned to Scott AFB, Illinois, and told to construct a database on all potential airlines. I was soon asked to serve as a consultant to this activity. Since this office began operation, the number of DoD charter-airline crashes has plummeted. This is inter-esting, given the military's continued problems with its own transport aircraft operations—evidenced by the Ron Brown accident.

In late 1996, Defense Secretary William Perry, the consummate Pen-tagon insider, announced he would not be staying on for Clinton's second term. Mr. Perry had epitomized the DoD status quo approach to safety is-sues. The president soon selected William Cohen, the retiring senator from Maine—a Republican. This choice surprised many people, partly because this guy was known to be an independent thinker, one who had previously criticized some of the Clinton administration's military policies.

Many safety experts had hoped that Cohen would bring a breath of fresh air to the long overdue need for military reform, for while Cohen was an outsider to the Pentagon bureaucracy, he was *very* familiar with military issues. He had studied these topics for nearly a quarter century from his perch on the House and later the Senate Armed Services Com-mittees. There, he gained a reputation as a soft-spoken but thoughtful person who did his homework—and asked tough questions.

Soon after he assumed his duties as Secretary of Defense, he made a number of decisions that must have surprised and even alarmed some

Pentagon insiders. These actions suggested that, unlike some of his predecessors and many of his subordinates, he had a *genuine* interest in improving military safety and accountability.

One incident involved fallout from a tragedy that happened on Secretary Perry's watch. On June 25, 1996, a truck bomb exploded outside the Khobar Towers dormitory in Saudi Arabia. The blast killed nineteen American airmen, but it was not the first time terrorists had used such tactics against our GIs there.[9]

A subsequent DoD investigation found that the USAF officer in charge, Brigadier General James Schwalier, had *not* taken all the appropriate measures to protect his troops. But Secretary Perry just ignored this finding and allowed him to stay on the promotion list. Senator Arlen Specter said, "The Department of Defense has become an excuse factory, as opposed to standing up and being accountable . . . "[10]

Soon after being sworn in as Defense Secretary, Mr. Cohen removed Schwalier's name from the promotion list. This apparently did not sit well with the Air Force chief of staff, General Ronald Fogleman, for he promptly announced that he just might have to resign from the service if his man, Schwalier, did not get promoted.

Thus, the new secretary was about to face his first test. He replied that he would accept General Fogleman's resignation. Suddenly, the brass and the bureaucracy discovered there was a new sheriff in town.

If that didn't cause aftershocks throughout the Pentagon, Cohen's interview with the *Boston Globe* soon would. That paper's Pulitzer Prize–winning reporters, Matthew Brelis and Stephen Kurkjian, had been doing a series on military safety and had interviewed Secretary Cohen. During that interview, the secretary indicated that " . . . he believes the military should make public the causes of mishaps."[11]

This was *absolute heresy*, given the fact his Pentagon associates had insisted on the exact opposite for decades. Such information was "privileged." Without this protection, the services argued, they just could not successfully obtain critical data from their GIs. Actually, they had insisted that the findings, recommendations, as well as the *causes* from mishap investigations could never be released outside the DoD without undermining the whole military safety process. Now Cohen, in one interview, had destroyed that long sacrosanct argument that had been used successfully to avoid accountability.

If the traditionalists in the Pentagon had not figured the new guy out yet, he would soon give them some more clues. Mr. Cohen was "displeased" with the Army's new FMTV trucks, which kept flipping over. The Army wanted to purchase another batch of the defective trucks—actually 9,350 more at a cost of $1.4 billion. But the new secretary stepped in and declared there would be no new order until the design problems were corrected.[12]

If the Army was too ready to throw good money after bad, the Air Force was doing just the opposite. After the 1996 Ron Brown crash, Congress had ordered them to install new safety equipment on *all* their transports. The Air Force had decided they had better things to do with their funds. Besides, some of these aircraft were going to the boneyard in five or ten years.

On September 13, 1997, a USAF C-141 was crossing the South Atlantic when a German Air Force TU-154 jet got off course.[13] The two transports slammed together and all thirty-three people aboard perished. The families of the American victims began asking why the C-141 did not have the required collision avoidance systems installed.

After some equivocation, the Air Force admitted it had ignored the Congressional directive because it did not want to spend money on such old aircraft. As with the Army trucks, Secretary Cohen insisted they do the right thing. He soon announced the Air Force had agreed to accelerate the program of putting the safety devices on such aircraft, at a cost of $20 million.[14]

Sometimes it wasn't what he said, but how he said it. In September 1997, there was a rash of seemingly unrelated military plane crashes involving all of the services. The secretary knew something dramatic needed to be done, pronto. So he decided to have a one-day "safety stand-down" for each of the services.

But he ignored the bureaucratic niceties of holding meetings to ask everyone's opinion if that would be okay. Reliable sources told me the brass was astounded that he did not consult with his military experts before announcing his decision. Perhaps it had occurred to the secretary that these same military "experts" had caused the problem in the first place.

During his tenure, Secretary Cohen would also be treated to a lot of in-house advice and several supposedly independent studies that often suggested things actually were not too bad from a safety standpoint. This was consistent, for example, with the picture conveyed a few years before by the Air Force's blue ribbon panel.[15] But then they had the Ron Brown crash and all these other problems.

The secretary was astute enough to know the devil was in the details. For example, the sources generally came to the same conclusions. On most measures, say the total number of crashes or the mishap rates, it appears there *has* been improvement over the last several decades. Ergo, things are not all that bad. These same studies, though, usually admitted the rate of improvement had stagnated in recent years.

Well, there are lots of ways to interpret statistics, and most of the inquiries did not bother to explain certain details. For instance, the number of deaths had dramatically decreased, but so had the number of people in uniform. Ditto the number of vehicles, ships, and aircraft. Furthermore, crew size for most weapons systems had decreased.

For instance, the number of crew members in each bomber aircraft has decreased. There were six people in the 1960s-era B-52s, down to four in the 1980s-era B-1s, and now there are only two in the current B-2s. Thus, fewer people are exposed to a risky flying environment.

Then, too, most accidents involve human factors issues. Thus, one should note the large improvements in the safety-related demographics of the military workforce. These important factors have dramatically changed, especially in the last few decades.[16]

Only a few decades ago, America had a young, usually unmarried, less educated, virtually all-male, draftee-based force—with a significant number of substance and alcohol abuse problems. Contrast that with the all-volunteer, usually married, better educated, drug-free demographics of today's military. I believe these factors alone can explain much of the safety-related improvements.[17]

Obviously, military equipment also improved along with its civilian counterparts, from airliners to automobiles. The modern technology, such as solid-state electronics and turbo-fan engines, are vastly more reliable and safer than their counterparts of only a few decades ago. Again, the statistics are just reflecting the overall technical trends.

Of course, the cost of this technology has skyrocketed. The price of those same bombers has risen from roughly $20 million for the B-52, to

$200 million for the B-1, to an astronomical $2 billion for the B-2. So, when they do crash, it is increasingly costly.

But the military accident cost-accounting system, as the DoD IG investigation into my complaint admitted, has "some problems."[18] Translation: We admit to losing $3 billion annually in accidents, but we do not really know what accidents cost. Furthermore, the secretary's handlers have made sure that he not see the real numbers.

I was informed that such an investigation was done secretly. It revealed the direct costs alone for all types of accidents was *at least* $7 billion annually. This rather comprehensive study included things not in the DoD budget, such as the expenses of paying pensions and long-term medical care for on-duty and off-duty injuries. Unfortunately, that $7 billion figure did not include the *indirect* costs, such as investigating crashes and purchasing extra "attrition" aircraft to cover those lost in crashes. Unfortunately, the author of the study was never allowed to present it to Cohen.

But deceiving the secretary about the real cost of mishaps was not the only problem. The basic barometer of military aviation safety is the so-called Class A flight mishap rate. Several times in recent years, the Pentagon has proudly proclaimed that this fundamental index has gone down—a sign that things are improving.

But in 1997, Russell Carollo, a Pulitzer Prize–winning reporter for the *Dayton Daily News*, obtained the computer tapes from the three military safety centers. After carefully studying this raw data for eighteen months, Carollo came to a shocking conclusion.

As noted earlier, the Pentagon allows the individual services some latitude in excluding certain types of accidents from counting against their critical Class A flight mishap rate, such as crashes that occur after an aircraft has landed. Of course, the NTSB for civilian crash statistics allows no such exemptions.

This brilliant reporter discovered that the military safety centers had been hiding increasing numbers of accidents in these special, non-rate-producing categories—and the problems were getting worse as time went on. He also discovered that they were doing this for the less severe Class B mishap rates, too. Furthermore, this deception involved at least 282 accidents over a seven-year period.[19]

Reporter Carollo stated, "The percentage of accidents not counted increased from 5.6 percent in 1990 to 23 percent in 1997—nearly one of every four incidents."[20] The Pentagon staff was more than happy to turn a blind eye to such deceptive practices by its three military safety centers. After all, these bogus improvements also made them look good.

The bottom line is, there have been some understandable improvements, but not enough, given the size of these problems. Then, too, the rate of improvement has leveled off in recent years. Not so the costs of these problems, which while poorly documented, are known to be growing rapidly.

Speaking of costs, it is interesting that the Air Force keeps asking the DoD to raise the dollar threshold for the definition of the all-important Class A mishap. Obviously, increasing this figure would decrease the number of crashes that are classified as Class A. That would help make it look as if things were getting safer.

Interestingly, this value was increased from $500,000 in the early 1980s to $1 million in the late 1980s. Now, they want to increase it to $3 million. DoD has so far resisted this scam. Obviously, recent inflation rates have not been bad enough to justify anything like this kind of an increase.

As if these safety issues were not enough, the new secretary of defense would soon be faced with a major health concern—the growing threats represented by biological weapons, especially the use of anthrax by several potential enemies. In response, Cohen ordered the inoculation of all 2.4 million active-duty and reserve military personnel.[21]

The difficulty here was that, because of past medical abuses by the Pentagon, many GIs were reluctant to take these shots. Hundreds openly refused, and some were court-martialed, while many others simply resigned from the service.

Ironically, "information warfare" was something the military has used to its advantage in recent campaigns. But now the troops are using the Internet to discuss reported problems with the anthrax shots, including questions about the manufacturer's previous quality-control difficulties. This situation has even led some in Congress to call for the suspension of the anthrax inoculation program.[22]

One *New York Times* interview captured the depth of the problem: "I think it speaks to the undercurrent of distrust of the government and the military," said Lieutenant General Ronald R. Blanck, the surgeon general of the Army, the service that oversees the vaccination program. "Agent Orange. Nuclear tests in the fifties. People say, 'How can you say this is safe?' Clearly, we have a credibility problem."[23]

William Cohen indeed had his work cut out for him. Obviously, convincing the rank and file that he would do everything in his power to protect them was not going to be easy, for our troops are very sophisticated and know that some defense secretaries and many other senior leaders have been AWOL on such issues.

After more than a year in office, the secretary took a very proactive step to help convince the skeptics in and out of uniform. On June 23, 1998, he issued an "accident prevention proclamation," giving his commitment to these vital matters. "I have stated that even one accident is too many, and I continue to advocate continuous improvement until we reach a goal of zero accidents, occupational illnesses. . . . Working together, I believe we can and will move toward this goal."[24]

Unfortunately, very disturbing signs would emerge in the waning months of the Clinton administration. The president, feeling the heat at home from Congressional impeachment, decided to take his family and friends on a world tour. This would require the overstretched USAF Air Mobility Command to provide dozens of transports to support the Clinton entourage in the manner to which it had become accustomed.

A major tragedy was narrowly averted during one stop in India. There, the air traffic control system put two giant USAF transports on a collision course. Fortunately, the craft missed each other by a mere two hundred feet, no thanks to the fact that they were among those military jets still awaiting the installation of collision avoidance systems mandated by Congress years earlier.[25]

Two foreign air traffic controllers, one in Manilla, another in Japan, each cleared the two transports to a refueling rendezvous at the same fix and same altitude. Fortunately, the alert aircrews saw each other's craft in time to take evasive action and avoid a certain collision.

Another more embarrassing incident involved the Thunderbirds, the elite USAF aerial demonstration team. These eight F-16 fighter pilots intended to depart Andrews AFB in Maryland and proceed westward over the city of Washington in marginal weather.

They planned to play "follow the leader" and depart in sequence in a so-called radar-assisted trail departure. This formation soon ran into difficulty when one of the pilots became disoriented. This caused the formation to break up, with various jets going in different directions. One F-16 was soon involved in a near midair collision with a private aircraft at nearby Dulles Airport, while a second nearly collided with an American Airlines MD-80 passenger plane. An alert FAA air traffic controller then noticed that a third F-16 was approaching a thirty-five-hundred-foot mountain and warned him in time.[26]

Later that year the Air Force congratulated itself on its banner year in safety. However, these two incidents suggest that but for the grace of God and a few hundred feet of empty airspace, this could have been an absolutely disastrous year.

Another safety debacle would occur as Cohen was beginning to pack his bags. The Marines were close to ordering their innovative but dangerous V-22 vertical takeoff and landing transport into full production when disaster struck.[27] On April 8, 2000, a V-22 crashed in Arizona, killing all nineteen Marines aboard.

I was soon contacted by a senior Pentagon official who was charged with evaluating the V-22 for the USAF. He was aware of my earlier whistle-blowing and wanted me assigned as a consultant to the Marine Safety Investigation Board. My presence was needed, in his words, "to keep the Marines honest"—because he heard the Marines were publicly suggesting the accident might be due to pilot error.

This official planned to send the request through an assistant secretary of the Air Force to the chief of staff, who would have to pass it on to the Marine Corps. It was not long before his plan came to naught. The request was declined.

As expected, the Marine investigation blamed the dead pilots. It claimed they had descended too rapidly and had run into the invisible downwash from the V-22 directly in front of them. The Marines and the manufacturer had apparently known that the V-22 design made it highly susceptible to such problems, but they had neglected to adequately warn the pilots.

As the Pentagon official had feared, this explanation got the Marine Corps off the hook—temporarily. The folly of this flawed mishap investigation was revealed on the evening of December 11, 2000.[28] Four more Marines died when their V-22 hydraulic system failed, just as it had done numerous times in earlier tests. This time a hidden software glitch compounded the problem, sending their craft out of control. It crashed into a North Carolina forest and burned for hours.

This exotic crash involved the Pentagon's first fly-by-wire passenger aircraft, which had many known safety deficiencies. Because of widespread criticism of this expensive program, and because of the two recent fatal crashes, Mr. Cohen announced he would recommend an "independent panel" review the program before committing it to production.

A problem occurred when the four members of this panel were announced. One was the CEO of a major defense contractor, another was a retired Marine general who had lobbied for the aircraft, the third was a retired Air Force general who had been hired earlier by ValuJet to fix their problems, and the fourth individual was a college professor whose academic chair had been partly paid for by one of the V-22's prime contractors. Thus, it appeared Cohen's group was all too typical of the kind of independent panels hired by the Pentagon to investigate itself.

Then, with thousands of troops on food stamps and shortages of everything including pistol bullets, Secretary Cohen decided to spend $300,000 on a gala bash in Hollywood, the ostensive purpose of which was to thank the film industry for doing movies like *Saving Private Ryan*.[29]

Secretary Cohen had earlier stated that he wanted the military to ". . . reconnect with the American people. . . ."[30] This is another tall order, one that will require the help of the *future* Congresses and presidential administrations, for the Pentagon's shameful past in the safety and health arenas has done much to isolate it from its own troops, not to mention the general population. But continuing to hide behind this "wall of shame" will only exacerbate the situation.

25

Saving Private Leland

Private First Class William A. Leland III is your typical GI. Tonight this U.S. Army paratrooper shuffles through the dark and noisy C-130 fuselage and steps through the open door into the black abyss. The windblast twists him around while he listens for the reassuring sound of his main parachute popping open.

He will *never* hear that unmistakable sound—as gravity sucks him ever faster toward the Fort Bragg drop zone a thousand feet below. Leland knows something is seriously wrong and grabs for his reserve chute handle. But before it can open, he hits the North Carolina soil at 120 miles per hour. Life is suddenly ripped from his shattered body, ending this young man's quest to "be all he can be."[1]

Only hours before Private Leland's death on January 29, 1998, President Clinton spoke at the National Defense University in southeast Washington, D.C.—America's finishing school for senior admirals and generals. As he spoke, Clinton did not know who would be the next victim, but he reminded the brass that we lose hundreds of troops in accidents every year.[2] These senior officers listened silently when the president said, "We must and will always make their safety a top priority."[3]

While Clinton spoke a few hundred miles away, Private Leland was diligently preparing for his night jump. As this trusting soldier went about his duties that afternoon, he was a dead man walking.

It is impossible to know if this particular twenty-three-year-old paratrooper would have been spared had the Pentagon leadership not ignored my 1994 complaint. However, one thing is certain: ignoring my plea was a *statistical death sentence* for him and more than a thousand other victims who have perished in the intervening years.

But the real question is how to stop this carnage—*now.* Specifically, what actions must occur to drastically reduce unnecessary military accidents and avoidable illnesses? This quest will require the active involvement of several groups.

The American people must say "enough is enough"—we simply will not support the continued slaughter of our finest men and women. Congress must hold hearings, pass legislation, and adequately fund the necessary equipment, training, and infrastructure enhancements to achieve this goal. The administration must provide leadership, initiate a series of executive orders, and insure that the laws be faithfully executed. Military commanders must acknowledge their fundamental responsibility for protecting subordinates and master those skills needed to accomplish this. Finally, the courts need to reexamine the government's assertion of absolute immunity in military disasters.

Today, the most vocal group on the issue of enhancing military safety consists of the accident and illness victims and their families. Understandably, many of these people are terribly angry and hurt, for they have cried out in vain for answers and justice like the civil rights advocates of a bygone era, only to be battered or ignored by those holding power.

But a government of the people, by the people, and for the people requires that all concerned citizens study these issues and contact their elected representatives. They should remind these officials that they do not want countless billions spent on defense unless adequate funds are made available to protect those who must go in harm's way.

These citizens should also insist they will not encourage their kids to join up unless a good-faith effort is made to reform this system. Last, when tragedies occur, they must demand to know *why*—no more closed-door investigations with "sorry, that's privileged" responses.

The summer of 2000 would see many hotly contested political campaigns. Interestingly, both Republican front-runners, Senator John McCain and Governor George W. Bush, were former military pilots who had seen comrades die in accidents. After winning the nomination, George W. Bush selected for his running mate Richard Cheney, a highly regarded military expert who had served as the elder Bush's Secretary of Defense. During the campaign, Cheney and Bush both discussed the need for "military reform."

Cheney had a well-publicized track record in that endeavor, which included canceling the Navy's star-crossed stealth bomber, the A-12. But Congress had ignored this Secretary of Defense's early objections to the Marine's V-22 aircraft. This helicopter-like craft was a collection of compromises when it came to safety, and by the time Cheney was sworn in, four V-22 crashes had claimed thirty lives.

George W. Bush promised to focus on military issues during the fourth week of his administration. This pledge took him to Fort Stewart in Georgia, where the former Air National Guard fighter pilot received a rousing welcome from camouflage-clad U.S. Army troops.

As President Bush carefully assumed the reigns of leadership, America's men and women in uniform finally felt they had a commander in chief who understood their problems. Bill Clinton's youthful remark that he "loathed the military" had always hurt them deeply. What's more, part of Clinton's legacy was a military that was still unsafe.

As he began his opening remarks, George W. Bush made a request of the assembled soldiers—to join him in a moment of silent prayer for the victims of the previous day's collision between a U.S. Navy submarine and a Japanese trawler. He then told them, "While you're serving us well . . . America is not serving you well enough."[4]

These words would be all too prophetic, for military safety problems haunted the early weeks of his administration. Perhaps the ugliest episode involved the relatives of the dead Marine Corps V-22 crew members pleading for an honest investigation into what killed their loved ones. For weeks, stories swirled through the media about two issues. The first involved reports of senior USMC officers concealing maintenance problems of the V-22 fleet.[5] Other stories challenged the inappropriate finding of "pilot error" in an earlier V-22 accident investigation.[6]

The Navy sub's collision with a Japanese trawler presented President Bush with his first foreign policy challenge. The president had to apologize to the Japanese premier for this sinking and for the deaths of several Japanese crew members. George W. Bush must have been as surprised as the rest of the nation when the Navy tried to limit damning information about the mishap.

Fortunately, American law requires that the National Transportation Safety Board conduct an independent investigation when accidents occur between a civilian vessel and a U.S. warship. The Navy efforts at damage control soon backfired as the embarrassing details dribbled out. NTSB statements and the diligent work by investigative reporters made headlines around the world—and a very disturbing picture emerged.

It seems that the nuclear attack submarine USS *Greeneville* was not on a military mission at all. Senior officers had arranged a ride for sixteen civilians who had contributed to a naval memorial fund. The grateful officers wanted to show these distinguished visitors just how a submarine operates. The *Greeneville* was demonstrating a risky rapid surfacing maneuver when it collided with the *Ehime Maru*, a fishing trawler used for training Japanese high school students.

The problem was that the space aboard this compact sub made it difficult to handle so many visitors. The entourage had to be fed in two shifts in the vessel's tiny galley, which caused the day cruise to run late. The ship's navigator reminded the captain of this, and the captain proceeded to hasten the climax of the day's festivities, an "emergency blow."

During this dramatic maneuver, the sub captain brings his vessel to periscope depth to scan surrounding waters for surface ships. He then dives to about four hundred feet and directs the crew to blow the water from its ballast tanks with compressed air. This forces the sub to pop to the surface and momentarily fly upward, like a playful dolphin.

Three guests were allowed to occupy critical crew positions while nearby sailors talked them through this dangerous maneuver. Other visitors were crowded into the same control room, which prevented the sonar technician from plotting the location of surface targets on a paper attached to a wall. This technician saw the sometimes inaccurate passive sonar returns from the nearby fishing vessel but decided they must be in error because the skipper had just finished his periscope sweeps of the surface and was going ahead with the emergency blow maneuver. On top of everything else, the sonar video scope located in the control room was inoperative.

The stage was set for disaster as the captain raced through the preparations to surface, and none of the crew members challenged his actions. The situation was eerily similar to that aboard cruiser USS *Vincennes* as it was about to shoot down an Iranian airliner thirteen years before.[7] In both situations, crew members who had vital information declined to challenge the flawed thinking of their captain at a critical juncture.

Tragically, the *Greeneville* crew, like most other military personnel, had never received the Crew Resource Management training as I had recommended to the Secretary of Defense in 1994. Now, just as the sub reached the surface, its aft vertical fin slashed through the engine room of the Japanese trawler. The smaller vessel sank almost immediately, drowning nine crew members including four who were high school students.

Moreover, this type of submarine accident had happened twice before, and the Navy had ignored the lessons from the earlier tragedies. In 1981, the nuclear submarine USS *George Washington*, en route to a liberty port, hastily surfaced in the East China Sea. It rammed and sank a Japanese freighter.[8] Unbelievably, the sub did not report this collision until the next day.

Then, in 1989, the Navy supplied a nuclear submarine, USS *Houston*, for the movie *The Hunt for Red October*. It was surfacing as it returned to port near San Diego when it snagged a towline from a tugboat pulling a barge.[9] The tug sank immediately, drowning one crew member. Interestingly, the NTSB, after investigating this accident, recommended that submarines use their more accurate active sonar when surfacing in crowded sea-lanes, but the Navy rejected this idea.

As it grappled with the USS *Greeneville* tragedy, a second blow hit the new administration. On March 3, a Florida Army National Guard C-23 transport, hauling Virginia Air National Guardsmen, crashed in stormy weather near Macon, Georgia. All twenty-one "weekend warriors" died instantly when the twin-turboprop craft plunged into an open field. Camera crews were quickly on the scene, and pictures of the shattered wreckage flashed across the nation that weekend.

Then, without warning, a third major military disaster occurred on the evening of March 16. A U.S. Navy F/A-18 flown by a squadron commander was making a practice bomb run at a range in Kuwait when coordination with USAF forward air controller broke down. This sergeant radioed the pilot that he was cleared to release his weapons, only to discover that something was very wrong. He hastily transmitted "Abort, abort."[10] But it was too late, for the three five-hundred pound bombs exploded within one hundred feet of an observation post.

Miraculously, he was only wounded. But five other GIs and a New Zealand major died. The prime minister of that country would soon demand "some explanations,"[11] and this won't be the last time an errant bomb would embarrass the new administration with a foreign head of state. On December 5, 2001, a two-thousand-pound smart bomb from a B-52 would kill three of our GIs and slightly injure Hamid Karzai, the head of the new Afghan government.[12]

Thus, the agonies would continue, especially for the new secretary of defense, Donald Rumsfeld who was no stranger to the job, having ably served in that post under President Ford decades earlier. Rumsfeld issued the following statement: "Tragedies such as this occur without warning and for reasons that are difficult to understand. . . . We will work hard to take care of the families involved and to find out how such an accident could occur."[13]

On the day of the Kuwait mishap, President Bush was visiting Panama City, Florida. For the second time in as many months, he had to request a moment of silence for the dead. A saddened commander in chief would then say, "I'm reminded today of how dangerous service can be."[14]

But President Bush now has the opportunity to change this situation, if he is willing to confront the Pentagon's entrenched bureaucracy. His best tool for bringing about change is to issue a series of executive orders. Minimally, these orders should cover several vital issues.

First, he should direct all personnel to fully cooperate with all efforts to overhaul the DoD safety and health systems. This includes testifying candidly during Congressional or judicial hearings.

Second, information on the real causes of all future mishaps must be released in a timely manner.[15] Similarly, mishap board findings and recommendations should also be made available. In addition, the causes, findings, and recommendations of formerly "privileged" reports need to be released upon request after the names and identifying information of witnesses are redacted.

There may be howls of protest over these actions by those who fear that the truth will hurt their careers. The president should hang tough and remind everyone that "privilege" has sometimes been suspended for major accidents, such as the Ron Brown crash. So why do you have to have it in the hundreds of smaller inquiries?

Last, the commander in chief should insist that the harassment of or retaliation against victims, witnesses, investigators, and whistle-blowers cease immediately. Furthermore, the withholding or the destruction of evidence related to military safety and health issues must be fully punished. These moves would signal our military decision makers that "the times, they are a changing."

Interestingly, the Pentagon already spends more than $50 million annually to recover and identify the remains of those killed in battle.[16] Now we are going to grant those whom *we* kill in accidents, and those still alive but ill, the same type of courtesy. The American government will thereby simply be meeting standards it demands of other countries, such as North Korea.

Congress should also hold hearings in preparation for a second "GI Bill of Rights." The earlier law was a testament to this nation's commitment to insuring those who so courageously served would have a fair chance at education, employment, and housing. New legislation is needed for something even more vital. The legislation must pledge America's commitment to protecting the safety and health of its servicemen and women. This is an idea whose time has come, and it is the least we can do.[17]

The cornerstone of the legislation would be the creation of a Military Safety Board, or MSB.[18] This new agency should be totally independent from the DoD. It would have several major functions: 1) investigate hazards, incidents, mishaps, and illnesses; 2) perform special studies related to such problems; 3) issue public statements on findings, causes, and recommendations; 4) advise the president, Department of Defense officials, and Congress on these matters.

Although new itself, the MSB could make maximum use of the facilities and expertise of other existing government and nongovernment agencies. Working agreements should be established with organizations like the NTSB, NASA, EPA, Public Health Service, Food and Drug Administration, Centers for Disease Control, National Academy of Science, the National Safety Council, and the Flight Safety Foundation. This will ensure the highest quality products while minimizing time and costs.

The MSB should also operate an anonymous reporting system designed to allow the organization to detect subtle hazards and otherwise unreported incidents. This is like having a "radar system" to identify potential problems *before* they turn into catastrophes. NASA and the Australian safety bureau have operated such systems for years and have shown their benefits.

Another useful feature for the MSB would be the capability, staff, and mandate to perform economic, operational, and environmental impact studies. That would allow the organization to quickly examine such issues before making recommendations. This could reduce the number of "yeah, buts"—recommendations rejected by the Pentagon as unrealistic.

The MSB would need to have in-house experts familiar with military equipment, tactics, procedures, and its unique customs. Thus, the board would undoubtedly recruit former military personnel, especially those with experience in the safety and health fields. It would also rely on some active-duty personnel to serve as subject-matter experts.

The agency would be responsible for investigating the vast majority of military accidents and illnesses. It would do so with great openness while respecting the concerns of the victims' families. It would, however, defer to the Defense and State Departments when such occurrences involve highly classified systems or especially sensitive national missions. Here, the president would make the call. Obviously, should he or she so direct, the expertise and facilities of the MSB could discreetly support such requests.

This agency would always strive for a lofty purpose—protecting those who have to go in harm's way. Perhaps a fitting motto for the organization might be the William Shakespeare quotation: "Times glory is to calm contending kings, to unmask falsehoods, and bring truth to light."[19]

Obviously, Congress needs to create the MSB and fund the necessary training and equipment to permit the military to better protect its troops. These legislators should also pass laws designed to facilitate such improvements. These laws would likely resemble those associated with the Environmental Protection Agency. They would thereby mandate that crimes against troops are as important as those against trees. This legislation must insure that those in leadership positions know that intentionally or unnecessarily endangering their subordinates will have real consequences.

Furthermore, such crimes would be tried in the federal courts instead of in the "good old boy" system of military justice. This is already the case for environmental crimes, as three Army officials discovered in 1989. They were threatened with jail time for allowing the dumping of deadly chemicals at Aberdeen Proving Grounds in Maryland. The trial of the "Aberdeen Three" in federal court sent a chilling message throughout the DoD.[20]

Obviously, this new legislation would not be intended to make scapegoats out of commanders for honest mistakes. Thorough, impartial, and timely investigations are the best defense against scapegoating—for all ranks. This should end the "blame games." By doing so, it will restore trust in the whole system. Thus, those who aspire to leadership positions will know they also will be protected from capricious actions of their associates and bosses. However, they must acknowledge their own fundamental roles and agree to always be accountable.

These military officials will *still* have the responsibility for functions such as training and operating their accident and illness prevention systems. They will need to master subjects like operational risk evaluation, just as they previously mastered the personnel skills needed to deal with sexual harassment. These are just other types of management skills, and most military leaders excel at such challenges.

The nation has placed great trust in their judgment and integrity, but now, for once, they will also have the resources needed to accomplish their *other* vital function—force protection. Incidentally, this process will not be limited to just protecting their troops, but will include civil servants, contractors, and the public.

Perhaps the last arena reached by such reforms will be America's judicial system. The Supreme Court has repeatedly invoked the Feres Doctrine to deny compensation to victims of military accidents, much as it ignored basic civil rights issues for decades—until the *Brown v. The Board of Education* ruling in 1955. Interestingly, the impetus for doing this may come from abroad—from our closest ally, Britain. When the European Convention on Human Rights was adopted, allowing all citizens to sue their governments, the British did *not* ask that its armed force members be exempt.[21] Hopefully, America will not fall too far behind on this vital human rights issue.

On the eve of the new millennium, *Time* published a list of the ten most influential people of the twentieth century.[22] These were the ultimate "shakers and movers," and their names included famous statesmen, entertainers, and scientists. The only one on the list who was not a *real* person was the nameless American GI. This was a fitting honor, for, with courage and chivalry, our troops fought tyranny and tried to restore justice to a troubled world—not once, but in five separate, major crusades of that century.

Unfortunately, the new century finds America's GIs once again embroiled in a war. This time, however, it is a war against evil incarnate—international terrorism.

America can never forget the humble GI's courage and sacrifice in combat. Hollywood accurately portrayed the plight of GIs with the fictitious characters in *Saving Private Ryan*.[23] But we must also remember the loss of very *real* people like Private Leland in accidents. These modern knights have needlessly suffered in silence for too long.

We should remember that since the founding of the republic, more than *one-half million* American troops have died from largely preventable wartime accidents and illnesses.[24] In fact, about half of this nation's combat casualties were *not* caused by our enemies.

Furthermore, "peacetime" offers little respite, as the fifty-five murdered GIs learned on September 11, 2001, when a hijacked airliner crashed into the Pentagon.[25] Interestingly, that is about the same number of troops we kill *every* few months in accidents. Indeed, during the last quarter century, operational accidents have actually killed ten times more GIs than hostile action.

However, the French philosopher Voltaire probably offered the best rationale for undertaking these reforms when he said, "To the living we owe respect, to the dead we owe the truth."[26]

Notes

Chapter 1

1. UH-60 is a standard twin-engine 14-place, utility helicopter manufactured by Sikorsky, United Technologies since 1974 for U.S. Army, Navy, and USAF.
2. Officially part of "Operation Provide Comfort," authorized by U.S. National Command Authority in April 1991.
3. F-15 is the primary USAF, twin-engine, supersonic air superiority fighter, manufactured by McDonnell Douglas and Boeing since 1972.
4. *Aircraft Accident Investigation Board Report*, U.S. Army, UH-60 Blackhawk Helicopters 87-26000 and 88-26060 (U.S. Air Forces Europe, 1994).
5. "Hind" is the NATO code name for the Mi-24 type of heavily armed, twin-engine, assault helicopter. Built by the Mil Design Bureau, they entered Soviet service in 1974 and were supplied to the Iraqis.
6. Joan Piper, *Chain of Events* (Dulles, Virginia: Brassey's, 2000), 168–169.
7. E-3, officially called the "Sentry," is a highly modified four-engine Boeing 707 jetliner, which was first flown in 1975.
8. The so-called QWERTY keyboard named after the physical arrangement of the letter keys.
9. The radar-guided AIM-120 AMRAAM (Advanced Medium Range Air to Air Missile) was the latest and most expensive such weapon in the USAF inventory.
10. The highly maneuverable, heat-seeking AIM-9 (Sidewinder) was originally developed by the U.S. Navy as a dog-fighting weapon.
11. The actual thoughts and actions of deceased victims such as Lt. Piper are, of course, known but to God, although the author's decades of interviewing crash

survivors and studying the physical evidence suggests these are the typical responses for such individuals.

12. Excerpt from DoD tape recording of the F-15s' radio transmissions.

13. Alan Diehl, "Crew Resource Management: It's Not Just for Fliers Anymore," *Flying Safety,* June 1994, 8–11.

14. The military intentionally selected two similar-sounding labels, "Safety" and "Accident," to confuse outsiders who request these documents so they will not realize they are not getting the report from the real investigation.

15. "Transportation Safety Act of 1974," 93rd Congress, 2nd Session, H.R. 15223, Public Law 93-633, approved January 3, 1975 (Washington, D.C.: Government Printing Office).

16. Public Use Aircraft Accidents Investigations Act, 106th Congress, 1st Session, H.R. 3036, Public Law 106-73, approved October 19, 1994 (Washington, D.C.: Government Printing Office).

17. A pseudonym. Some non-public-domain individuals, especially those still on active duty or employed in DoD-related positions, will not be identified by their real names. Everything else regarding such people is factually correct.

18. GIs: "Government Issue" is a term of endearment for U.S. soldiers, sailors, airmen, and Marines that refers to equipment they are given.

19. "Cockpit/Crew Resource Management Program," Air Force Instruction 36-2243, USAF, June 20, 1994.

20. *Aircraft Accident Investigation Board Report,* U.S. Army, UH-60 Blackhawk Helicopters 87-26000 and 88-26060 (U.S. Air Forces Europe, 1994).

21. John D. Morrocco, "Fratricide Investigation Spurs U.S. Training Review," *Aviation Week and Space Technology,* July 18, 1994, 23, 25.

22. Piper, *Chain of Events.*

Chapter 2

1. Bill Gunston, Editor-in-Chief, *Chronicle of Aviation* (Liberty, Missouri: Chronicle Communications Ltd., JL Publishing Co., 1992), 7.

2. This as well as other details referenced in this chapter obtained from induction award statement for Thomas E. Selfridge to the Aviation Hall of Fame, Dayton, Ohio, December 16, 1965, written by James E. Jacobs. Available from Air Force Museum Research Library, Wright-Patterson AFB, Ohio.

3. Ibid.

4. Ibid.

5. Frank P. Lahm, "The Report of the Accident to the Wright Aeroplane at Fort Myer, Virginia" (Washington, D.C., War Department Office of the Chief Signal Officer, February 19, 1909), 1.

6. This is now on display at the USAF Museum at Wright-Patterson AFB, Ohio.

7. Douglas J. Ingells, "The Fort Myer Incident," *The Saturday Evening Post,* September 13, 1958, 86.

Chapter 3

1. "Principal Wars in Which the United States Participated: U.S. Military Personnel and Casualties," Table 2-23, Office of Secretary of Defense, http://web1.whs.osd. mil/mmid/m01/sms223r.htm., March 1, 2000. Note that while the figures in this table represent the "official body count" for each of America's principal wars, one should not take them literally because of several inaccuracies in the accounting system. Furthermore, as will be discussed in this book, there are a number of systemic problems that artificially increase the numbers of "battle deaths" and decrease the real numbers of "other deaths." For example, many victims of accidents that occur in the war zone, including friendly-fire, are counted as "battle deaths." As was recently admitted in reference to the Korean War, troops who are killed outside of the war zone in accidents are not counted as "other deaths," as the author believes they should be. Similarly warzone suicides and murders are sometimes improperly counted as "battle deaths." Unfortunately the treatment of these and other causes of death, e.g., pre-existing disease, is neither clear nor consistent. Lastly, this table obviously does not include troop deaths occurring between our major wars. For instance, during the height of the Cold War, several hundred troops died annually in on-duty and off-duty accidents. Thus, the total number of American troops who died from accidents and illnesses probably exceeds the 552,870 figure suggested by this table. The author believes that half a million deaths is a very conservative estimate.
2. The author is aware of instances where battlefield mishaps were reported as combat losses during the Gulf War. This was done for a variety of reasons, e.g., to protect an inept commander who failed to properly train his troops.
3. Matthew Brelis and Stephen Kurkjian, "Confronting the Enemy Within: Safety in the U.S. Armed Forces," *Boston Globe,* June 8, 1997, A32.
4. Information from the United States Civil War Center, "Statistical Summary of America's Major Wars," Note: Confederate non-battle deaths (other) estimated. See www.cwc.1su.edu/other/stats/warcost.htm.
5. Mark Thompson, "Reports of Their Deaths Were Greatly Exaggerated," *Time,* June 12, 2000, 22. The figure for "other deaths" includes only deaths that occurred in the war zone. The U.S. military actually suffered over six times that number of casualties (20,617) worldwide during the same time period.
6. David Masci, "On Watch with Jesse Brown," *Air Force Magazine,* Vol. 79, No. 6, August 1996; 70–73.
7. W. A. Swanberg, *First Blood, The Study of Fort Sumter* (New York: Charles Scribner and Son, 1957), 328.
8. Geoffrey C. Ward, *The Civil War* (New York: Alfred A. Knopf, 1990), 208.
9. Ibid., 403.
10. Martin Blumenson, *Patton: The Man Behind the Legend* (New York: William Morrow Co.), 1995.
11. Paul W. Tibbets, *Enola Gay* (Columbus, Ohio: Mid Coast Marketing, 1998), 57–58.

12. John Donnelly, "Deaths in Military, Report Says," *Defense Week*, July 6, 1998, 1. Note: Until recently when vehicle deaths slightly exceeded those caused by aircraft accidents.

13. Oral history interview with General William Lecel Lee, Flight Instructor to Eisenhower stationed in the Philippines, dated December 9, 1970 (Abilene, Kansas: Eisenhower Library.)

14. Air Vice Marshal Ron Dick, RAF, *Reach and Power, the Heritage of the United States Air Force in Pictures and Artifacts* (Washington, D.C.: U.S. Government Printing Office, 1997), 229.

15. Hyman G. Rickover, *How the Battleship Maine Was Destroyed* (Washington, D.C.: Dept. of the Navy, Government Printing Office, 1976), 94.

16. Tom Miller, "Remember the *Maine*," *Smithsonian Magazine*, February, 1998, 46–57.

17. Rickover, *How the Battleship Maine Was Destroyed*, 94.

18. See Table 1, Chapter 3, 25.

19. Rickover, *How the Battleship Maine Was Destroyed*, 94.

20. Thomas B. Buell, *Master of Sea Power* (Boston: Little, Brown & Company, 1980), 419.

21. Approximately thirty miles per hour.

22. Buell, *Master of Sea Power*, 419.

23. Kermit Bonner, *Final Voyages* (Paducah, Kentucky: Turner Publishing, 1999). (FDR also quietly commuted the fourteen years at hard labor sentence given to the sailor who left the primer in the torpedo tube.)

24. Major General John W. Huston, *The World War II Diaries of General Henry H. 'Hap' Arnold* (Maxwell AFB, Alabama: Air University, in Press).

25. Ibid.

26. "Eagle Claw" was the official name for the overall operation, but the public came to know it as "Desert One," which was the base where it ended tragically.

27. Richard P. Hallion, *Storm Over Iraq* (Washington & London: Smithsonian Institution Press, 1992), 85–88.

28. Richard A. Gabriel, *Military Incompetence, Why the American Military Doesn't Win* (New York: Hill and Wang, a division of Farrar, Straus and Giroux, 1985), 96.

29. Hallion, *Storm Over Iraq*, 87.

Chapter 4

1. Richard G. Davis, *Hap - Henry H. Arnold - Military Aviator* (Washington, D.C.: U.S. Government Printing Office, Air Force History and Museums Program, 1997), 3.

2. Ibid., 5.

3. Omega G. East, *The Wright Brothers: The Wright Brothers of Dayton Ohio*, U.S. History, Volume Handbook 34, 1985.

4. Dick, *Air Force in Pictures and Artifacts*, 89.

5. Gunston, *Chronicle of Aviation*, 315.

6. A. F. Zeller, *Three Decades of USAF Efforts to Reduce Human Error Accidents 1947–1977*, paper presented at the 35th Aerospace Medical Panel Specialists Meeting, Paris: November, 1977.

7. www.quoteland.com.
8. Dave English, *Slipping the Surly Bonds* (New York: McGraw-Hill, 1998), 2.
9. *National Transportation Safety Board Aircraft Accident Report (NTSB-AAR-81-3) Redcoat Air Cargo Ltd., Bristol Britannia 253F, Billerica, Massachusetts* (Washington, D.C.: U.S. Government Printing Office, February 16, 1980).
10. Don Phillips and John Mintz, "Air Force Overflies FAA Safety Rules: Civil Standards Don't Apply," *Washington Post*, April 15, 1996, 1.
11. The name of this organization was later changed to the Air Force Safety Agency and finally to the Air Force Safety Center. It should also be noted that the Departments of the Army and Navy (which includes the Marine Corps) also have safety centers. While these other services use slightly different mishap investigation procedures, the processes are fundamentally similar in that junior officers are temporarily assigned to safety duties, which involve investigating their superiors.
12. Alan Diehl, "Human Engineering and the Cost Effectiveness of Air Safety Devices," Master Thesis, Wichita State University, Kansas, April, 1971.
13. Information derived from USAF safety agency database and production aircraft numbers.
14. Official Correspondence, Brig. Gen. Joel T. Hall, Air Force Inspection and Safety Center, to Gen. Merrill A. McPeak at Headquarters USAF, Pentagon, Washington, D.C., March 26, 1991, 1.
15. Official Correspondence, Gen. Merrill A. McPeak to Brig. Gen. Joel T. Hall, Headquarters USAF, Pentagon, Washington, D.C., April 1, 1991.

Chapter 5

1. Robert S. McNamara, *In Retrospect* (New York: Vintage Books, 1996).
2. H.R. McMaster, *Dereliction of Duty: Lyndon Johnson, Robert McNamara, the Joint Chiefs of Staff, and the Lies That Led to Vietnam* (New York: Harper Collins, 1997).
3. Matthew Brelis and Steven Kurkjian, "Kin of Air Crash Victims Fault U.S. on Safety Record," *Boston Globe*, March 15, 1998, A-04.
4. DoD Privilege Workshop, Kirtland Air Force Base, New Mexico, November 30 to December 3, 1993.
5. Alan Cullison, "Russian Sailor's Last Scribbled Words Signal an End to Culture of Silence," *Wall Street Journal*, November 14, 2000, A-22.
6. A pseudonym.
7. These are military physicians who have received post-graduate training in aviation medicine.
8. A pseudonym.

Chapter 6

1. John Nance, *Blind Trust* (New York: John Morrow, 1986).

2. David Gero, *Aviation Disasters* (London: Patrick Stephens Ltd., 1993), 110–113.

3. *Aircraft Accident Investigation Report: F-117A*, SN86-0822, 10 May 95, 49th Fighter Wing, Holloman AFB, New Mexico.

4. This type of psychological "compartmentalization" is not to be confused with the security procedures having the same label, which are described earlier in this chapter.

Chapter 7

1. NVG field of view is only 40 degrees across, versus almost 190 degrees for normal eyes.

2. "Investigators' Forum, Flight Fax," *U.S. Army Safety Magazine*, November 1995, 6.

3. Ibid.

4. *U.S. Army Accident Report*, Helicopter Accident, 15 August 1995.

5. Jeff Erlich, "Copter Engines Get Emergency Retrofit," *Defense News (USA edition)*, June 17–23, 1996.

6. The U.S. Army Accident Report stated that the in-trail helicopter radioed the lead helicopter that their right engine was on fire. However, Robert Rogers's widow was told that the in-trail helicopter initially radioed that the fire was in the left engine. Obviously, this misinformation could have confused the pilots in Rogers's aircraft and contributed to their mistakenly shutting down the wrong engine.

7. E-mail letter from Steve Darden to Mrs. Candida Rogers dated September 24, 1997.

8. Letter from Col. Juan V. Crayton, Dept. of the Army, Office of the Inspector General, Washington, D.C., to Ms. Debra C. Paton (mother-in-law of Sgt. Rogers), dated September 26, 1996.

9. *GAO Report on the GE-700/701 Engine Failures* (done after this crash) contradicted information presented to the families of the victims by the Army.

10. Ibid.

11. *60 Minutes*, CBS Television, December 13, 1998.

Chapter 8

1. Janet R. Daly Bednarek, "Damned Fool Idea," *Air Power History*, Winter 1996, 38.

2. Ibid., 44–45.

3. Ibid., 45.

4. Four-engine strategic airlift jet-transport manufactured by Lockheed Aircraft Co. since 1968.

5. Beryl Frank, *Plane Crashes* (New York: Bell Publishing Company, 1981), 72.

6. Gunston, *Chronicle of Aviation*, 728.

7. *Report: Investigation of Aircraft Accident, Alaska Air National Guard, KC-135E, SN 57-1481, Eielson AFB, Alaska*, 20 September 1989.

8. *Gray v. Lockheed Aeronautical Systems Co.*, 880, Fed. Supplement 1599 (U.S District Court, Georgia), March 31, 1995.

9. Ibid.

10. Federal Air Regulations, Part 23. U.S. Department of Transportation.

11. Mark Thompson, "The Deadly Trainer," *Time*, January 12, 1998, 42–44.

12. Ibid.

13. Bruce Rolfsen, "Death Trap, A Case Study on How Not to Buy an Airplane," *Air Force Times*, October 25, 1999, 14–16.

14. The Air Force is reportedly acquiring another type of trainer to replace the T-3, according to a recent article. See AOPA Pilot, October 2000, 44.

15. Thompson, "The Deadly Trainer," 42–44.

Chapter 9

1. Russell Carollo, "Falling From the Sky—Part 3 of 6: Poor Maintenance Linked to Hundreds of Mishaps," *Dayton Daily News*, October 26, 1999.

2. HC-130 aircraft are now designated MC-130 Combat Shadows.

3. Bob Young, "Why Did These 10 Men Die?" *Willamette Week*, June 18, 1997, 18.

4. Note that the location of the flight engineer's seat on the C-130 is unusual. On most civilian and military transports, it is behind the copilot, facing the right-side cockpit wall.

5. King 56 CVR Transcript, 22 November 1996, O-32.

6. Ibid., O-33.

7. "Weekend warriors" is a traditional term of endearment, but it does not reflect the reality that many of today's reservists and guardsmen serve every day on prolonged deployments around the world. Collectively they make a very significant contribution to America's total military force structure.

8. Bryan Denson, "Suit Says Bad Part Caused Air Crash," *The Oregonian*, November 21, 1997, D-1, D-16.

9. David Castellon, "Report: No Insensitivity Toward Crash-Victims' Families," *Air Force Times*, December 7, 1998, 8.

10. Bryan Denson, "Air Force Finds No Violation in King Inquiry," *The Oregonian*, May 25, 1999, E-1, E-5.

11. Jim Barnett and Bryan Denson, "Crash Report Inadequate Board Says," *The Oregonian*, July 23, 1997, A-1, A-12.

12. Brendan Sobie, "Air Force Maintains November C-130 Crash Was an Isolated Incident," *Inside the Air Force*, Vol. 8, No. 29, July 18, 1997, 13.

13. Ibid.

14. William Matthews, "Searching for Answers, At Senators' Urging, Air Force to Review C-130 Safety," *Air Force Times*, September 29, 1997, 18.

15. Ibid.

16. Denson, "Bad Parts Caused Air Crash," *The Oregonian*, D-1, D-16.

17. Bob Young, "King 56 Crash—Media Fly-By," *Willamette Week*, October 10, 1997.

18. David Castellon, "More C-130 Wreckage to be Retrieved," *Air Force Times,* February 2, 1998, 22.

19. As described in Chapter 18, Secretary of Commerce Brown was one of thirty-five victims in a 1996 USAF jet crash in Croatia.

20. Matthew Wald, "Tests Show Landing Beacon Functioned in Croatia Crash," *New York Times,* April 10, 1996, 16.

21. Associated Press, "Manuals May Have Misled Crew," *Air Force Times,* December 8, 1997, 8.

22. Bryan Denson, "C-130 Crew Unaware of Risks," *The Oregonian,* 1, A-16.

23. Ironically, General McPeak, who retired October 25, 1994, decided to move to Oregon.

24. The lack of CRM for AWACS and F-15 crew members was discussed in Chapter 1.

25. See Chapter 8 for a discussion of how poor Navy depot maintenance reportedly caused an S-3 crash.

26. Castellon, "More C-130 Wreckage to be Retrieved," 22.

27. Bryan Denson and Norm Maves Jr., "Air Force Reassigns Reserve Commander," *The Oregonian,* January 17, 1998, D-1, D-7.

28. Denson, "Air Force Finds No Violation in King Inquiry," E-1, E-5.

Chapter 10

1. Letter from USAF General Ronald R. Fogleman at Scott Air Force Base, Illinois, to Dr. Alan Diehl at Kirtland Air Force Base, New Mexico, August 8, 1994.

2. Matthew Brelis and Steven Kurkjian, "Ill-equipped Air Force Plane Haunts Widow," *Boston Globe,* December 3, 1997, 1.

3. Ibid.

4. Ibid.

5. Jerome Lederer, "Aviation Safety Perspectives, Hindsight, Insight, Foresight." Paper presented at the Nineteenth Wing Club "Sight" Lecture, New York, New York, April, 1982.

6. Note: I have personally lobbied people in the Pentagon to install such systems on the F-22 and F-16. I was told unofficially that the under secretary of defense has recently directed the USAF to reconsider installing such equipment. Hopefully this will happen in the near future.

7. Alan E. Diehl, "Human Performance and Systems Safety Considerations in Aviation Mishaps," *The International Journal of Aviation Psychology,* Mahwah, New Jersey: Lawrence Erlbaum Associates, 1991, No. 1, Vol. 2, 97–106.

8. "Draft Air Force Report Finds B-2 Cockpit Design 'Barely Acceptable,'" *Inside the Air Force,* Vol. 7, No. 50, December 13, 1996, 5.

9. Ibid.

10. Ibid.

11. Public Law 92–156, 92nd Congress, First session, dated 17 November 1971 (Washington, D.C.: U.S. Government Printing Office).

12. Russell Carollo, "Crash That Transfixed Nation Left No Trace in Air Force Data," *Dayton (Ohio) Daily News*, October 27, 1999.
13. Ibid.

Chapter 11

1. All of the tragic events described in this chapter really happened, but to prevent further embarrassment to the victims' families, I haven't identified the accidents.
2. Gregory Vistica, *Fall from Glory: The Men Who Sank the U.S. Navy* (New York: Touchstone Books, Simon & Schuster, September 1995), 237–238.
3. U.S. Navy Class A mishap rate jumped from 2.06 in 1986 (when the movie *Top Gun* premiered) to 5.84 in 1987 and 4.34 in 1988. These figures are from the U.S. Navy's own database.
4. Vistica, *Fall From Glory*, 224ff.
5. Ibid., 14.
6. Robert Alkov, *Aviation Safety: The Human Factor* (Casper, Wyoming: Endeavor Books, 1997), 50–52.
7. Technically, the USAF designates navigators who fly in fighter aircraft as "weapon systems officers."
8. 1963 movie by Columbia Pictures starring Steve McQueen.
9. William Shakespeare, *Julius Caesar*, Act I, ii, 139.

Chapter 12

1. Lieutenant Colonel Charles R. Shrader, U.S. Army, *Amicicide: The Problem of Friendly Fire in Modern War* (Washington, D.C.: U.S. Government Printing Office, December 1982).
2. Ann LoLordo, "Friendly Fire: A Question of How You Fix It," *Baltimore Sun*, April 25, 1994, 1. Note: Other research suggests that fratricide has caused over 15 percent of U.S. battlefield casualties since World War II.
3. Matt Miller, "Friendly Fire: 'Unfortunate' Part of War," *Harrisburg (Pennsylvania) Patriot*, August 27, 1991, 1.
4. CRM training would be very valuable for such individuals.
5. LoLordo, "'Friendly Fire'": 1.
6. Ibid.
7. All quotes related in this incident are from the actual U.S. Army cockpit audio/video tapes obtained by producer Daphna Rubin for the Discovery Channel, *Guardians of the Night*, January 20, 1996.
8. Twentieth Century Fox, *Courage Under Fire*, starring Meg Ryan, Denzel Washington.
9. Col. James G. Burton, *Pentagon Wars* (Naval Institute Press, September 1989).
10. Michael E. Ruane, "Troops Await Help on 'Friendly Fire,'" *Philadelphia Inquirer*, February 22, 1996, 1.

11. Geoffrey Regan, *Blue on Blue: A History of Friendly Fire* (New York: Avon Books, 1995), 4.
12. Report of Hearing Testimony before the Permanent Subcommittee on Investigations, The Investigation of a Friendly Fire Incident During the Persian Gulf War, U.S. Senate, 104th Congress, June 29, 1995 (Washington, D.C.: U.S. Government Printing Office), 34.
13. Ibid. In the heat of battle, the lieutenant launched the wrong color flare into the air.
14. Ibid., 81.
15. Ibid., 22.
16. Ibid., 22.
17. Ibid., 4, 72. Two reprimands were not made part of the officers' permanent records, and a third was withdrawn.
18. Ibid., 31.
19. Ibid.
20. Ibid.
21. Defense Condition One—the highest state of alert.
22. Testimony, U.S. Congress, Senate Permanent Subcommittee on Investigations, June 29, 1995, 4.
23. Ibid., 5–6.
24. Ibid., 7.
25. Ibid., 8.
26. LoLordo, "Friendly Fire," 1.

Chapter 13

1. The U.S. Air Force major mishap rate per one hundred thousand flying hours increased more than 35 percent (from 1.11 to 1.51 from fiscal years 1991 to 1994), U.S. Air Force Safety Center Data Base.
2. Most traditional USAF wings consist of three squadrons at one base, all flying the same type of aircraft. The general wanted to co-locate squadrons of different types of transport and fighter aircraft. The plan resulted in a tragic accident described in Chapter 16.
3. Robert Corchado, "How to fix tactical-aircraft maintenance," *Air Force Times*, July 7, 1997, 37.
4. The North Korean and Iraqi regimes have been making bellicose threats.
5. Ernest Blazar, "Wing of Fate: What Went Wrong?" *Navy Times*, July 14, 1997, 4.
6. U.S. Navy, *Mishap Investigative Report, F-14A, Oct. 25, 1994, USS Abraham Lincoln*, Military City Online.
7. Blazar, "Wing of Fate," 4.
8. George C. Wilson and Peter Carlson, "The Ultimate Stealth Plane," *Washington Post*, January 1–7, 1996, 6.

9. A. Ernest Fitzgerald, *The Pentagonists* (New York: Houghton Mifflin, 1989).
10. The conspirators even fooled a group of visiting congressmen during a junket to the factory when they showed them the mock-up of the A-12 and suggested it was the actual prototype aircraft. The latter was still months away from being assembled.
11. Wilson and Carlson, "The Ultimate Stealth Plane," 6–11.
12. Blazar, "Wing of Fate," 4.
13. Mark Thompson, "Way, Way Off in the Wild Blue Yonder," *Time*, May 29, 1995, 32–33.
14. Ronald Lewis, "Raising the Tomcat," *Air Forces Monthly*, March 1995, 58–59.
15. Blazar, "Wing of Fate," 4.
16. Lewis had served as USAF armaments system technician and worked with a wide variety of bomb racks. He also performed accident photo imagery interpretation during his military career.
17. It would be several years before the Bombcat became an effective weapon system. The original ungainly drag-producing racks, designed to carry several five hundred-pound unguided bombs were replaced with streamlined racks that carried individual laser-guided two thousand-pound bombs flush under the jet's fuselage.
18. Evan Thomas and Gregory L. Vistica, "Falling Out of the Sky," *Newsweek*, March 17, 1997, 26–28.
19. Certainly the individual who most deserves to know the whole truth about Lieutenant Hultgreen's death is her mother, Sally Spears. She wrote a compelling book about her daughter's struggle to become the Navy's first female fighter pilot. She also describes the hurdles Kara faced aboard the USS *Abraham Lincoln* during her combat readiness training in preparation for her first cruise. Sally Spears, *Call Sign Revlon* (Annapolis, Maryland: Naval Institute Press, 1998).
20. Brendan M. Greeley Jr., "TAC to Modify A-7's and F-16's for Close Air Support," *Aviation Week and Space Technology*, August 22, 1988, 41.
21. A close friend who flew with her in T-37s said she was one of the best aviators he ever knew.
22. Captain Svoboda, who had not flown for more than three weeks, received one short day flight before being assigned to her fatal night mission.
23. This instrument, sometimes called an artificial horizon, was discussed in Chapter 6.
24. Bryant Jordan, "Pilot Error Blamed in Fatal A-10 Crash," *Air Force Times*, September 29, 1997.
25. Gunston, *Chronicle of Aviation*, 442.

Chapter 14

1. Arnold Abrams, "The Final Patrol—Airmen's Families Dispute Navy Version of '87 Crash," *Long Island (New York) Sunday Newsday*, October 1, 1995, A-5, A-30.

2. Ibid.
3. C. E. Lewis, W. L. Jones, F. Austin, and J. Roman, "Flight Research Program IX, Medical Monitoring of Carrier Pilots in Combat-II," *ASEM Aerospace Medicine,* 1967, 38, 133–139.
4. Abrams, "The Final Patrol," A-5, A-30.
5. Barry H. Kantowitz and Robert D. Sorkin, *Human Factors: Understanding People-System Relationships,* Chapter 19 (New York: John Wiley & Sons, 1983), 604.
6. Abrams, "The Final Patrol," A-31.
7. Ibid., A-31.
8. Ibid., It was disclosed in an interview with members of the crew that the ship's officers thought it was too dangerous for the rescuers in the helicopter to go after the trapped crew members inside the EA-3, but rescuers disagreed.
9. Ibid.
10. Ibid.
11. Ibid.
12. Ibid.
13. See Chapter 4.
14. Vistica, *Fall from Glory.*
15. Ibid., 289.
16. Ibid., 289.
17. Charles Thompson II, *A Glimpse of Hell* (New York: W. W. Norton & Company, 1999), 280.
18. Ibid., 127.
19. Associated Press, "Iowa Explosion May Never Be Solved—GAO," *Washington Times,* August 29, 1991, 3.
20. Ibid.
21. Vistica, *Fall from Glory,* 290.

Chapter 15

1. Vistica, *Fall from Glory,* 274–275.
2. See Chapter 3.
3. Vistica, *Fall from Glory,* 273.
4. Ibid., 274.
5. Ibid., 275.
6. Ibid., 275.
7. Ibid., 275.
8. Ibid., 277.
9. *Formal Investigation into Circumstance Surrounding the Downing of Iran Air Flight 655 on 3 July 1988,* U.S. Central Command 28 July 1988, 33.
10. Will and Sharon Rogers, *Storm Center, The USS Vincennes and Iran Air Flight 655* (Annapolis, Maryland: Naval Institute Press, 1992), 14.

11. Ibid., 16.
12. Ibid., 14.
13. Vistica, *Fall from Glory*, 278.
14. Ibid.
15. Thompson II, *A Glimpse of Hell*, 21.
16. Larry Wheeler, "Student's Project Revives Effort to Clear Name of Court-Martialed Navy Captain," *Gannett News Service*, April 22, 1998, ARC.
17. "Paul Murphy and Harold Bray, Survivors of the USS *Indianapolis*," *Fresh Air*, National Public Radio, August 10, 2001.
18. Graham K. Yost, "CIA Classified Document Links Pan Am 103 Bomb to Iran," *Rumor Mill News Agency*, December 24, 1999. Note: Although one Libyan intelligence agent was recently convicted for the bombing of Pan Am 103, speculation still persists that the bombing was an act of revenge by Arab terrorists for the Iranian airliner shoot-down.
19. Rogers, *Storm Center*, 191ff.
20. Sherry Sontag with Annette L. Drew and Christopher Drew, *Blind Man's Bluff: The Untold Story of American Submarine Espionage* (New York: Public Affairs Press, October 1998).
21. Note: In such cases, the sub is also intentionally turned at least 180 degrees. This maneuver should theoretically shut the torpedo's motor off, because it is equipped with a sensor that prevents the weapon from turning around and homing back on its own sub.
22. Navy Ordnance Command quality-control procedures require that three out of every one hundred torpedo batteries in a production batch be tested. But because the Navy was behind schedule, they just ignored this requirement and had the units shipped to the fleet untested. They then discovered a problem with the batch of batteries aboard the Scorpion.
23. Captain C.A.K. McDonald, "Real Story of Scorpion?" *Proceedings*, June 1999, 28.
24. Dale Eisman, "Study Indicates Navy Risking Seawolf Crews," *The Virginian-Pilot*, February 16, 2000.

Chapter 16

1. *Aircraft Accident Investigation Report F-16D and C-130E at Pope AFB North Carolina on 23 March 1994*, N-7.
2. Ibid.
3. Ibid.
4. Stephen Watkins, "Inferno at Pope," *Air Force Times*, April 3, 1995, 12–14.
5. A pseudonym. Some non-public-domain individuals, especially those still on active duty or employed in DoD-related positions, are not identified by their real names. Everything else regarding such people is factually correct.

6. Watkins, "Inferno at Pope," 12.

7. John A. Tirpak, senior editor, "The Expeditionary Air Force Takes Shape," *Air Force Magazine,* June 1997, 32.

8. Philip Shenon, "Pilot Also Blamed for Air Force Crash," *New York Times,* June 21, 1997, 7.

Chapter 17

1. Vago Muradian, "A Tragic Loss for the Service," *Air Force Times,* May 1, 1995, 13.

2. "Human Systems Integration Requirements for the Air Force Acquisition Programs," Report No. 94–124, June 8, 1994, *Department of Defense Office of the Inspector General* (Washington, D.C.: U.S. Government Printing Office).

3. The aviation abbreviation for "passenger."

4. *Aircraft Investigation Report, C-21A (SN84-0136), Alexander City, Alabama, 17 April 1995,* includes all cockpit voice recorder and other quotations and data concerning crash.

5. Ibid., 16. The flight manual warns that "improper rudder input in conjunction with overly aggressive single engine power application may cause loss of aircraft control. Recovery may not be possible" (Tab AA-5). Simulator tests under these conditions revealed that attempting to coordinate flight by centering the ball on the slip indicator would cause the aircraft to roll uncontrollably. Recovery at such low altitude was not possible (Tab AA-18).

6. Steven Watkins, "C-21A Investigation Raises Questions," *Air Force Times,* July 31, 1995, 3–4.

7. Muradian, "A Tragic Loss for the Service," 13.

8. Letter from General Glenn Profitt to General James Cole, dated September 21, 1993.

Chapter 18

1. "Presidential Address to Commerce Staff," *Commerce People,* June 1996, 10.

2. ValuJet was a cut-rate airline that operated in the southeastern United States. In 1996, one of their DC-9s crashed into the Everglades killing all 110 persons on board after an in-flight fire in the cargo hold. It was later learned that this airline had violated numerous safety procedures to save money.

3. Bradley Graham, "Crash-Probe Depositions Speak Volumes," *Washington Post,* June 17, 1996, 15.

4. *Accident Investigation Board Report, United States Air Force CT-43A, 73-1149, 3 April 1996, Dubrovnik, Croatia,* 65.

5. These small maps were originally sized to fit into the pocket of military flight suits. Pilots always have the appropriate "approach plate" attached to the aircraft control wheel or to a special clipboard while they are making an instrument approach.

6. *Accident Investigation Board Report, United States Air Force CT-43A, 73-1149, 3 April 1996, Dubrovnik, Croatia*, 58.

7. When landing in bad weather, one receiver must stay tuned to the first beacon to provide the pilots with course guidance to the airport. The second receiver is required to tell them when they have arrived at the end of the instrument approach, the so-called missed approach point, where they must abort the landing unless they can actually see the airport.

8. *Accident Investigation Board Report, United States Air Force CT-43A, 73-1149, 3 April 1996, Dubrovnik, Croatia*, 58.

9. The accident investigation board report cited aircrew error along with other causes including the command's failure to comply with existing regulations on approved airport approaches and failure to provide theater-specific orientation training, as well as the improperly designed Dubrovnik NDB instrument approach procedures, 15e.

10. Alan Diehl, "Crew 'Recourse' Management," *Flying Safety*, December 1993, 20–21.

11. Julie Bird, "Would a Navigator, GPS Have Helped?" *Air Force Times*, May 13, 1996, 6.

12. U.S. Congress, Public Law 106-181, 106th Congress, First Session, April 6, 2000 (Washington, D.C.: U.S. Government Printing Office).

Chapter 19

1. Harold P. Van Cott, Ph.D. and Robert G. Kinkade, Ph.D., editors, *Human Engineering Guide to Equipment Design* (Revised Edition), Washington, D.C.: U.S. Government Printing Office, 608.

2. After General McPeak retired, his plans to eliminate most of these skilled maintenance technician jobs were largely abandoned, but not before many of the best mechanics had left the service.

3. Ironically, General Heflebower, Colonel Danny Piper (Lieutenant Laura Piper's father), and I were all in USAF Academy Class of 1967. (I never graduated with them, though. Having received a General Hap Arnold scholarship, I finished my undergraduate work in 1966 at the University of South Florida.)

4. Steven Watkins, "The High Cost of Accountability," *Air Force Times*, December 23, 1996, 10–14.

5. Ibid., 11.

6. Ibid., 12.

7. Alan Diehl, "Safety Problems Lead to More Losses," *Air Force Times*, June 12, 1995, 38.

8. See Chapter 21.

9. See Chapter 16.

10. Editorial, "Accountability Gone Awry," *Air Force Times*, December 30, 1996, 17.

11. Julie Bird, "Fogleman Defends Mechanics' Prosecution," *Air Force Times*, January 20, 1997, 6.

12. News in Brief, "Prosecutor Won't Be Punished," *Air Force Times*, June 9, 1997, 2.
13. Julie Bird, "Mechanic Is Cleared," *Air Force Times*, April 6, 1998, 8.

Chapter 20

1. The HH-60 Pave Hawk is a highly modified version of the H-60 Black Hawk.
2. Bryant Jordan, "Worked to Death," *Air Force Times*, March 29, 1999, 12–14.

Chapter 21

1. In 1999, the government also belatedly agreed to compensate the families of American victims.
2. Steven Watkins, "Scapegoat?" *Air Force Times*, March 6, 1996, 14–15.
3. Air Force Instruction 36–2243, "Cockpit/Crew Resource Management Program," dated June 20, 1994.
4. David Greene, "Military Justice Is Not Always Just," *Air Force Times*, May 22, 1995, 28.
5. Air Force Instruction 91–204, dated July 22, 1994, 26.
6. "Damaged" engines are normally sent back to a logistics center base, supposedly for "repair." Upon arrival, these shattered engines are simply scrapped, but the services rarely revise the intentionally underestimated dollar figures in their mishap reports. Note: DoD regulations allow mishap-damaged engines to be assessed at only 17 percent of the cost of destroyed engines.
7. Steven Watkins, "Beyond the Verdict," *Air Force Times*, July 3, 1995, 12–15.
8. Described in Chapter 12.
9. Thorson, incidentally, was a classmate of mine (and Danny Piper's) at the USAF Academy. Eric had also served with distinction as an assistant secretary of the Air Force under Ronald Reagan, after being medically retired from the service.
10. Robert Novak, "A Pentagon Whitewash," *Washington Post*, June 8, 2000, 31.
11. "Seeking Answers," *U.S. News and World Report*, September 23, 1996, 10.
12. "Operation Provide Comfort: Review of U.S. Air Force Investigation of Black Hawk Fratricide Incident," GAO Report B-266152.2, November 1997.
13. This GAO report did not discuss information on the homophobic aspects of the F-15/F-16 rivalry.
14. "United States Air Force Safety Blue Ribbon Panel Report," September 5, 1995, Appendix E; 5.
15. A. Ernest Fitzgerald, *The Pentagonists* (Boston, Massachusetts: Houghton Mifflin Company, 1989).
16. "GAO Slams Pentagon Fraud, Waste, Abuse," *Defense Week*, February 1, 1999.
17. Letter from USAF General Ronald R. Fogleman at Scott Air Force Base, Illinois, to Dr. Alan Diehl at Kirtland Air Force Base, New Mexico, dated 8 August 1994.
18. Julie Bird, "Accident-Probe Mismanagement Charges Rejected," *Air Force Times*, April 21, 1997, 4.

19. Ibid.
20. See Chapter 8.
21. Ibid., Recommendation 10. "Require an experienced AFSA representative to serve as a voting member on each Class A SIB," 21.
22. Ironically, many of these same issues would resurface in future years when the Air Force reinvestigated the T-3 (Secretary of the Air Force Inspector General, "Broad Area Review of the Enhanced Flight Screening Program," March 17, 1998, HQ USAF).

Chapter 22

1. Al Kamen, "Problems in the Air," *Washington Post*, July 1, 1996, 15.
2. Ibid.
3. While such aircraft do not transport the president per se, they do carry people and equipment needed to ensure his protection and effectiveness.
4. News in Brief, "Guardsman Dies in Sikorsky Crash," *Air Force Times*, May 20, 1996, 2.
5. Lisa Holewa (Associated Press), "Clinton Copter Destroyed," *Albuquerque Journal*, September 7, 1996, A7.
6. Steven Watkins, "President Orders a Review of Executive Fleet," *Air Force Times*, September 23, 1996, 6.
7. GPWS: Acronym for ground proximity warning system, an onboard electronic device to alert the crew to dangerous terrain as described in Chapter 10.
8. CRM: Acronym for Crew Resource Management, a comprehensive training program teaching crew coordination, judgment, and stress management, described in Chapter 1.
9. TCAS: Acronym for traffic advisory and collision-avoidance system, an onboard electronic device to warn pilots of nearby aircraft, described in Chapter 10.
10. Paul Bedard, "UPS Pilot: Clinton Encounter Too Close," *Washington Times*, June 5, 1997, 6.
11. Watkins, "President Orders a Review of Executive Fleet," 6.
12. Ibid.
13. Letter (via fax) from Mr. Fred Brugger, House Appropriations Committee, U.S. House of Representatives, Surveys and Investigation Staff to Dr. Alan Diehl dated December 3, 1996.
14. Letter of reply from Dr. Alan Diehl to Mr. Fred Brugger, House Appropriations Committee, U.S. House of Representatives, Surveys and Investigation Staff dated January 5, 1997.
15. Ibid.
16. Kenneth Bacon, ASD (Pennsylvania), DoD News Briefing, September 22, 1998, 2–5.
17. Ibid.
18. "A New Bomb Damage Report," *Newsweek*, December 20, 1999, 4.

19. Steven Lee Myers, "Chinese Embassy Bombing: A Wide Net of Blame," *New York Times,* April 17, 2000, 1.
20. Steven Lee Myers, "C.I.A. Fires Officer Blamed in Bombing of Chinese Embassy," *New York Times,* April 9, 2000, 1.
21. Patrick Eddington, "Get Ready for More Targeting Disasters," *Los Angeles Times,* July 5, 1999, 15.
22. Ibid.
23. Seth Faison, "U.S. to Pay China $4.5 Million for Embassy Bombing," *New York Times,* July 31, 1999.
24. Ibid.
25. Peter Grier, "Aerospace World - Deal Offered in Chinese Embassy Bombing," *Air Force Magazine,* February 2000, 16–17.
26. Juan O. Tamayo, "U.S. Bombing Range under Political Fire," *Miami Herald,* May 23, 1999.
27. Patrick J. Sloyan, "Brakes on Army Truck Contribute to Upsurge in Accidents," *Long Island Newsday,* June 18, 1998.
28. Patrick J. Sloyan, "Cohen Suspends Truck Contract," *Long Island Newsday,* June 3, 1998, 19.
29. Sloyan, "Brakes on Army Truck Contribute to Upsurge in Accidents," June 18, 1998. The article gave no details on the death toll for new FMTVs but said the old M939 trucks had killed 132 people and seriously injured "hundreds more" from 1983–1998.
30. Tamara Lytle, "Why Did Cape Rockets Fail? Human Mistakes," *Orlando (Florida) Sentinel,* June 16, 1999.
31. Associated Press, "Pentagon Study Blames Rocket Makers for Launch Failures," *Washington Post,* December 2, 1999, 13.
32. Associated Press, "Air Force Blames Latest Satellite Snafu on Mother Nature," CNN.com, May 11, 1999.
33. Jack Dorsey, "Saudi Ship Sounded Warning Before Collision," *Norfolk Virginian-Pilot,* March 18, 1999.
34. Ibid.
35. Ibid.
36. Jack Dorsey, "Navy Scapegoated Ex-Radford Skipper, Several Officers Say," *Norfolk Virginian Pilot,* July 19, 1999.
37. Thompson II, *A Glimpse of Hell.*
38. Richard L. Schwoebel, *Explosion Aboard the Battleship Iowa* (Washington, D.C.: Naval Institute Press, April 1999).
39. Robert L. Allen, *The Port Chicago Mutiny* (New York: Warner Books, 1989).
40. William Glaberson, "Convicted Mutineer's Bid for Pardon Poses Dilemma on Race and Military," *New York Times,* June 23, 1999.
41. Ibid.
42. Kevin Galvin, "Clinton Pardons Mutiny Convict," Associated Press, in *Albuquerque Journal,* December 24, 1999, A5.

43. Vera Haller, "Italy Criticizes U.S. Flights in Fatal Accident," *Washington Post*, February 5, 1998, 1.

44. Associated Press, "U.S. Settles in Gondola Crash for $40 Million," *Washington Post*, April 26, 2000, 8.

45. Testimony from House Committee on National Security, Military Procurement Subcommittee, *Accident Investigations of Recent F-14 and AV-8B Mishaps*, 104th Congress, 2nd session, 16 April 1996 (Washington, D.C.: U.S. Government Printing Office).

46. Tony Kern, *A Darker Shade of Blue, The Rogue Pilot* (New York: McGraw Hill, 1999).

47. "Verdict on a Tragedy," *Washington Post*, March 6, 1999, 20.

Chapter 23

1. Ironically, the U.S. military has played an important historic medical role. For example, the military demonstrated methods of controlling malaria and became the first widespread user of antibiotics.

2. Philip Shenon, "U.S. Jets Pounded Iraqi Arms Depot Storing Nerve Gas," *New York Times*, October 3, 1996, 1.

3. Bill Mesler, "Pentagon Poison: The Great Radioactive Ammo Cover-Up," *The Nation*, May 26, 1997, 17.

4. Willis Witter, "Uranium Bullets Could Wound U.S.," *Washington Times*, February 11, 1997, 1ff.

5. Art Pine, "Gulf Veteran's Clue Guided Search for Illness' Source," *The Los Angeles Times* (Washington Edition), October 6, 1996, 1.

6. Gary Matsumoto, "The Pentagon's Toxic Secret," *Vanity Fair*, May 1999, 82.

7. President Clinton's advisors would later convince him to sign an executive order on September 30, 1999, allowing the DoD to give experimental drugs to service members without their informed consent. (Keith J. Costa, "Clinton Order Guides How Experimental Vaccines Can Be Administered," *Inside the Pentagon*, October 7, 1999, 4).

8. Eileen Welsome, *The Plutonium Files: America's Secret Medical Experiments in the Cold War* (New York: Dial Press, 1999).

9. John Hanchette and Norm Brewer, "Most Gulf War Chemical Warfare Records Are Missing," *USA Today*, December 6, 1996, 4.

10. Philip Shenon, "Investigators Find Excerpts of Gulf War Chemical Logs," *New York Times*, October 24, 1997.

11. Philip Shenon, "Panel Says Pentagon Ignored Signs of Poison Gas," *New York Times*, October 31, 1997.

12. Ibid.

13. The author gained a deep respect for the complexity of these matters when he studied the subject under a U.S. Public Health Service fellowship at North Carolina State University, 1970–1973.

14. Dave Parks, "War Logs Record Gas Attack," *Birmingham (Alabama) News*, June 20, 1997, 1.

15. Dana Priest, "CIA Warned of Chemical Arms in '91," *Washington Post*, February 26, 1997, 1.

16. Shenon, "Panel Says Pentagon Ignored Signs of Poison Gas."

17. Philip Shenon, "Pentagon Says Inquiry Will Seek Missing Chemical-Weapons Logs," *New York Times*, March 4, 1997, 14.

18. Norm Brewer and John Hanchette, "Gulf War Chemical Arms: Deadline Set for Answers," Gannett News Service, *USA Today*, February 27, 1997, 1, 4.

19. Patrick G. Eddington, *Gassed in the Gulf* (Washington, D.C.: Insignia Publishing Co., 1997), 269.

20. Philip Shenon, "Seeking to Keep Jurisdiction, Pentagon Expands Gulf War Inquiry," *New York Times*, November 13, 1996, 1, 20.

21. Dana Priest, "Pentagon Retreats on Hiring of PR Firm," *Washington Post*, November 17, 1996, 4.

22. Eric Schmitt, "No Proof Is Found of Chemical Cause for Gulf Illness," *New York Times*, January 8, 1997, 1.

23. Ibid.

24. Philip Shenon, "Pentagon Reveals it Lost Most Logs on Chemical Arms," *New York Times*, February 28, 1997, 1.

25. Ibid.

26. Ibid.

27. John Hanchette, "Chemical Risk to Gulf Troops Was Forecast," Gannett News Service, *USA Today*, August 14, 1997, 1.

28. Richard Parker, "Congressional Panel Urges Independent Probe of Gulf War Ills," *Philadelphia Inquirer*, November 1, 1997, 3.

29. Ibid.

30. Norm Brewer, "Gulf Illness Treated 'Cavalierly,'" Gannett News Service, *USA Today*, September 15, 1997, 5.

31. Eddington, *Gassed in the Gulf*, 59.

32. Associated Press, "Gulf Risks Ignored, Chemical Officer Says," *Albuquerque Journal*, August 24, 1996.

33. Associated Press, "Defective Gas-Warfare Suits Recalled," *Los Angeles Times*, February 28, 2000, 5.

34. Ibid.

35. Mark Pazniokas and Dennis Williams (The Hartford Courant), "U.S. Sprayed Germs on Sailors," *Albuquerque Journal*, October 21, 2001, A-4.

36. Ibid.

37. Sheryl Gay Stolberg, "U.S. Reports Disease Link to Gulf War," *New York Times*, December 11, 2001, 1.

38. Leonard A. Cole, *The Eleventh Plague* (New York: W.H. Freeman and Company, 1997), 131.

39. Elmo Zumwalt Jr. and Elmo Zumwalt III, *My Father, My Son* (New York: The Macmillan Publishing Co., 1986).
40. "Study Links Defects, Gulf War," *Albuquerque Journal*, October 6, 2001, A-6.
41. *The Twentieth Century*, CBS Television, Mike Wallace commentator.

Chapter 24

1. Susan Page, "U.S. Mourns First Deaths in Conflict," *USA Today*, May 6, 1999, 1.
2. Marni McEntee, "Monteith Soldier Electrocuted in Antenna Accident," *European Stars and Stripes*, August 3, 1999, 3.
3. 1964 movie *Fail-Safe*, directed by Sidney Lumet and based on the book of the same name by Eugene Burdick and Harvey Wheeler published by McGraw Hill, 1962.
4. This name change occurred circa 2000.
5. Like Navy flight surgeons, these specialists receive medical service corps wings.
6. Pat Kostazewa, "B-1/B-52," *Flying Safety, USAF*, January/February 1999, 4.
7. I recently brought this deficiency to the attention of the Office of the Secretary of Defense in hopes that corrective action will soon be taken on future F-22 orders. Interestingly, the under secretary of defense for acquisition reportedly also ordered the USAF to consider retrofitting such systems on its F-16 fleet to fix the problem described in Chapter 10.
8. Roy Rowan, "Cover Stories: Gander Different Crash, Same Questions," *Time*, April 27, 1992, 33.
9. John Diamond, "Critics: Light Punishments Seem Common in Military Debacles," *Albuquerque Journal*, December 25, 1995, 7.
10. Ibid.
11. Matthew Brelis and Stephen Kurkjian, "Cohen Urges Safety Changes," *Boston Globe*, April 11, 1998, 6.
12. Daniel G. Dupont, "Army Stops Work on FMTV; Appropriators Ask Cohen to Terminate Contract," *Inside the Army*, October 26, 1998, 1.
13. Discussed in Chapter 10.
14. Jamie McIntyre, "Pentagon Orders Faster Action on Air Safety System," *CNN News*, March 30, 1998.
15. *United States Air Force Safety Blue Ribbon Report*, Memorandum for the Air Force Chief of Staff, Washington, D.C., September 5, 1995.
16. These facts were explained in my letter of reply to Mr. Fred Brugger, House Appropriations Committee, Surveys and Investigation Staff, dated January 5, 1997.
17. Recent assertions by organizations like the DoD IG indicating that current military death rates are now "comparable" to those of the U.S. general population may be challenged for several reasons. Today's military personnel are initially screened for physical and mental health, general intelligence, criminal behavior,

and so forth. They are then constantly monitored for dangerous behavior on and off duty, including drug and alcohol use, driving violations, and even financial problems. Military personnel also tend to be highly motivated individuals who are immersed in an environment containing strong support-group ties that discourage aberrant behavior.

These factors all tend to drastically reduce the number of accidents and illnesses, especially among youthful populations. Thus, it is very difficult to establish statistically representative groups with similar characteristics who are living in similar highly controlled environments, which are needed to make accurate comparisons. This reality limits the utility of saying military death rates are comparable to those in the general population.

John Donnelly, "Deaths in Military Down, Report Says," *Defense Week,* July 6, 1998, 1.

18. See Chapter 21, page 257.
19. Russell Carollo, "Official Statistics Mask Actual Number of Crashes," *Dayton Daily News,* October 27, 1999.
20. Ibid.
21. Steven Lee Myers, "Airman Discharged for Refusal to Take Anthrax Vaccine as Rebellion Grows," *New York Times,* March 11, 1999.
22. Ibid.
23. Ibid.
24. William S. Cohen, "Proclamation Accident Prevention," June 23, 1998.
25. Mike Glenn, "Planes Supporting Clinton's India Trip Nearly Collide," *Air Force Times,* April 3, 2000, 12.
26. David Moniz, "Not-So-Precise Flight Investigated: Thunderbirds Off Course Near Washington," *USA Today,* May 25, 2000, 3-A.
27. Paul Richter, "Osprey Hopes and Heartbreak," *Los Angeles Times,* February 19, 2001, 1.
28. Ibid.
29. Peter Grier (Aerospace World), "Cohen Pays Tribute to His Hollywood Heroes," *Air Force Magazine,* February 2001, 16.
30. Paul Craig Roberts, "Flotsam Flowing in Dalton's Wake," *Washington Times,* June 12, 1998, 20.

Chapter 25

1. The accident report narrative notes that his main parachute failed to deploy after the packing malfunctioned and the static line attached to the aircraft broke, and that his reserve parachute did not fully deploy. (Narrative from Army Safety Center Report Case Number 980129, 1998, 2–3.)
2. Ernest Blazar, "Inside the Ring, Glass Jaw," *Washington Times,* February 2, 1998, 9.
3. Ibid.

4. Brian Knowlton, "Bush Vows He'll Never 'Overextend' U.S. Forces," *International Herald Tribune*, February 13, 2001, 1.

5. Months later, the Pentagon would formally charge a general and several other officers with falsifying records to conceal these problems. Robert Burns (Associated Press), "Marines Charged in Osprey Case," *Albuquerque Journal*, August 18, 2001, A-4.

6. Mary Pat Flaherty, "Osprey Widows Plead for Aggressive Probe," *Washington Post*, March 10, 2001, 02.

7. See Chapter 15.

8. Greenpeace, "April 9, 1981, Aboard the USS *George Washington* (SSBN-598) in the South China Sea," *Selected Accidents Involving Nuclear Weapons - 1950–1993*.

9. Christopher Lehman, "Terror at Sea: A Submariner's Tale," *Washington Post*, March 19, 2001, B-1.

10. Robert Burns (Associated Press), "Controller Was Hurt in Bomb Drop," *Philadelphia Inquirer*, March 15, 2001.

11. CNN.com/World, "New Zealand Demands Explanation for Bomb Death," March 12, 2001.

12. John Pomfret, "For Incoming Chief, One More Close Call," *Washington Post*, December 6, 2001, 31.

13. James Dao, "Bombing Accident Kills 5 Americans at Site in Kuwait," *New York Times*, March 13, 2001, 1.

14. Ibid.

15. The president of an accident investigation board (which is convened primarily to establish disciplinary action) provides a statement of his opinion as to what caused the accident. This statement should not be confused with the formal safety investigation board's finding of cause.

16. John Diedrich, "U.S. Tries to Recover Remains of Personnel Missing Around World," *Colorado Springs Gazette-Telegraph*, April 19, 1999.

17. Two senators have personally known the horrors of military mishaps. Max Cleland was grievously disfigured in a grenade accident and described his experiences in his book, *Strong at the Broken Places: A Personal Story* (Marietta, Georgia: Longstreet Press, Inc., November 2000). John McCain was injured when a rocket hit his jet on the deck of the USS *Forrestal*. He then watched the ensuing explosions and fires claim 134 shipmates, as he noted in his recent book, *John McCain: Faith of My Fathers* (New York: Random House, 1999), 177–181.

18. This proposed Military Safety Board would also be heavily involved with health issues. In 1999, the National Academy of Sciences suggested that Congress establish an independent center on military health. (Associated Press, "Congress Urged to Form Military Health Center," *Baltimore [Maryland] Sun*, November 6, 1999).

19. William Shakespeare, *The Rape of Lucrece*.

20. Seth Shulman, "The Threat at Home: Confronting the Toxic Legacy of the U.S. Military," (Boston, Massachusetts: *Beacon Press*), 1992: 126–135.

21. David Bamber, "Soldiers to Be Given the Right to Sue Their Officers," *London Sunday Telegraph*, February 27, 2000, 1.
22. General Colin Powell, "Heroes and Icons—The American G.I.," *Time*, June 19, 1999, Vol. 153, No. 23; 70–73.
23. Movie *Saving Private Ryan*, produced by Dreamworks, directed by Steven Spielberg, 1998.
24. See Table 1, Chapter 3, page 25.
25. The miraculously low number of military casualties was due partly to the fact that the section of the Pentagon had recently been renovated and was not fully occupied. This figure did not include civilian victims in the building and aircraft. "The Pentagon Who We Lost," *Air Force Times*, October 1, 2001, 16.
26. Francois Marie Arouet Voltaire, 1694–1778.

Index

About the Author

Dr. Alan Diehl is an award-winning safety expert with more than thirty years' experience in aircraft design, aviation psychology, aircrew training, and accident investigation. He has degrees in psychology and management, as well as a Ph.D. in engineering. He is also a former Air Force reservist.

He has held positions with two aircraft manufacturers, the National Transportation Safety Board, the Federal Aviation Administration, and the Navy. Prior to filing a whistle-blowing complaint, he was the senior civilian at the Air Force Safety Agency.

His accomplishments include helping to design one of the first combat lasers and the Cessna Citation jet that received the Collier Trophy for its outstanding safety record. He also drafted the first government recommendation to implement Crew Resource Management, which revolutionized global aviation training.

Dr. Diehl has published dozens of technical articles and is often quoted by the national press and safety advocates. He frequently appears on national television to discuss such issues. He has also served as a consultant to Congressional and United Nations agencies.

He and his wife, Marlyn, reside in Albuquerque, New Mexico.